TOXIC COMMUNITIES

Toxic Communities

Environmental Racism, Industrial Pollution, and Residential Mobility

Dorceta E. Taylor

NEW YORK UNIVERSITY PRESS
New York and London

NEW YORK UNIVERSITY PRESS
New York and London
www.nyupress.org

References to Internet websites (URLs) were accurate at the time of writing.
Neither the author nor New York University Press is responsible for URLs
that may have expired or changed since the manuscript was prepared.

Library of Congress Cataloging-in-Publication Data
Taylor, Dorceta E.
Toxic communities : environmental racism, industrial pollution, and
residential mobility / Dorceta E. Taylor.
pages   cm
Includes bibliographical references and index.
ISBN 978-1-4798-5239-0 (hardback) — ISBN 978-1-4798-6178-1 (paper)
1. Environmental justice—United States. 2. Hazardous waste sites—
Social aspects—United States. 3. Hazardous waste sites—Location—
United States. 4. United States—Environmental conditions—Social
aspects.   I. Title.
GE230.T38 2014
363.72'870973—dc23   2014002556

New York University Press books are printed on acid-free paper,
and their binding materials are chosen for strength and durability.
We strive to use environmentally responsible suppliers and materials
to the greatest extent possible in publishing our books.

Manufactured in the United States of America

c 10 9 8 7 6 5 4 3 2 1
p 10 9 8 7 6 5 4 3 2 1

Also available as an ebook

Dedicated to my mother,
Dorothy Aileen Cameron Taylor,
and my grandmother,
Lucy Ann Cameron Stewart,

Black women
Strong women
Survivors extraordinaire
Your spirits live on!

CONTENTS

ACKNOWLEDGMENTS

I would like to thank the University of Michigan's School of Natural Resources and the Program in the Environment for providing me with the resources and inspiration to write this book. Many thanks also go to the university librarians whose tireless efforts made it easy for me to find the materials I needed to complete this project. I would also like to thank the reviewers of earlier drafts of this manuscript for their helpful feedback. Thanks also go to Ilene Kalish and the rest of the editorial staff at New York University Press for their help and guidance through this process. I am grateful to my husband, Ian, and daughters, Shaina and Justine, for their patience and kindness during the writing of this book.

ACRONYMS AND ABBREVIATIONS

AAEJ	African Americans for Environmental Justice
ACE	Alabamians for a Clean Environment
ACLU	American Civil Liberties Union
ACORN	Association of Community Organizations for Reform Now
AFL-CIO	American Federation of Labor–Congress of Industrial Organizations
ARCO	Atlantic Richfield Company
BFI	Browning-Ferris Industries
BIA	Bureau of Indian Affairs
CAC	Central Advisory Council
CDC	Centers for Disease Control
CERCLA	Comprehensive Environmental Response Compensation Liability Act
CHA	Chicago Housing Authority
CREB	Chicago Real Estate Board
DDE	dichlorodiphenyldichloroethylene
DDT	dichlorodiphenyltrichloroethane
DOE	Department of Energy
EDC	ethylene dichloride
EJ	environmental justice
EJM	environmental justice movement
EPA	Environmental Protection Agency
FHA	Federal Housing Administration
FmHA	Farmers Home Administration
FTI	Federal Technologies, Incorporated
GAO	General Accounting Office / Government Accountability Office (after 2004)
GM	General Motors Company

HOLC	Home Owners' Loan Corporation
HRS	Hazard Ranking System
HUD	Housing and Urban Development
IRA	Indian Reorganization Act
LDEQ	Louisiana Department of Environmental Quality
MAUP	Modifiable areal unit problem
mg/kg	milligrams per kilogram
MPHA	Myers Park Housing Association
MRS	monitored retrieval storage
NAACP	National Association for the Advancement of Colored People
NAREB	National Association of Real Estate Boards
ng/ml	nanograms per milliliter
NIH	National Institutes of Health
NORCO	New Orleans Refining Company
NPL	National Priorities List
PCBs	polychlorinated biphenyls
PEON	Protect the Environment of Noxubee
ppm	parts per million
PWA	Public Works Administration
RCRA	Resource Conservation and Recovery Act
RECA	Radiation Exposure Compensation Act
RIA	Resources Industries of Alabama, Incorporated
R.I.S.E.	Residents Involved in Saving the Environment
RSEI	Risk-Screening Environmental Indicators
SCOPE	Sumter Countians Organized for the Protection of the Environment
TCE	trichloroethylene
TDH	Texas Department of Health
TRI	Toxics Release Inventory
TSCA	Toxic Substances Control Act
TSDF	toxic storage disposal facility
TVA	Tennessee Valley Authority
UCC	United Church of Christ
USPCI	United States Pollution Control, Incorporated
VA	Veterans Administration
WMX	Waste Management

Introduction

Environmental Justice Claims

Two of the most controversial claims of the environmental justice movement (EJM) are the assertions that hazardous facilities are concentrated in minority and low-income communities in the United States and that those communities are exposed to inordinate amounts of environmental hazards. These claims are often used to spur mobilization around environmental issues in such communities. Though I have elsewhere (2009) documented a long history of noxious and hazardous facilities being located within or close to minority and low-income communities and evidence of minority environmental activism that predates the twentieth century, it is only in the past three decades that a sustained movement focused on environmental inequalities has arisen. The rise of contemporary EJM coincides with the emergence of environmental justice (EJ) scholarship, policies, legal challenges, and so on.

During the 1960s and 1970s, there was a marked shift in minority responses to environmental inequalities that laid the groundwork for the EJM. Minority activists became more deliberate in their environmental activism—they linked environment with racial and other kinds of social inequalities and framed the issues in terms of rights to safe and healthy environments. Minorities also agitated for more research on environmental inequalities, treatment of illnesses arising from exposure to environmental hazards, policies to facilitate improvement in conditions, and legal redress of harm suffered (D.E. Taylor, 2010, 2011). In addition, minority scholars and activists began to write and speak about environmental issues in the 1970s by linking them with race and social inequality (see for instance Hare, 1970).

Why Don't They Move?

Several events related to the siting of hazardous facilities, the dumping of hazardous wastes, and the contamination of minority communities led to the emergence of the EJM in the late 1980s to early 1990s. The movement asserted that minorities and the poor lived in the most degraded environments. Among other things, movement activists argued that minority communities hosted a disproportionate number of hazardous and noxious facilities, were destroyed for freeways or commercial development, were deprived of amenities such as parks and open space, and were saddled with poor transportation and garbage-removal services. EJ activists coined the term "environmental racism" to describe processes that resulted in minority and low-income communities facing disproportionate environmental harms and limited environmental benefits (D.E. Taylor, 2000, 2010, 2011).

In response to these claims, skeptics have asked the question, Why don't they move? This question is asked of rural and urban communities that articulate the aforementioned types of EJ claims. Famed civil rights activist and field secretary for the state of Mississippi's National Association for the Advancement of Colored People (NAACP) Medgar Evers reflected on this question in a 1958 essay titled "Why I Live in Mississippi." Evers said, "It may sound funny, but I love the South. I don't choose to live anywhere else. There's land here, and a man can raise cattle, and I'm going to do that some day. There are lakes where a man can sink a hook and fight the bass. There is room for my children to play and grow, and become good citizens" (Evers, 2005: 111).

Gail Small, a member of the Northern Cheyenne Tribe and executive director of Native Action in Lame Deer, Montana, responds this way:

> I've always known that this is the place I was meant to be. This is my source of strength here. This land that I live on today with my four kids, it's my mother's family's land. And her family, they're buried right behind us here in the hills. . . . The land is tied to the culture, to the language, to the view point. There's a tremendous spiritual connection to our homeland. (Katahdin Foundation, 2005)

Evers and Small are referring to access to land, ownership of it, and connection to it as reasons why people do not move. They are also referring to the challenges that poor rural residents face in considering relocation to places where they will not have enough funds to purchase land or a new home or must forgo supplementing their income with subsistence activities. Urbanites in communities exposed to environmental hazards also face an array of challenges if and when they consider relocation.

This book examines the underlying assumptions behind this and similar questions and analyzes the forces that constrain, compel, or encourage the movement of minorities. It examines the expulsion of minorities from desirable land and communities, the demolition of their neighborhoods, the relocation of minorities to segregated neighborhoods, and the construction of minority neighborhoods in undesirable locations. Moreover, the book examines how industrial processes expose minorities and low-income people to dangerous environmental conditions. Throughout, the book explores why minorities live in communities with hazardous facilities in them or close by. Hence, the book focuses on three key questions: Why do minorities live adjacent to hazardous facilities or become exposed to environmental hazards? Why do they not move? And who or what keeps them from moving?

Theories, Arguments, Research, and Evidence

EJM claims and activism have stimulated a robust area of research and inquiry. This book focuses on one of the largest and most contentious areas of EJ research—the exposure to environmental hazards and industrial activities in minority and low-income communities. The book reviews the research in the field. Though several scholars have published reviews of EJ research (Goldman, 1993; Pulido, 1996; Pinderhughes, 1996; Lui, 2001; Bowen, 2002; Rinquist, 2000, 2005; Noonan, 2008; Sze and London, 2008; Mohai, Pellow, and Roberts, 2009; D.E. Taylor, 2010, 2011), the review attempted in this book explores the relationship between exposure to environmental hazards and residential mobility more comprehensively and systematically than earlier publications have. It examines the theories and arguments that have been put forward to explain these phenomena and discusses the evidence presented to support or refute the claims of researchers, EJ advocates, and EJ skeptics.

This book urges EJ researchers to pay more attention to both rural and urban EJ issues and to refine their methods to account for the complexity of EJ issues. The book demonstrates that some of the same processes that have been identified and investigated in urban settings, such as segregation and displacement, also occur in rural contexts in ways that influence outcomes. Unlike Jeffreys, who argues that "the fact remains that environmental problems, from a minority perspective, are rather trivial in comparison to the larger economic and civil liberty issues" (1994: 679), this book illustrates that environmental issues are vitally important to minorities. Many minorities recognize this importance and are deeply engaged in environmental affairs.

Overview of the Book

Chapter 1 examines several landmark EJ cases occurring in Black communities in the South that led to activism around environmental issues. These cases help the reader to understand the mechanisms by which communities of color are found in close proximity to hazardous facilities. I examine the claim of disproportionate siting, racism, and discrimination in chapter 2. Chapter 3 examines the internal colonialism thesis in cases occurring in Native American communities in the West. Here, too, the processes by which hazardous facilities and industrial operations occur in or adjacent to minority communities are explored. In chapter 4, I examine several theses and arguments that can be grouped under the category of market dynamics. These theses examine several arguments related to residential mobility. They home in on the question of who moves or stays when people are confronted with the likelihood that they may be exposed to environmental hazards.

Chapter 5 examines how the legal, regulatory, and administrative contexts influence siting, exposure to hazards, and the ability of jurisdictions to enact and enforce environmental protections. Chapter 6 discusses the roles of manipulation, enticement, and environmental blackmail in the siting process and the operation of hazardous facilities.

The rest of the book focuses on the relationship between segregation, housing choices, and residential mobility. Chapter 7 examines residential segregation and the rise of racialized zoning, while chapter 8 explores the use of restrictive covenants to foster residential segregation.

Chapter 9 explores eminent domain, urban renewal, and contemporary forms of expulsive zoning. It also discusses segregation and public housing. Chapter 10 assesses whether housing discrimination is a thing of the past or still a contemporary phenomenon. The conclusion briefly discusses future directions of EJ research.

1

Toxic Exposure

*Landmark Cases in the South and the Rise of
Environmental Justice Activism*

As minorities grew increasingly concerned about exposure to environmental hazards in the late 1970s and early 1980s, two events led them to consider the broader implications of living in close proximity to hazardous industrial facilities. These were the contamination of the waterways around Triana, Alabama, with pesticides from a manufacturing facility and the siting of a hazardous waste landfill in Warren County, North Carolina. A third region—Cancer Alley in Louisiana—is also discussed in this chapter because of its significance in amplifying awareness of environmental hazards in minority communities. This chapter shows how rural communities played an important role in raising public awareness of EJ issues.

The cases discussed in this chapter are also important because they helped to establish the master frame for many of the EJ claims that arose vis-à-vis minorities and exposure to hazards. These landmark cases also helped to establish organizing and legal strategies, as well as policy agendas. The cases also provided some of the early opportunities for scholars to examine the relationship between environment and social justice.

Triana—DDT Contamination and Toxic Fish Consumption

When residents of the small, predominantly Black rural settlement of Triana, Alabama, discovered that they were poisoned with dichloro-diphenyltrichloroethane (DDT) in 1978, they wondered how race and poverty were related to their exposure. Beginning in 1947, DDT—an insecticide widely used to spray crops and kill mosquitoes—was manufactured in the Calabama Chemical Company facility located about six miles from Triana. Calabama operated on land leased from the U.S. Army at the sprawling Redstone Arsenal complex. In 1954, Olin purchased the Calabama Chemical Company and continued to manufacture DDT at the plant till 1970 (*Olin v. Insurance Company*, 1992; Roberts, Laughlin, Hsheih, and Legters, 1997).

While in business, the plant operated seven days a week producing between one to two million pounds of DDT monthly. Waste water contaminated with DDT was released into brick-lined trenches running alongside the factory. The trenches transported the effluents from the Olin factory to an acid-neutralization pit and a series of drainage ditches that emptied into a stream—the Huntsville Spring Branch. The two most contaminated streams were the Huntsville Spring Branch and Indian Creek. Both tributaries empty into the Tennessee River at Triana. Roughly 75% of the residents of Triana are Black (*Olin v. Insurance Company*, 1991; U.S. EPA, 1986b, 2002; Reich, Perkins, and Cutter, 1985).

The lives of Triana residents were inextricably linked to what went on in the DDT-manufacturing facility. Contaminated waste water from the factory traveled less than a mile before emptying into the Huntsville Spring Branch. Triana residents fished for and consumed contaminated fish from Indian Creek; they also used the creek and the Tennessee River for their drinking-water supply till 1967. That year a well was constructed in Triana, and water was piped to residents' homes (Kreiss et al., 1981; *Olin v. Insurance Company*, 1992). DDT is a chemical that poses danger to human health. It is associated with increased risk of pancreatic and breast cancer, non-Hodgkin's lymphoma, hypertension, impaired neural functions, liver disease, reduced psychomotor function, obesity, elevated cholesterol, and reduced fecundity and other reproductive problems (Kreiss et al., 1981).

Contamination of Local Waterways

Though Olin representatives testified in court that the company believed it operated a "closed plant," that is, a facility that did not allow its product (DDT) or byproducts to escape into the environment, the plant released DDT almost continuously during its operation. Records show that even before Olin acquired the plant, DDT was escaping into local tributaries. In 1948, Calabama's manager, Benton Wilcoxin (who continued to manage the plant after Olin bought it), discovered that DDT was settling in the waste-water trenches. In 1952, the Army, concerned about chemical leakage from the plant, set maximum levels of 10 parts per million (ppm) DDT for the effluents. The Army also established a zero permissible level of DDT for the Huntsville Spring Branch. Nonetheless, three years later, Olin engineers found DDT in the waste-water trenches. DDT was again found in samples analyzed from the trenches in 1957 and 1961. While events unfolded at Olin, research evidence was mounting that DDT was harmful to humans and the environment. By the mid-1950s, researchers and DDT manufacturers were aware that the chemical was very toxic. In fact, Olin began putting warning labels on some of its DDT products between 1957 and 1958 that alerted users that the products should not be used near children, fish, or wild fowl (*Olin v. Insurance Company*, 1991, 1992). As early as 1959, the U.S. Fish and Wildlife Service reported that there was a 97% drop in the number of double-crested cormorants at the Wheeler National Wildlife Refuge (parts of which abut the Redstone Arsenal). Fourteen hundred acres of the refuge were contaminated with DDT, and by 1963 there was also a 90% decrease in the number of red-shouldered hawks (Press, 1981; Maynard, Cooper & Gale, 1995; U.S. EPA, 1983). Rachel Carson's 1962 book, *Silent Spring*, also provided strong evidence that DDT was harmful to wildlife and humans.

During the 1960s, the Army increased the testing of nearby creeks as public awareness of the dangers of DDT grew. After a buildup of DDT was observed at the confluence of the Olin drainage ditch and the Huntsville Spring Branch in 1963, the Public Health Service was asked to conduct a study. The Public Health Service found toxic levels of DDT in the Huntsville Spring Branch and that the fish in the creek were dying from exposure to the chemical. The study also found traces of DDT at a dam more than 100 miles downstream of the Olin plant. Toxicity data in the Public Health Service report indicate that fish exposed to 25% concentration of Olin's effluents died within an hour of exposure. The study expressed concern for the health of fish and wildlife and for people consuming them. However, it was several more years before local Blacks who were subsistence anglers and who consumed large quantities of fish from the creeks around the Olin plant were tested and warned about DDT contamination. In 1964, the Tennessee Valley Authority (TVA—which has jurisdiction over the Tennessee River watershed) also conducted a study of the Huntsville Spring Branch and found that it was polluted with DDT. That same year, the Army notified Olin that it had lowered the limit of DDT permissible in the effluents to 80 parts per billion (*Olin v. Insurance Company*, 1991, 1992).

Nonetheless, the Olin plant continued to pollute the waterways with DDT throughout the 1960s. In 1965, Olin began running its effluents through a settling tank in an attempt to filter out contaminants and reduce water pollution. The tank filled up quickly, collecting more than 12,000 pounds of DDT-tainted materials in a four-month period. Court documents also show that Olin executives were notified that DDT was being released by the plant. A 1967 conference concerning pollution at the Redstone Arsenal concluded that pollution in the Huntsville Spring Branch was dangerous to aquatic life. Finally, in August 1969, the Army began procedures to close the facility on the grounds that Olin had violated its lease by releasing DDT into local streams. When a new filtering system failed to stem the flow of DDT from the plant, the Huntsville facility closed on June 30, 1970. Six months later, the federal government banned all DDT use in the U.S. except for emergency purposes (*Olin v. Insurance Company*, 1991, 1992; Reich, Perkins, and Cutter, 1985).

When Olin's manufacturing facility closed, the company left behind about 417 tons of DDT in the water and sediments of Huntsville Spring Branch–Indian Creek tributaries (U.S. EPA, 1983, 1986b). A 1972 Army study found extensive water pollution in the area around the defunct Olin plant. Fish in area streams also had high levels of DDT in their systems. Based on the results of the tests, the Environmental Protection Agency (EPA) ordered the Army to clean up the facility. In 1978, TVA conducted another study of DDT contamination in waterways downstream of the Redstone Arsenal and found very high levels of DDT in the fish. The report also expressed concern for the people in the area who ate the contaminated fish. The report was made public, and it was at this juncture that the residents of Triana learned that they might be contaminated with DDT (*Olin v. Insurance Company*, 1991, 1992; Maynard, Cooper & Gale, 1995; Press, 1981; Hollis, 1980; Reynolds, 1980; NIH, 1997).

Shortly after the 1978 TVA study was released, the EPA ordered the Army to develop a remediation plan for the Huntsville Spring Branch. The Army argued that it was not responsible for cleanup because the Wheeler Wildlife Refuge is just outside the Redstone Arsenal boundary. Eventually the Army acquiesced and collaborated with the EPA and the Fish and Wildlife Service to resolve the problem (Noland, 1979). The Centers for Disease Control (CDC) analyzed samples of fish caught in Indian Creek in 1979 and found they had an average of 226 milligrams per kilogram (mg/kg) of DDT residues. The Food and Drug Administration's action level for DDT is set at 5 mg/kg (Kreiss et al., 1981).

Residents Tested

The lack of concern for local residents shown by wildlife managers, some government agencies, the Army, Calabama Chemical Company, and Olin did not escape the notice of Triana's residents. Though evidence of DDT contamination was identified as early as 1948 and research indicating that the chemical might be harmful to humans began surfacing in the 1950s, Blacks who lived close to the Olin plant and who drank contaminated water and ate large quantities of toxic fish were not tested or alerted to the problem till three decades after the problem was first identified. Clyde Foster, then mayor of Triana and one of the plaintiffs in the lawsuits discussed in the following section, argued that the TVA knew of the contamination but did not warn or test Triana's residents (Haggerty, 1980: 14).

In another interview, Foster charged that state and federal agencies knew of the excessive levels of DDT in fish consumed by Triana residents for years but refrained from making the information public because they wanted to use Triana's residents as "guinea pigs." The police chief, Joe Fletcher, echoes Foster's sentiments. Fletcher thinks the Army knew of the contamination for a long time. He argues, "They knew it was there. . . . They should have come down and told us about it in 1964, when we were incorporated" (Noland, 1979: 15).

The first round of testing of residents began in December 1978. The

CDC collected blood samples from 12 residents. Analysis showed that one of the test subjects had DDT and DDE (dichlorodiphenyldichloroethylene) levels that were twice as high as any level previously recorded in the medical literature. The CDC conducted a more extensive study in 1979 in which 518 people were tested; 86.9% of the study participants were Black. Participants ranged in age from a few weeks to 90 years old. Adults had resided in Triana for an average of 24.9 years. There were several ways in which Triana residents were exposed to DDT. Routes of exposure included consumption of locally caught fish, imbibing water from local creeks, spraying of nearby cotton fields, and working in the pesticide-manufacturing facility. However, the primary source of exposure was through fish consumption. The median fish consumption was 4.3 fish meals per month; however, some study participants reported consuming fish once or twice daily (Kreiss et al., 1981).

The study found that the average DDT level in the study population was 159.4 nanograms per milliliter (ng/ml). However, six participants had between 1,000 and 2,820.5 ng/ml of DDT in their systems. A third of the sample had DDT levels that were greater than 500 ng/ml, and 28% had levels of DDT and its derivatives in their blood that were ten times the U.S. average. At the time of the study, the U.S. average for DDT levels in people 12 to 74 years was 15 ng/ml. The study found that DDT levels were higher in Blacks than in Whites and higher in males than in females. The study also found that age was the strongest predictor of DDT levels—the oldest respondents had the highest levels of DDT. Prior to this study, it was assumed that chronic exposure to DDT resulted in a steady-state condition in which intake of the pesticide would match the levels at which it is excreted from the body. The CDC study indicated that DDT continued to accumulate in the body over time (Kreiss et al., 1981).

Lawsuits

In July 1979, 32 commercial fishermen filed suit against Olin (*James v. Olin*, 1979). They argued that they suffered personal injury and property damage from the DDT contamination. Two months later, the state of Alabama also filed suit against Olin (*Alabama v. Olin*, 1979). A second CDC study was published in 1980 showing very high levels of DDT in the blood serum of Triana residents. The study also revealed that Triana residents had high levels of polychlorinated biphenyls (PCBs) in their blood stream. The discovery of PCBs in residents' bloodstream triggered a search for the source of the cancer-causing agent, but no major source of PCBs was found (Redstone Arsenal, 1980).

In 1980, three lawsuits were filed against Olin by residents and one by the U.S. government (*Freeman v. Olin*, 1980; *Parcus v. Olin*, 1980; *Charest v. Olin*, 1981; *United States v. Olin*, 1980). At the time, 866 of the 1,158 residents of Triana were Black (U.S. Census Bureau, 1980). The three citizens' suits (*Freeman v. Olin*, *Parcus v. Olin*, and *Charest v. Olin*) were brought on behalf of 1,200 residents living downstream of the Redstone Arsenal. The suits alleged that plaintiffs had eaten fish from the streams and had consumed water from the creeks and rivers. Plaintiffs were compensated $10,000 apiece. In all, 15 lawsuits (including class-action suits) were filed by individuals and government agencies (*Olin v. Insurance Company*, 1991, 1992; McGovern, 1997). The Redstone Arsenal site was declared a Superfund site in 1981. In December 1982, Olin reached an agreement with the EPA to clean up the Wheeler Wildlife Refuge as well as the Huntsville Spring Branch and Indian Creek tributaries. As part of the agreement, Olin promised to lower the level of DDT in catfish to 5 ppm by 1997 (catfish is used as an indicator species, and 5 ppm is the federal tolerance level for DDT), to excavate new channels and divert the flow of Huntsville Spring Branch and Indian Creek around the most contaminated portions of the tributaries, and to bury contaminated sediments in place. The agreement also called for Olin to provide $24 million ($19 million of which went to satisfy personal injury claims) to help residents in the contaminated area (U.S. EPA, 1983, 1986, 2002). Additional lawsuits were filed, and eventually more than 13,000 plaintiffs filed suit against Olin, the TVA, and the Army (residents of six counties were eligible to file claims). All the lawsuits were eventually settled for more than $80 million (*Olin v. Insurance Company*, 1991; McGovern, 1990, 1997).

Continued Monitoring

Federal agencies continued to monitor the waterways around the Olin plant for decades. A 1985 study of the aquatic ecosystem found that levels of DDT contamination in Indian Creek and Huntsville Spring Branch was still extremely high (Reich, Perkins, and Cutter, 1985). From 1980 to 1998, the TVA and other agencies collected fish samples in the lower Tennessee River basin (including samples from the Huntsville Spring Branch and Indian Creek). The Alabama Department of Environmental Management issued consumption advisories warning people not to eat the fish from Huntsville Spring Branch and Indian Creek because it was contaminated with DDT, dichlorodiphenyldichloroethane, DDE, and PCBs (Knight and Powell, 2001).

In 1997, the National Institutes of Health funded a study to examine the link between exposure to DDT and breast cancer (NIH, 1997). Breast exams and mammograms were conducted on 228 women aged 19 to 91; 80% of the study participants were Black. Though the study did not establish a link between breast cancer and DDT levels, it found that DDT and DDE levels in the blood serum of the study participants were very high (Rusiecki et al., 2006). Despite these results, community activists report that Triana women are dying from breast cancer (Associated Press, 2002).

Warren County—PCB Landfill

PCB Contamination

Though the Triana case was compelling, it was the events that occurred in Warren County, North Carolina, that changed everything. That is, the images of Black protestors lying face up across a rural road while a large dump truck filled with PCB-laced dirt inched toward them garnered much interest and shocked the nation. In 1982, residents of the predominantly Black Warren County (North Carolina) began protesting the construction of a chemical-waste landfill near Afton in which the state planned to bury 400,000 cubic yards of soil tainted with PCBs (LaBalme, 1988). The contamination occurred when a contractor (Robert Burns and his two sons) hired by Robert Ward of the Ward Transformer Company of Raleigh, North Carolina, to dispose of hazardous wastes sprayed approximately 12,850 gallons of PCB-tainted fluids along 210 miles of roads at 51 different sites in 14 counties in North Carolina in 1978. Ward Transformer bought, stored, rebuilt, and resold used electrical equipment including transformers (*United States v. Ward*, 1984, 1985).

At first, Burns was paid $1.70 per gallon to remove the adulterated fluids from Ward Transformer's facility and ship them to a Youngsville (Pennsylvania) warehouse for storage. When this proved too costly, Burns and Ward changed plans three months into the operation and decided to dump the remainder of the contaminated oil somewhere remote. They conjured up a plan to dispose of the oil at Fort Bragg's impact range. Two truckloads were dumped at Fort Bragg in late June 1978. However, Burns and Ward decided to dump the rest of contaminated oil elsewhere because the truck was getting stuck in the sandy soil at Fort Bragg and the oil was not readily absorbed by sand. Consequently, the two conspired to spray the contaminated fluids along remote, rural roads (*United States v. Ward*, 1982b; *United States v. Burns*, 1986).

All the modifications needed for the truck to carry out the operation were done at a Ward Transformer facility with the aid of company employees. PCB-laced fluids were dumped from an enclosed truck outfitted with a 750-gallon tank and piping connected to a nozzle which extended from the rear right side of the truck. The nozzle was opened to allow fluids to escape while the truck was in motion (*United States v. Ward*, 1985; *Warren County v. North Carolina*, 1981).

In July and August, Burns and his sons sprayed the contaminated fluids along secluded roadways in eastern North Carolina. The spill was first discovered at Fort Bragg when discolored grass and stained earth was noticed along 11 miles of roadway. Similar discoloration was spotted later on rural roadways in eastern counties. Test of soil samples showed that the concentration of PCBs was as high as 14,800 ppm in some samples (*United States v. Ward*, 1982b, 1982c, 1985).

Once the contaminated soil was discovered, the state considered several plans before deciding to bury the soil in a landfill. The state evaluated 90 sites in 20 counties as potential disposal sites before settling on the Warren County site. Many of the sites were ruled out because they did not meet two EPA criteria: the bottom of the landfill should be at least 50 feet above the groundwater level and the site should have thick, relatively impermeable soil formations such as large-area clay pans. The chosen landfill site, located about 3.5 miles south of Warrenton and about 2.5 miles north of Afton, is in a rural, agricultural area. In

December 1978, North Carolina applied for approval for the site to be used as a landfill. A public hearing—attended by hundreds of residents —was held in January 1979 in Warrenton. At the meeting, the state requested that the EPA waive three of its regulations—the requirement that the groundwater be at least 50 feet below the landfill bottom (the groundwater was seven feet below the surface at the chosen site), the need for an artificial liner (the state argued that soil compaction would be enough to prevent leaks), and the need for an underliner leachate-collection system (LaBalme, 1987; Exchange Project, 2006).

When residents voiced their concerns about the site, the state was ordered to conduct further soil tests. The results of the tests were submitted to the EPA in March. The Warren County site was approved on June 4, 1979 (*Warren County v. North Carolina*, 1981; *Twitty v. North Carolina*, 1987; LaBalme, 1987). Activists hired their own consultant— Dr. Charles Mulchi, a soil expert from the Department of Agronomy at the University of Maryland. Mulchi argued that the soil at the War-ren County site did not meet compaction criteria as it would not form a protective layer when compressed. He also argued that the kaolin-ite (soil/clay mixture) found at the selected site had a high chemical-exchange capacity (LaBalme, 1987; Exchange Project, 2006). Residents were also concerned about the landfill because PCB is known to cause cancer and other illnesses. Despite opposition to the landfill, Governor Hunt framed the siting of the landfill as a "public good" and assured residents that the health of North Carolinians would be safeguarded in "the finest manner possible" (LaBalme, 1987). Seeking to assure residents that the site would employ the best available technology in land-fill design, state and EPA officials referred to the facility as the "Cadillac of landfills" (Stocking, 1993).

Opposition to the Landfill

Opponents of the plan to bury wastes at the Warren County site filed two lawsuits in 1979 to halt plans for the landfill. One lawsuit was filed by landowners living adjacent to the landfill site (*Twitty v. North Caro-lina*, 1981) and the other by the Warren County Board of Commission-ers and the county manager (*Warren County v. North Carolina*, 1981). Warren County argued that the disposal of the PCBs in the landfill was a public nuisance and that the process by which the site was approved was defective as it allowed impermissible waivers of EPA regulations. The county questioned the timing of the preparation of the environmental impact statement and the level of detail it contained about the landfill design. The county also argued that the decision to establish the landfill was arbitrary and capricious. The county, which passed a law banning the disposal of PCBs within its limits (on August 21, 1978), argued that the plan to dump PCB-tainted soil in Warrenton violated its ordinances. In enacting the ordinance, the county noted that the area was "particularly unsuited for the disposition of PCB's because there is a generally high . . . water table in the county and most of the soils of the county are highly permeable, so that there is a substantial likelihood that, if stored or disposed of in the county, PCB's would eventually seep into the ground water supply" (*Warren County v. North Carolina*, 1981). The court, relying on EPA documents, struck down the Warren County ordinance by arguing that though states and local jurisdictions had some discretion in imposing more stringent disposal guidelines than those in federal regulations, states or local jurisdictions could not take action that would stymie the "national goal of properly disposing of hazardous chemical substances. . . . It would be a matter of national concern if . . . states [refused] to share in the national responsibility for finding safe means for the proper disposal of hazardous substances" (*Warren County v. North Carolina*, 1981).

The landfill site was designed so that excavation for the disposal site was no closer than seven feet above the water table and the contaminated soil at least 14 feet above the high-groundwater mark. A leachate-detection system would be put in place as well as both an artificial and a compacted-clay liner. After the PCB-tainted soil was buried, the landfill would be capped with three feet of compacted soil, an artificial liner, and a foot of topsoil. The case was decided in November 1981. The court ruled in favor of the defendants, the state of North Carolina. It argued that the environmental impact statement was in order as it provided enough details of the landfill design and that statutory and regulatory requirements were met by the state (*Warren County v. North Carolina*, 1981). The district court also ruled against the plaintiffs in another case—*Twitty v. North Carolina*—that made arguments similar to those made by Warren County. The plaintiffs argued that the bottom of the landfill should be at least 50 feet from the historical high-water mark. The court rejected the plaintiff's argument, claiming instead that the design of the landfill would be adequate to protect public health. The court came to this conclusion because it felt that since the landfill is located on a ridge that is above the 100-year flood level, the bottom of the waste would be a minimum of 10 feet above seasonal high waters (*Twitty v. North Carolina*, 1981).

The NAACP also filed a lawsuit in 1982 that explicitly linked race to exposure to environmental hazards. The organization argued that the driving force behind the decision to construct the landfill near Afton was the fact that the community was predominantly Black, rural, and poor. However, District Court Judge W. Earl Britt disagreed. He contended, "There is not one shred of evidence that race has at any time been a motivating factor for any decision taken by any official—state, federal or local—in this long saga" (*NAACP v. Gorsuch*, 1982).

The state acquired a 142.3-acre tract of land from Warren County residents Carter and Linda Pope, on which it built a 19.3-acre landfill to bury the 40,000 cubic yards of contaminated soil. In response to citizens' concerns about future landfill expansion, the county reached an out-of-court settlement with the state in which the county acquired the deed to the remainder of the property. There is also a restrictive covenant on the landfill site that bars any other kind of hazardous or radioactive wastes from being disposed of at the site (*United States v. Ward*, 1985; *Twitty v. North Carolina*, 1981, 1987; Exchange Project, 2006).

At the time the site was chosen, Warren County had the highest percentage of Blacks of any county in the state; it was also one of the counties with the lowest income. Warren County was 60% Black, and the unincorporated Shocco Township in which the landfill was located was 66% Black. Yet Blacks constituted only 22% of the state's population. Warren County was one of the four poorest counties in the state (LaBalme, 1988; U.S. GAO, 1983).

The dumping and capping took place quickly. Wastes began arriving at the landfill on September 15, 1982. By then, activists had organized an EJ group—the Warren County Citizens Concerned About PCBs. Five hundred protestors met the first truck at the Coley Springs Baptist Church in Afton; 55 people were arrested on the first day of protests by state patrol officers dressed in full riot gear. The protests received national attention. Army troops from Fort Bragg were also called in to quell the six weeks of protests in which 523 adults and children were arrested, including the congressional delegate from Washington, D.C., Walter Fauntroy, and members of the United Church of Christ Commission for Racial Justice (*Twitty v. North Carolina*, 1981; *Warren County v. North Carolina*, 1981; *United States v. Ward*, 1985; Thompson, 1998; LaBalme, 1988; *New York Times*, 1982a, 1982b, 1982c). These protests made headline news, and the pictures of residents blocking the road to the dump by lying down across it were printed in leading newspapers.

The last of 7,000 truckloads of tainted soil arrived at the landfill on October 27, and the landfill was capped by late November of that year. Even before the landfill was capped, there were signs of trouble. Heavy rains from a hurricane caused erosion and the accumulation of about 500,000 gallons of water at the site before the capping was concluded. Three months after the site was capped, residents photographed gas bubbles in the liner; they also reported a gurgling sound coming from the landfill (LaBalme, 1988; Exchange Project, 2006).

Problems continued to surface at the landfill, and the parties fought for a long time about additional remediation costs. By 1993, about 1.5 million gallons of water was trapped in the landfill. Warren County residents demanded and got the government to remediate problems at the site (Leavenworth, 1993; Exchange Project, 2006).

Criminal Charges and Cleanup Costs

Criminal charges were filed against the Burnses and the Ward Transformer Company. Robert Burns confessed to dumping the contaminated fluid along roadways and was arrested. On January 22, 1979, Robert Ward was indicted by a federal grand jury on eight counts of knowingly and willfully causing PCBs to be disposed of illegally. He was convicted on all eight counts in May 1981. Ward's conviction was upheld by the court of appeals in 1982. The U.S. Supreme Court denied Ward's petition to hear the case in 1982 (*United States v. Ward*, 1982b, 1982c, 1985).

In January 1982, the federal government brought suit against Robert Ward and the Ward Transformer Company to recover expenses incurred in the PCB cleanup. The state intervened in the case to recover its cleanup costs from the Ward Transformer Company also. Funding for the cleanup was provided from the EPA's Superfund program, which came about through the Comprehensive Environmental Response Compensation Liability Act (CERCLA) of 1980, and state funds. In all, $2.4 million was taken from the Superfund trust to cover the cost of cleanup. In addition, the U.S. Army spent $430,000 to remove contaminated soil from Fort Bragg, and North Carolina spent $450,000 on the cleanup. The case against Ward Transformer was finally settled in 1985. The court found that the company was liable for the cleanup costs (*United States v. Ward*, 1982a, 1984, 1985; CERCLA, 1980).

Studies Commissioned

During the protests, activists claimed that the landfill site was chosen because the township in which it was located was predominantly Black. Though activists did not succeed in blocking the landfill, their organizing led to important outcomes. They formed an effective EJ organization. They also formed a voter-registration foundation that resulted in Warren County becoming the first county in North Carolina where a majority of the members of the Board of County Commissioners were Black (Exchange Project, 2006).

Activists and protestors, including Representative Walter Fauntroy, also wondered whether the siting of the facility was a fluke or whether there was a tendency to site hazardous facilities in minority communities. This question led to the commissioning of two reports to examine the relationship between race, class, and the siting patterns of hazardous facilities. The first study, conducted by the U.S. General Accounting Office (GAO) focused on the southeastern United States (U.S. GAO, 1983), and the second—conducted by the United Church of Christ Commission for Racial Justice—was a national study (UCC, 1987). Both of these widely cited studies had a significant impact on mobilizing minority communities to organize around environmental issues and on the growth of the EJM. They were among the earliest studies to link race with the increased likelihood of living close to hazardous facilities and toxic waste sites. Unlike other early studies in the genre, they were widely circulated among minority activists and in minority communities.

Cancer Alley

Though events in Triana and Warren County took center stage in the late 1970s and early 1980s, during that time, rural communities in Louisiana were also trying to cope with an onslaught of industrial hazards that eventually garnered international attention. A 1978 *Washington Post* article used the term "Cancer Alley" to describe a heavily industrialized corridor where cancer occurred in high frequencies among the population. But the article was not describing southeastern Louisiana; it was referring to northeastern New Jersey (*Washington Post*, 1978). For the next nine years, communities such as Rutherford and Newark lived with the ominous-sounding moniker. Then, in 1987, the *Washington Post* published another article in which the tiny community of St. Gabriel, Louisiana, called Jacobs Drive—a street in the hamlet—Cancer Alley because there were 15 cancer victims in a two-block stretch. Half a mile away, there were seven cancer victims living on one block.

The meandering stretch of the Mississippi River from Baton Rouge to New Orleans used to be known as "petrochemical corridor," but since reports of the numerous cancer cases occurring in the small rural communities on both sides of the river surfaced, the entire area has become known as Cancer Alley. There are about 135 petrochemical plants in Cancer Alley. Cancer Alley includes the parishes (counties) of St. James, Ascension, East Baton Rouge, West Baton Rouge, Iberville, St. John the Baptist, St. Charles, Jefferson, Orleans, Plaquemines, and Assumption (Perlin, Sexton, and Wong, 1999; Maraniss and Weisskopf, 1987). Cancer Alley has hundreds of industrial facilities that include oil refineries, chemical-manufacturing facilities, and solid waste dumps (B. Wright, 2005; Lerner, 2005; Roberts and Toffolon-Weiss, 2001). A 2002 study found that Louisiana had the second-highest cancer death rate in the country (National Center for Health Statistics, 2002; Centers for Disease Control, 2002).

Cancer Rates

The most recent cancer data show that Louisiana has the second-highest male cancer rate in the country (trailing only Mississippi). While the national average for male cancers in 2008 was 532.6 per 100,000,

Louisiana's rate was 609.6 per 100,000. The state ranks twelfth overall for male and female cancers combined. The national combined male and female cancer rate is 462.1 per 100,000, while that rate is 490.4 per 100,000 in Louisiana. Louisiana has the third-highest male cancer death rate in the country. In 2008, the male cancer death rate was 261.1 per 100,000; at the time, the average U.S. male cancer death rate was 215.7. Louisiana has the fourth-highest female cancer death rate in the U.S. While the average U.S. female cancer death rate was 148.4 per 100,000 in 2008, it was 163.4 per 100,000 in Louisiana. Louisiana has the second-highest combined male and female cancer death rate. The combined cancer death rate is 203.0 per 100,000 in Louisiana; in comparison, the national average is 175.8 per 100,000 (U.S. Cancer Statistics Working Group, 2012).

Cancer is the second-leading cause of death in the U.S., causing one in four deaths in the country. A study of cancer death rates from 1999 to 2008 shows that Blacks are more likely to die from cancer than any other racial group is. In 2008, the death rate from all cancers was 472.3 per 100,000 for Blacks, 460.5 per 100,000 for Whites, 358 per 100,000 for Hispanics; 294.8 per 100,000 for Asians and Pacific Islanders, and 270.4 per 100,00 for Native Americans (U.S. Cancer Statistics Working Group, 2012; Eheman et al., 2012).

The Shell Oil Company (which has facilities in Cancer Alley) conducted its own research on mortality and cancer rates in Cancer Alley. The study, published in 2004, concluded that overall cancer and mortality rates for White males in Cancer Alley was significantly lower than rates for the corresponding Louisiana population. The study also argued that the incidence of lung cancer in Cancer Alley were similar to or lower than rates found elsewhere in Louisiana. White females in Cancer Alley had similar mortality patterns to White males. The mortality rates of non-White males and females in Cancer Alley were similar to corresponding populations elsewhere in the state. The study conceded that cancer rates were higher in Louisiana than the average for the U.S. as a whole (Tsai, Cardarelli, Wendt, and Fraser, 2004).

Another Shell-sponsored study compared the incidence of cancer among employees at two petrochemical plants in southern Louisiana and the general population of that part of the state. This study concluded that there was little evidence to indicate there was any association between the incidence of cancer and employment at the two petrochemical facilities. Though the study found an increased risk of bone cancer, the researchers concluded that the bone cancer is unlikely to be due to occupational exposures (Tsai, Chen, et al., 2004).

Toxic Releases

Public concern over exposure to hazardous compounds and materials is warranted. Though the overall on- and off-site releases and disposal of toxic chemicals and hazardous wastes have been declining, dropping by 30% between 2001 and 2010, there is still cause for concern. In 2010, the 20,904 facilities across the country that filed Toxics Release Inventory (TRI) information with the EPA reported releasing or disposing of 3.9 billion pounds of toxic chemicals in the air, in the water, on land, and through underground injection. The facilities also generated 21.8 billion pounds of production-related wastes (U.S. EPA, 2010).

Concern about toxic chemicals and hazardous wastes is high in Louisiana because a large number of industrial facilities are located in the state; many of these cluster along waterways such as the Mississippi River. The highest concentration of these facilities is found along Cancer Alley. The older facilities are much more egregious polluters than newer ones are (U.S. EPA, 2000b). In 2011, Louisiana's 361 TRI facilities reported releasing or disposing of 122.2 million pounds of toxic chemicals and hazardous wastes on-site and 8.6 million pounds off-site. These facilities also managed 2.4 billion pounds of production-related wastes. The 11 parishes in Cancer Alley account for 63.5% of the on- and off-site releases and disposal of toxic chemicals and hazardous materials in Louisiana. The parishes also account for 46.4% of the toxic chemicals found in production-related wastes managed in the state (see table 1.1) (U.S. EPA 2011d, 2011e).

The population of many of the small towns in Cancer Alley is primarily Black and low income. Despite the large number of industrial facilities, unemployment is high in many communities, and most residents do not have a college education. In Geismar and St. Gabriel alone, there are 18 industrial facilities in a 9.5-square-mile area. Industrial accidents and accidental releases are common occurrences in Cancer Alley. For instance, in 1994, Condea Vista (Conoco), located in Lake

Table 1.1. *Releases and Disposal of Toxic Chemicals and Hazardous Materials Cancer Alley*

Jurisdictions	Total on- and off-site disposal or release (in pounds)	Quantities of TRI chemicals in total production-related wastes managed (in pounds)
Louisiana	130,753,129	2,378,348,448
Cancer Alley parishes		
Ascension	18,035,670	186,226,585
Assumption	34,843	724,551
East Baton Rouge	9,183,812	141,476,012
Iberville	7,337,184	1,776,822
Jefferson	16,535,680	56,465,832
Orleans	28,543	120,043
Plaquemines	1,143,742	442,531
St. Charles	19,883,325	567,609,719
St. James	4,840,523	76,931,843
St. John the Baptist	4,943,883	49,380,072
West Baton Rouge	1,093,141	22,225,497
Parish total	83,060,346	1,103,379,507
Parish percentage	63.52	46.39

Source: Compiled from U.S. EPA 2011d.

Charles, reported 39 chemical accidents that released 129,500 pounds of chemicals. The following year, Condea Vista reported 90 accidental chemical releases. In 1997, the company was charged with contaminating local ground-water supplies with between 19 and 47 million pounds of ethylene dichloride (EDC—a suspected human carcinogen). In 1999, hundreds of unskilled laborers filed suit against Condea Vista, claiming they were exposed to EDC while cleaning up a spill from a leaking underground pipeline that carried the chemical inland from barges at Conoco's docks. On Christmas Eve, 1997, a 500,000-gallon storage tank at Borden Chemicals & Plastics in Ascension Parish blew up (the explosion was heard for miles), forcing the closure of Route 1 (the only entry and egress route for several communities) and the evacuation of residents (U.S. EPA, 2000a; Conoco EDC Litigation, 2002).

Exposure to pollution is high on the agenda of Louisiana's municipalities and parishes. A survey conducted by the Louisiana Department of Environmental Quality (LDEQ) found that local ordinances, water quality, and solid wastes were the top issues of concern for municipalities and parishes. More than 60% of them listed these as top concerns.

This is not surprising since the report indicates that more than 75% of the state's 480 regulatory water bodies are listed as "impaired." Most of the 11 parishes that did not meet the EPA's standards for ozone were in Cancer Alley (LDEQ, 2009).

Opposition to the Siting and Operation of Facilities

ALSEN — LANDFILLS AND HAZARDOUS WASTES AT THE NORTHERN GATEWAY

Though Triana and Warren County received much publicity, residents of Alsen began their fight for environmental justice earlier than either of the aforementioned communities. Alsen, an unincorporated village north of Baton Rouge, is the northern gateway to Cancer Alley. It is a small community of about 1,100 residents, 98.9% of whom are Black. Most of Alsen residents own their homes, and 77.4% are owner occupied; 19.4% of the residents are below the poverty level. In 1970, Rollins constructed what was at the time the fourth-largest hazardous waste landfill in the U.S. in Alsen; the facility also has an incinerator (Bullard 1990; Motavalli, 1998).

Longtime resident and leader of the Coalition for Community Action Mary McCastle began to organize the community in 1976 (Schwab, 1994). In a 1988 interview, the 72-year-old grandmother claimed that residents had no warning that Rollins was siting a facility and that once it was constructed, people did not know what was being dumped (Bullard, 1990). The Rollins facility was cited for violating federal and state environmental laws a hundred times between 1980 and 1985. Other industrial facilities can be found in Alsen; these include plastics plants, lead smelters, landfills, tank-car washers, petroleum coke yards, and resin makers. There are two Superfund sites in the community also. In late 1980, residents stepped up efforts to organize to reduce the contamination of their community. They founded the North Baton Rouge Environmental Association to oppose two landfills that were proposed for their community. In 1981, some community residents filed a $3 billion class-action lawsuit against Rollins and in 1987 reached a settlement with the company for a lot less. The litigants received between $500 and $3,000, and for that they gave up their rights to bring any further litigation against the company. However, when a wealthy White property owner who lived adjacent to Rollins sued the company for the death of his cattle after water spilled onto his pasture; he received $500,000 (Bullard, 1990, 1994; Motavalli, 1998).

After residents contacted the LDEQ about illnesses (such as skin rashes, irritation of the eye, and breathing problems) and pungent odors, the LDEQ found that Rollins was dumping in the landfill eight substances for which it had no permit. Cyanide was also found in every sample taken at the Rollins facility (Schwab, 1994). Hazardous waste is big business for Rollins; the company generates more than $69 million annually from this enterprise. When Rollins applied for a permit to burn PCBs at the Alsen incinerator during the mid-1980s, opposition grew, and national groups such as Greenpeace and the Sierra Club joined residents in their fight. Opponents succeeded in preventing Rollins from burning PCBs at the facility (Bullard, 1990).

ROLLINS DOWN THE RIVER — UNION'S PCB-DISPOSAL FACILITY

In 1984, Rollins began operating a PCB-disposal facility in Union, Louisiana, in St. James Parish. The facility was located about a quarter mile from the Romeville Elementary School. Obsolete electrical transformers—weighing as much as several thousand pounds—were brought to the facility by rail or truck. There PCB-laced fluids were drained from the transformers, which were then rinsed with diesel fuel. The spent PCB and diesel fuel were placed in containers and shipped to a Rollins incinerator in Texas, while the transformers were sent to a landfill in Nevada (*Rollins v. St. James*, 1985).

The first shipment of transformers arrived at Rollins's Union facility in November 1984. The next month, the St. James Parish Council passed an ordinance to regulate hazardous wastes and PCBs in the parish. The ordinance prohibited the treatment, storage, and disposal of PCBs at commercial waste-disposal facilities in the parish. The ordinance also stated that anyone transporting PCBs through the parish had to supply a manifest to or obtain a permit from the Sheriff's Department of the parish. Rollins filed suit on December 21, challenging the St. James ordinance on the grounds that it violated the Commerce Clause. On January 2, 1985, the St. James Parish Council repealed the ordinance and replaced it with another one that prohibited any businesses using commercial solvents from being conducted within one mile of any area of special concern (school, day-care center, nursing home, grain elevator, public building or auditorium, hospital, church, or theater) or being located in an area of special environmental concern (flood hazard area, flood plain, wetlands, and surface or subsurface drinking-water source). The new ordinance also prohibited such businesses from draining or discharging any spent solvents into any area of special environmental concern and specified that such businesses had to conduct their cleaning operations in a contained area (e.g., on a concrete slab at least two feet thick and sloped to collect spills). Rollins immediately challenged the new ordinance too. Though the district court felt that the ordinance "amounted to, and had the practical effect of, an absolute prohibition of Rollins' activities in the Parish," the court dismissed Rollin's case because it lacked subject-matter jurisdiction (*Rollins v. St. James*, 1985: 631).

Rollins appealed, and in 1985, the Fifth Circuit Court of Appeals ruled in favor of the company. Using the Warren County decisions as precedence, the Fifth Circuit Court argued that the St. James Parish ordinance was subject to the Supremacy Clause. That is, the Toxic Substances Control Act (TSCA) had supremacy over state and local waste-disposal ordinances. Though states and local jurisdictions can develop more stringent criteria governing the handling and disposal of hazardous wastes, such criteria are allowed only in very prescribed circumstances and cannot interfere with interstate commerce or discriminate against particular businesses (*Rollins v. St. James*, 1985).

The Fifth Circuit Court went on to call the St. James Parish ordinance a "sham" that would amount to "an outright prohibition of Rollins' PCB disposal activities or an unreasonably burdensome and restrictive regulation" of the company's business. The Circuit Court also argued that though "a hazardous facility appears to have been located almost deliberately on the most inauspicious possible site, one-quarter mile from a local elementary school, . . . if every locality were able to dodge responsibility for and participation in this program [TSCA] through artfully designed ordinances, the national goal of safe, environmentally sound toxic waste disposal would surely be frustrated" (*Rollins v. St. James*, 1985: 637).

DIAMOND — NORCO AND THE SHELL GAME

Originally a sugar plantation, Diamond morphed into a small Black community that was a segregated subdivision of Norco. The Diamond enclave consisted of four four-block-long streets on which Black families owned and occupied their property. Many of the Diamond residents have roots in the community that extend back to the times when their ancestors slaved away on the Trepagnier Plantation. The plantation was a land grant issued to the Canadian immigrant Pierre Trepagnier, who settled in the area in the 1740s. There were 16 such land grants in St. James Parish. Trepagnier eventually became the Diamond Plantation; the name was changed to Belltown and finally to the Diamond subdivision of Norco. The plantation owners abandoned the property after the Civil War, but the former slaves remained—some continued living in the slave quarters, while others took occupancy of the grand cypress main house perched on the banks of the Mississippi River (Lerner, 2005; Ottinger, 2005; Sternberg, [1996] 2001; Rolfes, 2000).

The dominance of petrochemicals is very evident in this small settlement. "Norco" is short for New Orleans Refining Company. Though Norco has a predominantly White residential section, Diamond is somewhat isolated from the rest of town, as it is shoehorned between the sprawling Shell/Motiva refinery and the Shell Chemical plant. Diamond is separated from the rest of Norco by a densely wooded buffer strip known as the Gaspard Line. Norco, which has about 3,300 residents, is 98% White, while Diamond has only Black residents (Lerner, 2005; Bazelon, 2003).

In 1911, the New Orleans Refining Company (NORCO—a proxy company for the Royal Dutch/Shell Group) purchased the 366-acre Good Hope Plantation for $21,000 and built its facility on it. The marine petroleum terminal was constructed adjacent to Belltown. NORCO built its first refinery near Diamond in 1916. Four years later, Shell began to process Mexican crude oil into asphalt at the plant. Shell purchased the facility in 1929. The company wanted to acquire more land to expand its production to include the manufacture of chemicals. Hence, in 1953, Shell bought up property in Belltown for a total of $109,000 to build Shell Chemical. The complex produces ethylene and propylene (building blocks of plastic) and methyl ethyl ketone (a solvent used in paints and medicines). The Black residents of Belltown were sharecroppers and farmers who had lived and worked on the land for a long time; some did not have title to the land. Some families were paid about $90 for their property, while others who lived in the "Big Store," the plantation's central building, received a pittance. Black families were essentially evicted or displaced to make way for industrial expansion. Those who could afford it purchased lots in the Diamond subdivision. Blacks thought they would be hired at the Shell plants, but few were among the 1,400 workers in the plant; and those who were hired were relegated to menial jobs. It is estimated that only about 3% of Diamond's residents were hired at the plant. Yet Diamond is literally on the fence line of the Shell complex, as the company expanded its operations till it was across the street from residents' homes (Lerner, 2005; J. Doyle, 2004; Louisiana Bucket Brigade, 2012; Bazelon, 2003).

Not surprisingly, Diamond residents live in fear of explosions from factories that dominate the landscape around them. They have good reason to be wary of the periodic explosions at the complexes. In 1973, an explosion killed Helen Washington and 16-year-old Leroy Jones, who was cutting Washington's grass when a ruptured pipeline released a plume of gas that ignited, engulfing Washington and Jones in flames. The Washington family sold the lot to Shell for $3,000 after the explosion, and Leroy Jones's mother received $500 in compensation. In 1988, seven Shell workers were killed and another 48 workers and residents were injured in an early morning explosion that destroyed some homes in Diamond and released about 159 million pounds of chemical wastes into the air. Shell admitted to paying $200 million to resolve the roughly 17,000 claims arising from the 1988 accident (Lerner, 2005; Doyle, 2004; Louisiana Bucket Brigade, 2012; Bazelon, 2003).

* * *

Why did residents not move? Diamond residents wanted to move, but without equitable compensation for their property, they would not have enough money to relocate. Realizing that their homes had lost virtually all their equity, a group of women began organizing in the 1970s to get Shell to purchase their homes. In 1990, residents organized a group—the Concerned Citizens of Norco—and began to picket Shell to force it to negotiate a buyout of the community. The Louisiana Bucket

Brigade began working with Norco residents to teach them how to collect air samples with EPA-approved buckets in 1999. Other regional and national environmental groups such as Greenpeace, Earthjustice Legal Defense Fund, the Refinery Reform Campaign, the Deep South Center for Environmental Justice, Commonweal, Environmental Health Fund, Coming Clean Campaign, and the Louisiana Environmental Action Network also collaborated with Diamond residents. The Concerned Citizens of Norco also got help from Wilma Subra of the Subra Company, who helped with the analysis of samples taken from Diamond (Lerner, 2005; Louisiana Bucket Brigade, 2012; CorpWatch, 2002).

While Diamond residents wanted Shell to purchase all the homes in the tract, Shell preferred to deal with each homeowner individually. During the time residents were campaigning to get a community buyout, Shell was acquiring individual lots in Diamond. From the 1970s onward, Shell paid an average of $26,933 for the Diamond lots it purchased. In 2001, Shell was offering a minimum of $50,000 to purchase a home. Around that time, three-bedroom homes a block away from Diamond were selling for $110,000. Eventually Shell purchased 48 of the 269 lots in Diamond through individual sales (Rolfes, 2000; Louisiana Bucket Brigade, 2012).

Two hundred and fifty Diamond residents brought suit against Shell, arguing that the facility was a nuisance that harmed their health, lowered their property values, and caused them to fear for their safety. The case went to trial in 1997, at which time Shell had pharmacology and toxicology experts testify on its behalf that the plant posed no health risks. One of Shell's lawyers argued, "We all live in a society that has to tolerate certain inconveniences." Addressing the jury for the closing argument, the lawyer continued, "Before you show them the money, they must show you the proof." The jury voted 10–2 against the Diamond residents (quoted in Bazelon, 2003).

Margie Richard, school teacher and leader of the Concerned Citizens of Norco, went all the way to United Nations Human Rights Commission in Geneva in 1999 to plead the residents' case. Richard also went to The Hague, Shell's international headquarters, to speak with officials about Diamond. Shell, a corporate behemoth with annual gross sales exceeding $175 billion, finally agreed to a buyout of the Diamond community in June 2002 (Lerner, 2005; Louisiana Bucket Brigade; 2012;

Swerczek, 2002; CorpWatch, 2002). Shell's website indicates that the Norco Refinery covers 1,000 acres. The company has a payroll of $50 million and pays more than $16 million in state and local taxes. Shell claims it pays $6 million in property taxes that fund local schools and the police and fire departments. The company also claims that in 2005 it infused the local economy with more than $26 million through its purchases of goods and services from vendors (Shell, 2012).

Shell compensated the Diamond residents who owned homes $80,000 minimum or the market value of their homes. Residents who lived in trailers were offered $50,000 minimum or the market value of their trailer. For anyone wishing to stay in Diamond, Shell offered a $25,000 home-improvement loan that was forgivable after five years. Shell did not agree to pay for the health insurance and medical bills of residents. Some residents such as Margie Richard's mother were able to sell their homes to Shell; Richard's mother sold hers for $114,000, and Richard herself sold her trailer to the company for $61,000. Shell spent about $30 million to purchase and then demolish 250 homes in Diamond (Lerner, 2005; Bullard, 2005; Doyle, 2004; CorpWatch, 2002; Bazelon, 2003).

WALLACE RESIDENTS OPPOSE FORMOSA

In 1988, the Gulf Coast Tenants Association and Greenpeace organized a march through the communities of Cancer Alley to raise awareness of environmental concerns in the region (Coyle, 1992b; 1992c). In 1992, the tiny settlement of Wallace—a town of about 750 people, 98% of whom were African American—fought a two-year battle with Formosa (a company with a history of environmental violations in Texas, Delaware, and Louisiana) before the company decided it would not build a $700 million facility that would have been the world's largest rayon and pulp processing plant. The parish rezoned 1,800 acres of residential and agricultural land to industrial uses, and the state and parish promised Formosa about $400 million in tax breaks if it built the Wallace facility (Coyle, 1992a; 1992b).

CONVENT AND SHINTECH

The most famous of these cases occurred in Convent. Both Wallace and Convent are in St. James Parish. The parish, which had a population of 21,216 people in 2000 and is 49.4% Black, straddles the Mississippi River (U.S. Census Bureau, 2000). St. James Parish has 12 petrochemical complexes. In 1996, Shintech announced plans to build a $700 million chlor-alkali vinyl complex (which would consist of three chemical plants and an incinerator) that was to produce 1.1 billion pounds of polyvinyl chloride annually. The plant was expected to emit 611,700 pounds of contaminants into the air. Shintech was promised almost $130 million in subsidies including a ten-year property-tax exemption worth about $95.4 million. The small town of Convent is 82% Black, and 40% of the residents live below the poverty level. An elementary school was located 1.5 miles from the proposed facility (Louisiana Environmental Action Network and Greenpeace USA, 1999; Coyle, 1992b, 1997b; R. Hines 2001).

In 1997, residents of the community filed a Title VI complaint with the EPA, objecting to the three permits the LDEQ issued to Shintech. Opponents of the planned facility alleged that the permits violated the Clean Air Act, Executive Order 12898, and Title VI of the 1964 Civil Rights Act. The EPA rejected some of the arguments in the petition regarding the Clean Air Act but agreed to an expedited review of the complaint concerning certain technical violations of the Clean Air Act. The EPA also urged the LDEQ to resolve potential EJ issues that arose because the permits were issued. In September 1997, the EPA rejected the state-issued air permits for Shintech on the grounds that the permits failed to regulate all potential sources of pollution and that the its review process had found 49 technical problems with the air permits that had to be resolved before the project could proceed (Chambers, 1998; Coyle, 1997a; R. Hines, 2001). The battle between Shintech and Covent garnered international attention. Finally, in 1998, Shintech decided to forgo plans to build in Convent and to build a smaller plant in Plaquemine (a small, heavily industrialized town also located in Cancer Alley) (Schelly and Stretesky, 2009).

Corporate Lobbying, Tax Breaks, and Incentives

Since the late 1970s, communities in Cancer Alley have been trying to limit the number of noxious facilities sited in their neighborhoods. While activists have generally organized to prevent a facility from siting in a particular location or to monitor the operations of a facility, the parishes and the state have had a much more ambiguous relationship with businesses. On the one hand, parishes have welcomed industries by offering tax exemptions and other incentives; on the other, they try to regulate the industries post hoc. Regulating the industries becomes particularly tricky if those industries generate income for the local or state governments. For instance, in 2002, industries operating in Cancer Alley generated 62,500 jobs and $1.14 billion in state taxes (Bazelon, 2003).

Louisiana has roughly 11% of the country's petroleum reserves, and the state is the second-largest producer of refined oil in the U.S. Consequently, the petrochemical industry is both an important driver of the state's economy and a powerful lobby in the legislature. Hence, it is no coincidence that one of the most influential groups in the state is the Louisiana Association of Business and Industry. The group recruits, trains, endorses, and supports political candidates who promote the association's interests. The Louisiana Chemical Association is another powerful industry lobbying group. Both of these associations coordinate their efforts at times (B. Wright, 2005).

Louisiana entices companies to establish facilities in the state by offering generous tax incentives through programs such as the Industrial Property Tax Exemption Program, which has been in effect since 1936. The Louisiana Economic Development website describes the program as offering "an attractive tax incentive for manufacturers" (2012). That is, manufacturing companies do not pay any local property taxes on the construction or renovation of buildings, machinery, equipment, improvements to the land, new investments, or annual capitalized additions at the manufacturing site for up to ten years. After this initial period, corporate taxes are reduced. Consequently, the amount of corporate tax relief in the state is staggering. Between 1988 and 1998, for instance, the state granted $2.5 billion in tax exemptions to corporations (B. Wright, 2005; Louisiana Economic Development, 2012). Mississippi has a similar Industrial Property Tax Exemption program (Mississippi Development Authority, 2012).

Thus, while much of this book is concerned with why communities do not move away from hazardous sites, it is clear why many corporations want to move in.

2

Disproportionate Siting

Claims of Racism and Discrimination

This book examines common claims made in EJ cases. It organizes the theses used to explain the claims about exposure to environmental hazards into seven major categories (see figure 2.1). It discusses the underlying assumptions of each thesis and traces the evolution of the research and arguments related to each one. The book also places these arguments and assumptions in historical context.

The Disproportionate Siting and Discrimination Thesis

The Premise

An early and oft-used explanation for exposure to environmental hazards is racial and class discrimination. Proponents of this thesis argue that hazardous facilities are disproportionately located in minority and low-income areas and that these patterns are the result of discrimination. Since the early 1980s, numerous studies have made this claim. These include landmark studies analyzing the siting of hazardous facilities in poor Black, Hispanic, and Native American communities (Bullard, 1983, 1990, 1993a, 1993b; Blumberg and Gottlieb, 1989; U.S. GAO 1983; UCC, 1987; Mohai and Bryant, 1992; H. White, 1992; Bailey and Faupel, 1992a; Robinson, 1992; LaDuke, 1993; Collin and Harris, 1993; Lee, 1993). Furthermore, scholars argue that discrimination can be institutional or noninstitutional, direct or indirect, intended or unintended (Feagin and Feagin, 1978, 1986, 2003; Knowles and Prewitt, 1970; Wellman, 1977). They also argue that disproportionate siting of hazardous facilities in minority and low-income communities forces residents

1. Disproportionate Siting and Discrimination
   - Unit of Analysis and the Modifiable Areal Unit Problem

2. Internal Colonialism
   - Center-Periphery
   - Militarism and Political Coercion
   - Radioactive Colonialism

3. Market Dynamics
   - Economic Rationality
     ○ Residential Sorting and White Flight
     ○ Hedonic Models, Property Values, and Willingness to Pay
       ▪ Compensating Host Communities
     ○ Clustering
   - Path of Least Resistance, Collective Efficacy, and Civic Vitality
     ○ Ethnic Churning
     ○ Neighborhood Life Cycle and Racial Succession
   - Chicken or Egg and the Minority Move-In Hypothesis
   - Relict Waste and the Accumulation of Hazards
   - Treadmill of Destruction
   - Vulnerability of Place

4. The Legal, Regulatory, and Administrative Context
   - Violations of Environmental Laws and the Pace of Cleanup
     ○ The Administrative Process
     ○ Inadequate Stakeholder Involvement
   - Scientific and Technical Rationality

5. Manipulation, Enticement, and Environmental Blackmail
   - Inviting Facilities In

6. Unique Biophysical Characteristics

7. Zoning and Residential Segregation
   - Racially Restrictive Zoning Laws
   - Private Racially Restrictive Covenants
   - Exclusionary and Expulsive Zoning
     ○ Heresthetics and the Structuring of Options
   - Segregation
   - Eminent Domain
   - Urban Renewal
   - Traditional Ecological Model and Dual Housing Model
     ○ Contemporary Housing Discrimination

Figure 2.1. Theories used to explain unequal exposure to environmental hazards

of such communities to accept greater risks than is deemed acceptable (Hird, 1994).

The disproportionate siting and discrimination thesis is one of the most contentious theories in EJ research, as many scholars are arrayed on both sides of the argument. Of the two claims of racial and social class discrimination, the claim of racism has been more controversial. Several early EJ studies claimed that race and class discrimination were important factors in explaining why hazardous facilities were located in minority and low-income neighborhoods (Bullard, 1983, 1990, 1993a, 1993b; Blumberg and Gottlieb, 1989; U.S. GAO 1983; UCC, 1987; Mohai and Bryant, 1992; H. White, 1992; Bailey and Faupel, 1992a, 1992b; Robinson, 1992; LaDuke, 1993; Collin and Harris, 1993; Lee, 1993; Goldman, 1993; Goldman and Fitton, 1994; Comacho, 1998). However, studies analyzing the racial and income disparities in exposure to air pollution and pesticides began appearing in the 1960s (see Goldman, 1993; and Mohai and Bryant, 1992). During the 1970s, researchers began publishing studies of racial and income disparities in exposure to hazardous wastes and proximity to hazardous waste facilities. For example, Berry et al.'s (1977) study found that both income and race were factors explaining proximity and exposure to environmental hazards but that race was more significant.

In 1983, Robert Bullard, a sociologist, published a landmark study that examined the siting pattern of waste dumps in Houston and asserted that the dumps "were not randomly scattered over the Houston landscape" (273). Instead, they were located in predominantly Black communities and near schools. Bullard found that four of five of the city's incinerators were located in predominantly Black neighborhoods, while the fifth was found in a predominantly Hispanic neighborhood. Two of the city's three mini-incinerators also operated in predominantly Black neighborhoods. Bullard also found that five of Houston's six municipal landfills were located in predominantly Black neighborhoods. At the time of the study, Blacks constituted only 27.6% of Houston's population. Bullard studied the relationship between landfill siting and schools and found that all ten of the landfills permitted by the city from 1920 to 1976 were near predominantly Black schools, so were 66% of the 47 solid waste sites and 77% of the municipal landfills permitted by the Texas Department of Health (TDH) between 1953 and 1978. Browning-Ferris Industries (BFI) also operated landfills in Houston, and 86% of the 21 landfills operated by the company between 1970 and 1978 were close to predominantly Black schools.

Another landmark study was released the same year Bullard's study was published. In 1982, Representative Walter Fauntroy, one of the

Black congressmen who participated in the Warren County protests, asked the General Accounting Office to conduct a study of the siting of hazardous waste landfills in EPA's Region IV. The study, published in 1983, found that three of the four communities in which off-site hazardous waste landfills were found were predominantly Black. The host communities also had lower incomes than surrounding census tracts (U.S. GAO, 1983).

A year later, Greenberg and Anderson (1984) published a study of hazardous waste sites in New Jersey in which they identified racial disparities in siting. Gould, of the Council on Economic Priorities, published a national study in 1986 in which he examined the production of toxic wastes in zip codes. Gould divided the population into five income categories and found that zip codes with the lowest income (i.e., where the average household income was $20,200) had the highest per-capita production of toxic wastes, 1,075 pounds per year. There was not a straightforward correlation between income and toxic waste production. Gould also found that zip codes with the second-highest average income ($29,500) had the second-highest per-capita production of toxic wastes (980 pounds per year). This study was followed by Bullard and Wright's (1986) article on waste facilities in Black communities in the South.

Of these early studies, none generated more attention than the 1987 United Church of Christ (UCC) study, *Toxic Wastes and Race in the United States*. This report was commissioned after some members of the church's Commission for Racial Justice participated in the Warren County protests. The report contained findings of two cross-sectional studies that examined the location of (a) commercial hazardous waste facilities and (b) uncontrolled toxic waste sites. The study, which relied on zip code analysis, found that race was the strongest predictor of the location of the commercial hazardous waste facilities. Though income was an important explanatory factor, race was more significant. The study found that three of the five largest hazardous waste landfills in the U.S. were located in predominantly Black or Hispanic communities. The findings were similar when uncontrolled waste sites were studied. The report found that three out of five Black and Hispanic residents lived in communities with uncontrolled toxic waste sites. Furthermore, large percentages of Blacks lived in metropolitan areas with the largest numbers of uncontrolled toxic waste sites. The study described the "inordinate concentration" of waste sites in Black and Hispanic communities and argued that "the possibility that these patterns resulted by chance is virtually impossible" (UCC 1987: xv).

Several studies employing spatial and nonspatial analytic techniques were published in the six years following the release of the UCC report. These studies supported the claims of *Toxic Wastes and Race in the United States*. These include Bullard and Wright's (1987a, 1987b) papers that examined hazardous waste disposal in Black communities in the South. Belliveau, Kent, and Rosenbaum (1989) analyzed Blacks' exposure to toxic releases emanating from industrial facilities in Richmond, California. Blumberg and Gottlieb published *War on Waste* in 1989. The book examined decisions to site incinerators in Black and Hispanic communities in California. The same year, researchers from Auburn University published the findings of their survey of residents' attitude toward the landfill in Emelle, Alabama (Bailey, Faupel, Holland, and Warren, 1989). Bullard's *Dumping in Dixie*, which chronicled the practice of hazardous waste disposal in Black communities in the South, was published in 1990. In 1991, K. Brown found that toxic-waste-emitting facilities were disproportionately located in Black communities in St. Louis and that such communities were exposed to higher toxic air releases. A Greenpeace report authored by Costner and Thornton in 1991 also examined racial disparities in exposure to incinerator emissions. Mohai and Bryant (1992) examined racial disparities in proximity to commercial hazardous waste facilities in Detroit and found that minorities were more likely than Whites to live in close proximity to such facilities.

An underlying assumption of the disproportionate siting and discrimination thesis is the idea that minorities resided in communities selected to host hazardous facilities *before* the facilities were built. In other words, minority communities are deliberately sought out and targeted for the placement of noxious facilities. Supporters of this thesis have provided many examples including Black communities such as Emelle (Alabama), Riceville (Texas), Alsen (Louisiana), and King and Queen County (Virginia), in which landfills were placed (Bailey and Faupel, 1992a, 1992b; Bailey, Faupel, and Gundlach, 1993; Bullard, 1983, 1990; Collin and Harris, 1993); West Dallas, where a lead smelter operated in a predominantly Black community and near a school (Bullard, 1990); the unincorporated community of Institute, West Virginia, where Union Carbide built a giant chemical plant that manufactured methyl isocyanate beside a historically Black university (Bullard, 1990); and the Diamond tract in Norco, Louisiana, that is sandwiched between the massive Norco Industrial Complex and two Shell Oil plants (Lerner, 2005). Communities such as South Central Los Angeles and Kettleman City (California) and Chester (Pennsylvania), where Black and Hispanic residents lived in neighborhoods before incinerators were placed in them, were also used as examples (Blumberg and Gottlieb, 1989; Pardo, 1998; Cole and Foster, 2001). Researchers also pointed to South Tucson, where Hispanics were exposed to trichloroethylene (TCE) that contaminated the groundwater supplies after Hughes Aircraft and other industries dumped wastes in desert arroyos on the city's Southside (Clarke and Gerlak, 1998). Native American reservations were also cited as places where minority populations lived before hazardous facilities were placed on them (LaDuke, 1993, 1999; Robinson, 1992; Angel, 1991; Cole and Foster, 2001).

Skepticism and Controversy

As EJ activism expanded and the publicity generated from the UCC report and subsequent studies grew, so did skepticism about EJ claims. Ergo, by 1993, studies refuting the claims of the UCC study were being published by scholars and representatives of the waste management industry. One of the earliest and most vocal critics of EJ claims was Charles McDermott, director of government affairs for Waste Management. He testified before a House subcommittee that "there is little evidence that emissions from waste facilities pose the greatest risk to the average minority community." McDermott criticized the UCC study's use of 1980 census data. He argued that while the UCC analysis told us about the postsiting demographic characteristics of host communities, it told us nothing about the demographic characteristics of the host communities *at the time the facilities were sited*. Arguing for the use of 1970 census data instead, McDermott stated that "to presume discriminatory intent, it is crucial that the demographic snapshot be taken as close to the time of siting as possible" (McDermott, 1993). Waste

Management conducted its own study of the demographic character-istics of the host communities of 130 of its solid waste and hazardous waste disposal sites and incinerators in 1991 (WMX Technologies, 1991). The study, completed a few months after the First National People of Color Environmental Leadership Summit was held in Washington, D.C., employed the same methodological techniques used in the UCC study. The Waste Management study found that 76% of the company's disposal facilities were located in communities with a White population that was equal to or greater than the average for the host state (McDer-mott, 1993, 1994).

Law professor Vicki Been was another early critic of the UCC report and other EJ scholarship. She published a series of articles between 1993 and 1997 in which she argued that hazardous facilities were not disproportionately sited in minority communities. She argued that the analysis should focus on the demographic characteristics of the neigh-borhoods at the time facilities were being sited (Been and Gupta, 1997; Been, 1993a, 1993b, 1993c, 1994a, 1994b, 1995).

Waste Management funded a group of researchers from the Social and Demographic Research Institute at the University of Massachusetts–Amherst to examine the siting patterns of toxic storage and disposal facilities (TSDFs) and abandoned waste sites. Between 1994 and 1997, the researchers, who also received funding from the EPA to conduct their study, published a series of articles critiquing the UCC study and other EJ scholarship. They critiqued the use of zip codes in the UCC report; they used census tracts instead in their analyses (Anderson, Anderton, and Oakes, 1994; Anderton et al., 1994; Anderton, Ander-son, Oakes, and Fraser, 1994; Anderton, Oakes, and Egan, 1997; Oakes, Anderton, and Anderson 1996).

The disproportionate siting and discrimination thesis has been chal-lenged on several levels, and alternative theories have been proposed (these are discussed in later chapters). For instance, researchers reported that they found no, weak, or inconsistent evidence that social class was associated with proximity to hazardous facilities (Anderson, Anderton, and Oakes, 1994; Anderton et. al., 1994; Anderton, Anderson, Oakes, and Fraser, 1994; Anderton, Oakes, and Egan, 1997; Bowen, Salling, Haynes, and Cyran, 1995; Brown, Ciambrone, and Hunter, 1997). They also reported finding no, weak, or inconsistent evidence that race was associated with the proximity to hazardous facilities (Been, 1993c, 1995; Zimmerman, 1994; Glickman, Golding, and Hersh, 1995; Pollock and Vittas, 1995; Hamilton, 1995; Oakes and Anderton, 1996; Yandle and Burton, 1996; Baden and Coursey, 1997; Sheppard, McMaster, Leitner, and Tian, 1999; Perlin, Wong, and Sexton, 2001; Bowen, 2002; Graham et al., 1999; Atlas, 2002). In fact, Downey (2005) argues outright that the racial characteristics of the neighborhoods around Detroit's manufacturing facilities do not result from income inequality or racist siting practices; they are a function of residential segregation, which has reduced Blacks' exposure to industrial pollution.

However, several scholars have found that race and class are significant predictors of past and future siting of hazardous facilities. In addition to national studies, such evidence has been found in studies conducted in metropolitan areas all over the country (Mohai and Bryant, 1992; Greenberg, 1993; Goldman and Fitton, 1994; Adeola, 1994; Hamilton, 1995; Krieg, 1995; U.S. GAO, 1995; Mohai, 1995, 1996; Goetz and Kemlage, 1996; Crawford, 1996a; Boer, Pastor, Sadd, and Snyder, 1997; Brown, Ciambrone, and Hunter, 1997; Markham and Rufa, 1997; Szasz and Meuser, 1997, 2000; Stretesky and Hogan, 1998; Clarke and Gerlak, 1998; Neumann, Forman, and Rothlein, 1998; Hird and Reese, 1998; Sadd, Pastor, Boer, and Snyder, 1999; Boone and Modarres, 1999; Faber and Krieg, 2000; Pastor, Sadd, and Hipp, 2001; Lejano and Iseki, 2001; Stretesky and Lynch, 2002; Pastor and Sadd, 2004; Mennis and Jordan, 2005; Downey, 2003, 2006; Ash and Fetter, 2004; Rinquist, 2005; Morello-Frosch and Lopez, 2006; Morello-Frosch and Jesdale, 2006; Pastor, Morello-Frosch, and Sadd, 2006; Saha and Mohai, 2005; Mohai and Saha, 2006, 2007; Bullard, Mohai, Saha, and Wright, 2007, 2008; Zahran, Hastings, and Brody, 2008; Wang and Filiberty, 2010).

As researchers continue to test the disproportionate siting and discrimination thesis, even scholars who have questioned the idea of racial discrimination in siting have found that facilities for hazardous materials handlers were located close to working-class neighborhoods and in areas with higher percentages of minority residents (Davidson and Anderton, 2000). Researchers have also found racial disparities when examining the siting patterns of specific kinds of facilities. For example, Graham et al. (1999) found that race was not a factor in predicting the location of oil refineries; however, the researchers found that the people living around coke plants were disproportionately poor and minority. Moreover, recent scholarship has identified immigrant minority communities as being particularly vulnerable to the siting of hazardous facilities (Greenwood, McClelland and Schulze, 1997; Hunter, 2000; Hunter, White, Little, and Sutton, 2003).

It should be noted that as EJ research grew more complex and sophisticated, not all studies or all researchers fell neatly on either side of the debate. Some studies provided partial support for the claims being made in support of or against the disproportionate siting and discrimination hypothesis. The same can be said for the investigation of other aspects of EJ claims.

The Unit of Analysis

The Modifiable Areal Unit Problem

The spatial unit of analysis (national, state, region, county, zip code, census tract, census block group, etc.) has been a major source of contention in EJ research since its inception. This is particularly true of research related to exposure to hazards. Yet despite the attention paid to the problem, the appropriate unit of analysis and the modifiable areal unit problem (MAUP) still remain as unresolved challenges. Scholars argue that reliance on aspatial units such as zip codes and census tracts to conduct analyses of spatial relations such as neighborhood segregation or racial and class disparities is problematic. They argue that such analyses rest on the assumption that census tracts approximate neighborhoods and that the tracts are similar in size. However, census tracts—which are determined by the number of residents in an area, not by real neighborhood boundaries—vary a great deal in size. Therefore, analyses based purely on census tracts can also miss pockets of microsegregation (or clustering) that occur *across* census tract boundaries (Reardon and O'Sullivan, 2004; Mohai and Saha, 2006; Reardon et al., 2008; Lee et al. 2008). Figure 2.2 illustrates the problems that can arise with using aspatial units in analyses and the logic behind using spatial techniques instead. As the figure shows, facilities 2, 3, and 4 are closest together, even though they are located in different tracts; the figure also represents microclustering across two

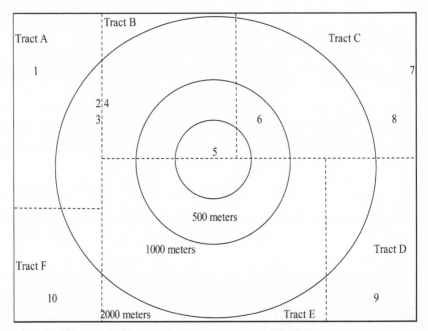

Figure 2.2. Spatial analysis of census tracts and local environments (adapted from Lee et al., 2008)

tracts. Facility 2 is closer to facility 4 than it is to facility 1, even though facilities 1 and 2 are in the same census tract.

The Edge Effect, Distance Decay, and Spatial Autocorrelation

Recognition of the edge effect is also important. Studies using fixed geographic boundaries such as counties, zip codes, or census tracts can run into problems with the edge effect. When the attribute being studied is located near the edge of the defined unit, the use of aspatial boundaries assumes that the effects being examined stop at the boundaries of the unit. It also assumes zero impact on populations living outside the boundaries. Since impacts do extend beyond the edges of counties, zip codes, census tracts, and so on, methods that can capture this have to be used. Accounting for the edge effect in EJ research is crucial. Mohai and Saha's (2006, 2007) national study of the siting pattern of TSDFs found that 49% of them were located within a quarter mile of the census tract boundary, and 71% were within half a mile of the tract boundary. They also found great variation in the size of the host tracts; the smallest was one-tenth of a square mile, while the largest was more than 7,500 square miles.

Research has found that neighborhood boundaries can be elastic and residents' perceptions of those boundaries differ markedly and are not always aligned with the contours of census tracts (Lee and Campbell, 1997; Sastry, Pebley, and Zonta, 2002). Other researchers such as Kaplan and Holloway (2001) and Raja, Ma, and Yadav (2008) have pointed to the importance of accounting for both scale and magnitude in spatial research. For these reasons, researchers are advocating methodologies that can handle microclustering and multigroup comparisons, reduce the MAUP, and allow for analyses across census tracts. Some advocate the use of techniques such as the spatial information theory index H (Thiel's H or spatial H) to analyze the spatial relationships in the siting of environmental amenities and disamenities. These researchers have used the technique in their study of residential segregation (Iceland, 2004; Lee et al., 2008; Farrell, 2008). Advocates of this approach recommend the use of a two-dimensional biweight kernel function that captures distance-decay dynamics by assigning more weight to nearby cells and less weight to distant ones. The biweight kernel function approximates a Gaussian normal curve (Lee et al., 2008; Reardon et al., 2008).

Mohai and Saha (2006, 2007) have used a proximity-weighted racial composition model in their study of hazardous waste sites in Michigan, while Downey (2006) uses a distance-decay model in his study of the impact gradient of TRI facilities in Detroit. Downey found that Black neighborhoods were disproportionately burdened by TRI facility activities in 2000. Recognizing the problem of spatial autocorrelation (the tendency for neighborhoods that are close to each other to have similar characteristics), Zenk et al. (2005, 2006) correct for this problem by using a moving average spatial regression model in their study of the locations of grocery stores in Detroit.

Relevance to EJ Research

The concern over the unit of analysis is not a trivial one. Some of the earliest and most widely cited studies supporting EJ claims used the county (U.S. GAO, 1983), zip codes (UCC, 1987), and census tracts

(Goldman and Fitton, 1994) as units of analysis. Researchers finding no evidence of racial discrimination in the siting of hazardous facilities or those critiquing the methodology of the U.S. GAO and UCC reports also used aspatial units such as counties (Hamilton, 1993) and census tracts (Been, 1993c, 1995; Anderson, Anderton, and Oakes, 1994; Anderton et al., 1994; Anderton, Anderson, Oakes, and Fraser, 1994). Census block groups have also been used (Chakraborty, Fokenbrock, and Schweitzer, 1999). Despite criticisms regarding the use of aspatial units, recent studies still use counties (Earnhard, 2004) and census tracts (Been and Gupta, 1997; Davidson and Anderton, 2000; Pastor, Sadd and Hipp, 2001; Downey, 2003, 2005) as units of analyses.

Different units of analysis persist in EJ research as scholars are still debating the issue of the scale at which inequities are most pronounced. Some believe that inequities are more visible when larger geographic units are analyzed (Cutter, Holm, and Clark, 1996; Rinquist, 2005), while others believe the opposite (Dolinoy and Miranda, 2004; Raja, Ma, and Yadav, 2008). Noonan, Turaga, and Baden (2009) demonstrate how results can vary by scale. They used logit regression models to conduct a national study of National Priorities List (NPL) sites at four geographic scales—counties, zip codes, census tracts, and census block groups. They found the strongest evidence of environmental inequities at the smaller scales—the census tract and census block group levels. The analysis indicated that areas with larger percentages of Blacks and Hispanics were more likely to have an NPL site than were other neighborhoods. Mohai and Saha's (2007) article also contains a detailed discussion of how results in their national study of NPL sites varied depending on the *geographic scale* (zip code, census tract, or census block group) and the *impact gradient* (within a one-mile radius, beyond a one-mile radius, within a three-mile radius, and beyond a three-mile radius).

Mohai and Saha's (2007) study is a replication of earlier studies that used the EPA's Resource Conservation and Recovery Information System and the Environmental Services Directory to identify the location of facilities (Anderson, Anderton, and Oakes, 1994; Oakes and Anderton, 1996; Been, 1995; Been and Gupta, 1997). By using the 50% areal containment method, Mohai and Saha (2007) found that the percentage of African American and Hispanic residents was a statistically significant predictor of TSDF location. Their study also found that the percentage of residents living in poverty, the percentage unemployed, and the percentage employed in precision manufacturing were also significant predictors of TSDF location.

Toward a More Nuanced Understanding of Exposure and Risk

Arguing that environmental impacts from hazardous or nuisance facilities are not always manifested in concentric circles (as the centroid-based methods assume), researchers are examining problems such as noise pollution by using integrated noise models to create computer-generated noise contours or footprints that can be analyzed (Sobotta, Campbell, and Owens (2007). Air and water pollution sometimes occur in plumes. Examination of these phenomena calls for models that can analyze such noncircular impacts.

Many of the aforementioned EJ studies focus on the question of whether it is race or class that is the strongest predictor of where hazardous facilities are located. The studies identify facilities that release toxins into the environment and correlate that with community demographic characteristics. However, this type of analysis does not tell us how *risks* are shaped by *exposures to multiple toxins* of *varying levels of toxicity*. Recent studies are using the EPA's Risk-Screening Environmental Indicators (RSEI) database to conduct more fine-grained analyses of *exposure* and *risk* (Ash and Fetter, 2004; Sicotte and Swanson, 2007; Downey, 2007; Grant, Trautner, Downey, and Thiebaud, 2010; Ard, 2013).

That is, understanding the impacts of hazardous facilities is not just a matter of assessing who is exposed to an environmental hazard or if a toxic facility is present in or absent from a particular neighborhood. It is also important to assess *how hazardous* the chemicals or facilities are. Researchers have also pointed to the importance of understanding how firm characteristics such as size, subsidiaries, and absentee management influence the toxicity of materials used and processed, the volume of toxics emitted, and a company's response to workers' and residents' claims (Pulido, 1996; Rosner and Markovitz, 2002; Cable, Shriver, and Mix, 2008; Grant, Trautner, Downey, and Thiebaud, 2010).

Grant and his colleagues conducted conventional regression analysis on RSEI data and found that the percentage of African American and the percentage of Hispanic residents were the strongest predictors of risky (toxic) emissions. However, when the researchers used fuzzy-set analysis on the same data set to examine how firm characteristics and community characteristics combined to produce impacts, they found that race interacted with firm characteristics (size and subsidiary status) to produce the significant effects (Grant, Trautner, Downey, and Thiebaud, 2010).

Despite considerable disagreements among researchers about the appropriate unit of analysis and the methodological techniques that should be used to study exposure to environmental hazards, the field of inquiry is evolving rapidly. Researchers are asking more complicated questions and employing more sophisticated models. In addition, some of the new techniques show great promise in helping us to understand more fully the factors that lead to and explain the siting of hazardous facilities.

3

Internal Colonialism

Native American Communities in the West

EJ activists contend that some parts of the country, such as Appalachia, the South, the Southwest, and Native American reservations, are seen and treated as internal colonies when it comes to the extraction and processing of hazardous materials, the operation of hazardous industrial facilities, and the exposure of residents to dangerous environmental conditions. They contend that companies seek out and locate their facilities in these areas because they have high unemployment and low wages and are rich in resources that can be extracted and processed. These same communities are also sought out as sites for hazardous extraction, manufacturing processes, and waste disposal activities. According to the colonial thesis, states such as those in the South that rank lowest on environmental protection and policy indices (Vig and Kraft, 2006) emerge as attractive sites for hosting noxious facilities. Sociologist Beverly Wright, who lives in New Orleans, describes the South as "backward because of its social, economic, and environmental policies." Consequently the region is an "environmental sacrifice zone, a dump for the rest of the nation's toxic waste[s]" (B. Wright, 2005: 88).

Colonialism

Robert Blauner (1969) defines colonialism as the process by which one country controls the political activities and economic resources of another less developed and less powerful country. The colonization complex has four main components: (1) forced entry of one country into the territory of another country, (2) alteration and destruction of the indigenous cultures and patterns of social organization of the invaded country, (3) domination of indigenous peoples by the invaders, and (4) the development of elaborate justifications for the invasion and subsequent behavior of the invaders.

Internal Colonialism and the Center-Periphery Thesis

The term "internal colonialism" is used by Blauner to describe the conditions and experiences of people of color in the United States. The term is also used to refer to territorial relations within a political entity. Blauner argues that the same dynamics that operate in the external colonial context operate with internal colonialism. In addition to overseas colonial expansion, major industrial countries such as the U.S. seek to bring their hinterlands or peripheral regions under the control of the core. Such moves toward internal colonization result in tensions or conflict between the core or center and the periphery of the country. The core develops exploitive relations with the periphery, using the hinterland's natural resources and cheap labor to enhance or sustain its development. If the periphery has indigenous or culturally distinct peoples, the core often discriminates against them. The core monopolizes trade and commerce, thus forcing the peripheral region to develop as a complementary economy of the core. The economic dependence of the internal colony is reinforced by legal, political, and military measures. The periphery is often characterized by lower levels of service and lower standards of living than the core (Blauner, 1969; Hechter, 1994).

In the past, the American South provided raw materials and labor. The northern states used laws and military action to ensure the South's compliance. Today, some people still describe the South and Native American reservations as internal colonies of the North, supplying natural resources, cheap labor, tax incentives, and land; serving as sites for noxious industrial facilities and military complexes; and hosting repositories for toxic wastes from other parts of the country.

EJ activists oppose industrial projects they consider dangerous to people's health and environmental quality. This being the case, they are particularly sensitive to projects that produce, process, or dispose of hazardous materials in minority communities. EJ activists also oppose corporations that split their operations—placing their corporate headquarters and administrative offices (the "clean" part of their operations) in the business districts or suburbs of major cities of the North, while placing the extractive, processing, manufacturing, and disposal (the "dirty" or "dangerous") parts of their operations in minority and low-income communities. Activists invoke the internal colonial frame when dealing with such corporations and facilities (Adeola, 2000; LaDuke, 1999; Jaimes, 1992; Churchill and LaDuke, 1992; Gedicks, 1993, 1998, 2001; Agyeman, Bullard, and Evans, 2003; D.E. Taylor, 2010). However, activists recognize that not all corporations are entirely domestic. Ergo, in cases such as Shintech in Convent and Shell in Norco—where multinational corporations headquartered in Japan and the Netherlands place their manufacturing operations in rural Louisiana—activists use the term "external colonialism" to describe these dynamics.

Militarism and Political Coercion

The frame of internal colonialism is also applicable to Native American reservations because these entities arose out of military conquest and subsequent military domination. The reservations are also entities that are geographically defined by and their locations chosen by the federal government. Indigenous populations were placed in these designated territories. The reservation system was one of the tools of military conquest that settlers used to get the upper hand over Native tribes.

The designation of fixed territories for indigenous peoples by invading groups is a common feature of the colonial model. There is a long history of military operations occurring adjacent to reservations. In fact, the United States War Department was created in 1789, in part to handle Indian affairs. Even after the Bureau of Indian Affairs (BIA) was created in 1824, Indian matters remained under the aegis of the War Department. The BIA was transferred to the newly created Department of the Interior in 1849 (BIA, 2012).

Hooks and Smith (2004) and Thomas, Fannin, and Rossman (2010) argue that militarism and political coercion explain both the location of Native American reservations and also the hazards tribes are exposed to. As later discussion will show, militarism is accompanied by exposure to environmental hazards.

Sovereignty

The question of sovereignty is also one that is tied to colonial relations. In the case of Native American tribes, they are sovereign nations. That means tribes are autonomous and have a legal right to govern and determine how their lands are used. However, the notion of sovereignty is a nebulous one when it comes to operating hazardous facilities. This is the case because the laws that govern tribal lands differ from those governing other lands in the country; therefore, those who wish to see hazardous facilities sited on reservations can bypass state regulators and deal directly with the tribes. Those who oppose tribal decisions also proffer their own definitions of sovereignty (Clarke, 2002; *Great Northern Paper v. Penobscot Nation*, 2001). While sovereignty allows the tribes greater decision-making authority, it also leaves room for manipulation by corporate interests.

Natural Resources on Native Lands

Native American reservations host many extractive industrial operations because tribal lands hold significant and strategic reserves of natural resources. There are 565 federally recognized tribes and 326 reservations in the U.S. The reservations occupy about 56.2 million acres or about 4% of the land area of the country. Native American reservations are located on about 3% of America's oil and natural gas reserves, 15% of the coal reserves, and between 37% and 55% of the uranium reserves. Substantial quantities of bauxite and zeolites also lie beneath Indian reservations. However, land bearing valuable resources is sometimes removed from reservations when such resources have been discovered. One such example is the massive copper deposit found on the Papago Reservation in Arizona in the 1920s. The ore-bearing part of the reservation was removed from Indian control by decree of the U.S. Congress. A second example is the colossal Fort Union coal deposit that underlies the territory reserved for the Lakota, Cheyenne, and Arapaho nations; 90% of the reservation land has been removed from Indian control (Amott and Matthaei, 1991; Nabokov, 1991; Jaimes, 1992; Churchill and LaDuke, 1992; Ambler, 1990; Thorpe, 1996; Eichstaedt, 1994; BIA, 2010a, 2010b; Thomas, Fannin, and Rossman, 2010).

Local Elites in the Colonialist Context

At times, minority elites act more in concert with corporate interests than those of fellow community residents. In essence, the global marketplace and multinational corporations have created incentives for elites, regardless of their social location, to act to reinforce elite and corporate interests rather than those of poor and marginal populations. So the relationship between corporations and reservations is not simply one of corporations exploiting the resources of the hinterlands; the exploitation is sometimes facilitated by local elites, some of whom are minorities (Bello, 1994; Escobar, 1995).

Another aspect of the colonialist complex is the manipulation of indigenous elites. In some cases, where local residents express strong opposition to corporate operations, handpicked locals or "tribal representatives" are installed as decision makers and spokespersons for the target community. For instance, the imposition of tribal councils through the 1934 Indian Reorganization Act (IRA) hastened the process of transferring resources from reservations to non-Indians. The institutionalization of the IRA resulted in a significant decline in the power and control of traditional leaders. This is the case because increasingly, under the IRA, tribal governments have been governed by corporatist tribal councils or boards answerable to the secretary of the interior. The tribal governments have been rooted not in traditional leadership but in constitutions and charters drafted by the BIA. Decisions have had to be approved by the secretary of the interior or the commissioner of Indian affairs. Hence, democratic majority rule replaced the traditional consensual method of decision making that tribes used (Robbins, 1992; Jaimes, 1992).

The model for the use of tribal councils was pioneered in the 1920s after a traditional Navajo tribal government blocked oil exploration on their reservation. Hence, in 1923, Commissioner Charles Burke issued *Regulations Relating to the Navajo Tribe of Indians*, which was intended to "promote better administration of the Navajo Tribe." Without consulting the tribe, the commissioner appointed a "Navajo Grand Council" composed of young, handpicked, prodevelopment, boarding-school-educated Indians to sit on the council. The traditional tribal government was excluded from the council. Despite the objections of the traditional tribal leaders, the handpicked council signed the leasing agreements sought by Standard Oil. Since then, tribal councils have been installed on reservations and have been used to circumvent the wishes of Indians all over the country. When the IRA administrators endorsed the use of tribal councils to supplant traditional tribal governments, many Native Americans objected strenuously (Robbins, 1992; Jaimes, 1992).

Radioactive Colonialism, Energy, and Hazardous Wastes

Nowhere are the problems of resource extraction and the dynamics of radioactive colonialism more evident than in the relationship between reservations, the Department of Energy (DOE), and corporations. Raw materials such as uranium and coal are extracted and processed on or near reservation land by Indian and non-Indian labor. The energy industry creates both a *split* and a *dual* labor market in this setting. In the split labor market scenario (Bonacich, 1994), Indian workers are paid less than non-Indian workers, though both sets of workers do the same work. Thus, the price of labor differs for the two sets of workers. In the dual labor market (Piore, 1994), Indian workers are relegated to the secondary labor market. This sector is characterized by low-wage, dangerous jobs and few benefits. Non-Indian workers occupy the primary labor market; they have high-paying managerial and supervisory jobs in the least hazardous parts of the industry.

So not only are reservations degraded by mining operations and contaminated from spills and the dumping of hazardous wastes; reservations are heavily courted to become the temporary and permanent storage sites of high-level nuclear wastes from all over the country. In 1982, Congress passed the Nuclear Waste Policy Act. The act considered Indian tribes as groups having equal power to the states. In 1985, judges in the Ninth Circuit Court of Appeals noted in a case involving the Washington Department of Ecology and the EPA that "Indian reservations may be considered as potential locations for hazardous waste disposal sites . . . because they are often remote from heavily populated areas" (*Washington Department of Ecology v. EPA*, 1985).

This view was also shared by corporations wanting to find a place to dispose of their toxic wastes. Ergo, during the mid 1980s, when the quest to find nuclear waste disposal sites took on a sense of urgency, reservations were considered for hosting temporary (facilities designed to hold nuclear wastes for up to 40 years) and permanent (facilities designed to hold nuclear wastes for up to 10,000 years) repositories. Because there was such large quantities of nuclear wastes to be stored and many utilities ran out of storage space, there was a strong desire to find temporary storage sites for these wastes till a permanent site could come on-line. During this time, 17 reservations were considered to host temporary monitored retrievable storage (MRS) facilities. Reservations receiving serious consideration for MRS facilities were the Mescalero Apaches of New Mexico, the Skull Valley Goshutes of Utah, and the Fort McDermitt Reservation (Paiutes and Western Shosnones) in Nevada. At the time, a consortium of 33 utilities controlling 94 reactors began taking aggressive steps to find storage sites for their nuclear wastes. The consortium courted Indian tribes to store the wastes on their reservations (Thorpe, 1996; Brook, 1998).

In 1991, DOE sent out a request to states, counties, and all the federally recognized tribes to submit proposals for grants to study the feasibility of hosting MRS facilities. These MRS facilities were intended to store some of the radioactive spent fuels that were housed at Yucca Mountain. Depending on the phase of the grant, awards ranged from $100,000 to $2.8 million. The Mescalero Apaches were the first tribe to submit a proposal; they did so in 1991, and the Skull Valley Goshutes submitted one the following year. Several other tribes expressed interest in the program. After several rounds of grants to fund feasibility studies, Congress halted the program in 1994 without siting any MRS facilities. However, this did not stop private utilities seeking to store their spent fuels from recruiting reservations to act as hosts for the radioactive wastes (Ishiyama and TallBear, 2001; Brook, 1998; Clarke, 2002).

According to the Worldwatch Institute, about 317 reservations are threatened by hazardous wastes. In recent years, more than 100 proposals have been made to dump toxic wastes on Indian lands. The proposed nuclear dumps would add to the exposure that Native Americans have already experienced, since residents of reservations have been exposed to radiation and nuclear wastes for more than half a century. For instance, between 1951 and 1992, there were more than a thousand atomic explosions on the Western Shoshone land at the Nevada Test

Site, and more than 1,000 slag piles and tailings from abandoned ura-nium mines sit on Navajo land (LaDuke, 1999; Eichstaedt, 1994; Ishiyama and TallBear, 2001).

Another dimension of internal colonialism is evident in these dy-namics. In many instances, tribes being courted as repositories of nuclear and other hazardous wastes are located on isolated reservations with high poverty and unemployment rates. During the early 1990s, when tribes were being asked to store nuclear wastes on their reser-vations, the Apaches—one of the tribes asked to host nuclear waste facilities—had the following demographic characteristics: 6.9% of the population had a college or graduate school education, 33.1% lived in single-parent households, the median household income in 1990 was $18,484, and 37.5% of the tribal members lived below the poverty level. In contrast, 20.3% of the U.S. population had a bachelor's or graduate degree, 6.3% of the civilian labor force was unemployed, the median household income was $30,056, and 13.1% of the population had incomes below the poverty level in 1990 (U.S. Census Bureau, 1990).

Radioactive Waste Dumping on the Skull Valley Goshute Reservation

In the energy production cycle, corporations tend to concentrate the most hazardous and radioactive elements of their industry on or near Indian lands. In short, the corporations extract resources, which are converted into wealth, while Indians labor in unsafe conditions, live in poverty, and inherit perilous wastes. The Skull Valley Goshute reser-vation in Utah provides evidence of this. The reservation and Tooele County, in which it is located, have been described as the "nation's greatest concentration of hyper-hazardous and ultra-deadly materials" (M. Davis, 1998) and a "national sacrifice zone" (Kuletz, 1998). These descriptors are used because several military installations surround the reservation. Some of these facilities conduct open-air nerve-agent tests and chemical and biological weapons tests, and hazardous materials are stored and incinerated at these facilities. For instance, the Deseret Chemical Depot stores artillery shells containing sarin and mustard gas, as well as land mines filled with VX gas. VX is such a powerful nerve agent that a single drop on the skin can result in death within 15 minutes of contact (Boffey, 1968; Center for the American West, 1997;

Wilson, 1998; Ishiyama and TallBear, 2001). The Goshute reservation, located about 65 miles west of Salt Lake City, covers about 18,000 acres. The tribe has about 134 people, about 15 to 20 of whom live on the reservation (Utah Division of Indian Affairs, 2012).

Area residents fear for their lives, as the Pentagon estimates that an accident involving hazardous gases could kill as many as 89,000 people living close by. Residents recall an accident that occurred in 1968 when more than 6,000 sheep died after nerve gas escaped from the U.S. Army Dugway Proving Ground during open-air aircraft tests. Sheep grazing up to 45 miles away from the facility died. The dead sheep were buried on the Goshute reservation. Traces of VX were found in the snow and grass samples collected about three weeks after the sheep were killed. The Army denied that anything untoward happened at Dugway for decades (Boffey, 1968; Ishiyama and TallBear, 2001; Wilson, 1998)

In the face of mounting criticism about the hazardous industries the county hosts, local officials trumpet the benefits of such industries — job creation and keeping property taxes low. County officials laud the West Desert Hazardous Industry Area that created more than 900 jobs and generates about $2 million annually in mitigation fees. These fees allowed the county to freeze its property taxes (Ishiyama and Tall-Bear, 2001).

Originally, the Mescaleros were asked to store up to 40,000 metric tons of spent nuclear fuels for 40 years on their reservation. The facility was expected to generate about $2.3 billion in revenues, and the Mescaleros would receive about $250 million in return (Thorpe, 1996). However, in 1996, after the Mescalero Apache tribe decided not to build an MRS facility on their reservation, a consortium of eight nuclear utility companies, Private Fuel Storage, sought to temporarily store about 44,000 tons of high-level radioactive wastes on the Skull Valley Goshute reservation. This tonnage would account for about 80% of the commercial irradiated nuclear fuel in the country in 2004. The Skull Valley Goshutes' decision to pursue the spent-fuel storage option was highly controversial. In the search for storage places for the nuclear wastes, utility companies courted 60 Indian reservations; 59 of them turned the utilities down. So not only was there a disagreement among the Goshutes themselves; the governor of Utah, as well as mainstream and EJ groups from around the country, also opposed the development of the facility on the reservation. The Goshute's tribal chairman, Leon Bear, was a staunch advocate of the MRS facility; however, tribal members such as Margene Bullcreek and her organization—Ohngo Gaudadeh Devia Awareness—and others doggedly opposed it. Native American EJ groups such as Indigenous Environmental Network and Honor the Earth also opposed the Goshutes' MRS facility. The controversy raged for a decade, during which time about half the members of the Goshute tribe living on the reservation sued to prevent the development of the facility. Finally, in September 2006, the Bureau of Land Management rejected the transportation plans for shipping the radioactive wastes to the reservation. The BIA also rejected the lease arrangement between Private Fuel Storage and the tribe (Costanzo, 1999; TallBear, 2000; Ishiyama and TallBear, 2001; Nuclear Information and Resource Service, 2006; Kamps, 2006).

Uranium Mining and the Navajos

The development of energy resources on Indian reservations has brought its share of problems—toxic contamination, relict waste, low wages, deplorable working conditions, and health problems for Native Americans. The most significant uranium deposits in the U.S. are on Navajo, Laguna Pueblo, Havasupai, and Colville Confederated tribal lands, as well as in the Cebolleta and San Mateo Springs areas. More than 60% of the known deposits of uranium are on Indian lands; hence, between 80% and 90% of the mining and milling of uranium has occurred on or near reservations. More than a thousand of the mines were on the Navajo reservation. Between 1950 and 1980, about 15,000 people worked in uranium mines; about a quarter of them were Native Americans. Many of the Indian uranium mine workers were Navajos. From 1944 to 1986, nearly four million tons uranium ore was mined on Navajo lands (J. Weaver, 1997; Churchill and LaDuke, 1992; Brugge, Benally, and Yazzie-Lewis, 2006; U.S. EPA, 2011b).

Luebben (1972) describes the hiring practices and work conditions in the mines in 1953. He explains that, when possible, Whites were hired before Navajos, but Navajos were always a readily available labor source if there was a shortage of White laborers. Moreover, Navajos were hired almost exclusively into the lowest grade jobs (as underground helpers and miners) regardless of their capabilities and work experience. Navajos did not hold any skilled or supervisory positions. Navajos were paid less than Whites doing the same work, and while most Whites were paid directly, Navajo paychecks (and those of a few Whites of "questionable character") were sent to a local mercantile manager. The merchant extracted all monies owed for goods obtained on credit at local stores before giving the worker the remainder of the wages. Since most Navajos overextended their credit at the overpriced stores, quite often they did not see a penny of their wages.

In 1952, the Navajo Tribal Council, in collaboration with the BIA, entered into an agreement with Kerr-McGee Corporation. In return for access to the reservation's uranium deposits located near Shiprock (Four Corners), Kerr-McGee employed 100 Navajo men for the underground mining operations. The nonunionized Navajo workers were paid an average of $1.60 per hour (approximately two-thirds of the off-reservation wage rate at the time). In addition, between 300 and 500 Navajos were involved in independent operations that mined shallow (50 feet or less) uranium deposits or rich uranium ore that were sold to the Atomic Energy Commission's buying station located at the Kerr-McGee facility. Kerr-McGee operated with lax safety standards. In 1952, a federal mine inspector found that ventilation units in the mine shafts were not operating. Two years later, an inspection revealed that fans were operating for only half of the shift. In 1955, the ventilator ran out of gas during the visit of an inspector. In addition, a 1959 report noted that radiation levels in the mine shafts were 90 times the permissible limits. The Shiprock facility closed in early 1980 after uranium reserves were exhausted. Kerr-McGee left behind about 71 acres of raw uranium tailings—waste products from the uranium refining process that retain about 85% of the original radioactivity of the ore. The tailings pile is located about 60 feet from the San Juan River, the only significant surface water source in the Shiprock area. This resulted in radioactive contamination of downstream communities. In addition, the surface mining operations left behind between 100 and 200 open shafts (Weaver, 1997; Churchill and LaDuke, 1992; Tso and Shields, 1980; LaDuke, 1979; Robinson, 1992; Brugge, Benally, and Yazzie-Lewis, 2006).

HEALTH IMPACTS AT SHIPROCK

Uranium mining at Shiprock took a staggering toll on the lives and health of the Navajos. Of the 150-plus workers who toiled in the underground mines, 38 died of lung cancer by the time the facility closed. Another 96 suffered from respiratory ailments and cancers. Leukemia, birth defects such as cleft palates, heart defects, pneumoconiosis, tuberculosis, and other diseases commonly linked to radiation exposure were prevalent in the area. The risk of lung cancer for residents living close to a uranium tailings pile was approximately twice as high as that of Navajos living farther away from the pile. Furthermore, the rate of lung cancer was also higher among shaft miners than among others on the reservation. Between 1964 and 1974, the rate of birth defects among Navajo newborns in the Shiprock area was two to eight times higher than the national average. Microencephaly was also 15 times higher than the national average. Though the rate of birth defects remained higher than the national average, it declined significantly after 1975. This decline occurred after the company covered a 40-acre uranium tailings pile. There was also a significant decline in mining and milling in the area after 1974. The installment of electrostatic precipitators at the nearby Four Corners Power Plant and the closure of the Shiprock electronics plant that exposed Navajo women to substances such as Cobalt-60 and Krypton-85 were also factors contributing to the decline (Samet, Kutvirt, Waxweiler, and Key, 1984; Churchill and LaDuke, 1992; Roscoe, Deddens, Salvan, and Schnorr, 1995).

RADIOACTIVE WASTES AND SPILLS AT CHURCHROCK

The Churchrock Reservation on the Arizona–New Mexico border has been left with tailing piles too, and the results are similar. For years, the Kerr-McGee mine at Churchrock and United Nuclear together discharged from their mines 2.8 billion gallons of radioactive water laden with heavy metals per year; this discharge contaminated local water supplies. In July 1979, an accident occurred at United Nuclear's Churchrock facility. The mill tailings dam broke, releasing more than 100 million gallons of highly radioactive water into the Rio Puerco River. The contaminated plume extended for 40 miles downstream of the facility. Although United Nuclear knew about serious problems with the dam for two years and that there were cracks in it for two months before the accident, it did not make needed repairs. The only source of water for 1,700 Navajos was contaminated. A Navajo woman and several animals that waded into the river the morning of the spill developed sores on their legs and died later. In all, over 1,000 sheep and other livestock that ingested the water from Rio Puerco died. United Nuclear was slow in getting emergency water and food to local residents. It took more than a year to reach an out-of-court settlement for damages—a paltry $525,000 split among 240 plaintiffs and their lawyers (Churchill and LaDuke, 1992; Gedicks, 1993; Robinson, 1992; Weaver, 1997; Ambler, 1990; Brugge, 2002; Brugge, Benally, and Yazzie-Lewis, 2006).

COMPENSATION, MAPPING, AND REMEDIATION

In October 1990, the Radiation Exposure Compensation Act (RECA) was signed into law. The U.S. Department of Justice determined who was eligible for benefits and compensation and set guidelines for identifying claimants. Some Navajo did not have marriage licenses or birth certificates to establish their eligibility. RECA was amended in 2000 to broaden the umbrella of eligibility. As a result, uranium mill workers and uranium transporters became eligible for benefits and compensation. The time period for which claims could be made and the geographic scope of where claims could originate were also broadened. As of November 2009, the government has compensated 21,810 people for a total of $1.5 billion, while 8,789 claims were denied (U.S. Department of Justice, 2009).

The EPA and the Navajo nation have been mapping the reservation since 1994. In 2007, they compiled a "Comprehensive Database and Atlas" of 520 abandoned mines. The EPA began implementing a five-year remediation plan in 2008. Cleaning up contaminated water sources took a high priority, since about 30% of the Navajos lack access to piped water. Cleanup efforts also involve the removal of contaminated soil and the screening of 683 structures for contamination (many homes were uninhabitable as the rocks used to build them were contaminated with uranium). Thus far, 34 structures have been demolished and 14 new homes built (U.S. EPA 2008, 2011b).

Laguna Pueblo Reservation

Similar events unfolded at the Laguna Pueblo reservation, located about 45 miles west of Albuquerque, New Mexico. The 530,000-acre reservation currently is home to about 8,200 residents living in six different villages. In 1952, the Anaconda Mining Company (later Atlantic Richfield or ARCO) signed a lease with the Pueblos to mine uranium on 4,900 acres of reservation land. Additional leases were signed in 1963 and 1976, bringing the total acreage leased to 8,000 acres. In 1953, ARCO began operating one of the largest open-pit uranium mines in the world on the reservation. The 625-feet-deep pit, which operated 24 hours every day for 30 years, employed about 800 tribal members. ARCO produced 24 million tons of uranium-bearing ore and 23.7 million tons of radioactive waste during its operation. Blasting caused nearby stone and mud houses to crack open, while dust coated the houses, crops, and people's belongings. The company closed the 2,800-acre Jackpile-Paguate Mine in 1982 (Luarkie, 2012).

When the mine closed, ARCO left behind contaminated, irradiated surface water and groundwater. Low-grade uranium ore was used to construct roads, houses, and other buildings on the reservation (Weaver, 1997; Churchill, 1993). The pit remained dormant for seven years before any remediation efforts got under way. In addition, stockpiled wastes blew over surrounding areas, including the Paguate Village, a community of about 1,500 people that is located about 30 yards from the mine. When it rained, contaminated water flowed from the waste pile into nearby tributaries. Two local streams, the Rio Moquino and Rio San Jose, have tested positive for radiation contamination. Reclamation work began in 1989 when ARCO and the Pueblo tribe reached an agreement. The Pueblos were contracted to do the reclamation work; however, the $43 million provided by ARCO was inadequate to fully reclaim the roughly 2,000 acres needing remediation. Though reclamation activities ceased in 1995, high-grade uranium ore still remains on the surface as well as in some of the exposed open pits on the reservation. The EPA began working with the tribe to assess contamination on the reservation in 2009. Three years later, the agency recommended that the Jackpile-Paguate Mine be placed on the NPL and receive Superfund designation. The Pueblos are opposed to any new mining on or near their lands. As a result, in 2007, the tribal council passed a resolution to establish a moratorium on uranium mining or development on the reservation (Luarkie, 2012).

Pine Ridge Reservation

The story repeats itself in the energy-industrial complex in the Black Hills region. On June 11, 1962, 200 tons of radioactive mill tailings washed into the Cheyenne River, an indirect source of water for the Pine Ridge Reservation. In 1980, the Indian Health Service announced that well water at Slim Buttes had gross alpha levels three times the national safety standard. A new well in the community had 14 times the radioactive level of national safety standards. Subsurface water on Pine Ridge's Red Shirt Table tested at several times the acceptable levels of radioactivity. Because the water source of the entire Pine Ridge Reservation was contaminated, the tribal president requested money to obtain emergency water supplies. The BIA stipulated that the water could be obtained but only for consumption by cattle. About 3.5 million tons of exposed tailings from the former army ordnance depot at Igloo, South Dakota, sit astride the banks of the Cheyenne River and Cottonwood Creek near downtown Edgemont. Though tailings contaminated the water supply, it was considered "cost prohibitive" to clean up the site. Between 1987 and 1989, the government claimed to have remedied the situation by digging up the pile from the center of the village and dumping it in a fenced vacant area on its fringes. Government experts also argued that the site is so contaminated that it is best suited for a national nuclear waste dump. As the cancer death rates in the area skyrocket, politicians such as a former governor of South Dakota have argued that a national nuclear dump would be an economic boom for the area's depressed economy. There are reports that there has been a significant increase in the number of still births, teratogenic effects such as cleft palates, and cancer deaths since 1970 (Churchill and LaDuke, 1992).

PCBs on Mohawk Land

Between 1898 and 1903, the Power Canal was constructed. Even before the canal was completed, the Aluminum Company of America

(ALCOA or Alcoa) began construction of its facility about eight miles west of the Akwesasne (St. Regis) Mohawk reservation. Alcoa opened its plant in 1903 (U.S. EPA, 2012a, 2012b, 2012d). The completion of the St. Lawrence–Franklin D. Roosevelt Power Project—a joint venture with Canada—resulted in the generation of massive amounts of hydroelectricity on the St. Lawrence River in 1958 (New York Power Authority, 2012). This had an *agglomeration effect* of other major industries clustering around the reservation to take advantage of hydropower infrastructure that was in place. Hence, in 1959, General Motors (GM) Corporation's Central Foundry Division set up an engine-parts factory less than 100 feet from the western border of the Akwesasne Mohawk reservation. Other facilities such as Reynolds Metals (Alcoa East) is located close to the reservation and also contributed to its contamination (Sengupta, 2001; Schell and Tarbell, 1998; Quigley, 2001).

Alcoa's 2,700-acre Massena facility (Alcoa West) is the longest continuously operating aluminum plant in the world. It includes a fabricating area, an ingot-extrusion area, and a smelting plant. The facility released PCBs and other hazardous substances such as polyaromatic hydrocarbons, volatile organic compounds, metals, fluoride, and cyanide on the property and into the Grasse River for years. Though Alcoa stopped using oil containing PCBs in the mid 1970s, the contamination extends about seven miles downstream of the facility. This stretch of the river contains about 1.25 million cubic yards of PCB-tainted sediments. The PCB levels in fish in the Grasse River was so high that the New York State Department of Health issued a consumption advisory that fish from the river should not be eaten. In 1989, the EPA ordered Alcoa to determine the extent of the contamination and develop a plan of remediation (U.S. EPA, 2012a, 2012b, 2012d).

New York State won its case against Alcoa in 1991, and the company agreed to pay $7.5 million in civil and criminal penalties for an array of environmental offenses. Violations included piling PCB-contaminated soil on company property and leaving it there for more than 90 days in 1989. The contaminated soil was eventually shipped to Alabama but was mislabeled as nonhazardous material. Further offenses included pouring acidic and caustic solutions used in the aluminum-cleaning process down a manhole, where they became part of the wastewater that flowed into the Grasse River (Sack, 1991).

In 1995, the company removed about 3,000 cubic yards of contaminated soil containing about 8,000 tons of PCBs. Fourteen contaminated areas were identified and cleaned up by 2001; however, contamination persisted. In 2001, Alcoa began capping parts of the site, but in 2003, assessment of those efforts showed that the capping material had been lost and sediment had been eroded in some areas. The company tried other forms of remediation, including the dredging and removal of 24,000 cubic yards of sediment, boulders, and debris in 2005; the material was disposed of in Alcoa's on-site landfill. Though the PCB levels have declined by 90% for smallmouth bass and brown bullhead and by about 60% for young spottail shiners since the 1990s, these fish are still too toxic for human consumption (U.S. EPA, 2012a, 2012b, 2012d).

In October 2012, the EPA released a "Proposed Remedial Action Plan" for Alcoa's Grasse River site. The planning phase will last three to four years and will be followed by site remediation between 2016 and 2020 at a cost of about $243 million—if the EPA-recommended alternative is chosen (U.S. EPA, 2012a, 2012d; *Business Wire*, 2012). Alcoa currently employs about 1,100 people and has a payroll of about $340 million annually. The plant produces 252,000 metric tons of molten aluminum yearly (ALCOA, 2012b).

GM's 270-acre plant that sits on the fence line of the St. Regis Mohawk Reservation is also an egregious polluter. The plant, originally built to manufacture aluminum cylinder heads for the Chevrolet Corvair, operated as an aluminum die-casting facility from 1959 to 2009. PCBs were a component of the hydraulic fluids used in die-casting machines at the facility till 1980. Wastes generated from this facility were disposed of on-site in a landfill and four lagoons. PCBs adulterated the soil and water and have been found in the St. Lawrence and Raquette Rivers, Turtle Cove, and Turtle Creek (U.S. EPA 2011a, 2012c). There was a huge dump on GM's property that Mohawk children foraged through to find scrap metal and wood that they could sell or reuse. Mohawks also used the discarded oil drums to collect rainwater for bathing. However, unbeknownst to them, the trash heap was a toxic dump filled with PCBs, mirex, and other hazardous compounds (Sengupta, 2001; Schell and Tarbell, 1998; Quigley, 2001).

PCB was used by many of the industries around the reservation till it was banned in 1977; consequently, the water, soil, air, and food is tainted with the chemical. For instance, snapping turtles on the reservation were found to contain up to 3,067 ppm of PCBs. Studies conducted on the tribe found that Mohawk women's breast milk had a significantly higher percentage of PCBs in it than did the breast milk of area White women (LaDuke, 1999; Rice and O'Keefe, 1995; Bristol, 1992; Schell and Tarbell, 1998; Johansen, 1994; Quigley, 2001).

In 1981, the New York State Department of Environmental Conservation reported that the groundwater was highly contaminated with PCBs. About 45 families drink area well water. and another 200 get water from the St. Lawrence River (located half a mile from the GM plant). Water in the area is also contaminated with heavy metals such as lead, chromium, mercury, cadmium, methylmercury, and antimony. Fish and local wildlife are critical components of the Mohawk diet, and these are heavily contaminated (Schell and Tarbell, 1998; LaDuke, 1999; Quigley, 2001).

In 1983, the EPA fined GM $507,000 for 21 violations of the TSCA. A year later, the 35-foot-high toxic mounds were covered with temporary, impermeable caps. The site was put on the NPL in 1984. Residents formed the Akwesasne Task Force on the Environment in 1987 to address ongoing problems. That same year, the EPA oversaw the placement of cap on the facility's landfill; the landfill contains an estimated 297,000 tons of PCBs. Cleanup costs were estimated at $138 million (Schell and Tarbell, 1998; LaDuke, 1999; Sengupta, 2001; Johansen, 1994; U.S. EPA 2011a, 2012c).

For several years, GM tried to contain the site by sealing the dumps and building a wall the company claimed would prevent PCBs from contaminating Mohawk land. To proceed with the plan, GM needed tribal approval to go onto Mohawk land to build the wall. The Mohawks rejected the plan because the tribe wanted GM to excavate the toxic sludge from the reservation and the factory site and remove it from the area. In the meantime, the government urged families on the reservation not to eat the fish, drink the water, or breastfeed their infants. In 1995, GM dredged and removed about 23,000 tons of PCB-contaminated sediments from the St. Lawrence River. The sediments were shipped off-site to be buried. Remediation of the Raquette lasted from 2002 to 2003, and about 16,900 cubic yards of tainted soil was removed. Contaminated soil was also removed from the slope of the landfill in 2003, and remediation work began in Turtle Cove the following year (U.S. EPA, 2011a; Sengupta, 2001; Johansen, 1994).

Samples taken from in, around, and under the buildings at the plant from 2008 to 2010 still show elevated concentrations of PCBs in the buildings, tunnels, and soil under the facility. GM (renamed Motors Liquidation Corporation) filed for bankruptcy protection in 2009. The site is currently owned by RACER Trust, which is overseeing demolition activities at the site as well as remediation. Demolition began in 2011 and will be completed in 2013 (U.S. EPA, 2011a, 2012c).

The Internal Colonial Frame in EJ Research

The concept of internal colonialism is more amorphous than other theories used to explain minority exposure to environmental hazards, and this could partly explain why it has not received as much scholarly attention in the EJ literature as other explanations. Thus far, most of the research using this thesis takes the form of descriptive case studies (Churchill and LaDuke, 1992; LaDuke, 1999; Weaver, 1997; Adeola, 2000; Jaimes, 1992; Gedicks, 1993, 1998, 2001). However, some scholars are approaching the colonialism framework from a theoretical perspective. For instance, Clarke (2002) explored the literature on rhetoric to examine how the framing of sovereignty evolved during the Skull Valley Goshute controversy. Martino-Taylor (2008, 2011), who embeds her work in the theories of C. Wright Mills, identifies what she calls a "military-industrial-academic" complex that uses chemical and biological weaponry on Blacks and other marginalized peoples for the purposes of military supremacy.

Spatial analyses of the relationship between exposure to environmental hazards and Native reservations are emerging. Hooks and Smith's (2004) study of militarism, environmental hazards, and reservations analyzed sites that contained unexploded ordnances (landmines, nerve gases, and toxic and explosive shells). They found that Native Americans tended to live in counties with sites deemed to be extremely dangerous because of the presence of unexploded military ordnances. There was a positive correlation between the presence of tribal land and the location of extremely dangerous military sites. That is, the more acres owned by Native Americans, the greater the number of such facilities. Hooks and Smith argue that Native American exposure to environmental hazards is the result of militarism rather than economic competition. They argue that coercive government policies of placing reservations in certain locations are important drivers of exposure to hazards. The researchers argue that as the military-industrial complex expanded in the 1940s and during the Cold War, remote locations were used as bombing ranges, testing grounds, and storage sites. These sites were located primarily in the western portion of the U.S.

TRI Releases on Reservation Land

Thomas, Fannin, and Rossman (2010) have also conducted a spatial analysis of the toxins on Native American reservations. Their study spans the period 2000 to 2002. They used government metadata files to study the census tracts in which reservations, trust lands, and military installations are located. The study found that one in eight census tracts with TRI facilities were located on reservations, trust lands, and military installations abutting tribal lands. Moreover, the facilities located in these tracts released toxic chemical wastes that amounted to about 345 pounds per Native American living in the United States. Census tracts that had military installations adjacent to Native American lands were responsible for 18.3% of the on- and off-site releases.

Table 3.1 shows that in 2011 a total of 10,752,510 pounds of toxic chemicals were released from and disposed of by 46 TRI-reporting facilities located on Indian reservations and in Alaska Native villages. There were 1,676 TRI-reporting facilities located within ten miles of Indian reservations and Alaska Native Villages. The top 100 of these had a total on- and off-site disposal and release of 224,149,940 pounds of toxic chemicals. In addition, almost 44 million pounds of production-related wastes were managed on reservations, and about 637 million pounds were managed near the reservations (U.S. EPA, 2011d).

What Keeps Them There?

Gail Small lives on a reservation in Lame Deer, Montana, that is surrounded by power plants, strip mining, and the extraction of coalbed methane gas—all of which befouls the only water source of the

Table 3.1. Releases and Disposal of Toxic Chemicals and Hazardous Materials on Native Reservations and in Alaska Native Villages

Jurisdictions	Total on- and off-site disposal or release (in pounds)	Quantities of TRI chemicals in total production-related wastes managed (in pounds)
On reservations	10,752,510	43,750,319
Top 100 companies located within 10 miles of reservations	224,149,940	637,311,982
Total	234,902,450	681,062,301

Source: Compiled from U.S. EPA 2011d.

Northern Cheyenne tribe. Despite all this, Small—a lawyer—stays in the community and fights for redress and to prevent future environmental degradation. Barry Dana, former chief of the Penobscot Reservation in Maine, is not trying to leave his small reservation on Indian Island in the Penobscot River either. Dana stays even though the river is contaminated by effluents from the Lincoln Pulp and Paper Mill located just 30 miles upstream (Native Action, 2012; Katahdin Foundation, 2005; *Great Northern Paper v. Penobscot Nation*, 2001).

Why do they stay? Reservations were established by the federal government in fixed locations. Moving away from the reservations has significant ramifications for Indians, including loss of land. Native Americans experienced this firsthand when the federal government embarked on a program to depopulate the reservations. During the 1950s, the BIA developed programs to remove Indians from the reservations, sell the land, and terminate the tribal system. The massive relocation program placed thousands of Indians in low-paying jobs in urban areas. Between 1952 and 1972, more than 100,000 Indians were relocated to low-rent apartments and housing projects in cities. This resulted in increased landlessness among Indians (Nabokov, 1991; Luebben, 1972).

Fishing, hunting, and gathering are important aspects of tribal culture and subsistence living that Native Americans lose if they leave the reservation. The reservations also hold important Native American cultural artifacts, burial sites, archeological features, and sacred sites. As many Native Americans assert, many of the reservations represent significant ties to their ancestral lands that they want to nurture. They have strong connections to the land that they do not want to sever. Moreover, many Native Americans are embedded in strong kinship networks and have built social and educational institutions on the reservations. Moving from the reservation is not at all like moving across town or from a city to the suburbs. Most reservations are in remote locations, so moving away from them will mean a significant disruption in many aspects of life. Indians who were moved from the reservations during the federal termination program and resettled in urban areas experienced this as they struggled mightily to craft new lives and build communities from scratch. For these and other reasons, Native Americans stay on the reservations despite their exposure to environmental hazards.

4

Market Dynamics

Residential Mobility, or Who Moves and Who Stays

Researchers in the EJ field have offered a range of theses to explain the siting patterns of hazardous facilities and the exposure to dangerous environmental conditions that are discussed in this chapter under the general heading of market dynamics. The decision making and the *economic behavior* of corporate actors and community residents is at the core of these arguments. This aspect of EJ research focuses on the following questions: (1) What are the current demographic characteristics of communities hosting hazardous facilities? (2) What were the demographic characteristics of the host community at the time the facility was sited? (3) How do residents of host communities respond to facility siting, Superfund and brownfield designation, and site remediation? (4) Who moves? (5) How are citizens' responses related to demographic changes in host communities? (6) What are the economic impacts of hazardous facilities on host communities?

Economic Rationality

Economic rationality is one thesis advanced by researchers to counter claims of discrimination in the siting patterns of hazardous facilities. Some scholars argue that companies are driven to control costs; therefore, they act in an economically rational way and place their facilities where it is cheapest to do so. For instance Jeffreys contends, "Poor people and minorities do not necessarily attract polluters merely because they are poor or people of color or because the polluters are racists. Low-cost land attracts industry for some of the same reasons that it attracts poor people" (1994: 682). According to this line of argument, the facilities are placed where there is easy access to transportation; land is cheap; specialized infrastructure and services can be shared; companies can bargain for reduced costs in fees, taxes, and other subsidies; operational costs are lowest; and there is access to labor, raw materials, and markets. For these reasons, TSDFs seem to cluster in certain locations. Commercial TSDF operators argue that *cost containment* is their primary motivation for selecting a site (Erickson and Wasylenko, 1980; Greenberg, Anderson, and Rosenberger, 1984; Newman and Sullivan, 1987; Blair and Premus, 1987; H. Freeman, 1989; Hannink, 1997; Zahran, Hastings, and Brody, 2008).

However, disproportionate siting can occur even if companies *do not intend* to discriminate. That is, disproportionate siting in minority and low-income areas can be an *unintended consequence* of profit maximization and cost containment. Disproportionate siting can occur because neighborhoods with low commercial property values often abut neighborhoods with low residential property values (Saha and Mohai, 2005; Been, 1994b). Hamilton takes this argument further by contending that companies are attracted to areas with low housing prices and a high proportion of minorities because such locations lower any potential compensation that polluters might be required to pay (Hamilton, 1993, 1995).

Studies testing the economic rationality thesis have found that TSDFs are located in areas with higher percentages of industrial workers (Anderton et al. 1994). Studies have also found a negative association between property values and the location of TSDFs (Anderton, Anderson, Oakes, and Fraser, 1994).

Campbell, Peck, and Tschudi (2010) argue that strategic firms might choose to adopt a *divide-and-conquer* strategy and locate their facilities near political boundaries such as the border between two cities. By locating on the boundary between two cities rather than in the middle of one, a firm impacts half the residents in each. The researchers' study of Maricopa County, Arizona (in which Phoenix is located), shows that census tracts with greater percentages of minority residents are located closer to new TRI facilities than are tracts with large percentages of Whites. The percentage of Asians was statistically significant in all the models; the percentage of Hispanics and the percentage of Native Americans were also positively associated with the presence of new TRI facilities. However, the researchers found no support for the *jurisdictional-divide* thesis; neither the city boundaries nor the boundaries of Native American reservations were significant in the models. They also examined poverty and argued that poverty was insignificant in predicting the location of TRI facilities.

Mohai and Saha's work (2006, 2007) could shed some light on the dynamics of placing hazardous facilities on or near jurisdictional boundaries and the role of scale in identifying whether the jurisdictional-divide argument is applicable. As mentioned before, Mohai and Saha found that 71% of the TSDFs they studied were located within half a mile of the census tract boundaries. It seems as if one would also find facilities on jurisdictional boundaries at smaller scales. Researchers have yet to explore the implications of this fact. In places where census tracts approximate neighborhood borders, placing facilities close to the boundaries could have a divide-and-conquer effect. However, as discussed earlier, census tracts do not always adhere to neighborhood boundaries.

Though Campbell, Peck, and Tschudi (2010) did not find support for their jurisdictional-divide argument in Maricopa County, their research, coupled with the findings of Mohai and Saha (2006, 2007), points to the need for larger multiscale analysis that probes this argument more fully. In addition, researchers should probe at what scale siting hazardous facilities on or close to jurisdictional boundaries is important and in what way. That is, is the jurisdictional-divide thesis supported when larger political units such as the county or the state are examined?

Residential Sorting and White Flight

Residential Sorting

Economic theorists argue that the presence of facilities in minority communities is *not* the result of intentional discrimination. Instead, people move into and out of communities in response to neighborhood characteristics. That is, the spatial arrangement of environmental amenities and disamenities induces residential sorting or neighborhood racial change that might appear on the surface to be discriminatory

(Cameron and McConnaha, 2006; Banzhaf and Walsh, 2008). Downey refers to the process of neighborhood racial change as *racial succession*. He argues that facility siting has "relatively little impact on neighborhood racial change" (2005: 978). Hence, the characteristics of host communities are the result of general processes of demographic change and racial succession.

White Flight

RACE AND CLASS

White flight can be seen as particular kind of residential sorting in which White residents move out of racially mixed neighborhoods or from White neighborhoods that abut Black neighborhoods. The move could be motivated by racial prejudice, lack of desire to live amid a particular racial group, desire to live among others of one's own race and culture, or class differences (Farley et al., 1978; M. White, 1984; W. Clark, 1992; Massey and Denton, 1993; Bobo and Zubrinsky, 1996; Farley, Fielding, and Krysan, 1997; Harris, 1999; Crowder, 2000; Krysan, 2002).

A White female respondent in Farley et al.'s study of segregation in Detroit commented, "It seems like the property values drop when [B]lack families move in," explaining further, "because they [Blacks] do not keep up their houses" (1994: 775). The respondent is expressing a sentiment that is fairly widespread. Farley, Danziger, and Holzer's (2000) analysis of data collected in the 1976 and 1992 Detroit Area Study indicates that Whites are more willing to live in neighborhoods with Black neighbors over time (see table 4.1). However, the analysis shows that in 1992 only 35% of Whites felt comfortable living in a neighborhood that was 53% Black. The study also showed that 53% of Whites would try to move if the neighborhood was 53% Black, while 73% said they would not *move into* a neighborhood with that composition of Blacks. Even in a neighborhood that was a third Black, 59% of Whites would refrain from moving into such a neighborhood in 1992.

Other researchers have also found that Whites are reluctant to move into neighborhoods perceived as "Black." Whites in Los Angeles were found to prefer neighborhoods that were 75% White and 25% Black; virtually no Whites wanted to live in a neighborhood that was more than 60% Black (W. Clark, 1992). Whites in Oklahoma City rated

Table 4.1. *White Respondents' Willingness to Live in Racially Mixed Neighborhoods, 1976 and 1992*

Neighborhood composition	Percentage indicating they would feel comfortable in the neighborhood		Percentage indicating they would try to move out of the neighborhood		Percentage indicating they would not move into such a neighborhood	
	1976	1992	1976	1992	1976	1992
7% Black	76	84	7	4	27	13
20% Black	58	70	24	15	50	31
33% Black	43	56	41	29	73	59
53% Black	28	35	64	53	84	73

Source: Compiled from Farley, Danziger, Holzer, 2000: 190.

neighborhoods less favorably as the percentage of Blacks increased—even when other factors such as distance from downtown, neighborhood cleanliness, crime, and neighborhood cohesion were held constant (St. John and Bates, 1990). Yinger (1979) studied the relationship between race and home prices and found that Whites had an aversion to Black neighbors. Emerson, Yancey, and Chai (2001) also found that Whites were unwilling to purchase homes in neighborhoods that were more than 15% Black. Bobo (1997) asserts that people's assessment of neighborhood desirability is influenced by the racial composition of a given neighborhood. Bobo and Zubrinsky (1996) also report that Whites prefer not to have Blacks as neighbors.

Frey (1979) argues that the racial composition of a neighborhood is not a big factor when Whites are deciding whether to move; however, racial composition is a major factor when White are selecting a new neighborhood to *move to*. Ellen (2000) reports that Whites stereotype neighborhoods on the basis of the racial composition when deciding which ones to move into. Cutler, Glaeser, and Vigdor (1999) posit that Whites are willing to pay a premium to avoid living in neighborhoods with Blacks. However, Harris (1999, 1997) also supports the argument that the residential mobility of Whites is unrelated to the proportion of neighborhood residents who are Black. So do South and Crowder (1998, 1997) and South and Deane (1993).

Is the feeling mutual? Do Blacks want to live in all-Black or predominantly Black neighborhoods? Researchers such as Thernstrom and Thernstrom (1997) and Patterson (1997) argue that segregation persists because *both* Blacks and Whites prefer to live among people of their own race. However, Farley, Danziger, and Holzer's (2000) analysis of the Detroit Area Study data shows that Blacks prefer racially mixed neighborhoods. In 1992, most Blacks preferred communities where between half and 71% of their neighbors were Black. Only 20% of Blacks chose a neighborhood that was 100% Black as their first- or second-choice neighborhood to live in, and 31% of Blacks were willing to move into an all-White neighborhood.

But is it true that property values fall when Blacks move into a neighborhood? Or are property values lower in Black neighborhoods than in other neighborhoods? Boston, Rigsby, and Zald (1972) argue that minority occupancy does not decrease property values. However, Harris (1999) found that nationwide housing lost 16% of its value when neighborhoods went from less than 10% Black to between 10% and 60% Black. When neighborhoods are at least 60% Black, housing loses 46% of its value. Harris examined the effects of both race and class in his Hedonic model and found that for 96% of the housing units, the price of housing declined as the percentage of Blacks in the neighborhood increased; but this occurred not because of race but because of the class of the residents. That is, once socioeconomic status of the neighborhood is controlled for, the relationship between neighborhood racial composition and housing value becomes insignificant. Harris concludes that housing in neighborhoods with a high percentage of Blacks is less valuable not because of an aversion to Blacks per se but because of people's preference for neighbors who are affluent and well educated. Harris's results support earlier findings reported by Pettigrew (1973). Pettigrew reported that by 1972, 85% of Whites agreed with the statement that it made no difference to them "if a Negro with just as much income and education" moved onto the block on which they lived.

Lee and Wood (1991) studied four cities from 1970 to 1980 and found that 90% of the integrated census tracts in Detroit and Atlanta and a third of those in Boston and Los Angeles underwent racial succession. Galster (1990) found that the extent of White flight varied within a given city also. In his study of Cleveland, Galster found that White flight was highest in census tracts where residents expressed the strongest *segregationist sentiments*.

Krysan (2002) used the Multi-City Study of Urban Inequality database to study factors contributing to White flight in Boston, Detroit, Atlanta, and Los Angeles. She found that 38% of Whites in Atlanta, Boston, and Detroit indicated they would consider moving out of neighborhoods that had Black residents. The percentage of Whites who would consider moving increased as the percentage of Blacks in a neighborhood increased. Whites who held *stereotypical views* of Blacks were the ones who were most likely to say they would consider moving out of a neighborhood if Blacks were living there. Detroit was the city where Whites were most likely to indicate they would move from neighborhoods where Blacks were living.

NOXIOUS FACILITIES

White flight can be triggered by factors other than the racial and class composition of the neighborhood. It can be triggered by the siting of noxious or hazardous facilities in a community (if Whites are the only ones or primarily the ones with means to move from the community). Under the White-flight scenario, communities that might have been racially mixed at the time of the siting of a facility become predominantly minority over time, as Whites move out and only minorities remain or minorities move in to replace those moving out. The extent to which White flight occurs varies by city.

Hedonic Models, Property Values, and Willingness to Pay

The Effects of Hazardous Sites on Property Values

Neighborhood change is related to property values and people's ability or desire to pay to live in certain neighborhoods. Hence, some researchers have examined the relationship between hazardous waste sites and property values by using hedonic models. Hedonic regression models are used to evaluate the demand for and value of goods. They are used to analyze the statistical relationship between the price of multiattribute goods such as homes with environmental factors such as the location of a hazardous facility, cleanup of hazardous waste sites, and the location of parks. In the case of residential property values, researchers compare the various attributes of a home (such as size, type of construction, age, etc.) to determine how the prices of comparable units vary with distance from an environmental *amenity* or *disamenity* (Palmquist and Smith, 2002).

Though companies trying to site hazardous facilities point to research indicating that landfills and other waste disposal sites do not have negative impacts on property values (Gamble, Downing, Shortle, and Epp, 1982; Zeiss and Atwater, 1989; Reichert, Small, and Mohanty, 1992; Bouvier, Halstead, Conway, and Malano, 2000; Parker, 2003), most of the research on this topic has come to the opposite conclusion. Most studies find that property values decline in areas adjacent to Superfund sites (McClelland, Schulze, and Hurd, 1990). Nelson, Genereux, and Genereux (1992) found that property values were lower within a two-mile radius of a landfill and that there was a *property value gradient* of 6.2% per mile.

Kohlhase (1991) studied property values in Harris County (where Houston is located) by looking at how home prices changed before (1976 and 1980) and after (1985) ten sites in the county were placed on the NPL. The study found that home prices dropped significantly in neighborhoods within six miles of the Superfund sites in 1985. Housing prices did not drop outside the six-mile radius from the NPL site. Kohlhase argues that the placement of the sites on the NPL created a market wherein houses near the NPL sites were perceived as disamenities and those further away as safe. In 1976, there was no premium on neighborhoods far from toxic sites. The magnitude of the decline in property values is unrelated to the severity of the site risk as measured by the EPA's Hazard Ranking System (HRS) score. (The HRS scores range from 1 to 100. A site must score more than 28.5 to be placed on the NPL.) The declines in property values ceased once NPL sites were remediated.

Aydin and Smith (2008) replicated Kohlhase's study and found that prices were depressed in a more restricted area than that reported by Kohlhase. Aydin and Smith found that prices were depressed in a 3.7-mile radius. They also found that prices rebounded after Superfund cleanup was completed on the sites. Noonan, Turaga and Baden (2009) also replicated Kohlhase's study and did a detailed assessment of the race effect at the South Cavalcade Street NPL site in Harris County. They found that the percentage of Blacks and minorities living within 4.76 miles of the site was higher than in the rest of the county. They also found that household incomes were lower inside the 4.76-mile radius than in the rest of the county.

McMillen and Thorsnes (2003) found similar market dynamics for housing around a copper smelter in Tacoma. They used an average derivative estimator to analyze the change in home prices before a site was placed on the Superfund list, during evaluation and cleanup, and after the site was cleaned. They found that home prices close to the smelter were depressed before the facility was designated a Superfund site. Once the plant closed, property values increased. After the site was cleaned up, real estate values were at a premium in the neighborhood; since the neighborhood was close to the water and the central business district, it became a desirable residential area when the risks were reduced.

Hurd (2002) also found that property values in neighborhoods adjacent to Superfund sites rebounded in Monterrey Park (located ten miles east of Los Angeles) when the sites were cleaned up. He found that home prices closest to the cleaned-up site rose faster than did others in the general area. In contrast, Reichert (1997) found that property values in Uniontown, Ohio, remained permanently depressed in neighborhoods close to a Superfund site. Kiel (1995) studied Woburn, Massachusetts. She argued that the identification of a site by the EPA as a Superfund site was accompanied by a drop in property values in neighborhoods around the hazardous waste site and that the home prices did not rebound.

Smolen, Moore, and Conway (1992) used a centroid-based method to study the effects of two hazardous waste landfills on property values in Toledo and found that they had adverse effects on property values within a 5.75-mile radius of the sites. Property values fell by about $12,100 per mile from each waste site. Greenstone and Gallagher (2008) found that placement on the NPL was associated with only small and statistically insignificant changes in property values (within a two- and three-mile radius of the sites). They also found that completed Superfund cleanups resulted in a small and statistically insignificant increase in property values and rental rates in neighborhoods close to hazardous waste sites. They examined a race variable and found that the percentage of Blacks declined in areas where sites were placed on the NPL. However, the change was statistically insignificant.

Ketar (1992) studied the relationship between hazardous waste sites and property values in New Jersey. The study found that property values declined in neighborhoods around hazardous waste sites. Greenberg and Hughes (1993) surveyed tax assessors about property values in New Jersey. Almost 20% of them reported that close proximity to hazardous waste sites depressed property values, and the effects were most pronounced within a quarter-mile radius of the sites.

Ready (2010) studied how the presence of landfills and the *volume of waste processed* affected nearby property values in several states. He found that landfills processing high volumes of wastes (500 tons per day or more) decreased nearby residential property values by an average of 13.8%. More specifically, property values increased by 5.9% per mile as one moved away from the landfills. The landfills processing low volumes of wastes (under 500 tons per day) decreased adjacent property values by an average of 2.7%. The impact declines with distance from the landfills at a gradient of about 1.3% per mile. While almost all the high-volume landfills lowered property values, about 74% of the low-volume landfills had a similar impact.

Kiel and Williams (2007) investigated how the *size of Superfund sites* affected property values. They found that larger Superfund sites depressed adjacent property values more than smaller ones did. Neighborhoods with depressed housing values before perilous sites were listed on the NPL continued to have depressed values after placement on the NPL. The researchers studied four NPL sites in detail and found one site (the Hollingsworth Solderless Terminal in Fort Lauderdale) that was viewed as a negative amenity before being cleaned remained so after remediation. However, another site (the Miami Gold Coast) rebounded to be viewed as an amenity after cleanup. For two sites (Jibboom in Sacramento and Intel in Santa Clara), cleanup appeared to have had no impact on property values adjacent to the sites.

Noonan, Turaga, and Baden (2009) summarize the findings of 15 studies that examine the distance that NPL sites have an effect on property values. Overall, studies find that the effects of hazardous facilities rarely extend beyond six miles. Other researchers have also found that close proximity to hazardous waste sites and other locally unwanted land uses is associated with reduced property values (Havlicek, Richardson, and Davies, 1971; Smith and Desvousges, 1986; Thayer, Albers, and Rahmatian, 1992; Hite, 1998; Dale, Murdoch, Thayer, and Waddell, 1999; McCluskey and Rausser, 2001; Boyle and Kiel, 2001; Deaton and Hoehn, 2004; Simons, Bowen, and Sementall, 1997).

So how does the presence of multiple dangerous sites affect property values? Researchers have found that when multiple hazardous waste sites exist in an area, the main *spillover effects* arise from proximity to the closest site (Ihlanfeldt and Taylor, 2004; Deaton and Hoehn, 2004). Ihlanfeldt and Taylor's (2004) study of Fulton County (where Atlanta is located) also found that even when waste sites are not deemed unsafe enough to be placed on the NPL, they still depress property values. Hite, Chern, Hitzhusen, and Randall's (2001) as well as Hite's (2009) study of four landfills in Franklin County, Ohio, revealed that nearby property values were depressed regardless of whether the landfills were operational or closed. This discussion points to overwhelming evidence that hazardous facilities have a detrimental impact on nearby property values.

Willingness to Pay and Environmental Tradeoffs

Do people vote with their feet and pocket book? EJ activists claim that when risks are perceived from hazardous sites, those who are *able to move* out of the affected community do so, leaving those who are unable to move behind. This is a willingness-to-pay or an environmental-tradeoff thesis. This argument assumes that people are either unwilling to pay for safer, more expensive housing or are *trading off* living with higher risks for more affordable housing. Scholars studying this phenomenon have found that people *will pay more* for housing to avoid risks; they will also pay a premium once sites are cleaned up and disamenities are transformed into desired amenities. For example, Smith and Desvousges's (1986) study of suburban Boston found that residents were willing to pay more for housing in order to live further away from hazardous waste sites.

Chattopadhyay, Braden, and Patunru's (2005) study of Waukegan, Illinois, found that residents were willing to pay more for housing when NPL sites around Waukegan Harbor were cleaned up. Similarly Gayer, Hamilton, and Viscusi's (2000, 2002) study of risk indicators in Grand Rapids, Michigan, found that residents were willing to pay more for housing to avoid perceived cancer risks from Superfund sites. Residents were willing to pay $1,085 to live an additional mile away from the closest Superfund site and $1,588 extra to have fewer hazardous sites within a quarter mile of their homes.

Gayer (2000) explored how race and class was related to voting with one's feet or pocket book in Grand Rapids. He found that the tradeoff between risk from hazardous waste sites and housing prices varied by levels of neighborhood income and education as well as the racial composition of the neighborhood. When Gayer controlled for endogeneity, he found that the risk tradeoff was $582 higher for a home in a neighborhood with a high percentage of college-educated residents, $270 more for a home in a high-income neighborhood, and $155 less for a home in a neighborhood with a large proportion of minorities.

Despite the promise of hedonic regression models, some researchers urge caution in their use because they are particularly susceptible to the *omitted variable bias*. In addition, such models can be difficult to estimate since the amenities or disamenities being studied are not distributed randomly across locations. There is some autospatial correlation. For example, locations with health risks arising from air pollution are often urban and industrial. In such cases, housing prices covary with other factors being measured; hence, it is difficult to disaggregate the price effects of health risks from the price effects of other locational factors being measured (L. Davis, 2004; Greenstone and Gallagher, 2005; Noonan, Krupka, and Baden, 2007). Noonan, Krupka, and Baden (2007) have responded to this critique by conducting a study of Superfund site cleanup in which they use panel data to examine changes in neighborhood demographic composition after cleanup. They found that sorting took place in neighborhoods after Superfund site cleanups. That is, after a Superfund site is remediated and removed from the NPL, increased percentages of minorities and renters move into the neighborhood.

Clustering

Studies have found that hazardous waste facilities tend to cluster spatially, concentrating in central business districts or in older industrial parts of cities, near transportation routes, and in locations with cheaper property (Krieg, 1995; Boer, Pastor, Sadd, and Snyder, 1997; Markham and Rufa, 1997; Pastor, Sadd, and Hipp, 2001; Baden and Coursey, 2002; Zahran, Hastings, and Brody, 2008). Examining the phenomenon of clustering in EJ research is important, as clustering may or may not be an indicator of discriminatory siting. Bolin et al. (2002) studied the geographic distribution of risk in Phoenix and found that the results varied depending on the hazard and cluster measures employed. Schweitzer and Stephenson (2007) argue that EJ scholars should pay more attention to clustering and the "agglomeration economy," which are related to siting patterns. Recognizing the role that clustering might play in siting patterns, scholars such as Fricker and Hengartner (2001) have analyzed coclustering between industrial sites and neighborhood demographic characteristics. Heitgard and Lee (2003) have also used cluster analysis to study NPL sites and surrounding neighborhoods. Bullard, Mohai, Saha, and Wright (2007) also studied this phenomenon in the report *Toxic Wastes and Race at Twenty* and found that neighborhoods in which multiple facilities were clustered close together had higher percentages of minorities (69%) than did those with little or no clustering (51%).

Fisher, Kelly, and Romm (2006) studied air-pollution impacts arising from the clustering of industrial facilities in West Oakland. They coupled an air-pollution dispersion model with spatial analysis. They also applied a statistical technique that used Ripley's K to incorporate point pattern analysis in their examination of pollution emanating from stationary sources. The technique is used to detect clusters and is commonly used in epidemiological and ecological spatial analyses.

Path of Least Resistance, Collective Efficacy, and Civic Vitality

The Path of Least Resistance

EJ researchers have also put forward another market-dynamics thesis to explain the presence of hazardous facilities in minority and low-income areas. They contend that increased community opposition to hosting hazardous facilities has constrained industry options; consequently, companies *seek out* and *exploit* the path of least resistance. As the argument goes, because minority and low-income communities are—at times—the least likely or able to resist, it is easier for industries to site their facilities in such communities (Morell and Magorian, 1982; Greenberg, Anderson, and Rosenberger, 1984; Bullard, 1983, 1990; Portney, 1991; Crawford, 1996a; Cole and Foster, 2001; Saha and Mohai, 2005). Campbell, Peck, and Tschudi (2010) found that TRI facilities were significantly more likely to be located in neighborhoods with children than in other neighborhoods. However, it is not just siting that is at stake—the *processing capacity* and *pollution output* of a facility are also important. Hamilton's (1993) study found that though race was not significant at the county level in determining where TSDFs were located, the variable was significant in determining whether production capacity would be reduced. That is, the higher the minority population of a county, the lower the likelihood that TSDFs reduced their production capacity. The finding was similar when zip codes were used as the unit of analysis (Hamilton, 1995).

Documents such as the Cerrell Report, which was commissioned by the California Waste Management Board and written in the mid 1980s, encouraged the path-of-least-resistance strategy. Though the report did not say that industries should target minority communities, it listed characteristics of communities that were low income and quite likely minority. The report identified characteristics that signify a locality as *least likely to resist*: having low income, lacking involvement in voluntary associations or social issues, being open to promises of economic benefits, and having high school or less education (Cerrell Associates and Powell, 1984).

Community opposition can be costly for companies; therefore, they seek to avoid it (Dear, 1992). Allen (2001) found that neighborhoods with higher levels of environmental engagement were associated with lower toxic releases. Home-ownership status also matters. Hamilton (1995) found that the zip codes with a high percentage of renters were more likely to be slated for expansion in production capacity of TSDFs than were those with low percentages of renters. Another variable of significance was a neighborhood's likelihood to engage in political opposition. Voter turnout was higher in zip codes where TSDFs had no production expansion plans. Hamilton argued that voter turnout was a significant factor in a firm's siting and operating decisions.

Collective Efficacy and Civic Vitality

Scholars argue that companies looking for the path of least resistance tend to place their facilities in communities that have little or no political power, *social capital*, or *community efficacy* (Hamilton, 1993, 1995; Pastor, Sadd, and Hipp, 2001). Community efficacy is a kind of collective efficacy wherein residents of an area are able to organize to bring about the changes and *outcomes they desire*—in this case, to resist the placement and operation of hazardous facilities in their neighborhoods and to reduce their exposure to pollution. Communities that have voluntary associations and residents who participate in them are more likely to resist the siting and operation of dangerous facilities, since the collaboration that is required to participate in voluntary community institutions builds *trust* and *reciprocity* among residents. Trust and reciprocity are important precursors of being able to resist the incursion and operation of unsafe facilities into one's neighborhood. Therefore, the ability to resist is influenced by residents' social capital, level of civic engagement, and social status (Coleman, 1988; Cole, 1992; Lowry, 1998; Putnam, 2000; Schlosberg, 2007). Sampson, Raudenbush, and Earls (1997) contend that higher neighborhood collective efficacy is related to greater *social cohesion* and the ability of neighbors to exert *social control* on each other.

Zahran, Hastings, and Brody (2008) examined the relationship between civic vitality and the location of TSDFs. They used the capital assets of nonprofits as a measure of civic vitality and found that TSDFs tended to avoid areas with higher than average potential for collective action. Gayer (2000) reports a similar finding—he found that polluters placed their facilities in communities less likely to engage in collective action and that cleanup priority was focused on neighborhoods most likely to engage in collective action.

Schelly and Stretesky (2009) used another approach to test the path-of-least-resistance thesis. The researchers studied three cases wherein hazardous facilities were proposed for low-income, minority communities in Michigan and Louisiana. The three communities organized and successfully opposed the facilities. Hence, Select Steel decided not built its minimill in Flint, Michigan; the scrap steel intended for Flint ended up at Bayou Steel Corporation's expanded minimill near Laplace, Louisiana, instead. Shintech halted plans to build a polyvinyl chloride plant in Convent, Louisiana, and placed it in Plaquamine, Louisiana, instead. In the third case, the consortium Louisiana Energy Services decided not to construct a uranium-enrichment plant near Homer, Louisiana; it instead built a facility near Eunice, New Mexico. In studying the Louisiana Environmental Services case, Bullard and Johnson (2000) found that as the list of potential sites narrowed, the percentage of African Americans in the community grew higher. Schelly and Stretesky (2009) compared the demographic characteristics of the original siting locations and the new ones that were chosen after community opposition forced a change of plans. The researchers found that the companies ended up settling in communities that were demographically similar to the communities that stymied the original siting. However, they found that community opposition had an impact on alternative siting decisions. In all three cases, the facilities emitted less pollution in the alternate locations than was initially proposed at the original sites.

Lashley and Taylor's (2010) study of the Continental Aluminum Recycling Company's (Continental Aluminum) case in southeast Michigan provides only partial support for Schelly and Stretesky's arguments. Lashley and Taylor found that Continental Aluminum closed its plant in the impoverished neighborhood of Riverbend in Detroit, which was 89% Black, and opened a new facility in the middle-class, rural community of South Lyon, which was 97% White. While the per-capita income in Riverbend was $14,533 in 2000, the per-capita income in South Lyon was $27,414. This does not match the pattern found by Schelly and Stretesky (2009), as Continental Aluminum moved its facility to a community that was demographically different from the one it was previously operating in. However, Lashley and Taylor's (2010) study supports Schelly and Stretesky's second argument, that movement to an alternative location was accompanied by a reduction in the amount of pollution emitted. Continental Aluminum ignored pleas from Riverbend residents to lower pollution. However, when activists in South Lyon demanded that the company reduce its pollution output and take measures to abate noise and other nuisances emanating from the factory, Continental Aluminum took measures to reduce noise and pollution.

Lashley and Taylor (2010) and Krieg (1995) are also identifying a phenomenon that EJ scholars are beginning to study. That is, the impact of *deinstitutionalization* on exposure to pollution. As older facilities in inner cities age and become defunct, some owners opt to build newer, high-tech facilities in the suburbs or rural areas rather than upgrade or pay for expensive pollution-control equipment for urban facilities. This phenomenon could ultimately result in a shift in pollution burdens and other environmental hazards, which will be reduced in the cities. However, since the newer facilities are less polluting, it is unclear what the overall net effect of this will be on the suburbs and rural areas.

Ethnic Churning

Pastor, Sadd, and Hipp (2001) contend that ethnic churning can render communities more vulnerable to the siting of hazardous facilities in their midst. That is, ethnic churning reduces the ability of residents to resist the siting of hazardous facilities. Ethnic churning is a particular type of residential sorting. It is the process by which one ethnic group replaces another in the demographic transitions that neighborhoods undergo. When racial and ethnic minority groups replace either Whites or each other, that process weakens the social bonds, trust, and reciprocity that traditionally connected residents with each other. The replacement process might be accompanied by conflicts and heightened tensions—this makes it more challenging to organize such communities. Pastor and his colleagues found that ethnic churning in communities in Los Angeles County—whereby Hispanics replaced Blacks in neighborhoods—was associated with the increased siting of TSDFs.

This thesis assumes that that regardless of socioeconomic status, racially or ethnically *homogeneous neighborhoods* have greater ability to resist incursions from hazardous facilities than heterogeneous ones do. Sobotta, Campbell, and Owens (2007) provide some support for this thesis. In their study of Phoenix, they created a noise footprint using an integrated noise model. The researchers found that when they controlled for Hispanic ethnicity and income, areas with a high percentage of Spanish-only speakers had a lower likelihood of being impacted by airport noise. Campbell, Peck, and Tschudi (2010) also tested this thesis and found some support for the idea that increased homogeneity was associated with increased likelihood for collective action.

Chicken or Egg and Minority Move-In

Moving to the Hazard

Several scholars who disagree with the disproportionate siting and racial discrimination thesis have raised an intriguing question and put forward an alternative hypothesis. They raise the chicken-or-egg question—*which came first*, the facilities or the people? They contend that the presence of hazardous facilities in minority and low-income neighborhoods could be a function of people moving to live close to facilities after they had been constructed because the presence of such facilities depresses land values. That is, falling property values impel people with means to abandon such neighborhoods. The exodus of residents who can afford to flee is followed by an influx of minority residents who have fewer housing options and who find the industrial neighborhoods affordable (Been, 1993c, 1994b, 1995; Been and Gupta, 1997; Oakes, Anderton, Anderson, 1996; Graham et al., 1999). Underpinning this market-dynamics argument is the notiion that minorities are *not* being discriminated against in the siting process or housing market; they are *choosing* to live in neighborhoods that already host hazardous facilities.

Oakes, Anderton, and Anderson examined this theory in a 1996 paper. The researchers found no evidence of either disproportionate siting of TSDFs in minority neighborhoods between 1970 and 1990 or minority move-in after the facilities were sited. Been and Gupta (1997) also examined this theory. They found that mean housing values and mean incomes grew at a slower pace in host tracts than in non-host tracts. However, they also found that the siting of TSDFs did not change the racial, ethnic, or socioeconomic composition of host tracts in any significant way.

Shaikh and Loomis (1999) studied this phenomenon in Denver. The researchers found no evidence of minority move-in after a stationary source of air pollution was placed in a zip code. Instead, they found evidence of increasing minority presence in zip codes that did not host polluting facilities. Pastor, Sadd, and Hipp (2001) have also examined the minority move-in hypothesis. They studied the siting of TSDFs and changes in the demographic composition of Los Angeles County from 1970 to 1990 to see if there was evidence of minority move-in after the facilities were built. Their study found that TSDFs were built in neighborhoods with a high percentage of minorities and that percentage minority was associated with future siting. Their data suggested that minorities were not moving into host neighborhoods; instead, minorities were more likely to *move out* of areas hosting TSDFs. The researchers also found that ethnic churning—change in the type of ethnic minorities living in a neighborhood—was associated with the siting of TSDFs. Downey (2005) also found that Blacks were not moving into neighborhoods with manufacturing facilities in Detroit. He argued that Black neighborhoods expanded along their edges and did not make incursions into manufacturing corridors. Hunter and Sutton (2004) examined demographic shifts in rural counties that contain hazardous waste sites and concluded that the outmigration of minorities—especially Asians—from such counties was significant.

Gentrification, Race, and Moving to Cleaned-Up Neighborhoods

Lee and Mohai (2011) studied 389 brownfield sites in metropolitan Detroit (Wayne, Macomb, and Oakland Counties) to find out who lived closest to them. They found that Blacks were significantly more likely than other racial groups to live within a half-mile radius of brownfield sites. Even in the suburbs, Blacks were more likely than others to live in close proximity to such sites.

But do minorities move in or out of neighborhoods once brownfield sites have been mitigated and redeveloped? To understand these dynamics, Gamper-Rabindran and Timmins (2011) examined residential sorting and demographic changes in neighborhoods within five kilometers of NPL sites. The researchers compared neighborhoods close to sites that were cleaned up as well as ones close to sites that were not cleaned up. They found that cleanup was associated with increases in population density, housing-unit density, mean household income, the percentage of college-educated residents, and percentages of Blacks and Hispanics. They found that housing values increased by 18.5% in neighborhoods that were one kilometer or less from a cleaned NPL site but increased by only 8.2% in neighborhoods that were two to three kilometers away. The researchers concluded that cleanup of NPL sites was associated with residential sorting that resulted in gentrification of the sites as higher-income residents moved into neighborhoods close to where hazardous sites were remediated. However, despite the influx of higher-income residents, such residents did not appear to displace minority residents from the area. The researchers argue that income—not race—was the driving force behind the sorting.

Gamper-Rabindran and Timmins's (2011) finding that minorities were not displaced after the remediation of NPL sites is not consistent with those of Essoka (2010), who found that Blacks and Hispanics were displaced in neighborhoods where brownfield sites were cleaned up. Essoka examined demographic changes in neighborhoods where 272 brownfield sites had been cleaned up and redeveloped. He found evidence of gentrification and that brownfield cleanup and redevelopment was associated with the displacement of minorities. The study found that Blacks were displaced 61% of the time and Latinos 14% of the time in brownfield redevelopment projects. Noonan, Krupka, and Baden (2007) found that increased percentages of minorities and renters moved into neighborhoods after Superfund sites were cleaned up. Eckerd (2011) found no correlation between gentrification of neighborhoods in Portland, Oregon, and cleanup of hazardous sites in neighborhoods that had them.

The work of other scholars might help to explain these findings. Results of studies suggest that residential sorting in gentrifying neighborhoods is no greater than that found in other neighborhoods. These researchers report that gentrification causes only minor displacement of low-income urban residents. These studies suggest that there might be a period of time that neighborhoods *absorb* the gentrifiers without *displacement* of longtime low-income residents (L. Freeman, 2005; Freeman and Braconi, 2002a, 2002b, 2004; Vigdor, 2002; McKinnish, Wals, and White, 2008). If this is the case, then gentrification-displacement studies should be conducted with a long-enough time interval in mind so that the impacts of gentrification can be identified and studied properly. Freeman and Braconi's (2002a, 2002b, 2004) study of the New York City Housing and Vacancy Survey found that between 1996 and 1999, 5.47%, or 37,766, of the renters who moved were displaced. They found that disadvantaged households in areas that were gentrifying were less likely to move away than were similar households in nongentrifying areas. Hence, the researchers concluded that gentrification does not result in the displacement of low-income residents.

Newman and Wyly (2006) also used the New York City Housing and Vacancy Survey to study gentrification and displacement. However, they studied the phenomena for a much longer period than Freeman and Braconi did. Newman and Wyly studied the time period 1989 to 2002 and found that displacement ranged from 5.4% (in 1995) to 11.6% (in 2001) of local moves among renters. In other words, 46,606 renters were displaced between 1999 and 2002, when the displacement rate was 9.9%. Newman and Wyly calculated the displacement for the time period (1996–1999) studied by Freeman and Braconi and found the displacement rate to be 8.9% (or 43,067 renters). Freeman and Braconi included renters who moved from outside New York City in their analysis, and Newman and Wyly did not. When Newman and Wyly examined displacement in specific subboroughs, they found that more than a third of the renters moving into Bushwick were displaced; so were a fourth of those moving into Brooklyn Heights / Fort Greene, and Brownsville / Ocean Hill. They also found that the displacement rates were highest among people in poverty—50% of such households moving into Stuyvesant Town and 40% of those moving into Co-op City were displaced. Newman and Wyly's multivariate analysis showed that after income and other factors are accounted for, Blacks, Hispanics, and Asians were less likely to be displaced than others.

Sullivan (2007) studied residents' attitudes toward gentrification in two predominantly Black neighborhoods of Portland, Oregon. The study of 460 residents found that, overall, respondents were satisfied with the changes occurring in the neighborhood. Both neighborhoods (Alberta and Eliot) had changed from being majority Black to majority White. The study found that Blacks were less likely to approve of the changes than Whites were. However, not all Blacks had the same level of disapproval. The study found that longtime Black residents were more likely to disapprove of the changes than were Black newcomers who had moved into the neighborhoods while they were undergoing gentrification. Analysis also showed that the Black newcomers had roughly the same level of approval for neighborhood change as Whites did.

Betancur (2011) focused on Hispanics as he studied gentrification in five Chicago neighborhoods: West Town, Lincoln Park, Lake View, Uptown, and Pilsen. Lincoln Park and Lake View are already gentrified, while the other three neighborhoods are in varying stages of gentrification. Betancur found dense networks of self-help and ethnic institutions in each enclave of Mexicans and Puerto Ricans. He also found differences in the way in which gentrifiers and longtime residents perceived each other and the neighborhoods. Gentrifiers tended to describe longtime residents as riff-raff, gangs, unruly, dirty, noisy, ill mannered, uncultured, and unappreciative of aesthetics. They felt that Puerto Ricans did not deserve to live in West Town and that Mexicans and Puerto Ricans should "go back home." The gentrifiers also believed that wealth was based on merit; hence, each individual got what he or she deserved. They did not feel that gentrification resulted in displacement; for them, it was a race- and class-neutral process in which people either chose to relocate or did not belong in the neighborhood in the first place (Betancur 2011: 392). Gentrifiers tended to emphasize *exchange values* for the communities that could be easily translated into commodified market values (see Logan and Molotch, 1987).

In contrast, longtime residents and grassroots activists emphasized the *social networks* that sustain the communities. They identified with living in the neighborhoods and felt a sense of belonging. Longtime residents saw each neighborhood as a "community" and tended to stress *use values* such as informal exchanges, solidarity, and informal economies. These residents saw gentrification as deleterious, as it contributed to displacement of minority residents (Betancur, 2011; Logan and Molotch, 1987).

Studies conducted by Gamper-Rabindran and Timmins (2011) and Essoka (2010) examined whether the demographic characteristics of neighborhoods changed after cleanup of an NPL or brownfield site and how, while Bostic and Martin (2003) analyzed if and how one racial group contributed to gentrification. However, none of these studies shed any light on the question of how gentrification is related to the *level* of residential segregation in a neighborhood. That is, are minorities and low-income residents more likely to be displaced from highly segregated neighborhoods where hazardous sites have been remediated than from neighborhoods with low levels of segregation? This question is of paramount concern to EJ activists as they ponder the impacts of site remediation and other urban revitalization projects. Though Byrne argues that "gentrification is good on balance for the poor and ethnic minorities" because cities that attract affluent residents are better placed to finance affordable housing (2003: 406), he does not provide any evidence to support his claim that cities that have been gentrified finance affordable housing more "aggressively" than other cities do.

L. Freeman (2009) examined the relationship between segregation and gentrification, looking at tracts that showed signs of gentrification in 1970, 1980, and 1990. He studied the impacts of education, race, and income on gentrification and found that gentrifying neighborhoods were typically more racially diverse at the start of the study period than were other neighborhoods. Moreover, the level of racial diversity increased more over the course of the study period in gentrifying tracts than it did in other census tracts. Gentrifying tracts also displayed more educational diversity over the study period than did other tracts. However, the study found that income diversity declined over time in gentrifying tracts. The bivariate models indicate that gentrification results in less income segregation, while racial segregation increases. The relationship between educational segregation and gentrification was insignificant in the multivariate model, but the relationship between income segregation and gentrification was statistically significant. There was also a significant relationship between racial segregation and gentrification. That is, gentrifying areas had increased racial segregation and decreased income segregation.

Much of the literature on gentrification assumes that Whites displace Blacks and other minorities as property values increase. However, do Blacks act as a gentrifying force? Bostic and Martin (2003) examined this question by studying several U.S. cities from 1970 to 1990. The researchers found that Black homeowners were a gentrifying influence in the 1970s but not in the 1980s. More research should be conducted on the extent to which ethnic-minority renters and homeowners act as gentrifying forces.

Hedonic models could be combined with traditional EJ research to test the minority move-in and other market-dynamics theses, but this approach is still in its infancy. For instance, though Kohlhase (1991) has a race variable in her paper, she does not discuss how race is related to move-in or move-out after sites are placed on the NPL and changing property values. Researchers studying residents' willingness to pay more for homes near remediated sites (Chattopadhyay, Braden, and Patunru, 2005) or to live further away from a hazardous waste site (Smith and

Desvousges, 1986) did not include race as a variable in their hedonic models. Hurd (2002) did not discuss race in his study of the recovery of property values after Superfund cleanup either. Greenstone and Gallagher (2008) did investigate the race variable and acknowledged the difficulty of testing EJ hypotheses in this context. They found that the percentage of Blacks declined when the waste sites were put on the NPL, but the magnitude of the change was small and statistically insignificant. Though researchers doing this type of research use distance-based techniques to study the effects of waste sites on property values, some still use aspatial units such as census tracts in their analyses. Some such as Hurd (2002) are using centroids and analyzing smaller distances, such as 1,000 feet from the site of the facility, as the unit of analysis.

On the other hand, traditional EJ research that is beginning to recognize and explore the effects of clustering and the agglomeration economy could benefit from incorporating techniques employed by researchers such as Ihlanfeldt and Taylor (2004), who recognize that multiple hazardous waste sites might have different impacts on a community than a single site will.

It is also interesting to note that none of the studies examining the minority move-in or vote-with-your-feet hypotheses account for the number of births or deaths in the study areas. That is, the researchers do not consider what portion of the increased population seen in an area is due to babies being born in an area or to people who had not lived there before moving in. Similarly, studies do not account for deaths in the examination of population declines. Population increase can result from an excess of births over deaths or from people migrating into an area. A decline in population can result from an exodus of residents but also from excess deaths over births. Researchers should attempt to account for the number of births and deaths in an area when studying population-dynamics hypotheses such as these.

Relict Waste and the Accumulation of Hazards

The issue of relict waste has emerged as an area of study in EJ research. It is important and relevant to this discussion, as the assertion that minorities move to live beside hazardous facilities implies that those who live adjacent to hazardous facilities have full knowledge of the hazards lurking in the air, on the land, and under the ground or in the waterways in their neighborhoods. As cases such as Love Canal (New York), Texarkana (Texas), Triana (Alabama), and Woburn (Massachusetts) show, residents are often unaware of the industrially generated risks and perils that lie underground or taint the waters in their neighborhoods. Relict waste can go undetected for lengthy periods as land uses change and hazards are buried in the conversion process. Hazards do not always emanate from large industrial facilities but can also come from small neighborhood operations such as dry cleaners, gas stations, auto-repair shops, metal plating businesses, small manufacturers, processors, and the like.

Colten (1990) demonstrated the importance of this line of research when he studied relict industrial wastes in Illinois and found that it was extremely challenging for anyone to assess the risks that recycled industrial land posed. Elliott and Frickel (2011) also studied relict industrial waste in the cities of Portland, Oregon, and New Orleans, Louisiana, for the period 1955–2008. The researchers studied 716 historical industrial sites in Portland and 215 in New Orleans. They found that the vast majority of former industrial land—properties with the greatest likelihood of containing relict waste—do not appear on government hazardous waste site lists or receive brownfield designation. None of the sites identified by Elliott and Frickel in New Orleans appeared on government hazardous sites list in Louisiana, and only 16% of the sites studied in Portland appeared on government listings in Oregon. The researchers found that lower-income census tracts were more likely to contain historical sites of hazardous manufacturing than were high-income tracts. In both cities, researchers found that Whites were more likely to live in tracts with historical hazardous manufacturing than were minorities.

Elliott and Frickel (2013) argue that it is important to conduct longitudinal studies to help us understand the historical dimensions of exposure to hazards. This is the case because relict wastes build up in cities as industrial land uses are introduced and industrial lands are reused and recycled. This process results in the *accumulation of hazards* that people are unwittingly exposed to. The accumulation of hazards and the concomitant exposure to them occurs independent of neighborhood demographics or existing regulatory apparatus. The researchers visited 120 of the historical industrial sites in Portland and found that 17% were still being used for hazardous manufacturing operations, 21% were converted to private residences, and 62% were being used for commercial purposes (restaurants, offices, and retail outlets).

Treadmill of Destruction

Scholars have borrowed from C. Wright Mills's (1994) concept of the power elites to examine how politics and economics converge to produce environmental inequalities. Mills includes the military as an important element of power. Hooks and Smith (2004, 2005) rely on Mills's work to examine the role of militarism and political coercion in the production and perpetuation of environmental inequalities. Hooks and Smith argue that there is a treadmill of destruction that is related to the geopolitics of arms races and that cannot be reduced to capitalism. They argue that growth in research, testing, storage, and deployment of arms contributes to the treadmill of destruction. They focus on Native Americans; the combination of industrialization, militarism, and segregation on reservations makes this group particularly vulnerable to exposure to environmental hazards. The researchers argue that coercive state policies help to shape the spatial distribution of environmental hazards that people are exposed to. Martino-Taylor (2008, 2011) also uses this framework but adds educational institutions as key actors in her study of environmental inequalities and exposure to toxics.

Downey, Bonds, and Clarke (2010) and Downey and Strife (2010) also evoke the treadmill-of-destruction argument in their attempt to theorize the links between natural-resource extraction, armed violence, and environmental degradation. They argue that armed violence is one mechanism used by power elites to gain control over others in natural-resource conflicts. Armed violence is also used to ensure that the natural resources needed for capital accumulation, industrial growth, and the maintenance of state supremacy continue to flow toward the power centers.

Environmental Hazards and the Vulnerability of Place

Cutter (2006) and Cutter, Boruff, and Shirley (2003) argue that the geographic distribution of risks, hazards, and disasters is contingent on

where one lives (place). Environmental injustices arise from the distribution of these hazards and risks that leave the poorest people—those
least able to adapt—quite vulnerable. Hence, biophysical and social factors interact to create a vulnerability of place.

Cutter, Boruff, and Shirley (2003) identify three main tenets of the
research on vulnerability: the identification of factors that make people
or places vulnerable to extreme natural events, resistance to or resilience
in the face of hazards, and exposure to hazards. The researchers use the
hazards-of-place model of vulnerability to determine the components
of social vulnerability. That is, risk (the likelihood of a hazard event)
interacts with mitigation (steps taken to reduce risks or their impacts)
to create the *hazard potential*. The hazard potential is influenced by geographic factors (such as location and proximity) and the social characteristics of the place. Hence, the biophysical and social factors interact
to produce the overall vulnerability of place. The researchers studied the
social vulnerability of 3,141 counties in 1990. They found that the most
vulnerable counties were in the southern half of the country—stretching from south Florida to California. This region of the country also had
greater ethnic and racial inequalities as well as rapid population growth.

Hurricanes Katrina and Rita demonstrated the extent to which vul-
nerabilities are layered and have devastating impacts on people of color
and the poor (Bullard and Wright, 2009, 2012). Not only did the storms
unleash their fury on the region; they exposed inadequate storm-
protection systems and disaster responses. Moreover, the hurricanes
disturbed 29 Superfund sites, adding to the toxic burden that residents
were exposed to (Neal, Famira, and Miller-Travis, 2010).

A less dramatic, but nonetheless important, example of *layered vul-
nerabilities* can be found in the Black enclave of Hyde Park in Augusta,
Georgia. In the 1940s, Black sharecroppers began purchasing lots and
building homes in the wetlands on the outskirts of Augusta. At the
time, there were a few industrial facilities already operating close by,
but the area was still primarily marsh land. As Hyde Park expanded to
encompass seven streets housing about 250 residents, the number of
hazardous facilities ringing the neighborhood multiplied. The area was
prone to floods; at times, the water rose so high that residents had to use
canoes to go about their business. However, like other Black enclaves
discussed later and Native American reservations, the roads were not

paved, and there were no street lights, sewers, or garbage services. Though Hyde Park residents paid city taxes, they did not get such services till 1970—and only after demonstrations. Residents were exposed to foul-smelling toxic air and soil, as well as surface- and groundwater contamination. The neighborhood was contaminated with PCBs, creosote, arsenic, chromium, and other chemicals (Checker, 2005).

Residents of the Virginia Subdivision, a predominantly White neighborhood adjacent to Hyde Park, began complaining to the Georgia Environmental Protection Division in the 1970s about foul-smelling water in their taps and wells. They also documented the number of cancers in their community. In 1987, the Agency for Toxic Substances Disease Registry suggested that Virginia Subdivision residents stay away from the ditches and refrain from using their well water. The residents filed a class-action lawsuit against Southern Wood Piedmont for trespass, nuisance, and neglect. In the mid 1990s, the company settled the suit for about $6.8 million. Despite the fact that the Virginia Subdivision is beside Hyde Park and the contaminated ditches run through both communities, none of Hyde Park's residents were apprised of the class-action suit. It was not till 1990 that Hyde Park residents heard about the lawsuit and became fully aware of the extent of the contamination and the health threats it posed. In 1991, Hyde Park residents filed a $700 million class-action lawsuit that was based on the same principles used in the Virginia Subdivision case (Hyde Park residents filed two additional suits). Though Hyde Park residents felt that discrimination was involved in their exposure to chemicals and exclusion from the lawsuit and subsequent settlement, they did not feel they had enough evidence to prove discriminatory intent. Hence, they used the same approach that was successful in the Virginia Subdivision case. Hyde Park residents were bombarded with studies producing conflicting results regarding the extent of the contamination and the danger it posed to their health. Hyde Park residents pushed for relocation—they wanted to move out of the neighborhood. The court disqualified many of the plaintiffs, and eventually the lawsuits were dropped between 1998 and 2000 (Checker, 2005; McCord, 2012).

Hyde Park residents were left to languish in the neighborhood even after one of the factories was cleaned up for $46 million and a neighborhood junkyard was designated as a Superfund site and remediated for $10 million. Finally in 2011, Augusta city commissioners voted to reallocate about $2.3 million in sales taxes to the purchase of Hyde Park homes and the construction of a 44-acre detention pond in an effort to reduce flooding in nearby areas. The entire project will cost about $18.2 million (McCord, 2011, 2012).

Why did Blacks settle in a place that already had industrial facilities? The sharecroppers who settled in the community could not gain ownership of the lands they farmed, so they sought affordable land they could buy. Hyde Park was one of the few places that Blacks could afford to purchase land; because of segregation, it was also one of the few places they were *allowed* to live in and around the city. Living in close proximity to the industrial facilities meant that men could walk to work, while women had a short bus ride to jobs as domestic servants in town. Hence, moving to Hyde Park meant homeownership, two jobs for young Black couples raising families, and practice of a rural lifestyle. Hyde Park families raised animals, and everyone had a vegetable garden that they were immensely proud of. The gardens were a source of male identity and pride. Neighborhood men felt they provided a home for their family as well as food. Living in this community also provided an opportunity to build one's home through sweat equity. This meant families built their homes slowly over a period of years as their finances allowed. Hyde Park was also a tight-knit community of strong friendship and family networks (Checker, 2005).

So what keeps residents there? The residents of Hyde Park want to move. However, once the contamination of the neighborhood became public, their properties lost most of their market value. When residents die or leave, the abandoned homes fall into disrepair, further depressing property values. Since the lawsuit did not proceed, residents did not have enough income to purchase homes elsewhere until the city approved a relocation plan (Checker, 2005; McCord, 2011, 2012).

While much of the EJ research has been focused on the question of who moves or who stays in neighborhoods where people have been exposed to industrial hazards, this chapter points to the need to broaden the questions being asked and undergird the research with explicit theoretical analysis. The discussion also points to avenues of inquiry in EJ and related fields that show promise in helping us to understand phenomena of concern to EJ scholars and activists.

5

Enforcing Environmental Protections

The Legal, Regulatory, and Administrative Contexts

Activists and policy analysts contend that the context in which EJ cases are adjudicated, regulated, and administered has significant impacts on outcomes. Ergo, this chapter focuses on the ways in which the legal and regulatory systems as well as the administration of environmental affairs affect cases related to facility siting and exposure to hazards.

The Commerce Clause and Inundation with Toxics — For the Good of the Nation

The Constitution's commerce clause is one of the most effective weapons that waste management companies wield to force communities to accept hazardous wastes or to prevent jurisdictions from developing or enforcing waste regulations that are more stringent than the federal ones. Waste management companies have invoked the clause and have been successful in using the courts to prevent state and local jurisdictions from banning the manufacturing, processing, or disposal of hazardous materials in their territory. The commerce clause has also been used successfully to prevent communities from levying additional fees on wastes originating outside their boundaries. This has had a chilling effect on communities' attempts to control the movement, processing, and disposal of hazardous wastes in their jurisdiction. With the exception of the Warren County case, the laws discussed in the case studies contained in this book did not even seek to ban wastes from the jurisdictions outright (they seek to charge fees that would help to compensate the state for the risks involved in being a repository for hazardous wastes, limit the volume of wastes processed, and ensure safer handling

of toxic products), yet the ordinances failed to withstand legal challenges. The courts have consistently argued that local legislation cannot
hinder the movement of articles of commerce across state lines. They
have also held the position that federal waste legislation has supremacy
over local laws. Local laws can supersede the relevant federal legislation only under very carefully prescribed circumstances (*Rollins v. St.
James*, 1985; *National Solid Wastes Management v. Alabama Department
of Environmental Management*, 1990a, 1990b; *Twitty v. North Carolina*,
1981; *Warren County v. North Carolina*, 1981).

   In striking down ordinances in which jurisdictions try to block
hazardous wastes generated outside their boundaries from being processed or buried within it, the courts have argued that the safe disposal
of hazardous wastes is a *national interest* and they have signaled that
any attempt to impede that interest—even if the ordinances are aimed
at blocking wastes from states that have not developed adequate disposal facilities or even if the community receiving the waste is already
inundated with hazardous wastes and has disposed of more than its
fair share—will not be upheld. The courts argue that the *good of the
nation* is a concern that is paramount to *local concerns* about health and
environmental risks (*Rollins v. St. James*, 1985; *National Solid Wastes
Management v. Alabama Department of Environmental Management*,
1990a, 1990b; *Twitty v. North Carolina*, 1981; *Warren County v. North
Carolina*, 1981).

   Hence, minority communities with gargantuan waste disposal facilities in their midst are in the unenviable position of bearing the risks
of hosting these facilities for the greater good of the nation, yet as the
courts have signaled, these communities have little hope of enacting
stringent regulations that can protect residents, compensate them for
the risks they are undertaking, help them to deal with disasters if and
when they occur, or stop the wastes from entering their communities
in the first place. This line of reasoning has left minority communities
shouldering a big share of the nation's solid waste disposal burden.

Violations of the Law and the Pace of Cleanup

The legal and regulatory climate can influence siting patterns. This is
the case because environmental legislation can result in discriminatory

outcomes resulting from the way the laws are interpreted and administered (Kraft and Kraut, 1988; Gerrard, 1999). Legal scholars such as Lavelle and Coyle (1992, 1993) have studied the EPA's handling of the Superfund process to see whether the policies and the administration of the program had discriminatory outcomes. They concluded that the agency favored White communities over minority communities in the cleanup of hazardous wastes and in the penalties levied against polluters. They studied environmental lawsuits and penalties assessed from 1985 to 1991 and found that fines assessed against polluters in minority zip codes were significantly lower (about 46%) than those assessed for violations of environmental laws occurring in White zip codes ($105,000 compared to $153,067). While the average fines were $95,664 in low-income zip codes, they were $146,993 in high-income zip codes. Their assessment of the administration of the toxic waste sites in the Superfund program found that it took longer to address hazardous sites in minority communities than in White communities; once addressed, it took longer for sites in minority communities to get on the NPL for cleanup, less stringent cleanup options were recommended for minority communities, and it took longer to start cleanup in minority communities than in White communities.

Hird also studied the Superfund process and reported that there were more sites in affluent neighborhoods than in poor neighborhoods (1993, 1994). He reported that there was no statistical relationship between poorer counties and the number of Superfund sites contained in them. However, he found that counties with a higher percentage of minorities had more Superfund sites than others. He also found that the number of Superfund sites was positively correlated with a greater manufacturing presence, a higher percentage of college-educated residents, a greater percentage of owner-occupied residences, and a greater percentage of new homes. Hird also examined the argument that the most hazardous sites were in minority communities. He examined sites with high HRS scores (61–100) and found that they tended to be located in areas with lower poverty rates, lower unemployment, lower percentages of minorities, and higher median housing values.

Regarding the pace of cleanup, Hird found that political representation or pressure (having a legislator in the county on congressional Superfund-oversight subcommittees) was insignificant in determining the pace of cleanup (Hird, 1993). However, in an earlier study, Hird found that states that had legislators who sat on these subcommittees were more likely to have a large number of hazardous sites on the NPL (Hird, 1990). The socioeconomic status and the racial composition of the county had no relationship to the cleanup pace either. However, a higher percentage of long-term residents was associated with slower cleanup pace (Hird, 1993).

Rinquist tried to replicate Lavelle and Coyle's study and found methodological problems with it. Rinquist found that the penalties were not significantly different in minority and White communities (1998). Atlas (2001) also attempted to replicate the Lavelle and Coyle study. The findings were published in a paper that contained an extensive critique of the methodological flaws in both Lavelle and Coyle's and Rinquist's research. The critique of Lavelle and Coyle included the use of zip codes as a unit of analysis, misclassification of multilocation cases (individual cases where violations occurred in more than one location), misclassification of the Hispanic population, use of means instead of medians, the use of quartiles to identify minority and White areas, no analysis of the severity of the violation or the violation history of the company, no analysis of whether fines were negotiated or based on the defendant's ability to pay, no accounting for the time periods in which the fines were levied (fines could increase over time), and lack of verification of the information contained in the EPA's docket of cases. In multilocation cases (for example, contractors of a particular company violating the law at several building sites), the EPA usually creates a separate record for each violation location, but it records only the total penalty for the all the company's violations. Atlas (2001) argues that though Rinquist recognized Lavelle and Coyle's errors regarding the classification of multilocation violations, tested for the severity of the violations and accounted for a company's violation history, extended the time line of his study to look at cases from 1974 to 1991, and used minority percentage in zip codes rather than quartiles, he also made several critical errors in the analysis, including his analysis of the role of the judges in the setting of fines, use of zip codes, and the way he defined prior violations. Atlas questioned the reliability of the findings of both studies (Atlas, 2001; see also Rinquist, 1998; Bryant, 1993; Kuehn, 1994; U.S. EPA, 1986a, 1998). Others such as Lynch, Stretesky, and Burns (2004) have also critiqued Lavelle and Coyle's study.

Atlas (2001) found no significant correlations between race or income and the penalties for violations. When he examined the mean differences in penalties, the results were $100,797 for the Black quartile, $113,632 for the Hispanic quartile, and $113,791 for the White quartile. Despite the finding of no significant correlation between race and penalties, the pattern of fines in Atlas's study (lowest penalties in Black communities and highest in White communities) mirrors the pattern that Lavelle and Coyle found. In multivariate models, Atlas found that the size of the penalties increased as the proportion of minorities in an area increased. He also found that the recency of the case had a significant impact on penalties—the fines were higher for more recently concluded cases. Fines levied against public defendants were lower than those assessed against business defendants. Moreover, cases that ended in litigation had smaller fines than those resulting from a settlement.

Other scholars have investigated if fines for violating environmental laws vary depending on the racial characteristics of the communities in which companies are located. Lynch, Stretesky, and Burns (2004) studied fines levied against oil refineries for violating environmental laws in 1998 and 1999. They give support for Lavelle and Coyle's findings. They found that the mean fines were lowest in Black census tracts, somewhat higher in Hispanic tracts, and highest in White tracts ($108,563, $126,136, and $341,590, respectively). Moreover, the study found that the penalty amounts decreased as the percentage of Blacks in the census tracts increased. The mean fines were much lower in poor communities than in affluent ones ($259,784 compared to $334,267). The disparities were also evident when the median fines were analyzed: the median fines were $38,125 in Black census tracts, $61,004 in Hispanic tracts, and $80,000 in White census tracts. The researchers found that the differences in these fines were not attributable to the severity of the violations, the number of past violations, the inspection history of the facility, or the EPA region in which the refinery is located.

Anderton and his colleagues, researchers producing several studies challenging and critiquing EJ claims, concluded in a 1997 paper that as the percentage of Blacks, Hispanics, and low-income residents of a neighborhood increases, the likelihood of a site being placed on the

NPL decreases (Anderton, Oakes, and Egan, 1997). O'Neil (2007) also studied the likelihood of a site being listed as a Superfund site and found that neighborhoods with a high percentage of minorities, low-income families, or residents without a high school diploma had lower chances of getting a Superfund listing for hazardous sites in their communities. The study found that a 1% increase in the percentage of minorities was associated with a 2% decrease in the likelihood of getting a Superfund listing. That being said, hazardous sites in Hispanic and Native American communities had a higher chance of being placed on the Superfund list than did sites in other communities. O'Neil also found that a 10% increase in the poverty rate resulted in a 13% less chance of a site being listed. She also found that the chances of a site being placed on the Superfund list worsened after the EJ Executive Order 12898 was enacted in 1994 by President Bill Clinton.

The Administrative Process

Daley and Layton (2004) studied three theoretical models (administrative convenience / transaction costs, problem severity, and political pressure) to see how they influenced the remediation of Superfund sites. Their study found that despite the EPA's claim of cleaning up the most hazardous sites first, it was the contaminated sites that had lower hazard ranking scores and were *easiest* and *cheapest* to clean that were being cleaned up first. The researchers claimed that the agency was cleaning up the *most convenient* cases and the ones with the *lowest transaction costs* first. The agency was also dealing with the sites with the least severe problems first. The researchers also examined two aspects of civic vitality—the presence of a community advisory group and the receipt of technical assistance grants—and found that these had a negative association on cleanup pace. That is, these two factors were related to a slower pace of cleanup. The authors did not study the effect of other kinds of community groups on the remediation process. They speculate that the community advisory groups might be inadvertently impeding the process by seeking the most stringent cleanup standards. It could also be that community advisory groups are formed and technical assistance grants given to communities with the most severe hazardous sites. While the community advisory groups and technical assistance grants might not have applied the most effective form of pressure to facilitate cleanup, legislators did. Daley and Layton found that Superfund sites in congressional districts that had a legislator who sat on a Superfund-oversight subcommittee were cleaned up faster. The study did not examine how the racial composition of host communities was related to site remediation.

Daley and Layton's (2004) research corroborates some of the findings in Sigman's study. Sigman (2001) concluded that there was little evidence that the EPA prioritized sites according to the severity of the hazard. Instead, the agency seemed to prioritize the sites based on the number of responsible parties and private interests in local communities. Though higher-income communities appeared to have sites in their jurisdiction listed on the NPL faster and got quicker cleanup, such communities can push for more extensive cleanups, and this could inadvertently slow the pace of cleanup. Sigman did not find evidence to support the claim that legislators affected the bureaucratic priorities of the agency.

Other researchers studying the choice and cost of cleanup options at Superfund sites report that the evidence does not suggest that the EPA opted for less permanent remedies in communities that had sizeable minority residents or in poor areas. They found that decisions related to the cleanup of NPL sites were more related to cleanup costs and risk factors rather than the demographic characteristics of a neighborhood (Gupta, van Houtven, and Cropper, 1996).

Inadequate Stakeholder Involvement

Scholars argue that ethnic minorities and the poor are underrepresented in the planning and regulatory process. They usually do not hold positions on planning and zoning commissions or city councils and are not regular participants in public hearings or other planning events. Studies find that the land-use decision makers tend to be White, male, and middle-aged or older. Many of those who participate regularly in the planning process are real estate professionals or have vested interests in land-use decisions. The low participation of people of color and the poor in the planning process stems from a variety of factors including lack of access to information, inconvenient timing and location of meetings, inadequate notification of land-use-related events, language and educational barriers, and perceptions of inefficacy (C. Arnold, 2007; Sanders and Getzels, 1987; Anderson and Sass, 2004).

Ferris (1993) suggests that stakeholder participation can be broadened by providing a larger number of technical assistance grants to EJ communities, increasing the amount of the grants, providing assistance with the grant process, and including more EJ activists in the stakeholder process.

Scientific and Technical Rationality

The EPA is responsible for establishing the scientific and technical criteria guiding the operation of TSDFs. The agency argues that the siting patterns of TSDFs are driven by scientific and technical decisions aimed at maximizing environmental protection and public safety (U.S. EPA, 2003). This thesis has also been espoused by researchers such as Been (1995) and Rinquist (2000). Others refine this argument by contending that public participation in the siting process is crucial because, barring effective community opposition, proposals that meet technical and regulatory requirements are likely to be approved for siting (Davy, 1997; Kraft and Kraut, 1988). Zahran, Hastings, and Brody (2008) tested the scientific and technical rationality thesis and found mixed results. They found that facilities were built in areas of peak ground acceleration and increased risk of seismic activity. That is, a one-unit increase in the peak ground activity acceleration increased the odds of TSDF siting by 7.2%.

Disparate Impact versus Discriminatory Intent

The Fourteenth Amendment of the Constitution provides that the states may not "deny to any person within [their] jurisdiction the equal protection of the laws." However, several criteria have to be met in order to base EJ cases on this amendment. That is, (1) governmental action must be involved for the equal protection clause to be violated; (2) the clause applies to local, state, and federal government action; (3) private acts of discrimination are not covered under the equal protection clause, unless they are somehow aided, mandated, or abetted by state law; (4) proof of governmental *intent* to discriminate is required to show that equal protection is denied; and (5) only insidious or unjustifiable discrimination is prohibited. Mere evidence or proof that there is *disparate or disproportionate impact* on one or more groups of people in an EJ case is not sufficient to prove intent to discriminate. The proof of intent to discriminate has been such a difficult standard to meet that few EJ cases are being brought forward as Fourteenth Amendment challenges anymore (Mank, 1999; Weinberg, 1999; Cory, 2008).

The Equal Protection Clause and EJ Cases

The 1886 *Yick Wo v. Hopkins* case involving Chinese laundries was an early EJ case that was successful. Cities began experimenting with zoning as a mechanism for constraining the land uses of racial and ethnic minorities in the 1880s. During that time, California cities such as San Francisco and Modesto began to ban the construction of laundries in "Caucasian" neighborhoods or the operation of laundries in wooden buildings. In San Francisco, 310 of the 320 laundries were constructed of wood; 240 of the laundries were owned by Chinese. More than 150 of the Chinese laundry owners were prosecuted under the ordinance, while non-Chinese owners were spared prosecution. Though the statute appeared to be race neutral on the surface, the enforcement of it had a discriminatory effect on the Chinese (*Yick Wo v. Hopkins*, 1886; Weinberg, 1999).

However, other EJ cases have not fared as well because intent is very difficult to prove. This section discusses four high-profile EJ Fourteenth Amendment cases that came before the courts between 1979 and 1995. It examines how the courts distinguished between discriminatory intent and disproportionate impact in deciding against plaintiffs filing EJ law suits.

Bean v. Southwestern Waste Management

BACKGROUND
The case of *Bean v. Southwestern Waste Management* was brought before the courts in Texas in 1979. On October 26 of that year, attorney Linda McKeever Bullard filed a motion for a temporary restraining order and preliminary injunction on behalf of Margaret Bean and

other Black residents of Houston, contesting the decision of the Texas Department of Health to grant a permit to Southwestern Waste Management to operate a solid waste facility in the East Houston–Dyersdale Road community. In seeking to revoke the permit, the plaintiffs argued that racial discrimination occurred in the issuance of the permit. Plaintiffs asked Robert Bullard to provide statistical data for the case.

The case relied on the discrimination thesis vis-à-vis the siting of the facility. Plaintiffs argued that the TDH's granting of the permit was part of a larger pattern of discrimination in the siting of solid waste facilities in the city. The court was interested in examining the racial characteristics of the host communities at the time the facilities that the TDH granted operating permits were opened; 17 such facilities operated in Houston. The data indicated that 58.8% of the permitted facilities were located in census tracts that were 25% or less minority at the time of opening; 82.4% of the facilities were in census tracts that were 50% or less minority at the time of their opening. The plaintiffs showed that roughly 60% of the residents in the census tract in which the waste facility at issue was being proposed were minority. At the time this case was brought before the courts, Houston's population was 39.3% minority. Using this percentage, the parties in this lawsuit determined 42.5% of the city's census tracts to be "minority" tracts, while the remaining 57.5% were considered as "Anglo" tracts. A citywide analysis found that 42.3% of the solid waste sites were located in minority census tracts, and 57.7% were in Anglo tracts. Moreover, 42.2% of minority census tracts had more than one solid waste site, compared to 57.8% of Anglo tracts that had more than one solid waste site (*Bean v. Southwestern Waste Management*, 1979).

The plaintiffs provided additional statistical data in the case. They argued that in 1975, 11 solid waste sites were located in census tracts that were 100% minority, but none were located in tracts that were 100% Anglo. However, it was shown in court that there were two solid waste sites in census tracts that were 100% Anglo in 1975 and 18 other solid waste sites in census tracts that were 90% or more Anglo in 1975. But *where* were the facilities located in the census tracts? Recognizing that the unit of analysis was important—and foreshadowing some of the more fine-tuned analysis that was years away—plaintiffs pointed out that in census tract 434, a predominantly Anglo tract, the hazardous waste site was located adjacent to the Black community of Riceville (*Bean v. Southwestern Waste Management*, 1979).

The plaintiffs also presented supplemental evidence in the case. They pointed out that in 1971 the county commissioners (who were then responsible for issuing permits) refused to grant a permit for a site that was proposed in almost the identical location as the one for which the preliminary injunction was being sought. At the time, Smiley High School, located about 1,700 feet from the proposed site, was an Anglo school. By the time the permit in question was issued, Smiley High School was a predominantly Black school with no air-conditioning. A residential area was almost as close to the proposed solid waste facility as the school.

THE DECISION

District Judge Gabrielle McDonald (the first African American appointed to a federal court in Texas and the first woman appointed in the district) presided over the case (U.S. District and Bankruptcy Courts, 2011). She stated that in order to get a preliminary injunction, the plaintiffs must meet four prerequisites. They had to establish (1) a substantial likelihood of success on the merits of the case, (2) that a substantial threat of irreparable injury existed, (3) that the threatened injury to the plaintiffs outweighed the potential harm the injunction may have caused the defendant, and (4) that granting the preliminary injunction would not be a disservice to the public interest (see *Canal Authority of the State of Florida v. Callaway*, 1974: 572). Judge McDonald concluded that there was a substantial threat of irreparable injury. She stated that the operation of the facility would affect "the entire nature of the community"—"its land values, its tax base, its aesthetics, the health and safety of its inhabitants, and the operation of Smiley High School, located a short distance from the site. Damages cannot adequately compensate for these types of injuries" (*Bean v. Southwestern Waste Management*, 1979: 677).

However, Judge McDonald did not believe that the plaintiffs established a substantial likelihood of success on the merits. The burden of proof was on the plaintiffs to show that there was discriminatory intent in issuing the permit (*Washington v. Davis*, 1976; *Village of Arlington Heights v. Metropolitan Housing*, 1977). That is, the plaintiffs needed to show more than the fact that they objected to the issuance of the permit or that issuing the permit was wrong; they needed to also show that there was an intent to discriminate on the basis of race (*Bean v. Southwestern Waste Management*, 1979). McDonald argued that statistical proof can be used to establish discriminatory intent, as in the cases of *Yick Wo v. Hopkins* (1886) and *Gomillion v. Lightfoot* (1960), or it can be supplemented with other types of evidence to establish *purposeful discrimination* (*Village of Arlington Heights v. Metropolitan Housing*, 1977). The judge felt that neither the statistical data presented in court nor the supplemental evidence was sufficient to show proof of discriminatory intent (*Bean v. Southwestern Waste Management*, 1979).

In reviewing the evidence, Judge McDonald concluded, "the plaintiffs have established that the decision to grant the permit was both unfortunate and insensitive." However, she added, "I cannot say that the plaintiffs have established a substantial likelihood of proving that the decision to grant the permit was motivated by purposeful racial discrimination." Consequently, the judge denied the motion for a preliminary injunction (*Bean v. Southwestern Waste Management*, 1979: 678).

East Bibb Twiggs Neighborhood Association v. Macon-Bibb County Planning and Zoning Commission

Another important equal protection EJ case involving the siting of a landfill came before the courts in Georgia in 1989. The plaintiffs in this case, the East Bibb Twiggs Neighborhood Association, alleged that they were deprived of equal protection when the Macon-Bibb County Planning and Zoning Commission granted permission to the Mullis Tree Service and Robert Mullis to create a private landfill in the neighborhood. The Neighborhood Association argued that the commission's decision was motivated by racial considerations (*East Bibb Twiggs v. Macon-Bibb County Commission*, 1989).

BACKGROUND

Robert Mullis and the Mullis Tree Service applied for a conditional-use permit to operate a nonputrescible waste landfill (to dispose of wood waste from the tree service) at a site located at Davis and Donnan Davis Roads on May 14, 1986. The site is in a census tract containing 5,527 residents, 60.9% of whom were Black. The only other private landfill approved by the commission (in 1978) was located in the neighboring census tract (no. 133.01). This census tract had 1,369 residents, 23.4% of whom were Black (*East Bibb Twiggs v. Macon-Bibb County Commission*, 1989).

About 150 residents attended a hearing held by the commission on June 23. Opponents of the landfill made a number of arguments based on theses of market dynamics, discrimination, disproportionate impacts, and the biophysical characteristics of the area. Attendees objected to the siting of the landfill on the grounds that it posed a threat to the residential character of the neighborhood, would lower property values, and would endanger the ecological balance of the area. Residents were also concerned about the potential for the expansion of the landfill into a public dump and about hazards to residents and children from increased truck traffic; and they expressed dissatisfaction with the perceived inequitable burden borne by the East Bibb area in terms of "unpleasant" and "undesirable" land uses. Robert Mullis and his representative, Charles Adams, were also at the meeting. Mullis and Adams relied on market-based and public-good arguments in asserting that there was a need for additional landfill space. They also argued that the landfill would be managed in compliance with existing regulations and under close supervision. After the hearing, the commission voted to deny the permit on the grounds that the proposed facility would be located adjacent to a predominantly residential area, that the increase in heavy truck traffic would increase noise in the area, and that such noise was undesirable in a residential setting (*East Bibb Twiggs v. Macon-Bibb County Commission*, 1989).

Robert Mullis, Charles Adams, and Tribble and Richardson (the firm producing the reports on which the petitioners relied in earlier hearings) asked for a rehearing and were granted one in July. During the rehearing, Mullis and his representatives responded to the concerns raised by residents. Mullis argued that his company had met all the requirements needed for the permit and that the site had been tested by engineers who found it to be geologically suitable for a landfill. He reiterated that the site would be operated in accordance with existing laws and carefully supervised at all times. Mullis also informed those who attended the hearing that the company would increase the buffer

zone around the landfill from 100 to 150 feet in areas where it abut-
ted residences. Mullis noted that there were only five homes adjacent
to the landfill site, and 25 homes were within a one-mile radius of the
site. Residents attending the rehearing expressed new concerns. They
questioned the adequacy of the buffer strip and raised questions about
health threats arising from vermin and insects and about the safety of
their wells. The Neighborhood Association argued that both the landfills approved by the commission were located in District 1; that district is roughly 70% Black. The Neighborhood Association also asked
the court to consider the historical practice of locating undesirable land
uses in Black communities. After the rehearing, the commission voted
to grant Mullis a permit to operate the landfill. The final site plan for the
landfill was approved in November 1986 (*East Bibb Twiggs v. Macon-
Bibb County Commission*, 1989).

THE DECISION

Upon hearing the arguments in this case, Chief Judge Wilbur Owens
concluded that the East Bibb Twiggs Neighborhood Association had
not presented enough evidence to prove that there was a violation of
the equal protection clause (*East Bibb Twiggs v. Macon-Bibb County
Commission*, 1989). In other words, the plaintiffs failed to meet the standards set in *Village of Arlington Heights v. Metropolitan Housing Department* (1977). Judge Owens argued that the commission's decisions were
not motivated by an intention to discriminate against Blacks. The judge
pointed out that though the census tract in which the proposed landfill
would be located was 60.9% Black, the commission had also approved a
landfill in the adjacent census tract, which was 76.6% White. According
to Owens, the Neighborhood Association had not shown that there was
a "clean pattern, unexplainable on grounds other than race" that the
commission discriminated against Blacks (*East Bibb Twiggs v. Macon-
Bibb County Commission*, 1989: 5). With this in mind, Judge Owens
upheld the commission's decision.

R.I.S.E. v. Kay

Yet another EJ case involving the siting of a landfill and the equal protection clause was filed in Richmond, Virginia, in 1990. In December of

that year, a community group, Residents Involved in Saving the Environment (R.I.S.E.), composed of King and Queen County citizens, sued the County Board of Supervisors (Kay et al.). The plaintiffs, R.I.S.E., argued that the siting of the landfill would have an adverse impact on Blacks, which would be a violation of the equal protection clause. They also alleged that there was a conspiracy to deny Blacks equal protection of their rights under the county's zoning ordinance, that the County Board of Supervisors failed to comply with the Virginia Public Procurement Act, and that the board violated the due process clause of the Fifth Amendment by acting in an arbitrary and capricious manner (*R.I.S.E. v. Kay*, 1991, 1992).

BACKGROUND

The conflict began in 1987 when the state of Virginia announced new regulations for solid waste disposal in landfills. These regulations presented a fiscal challenge to King and Queen County, as closing the three existing county landfills (which did not meet the new environmental standards) would cost an estimated $1.7 million. The county argued that it was in no position to close its existing landfills and develop a new one that could comply with the new regulations. Decisions regarding landfills were made by the King and Queen County Board of Supervisors, of which there were five members (*R.I.S.E. v. Kay*, 1991; Collin and Harris, 1993).

Members of the County Board of Supervisors tried to resolve the problem by initiating negotiations with the Chesapeake Corporation to operate a joint-venture landfill. The company identified 420 acres of the Piedmont Tract as a potential landfill site and hired the Law Engineering Company of Charlotte to test the site for suitability. The engineers concluded that the site was suitable for a landfill. The Chesapeake Corporation applied for a landfill permit in April 1988. However, the company halted negotiations for a joint-venture landfill and opted to expand the already-existing Prince William landfill for its own waste disposal purposes (*R.I.S.E. v. Kay*, 1991).

In January 1989, the County Board of Supervisors sought to purchase the Piedmont site from the Chesapeake Corporation, at which point the company presented two options to the board—the Piedmont Tract or the Norman-Saunders Tract. Since the Piedmont Tract was already tested and found suitable for landfill development, the board entered into negotiations to purchase that site for $420,000. The County Board of Supervisors also began discussions with Jeffrey Southard of BFI Engineering about the waste disposal problems in the county. In a board meeting held in November, the Planning Commission recommended rezoning the property to accommodate landfill development. The board finalized the purchase of the Piedmont Tract in December 1989 (*R.I.S.E. v. Kay*, 1991).

By this time, public opposition was brewing. Though the County Board of Supervisors did not refer to the proposed landfill as a regional facility, area residents and the media perceived and framed it as such. The Second Mount Olive Baptist Church became a key player in the events that unfolded. The historic church and graveyard—founded in 1869 by freed slaves—was located close to and on the main route to the dump. Though BFI promised to pave the road and leave a large buffer strip between the graveyard and the landfill, residents were not satisfied. A public meeting was held at the church on January 25, 1990. Residents argued that the landfill would reduce the quality of life of area residents because of the increased noise, dust, and odor; cause property values to decline; interfere with worship and social activities at the church and graveyard; result in blighting a historic church and community; and require major improvements to local roads. The Second Mount Olive Baptist Church meeting was followed by a public hearing (attended by BFI) held by the County Board of Supervisors on February 12; 15 of the 225 people attending the hearing testified against the proposed landfill. A petition signed by 947 residents opposing the landfill was also presented to the board. After the public hearing, the County Board of Supervisors voted unanimously to authorize the development of a landfill and to continue negotiations with BFI (*R.I.S.E. v. Kay*, 1991).

In response, residents formed the Concerned Citizen's Steering Committee (the precursor of R.I.S.E.). The group presented the County Board of Supervisors with a list of four potential alternative landfill sites in March. BFI and County Administrator Charles Smith inspected one of the alternative sites—Mantapike. However, they concluded that the site was unsuitable because of the slope of the land and a stream that traversed the site. Furthermore, 85% of the residents living in the vicinity of that site were Black. In May, residents formally formed a biracial organization, R.I.S.E. Many of the members of R.I.S.E. owned property in the vicinity of the proposed landfill. Race was not the main focus of R.I.S.E. at the time of its founding (*R.I.S.E. v. Kay*, 1991).

Approximately 50% of the population of King and Queen County was Black; however, 64% of the 61 people living within a half-mile radius of the proposed landfill were Black. Moreover, 80.8% of the 26 families living in 3.2-mile stretch of Route 614, which would be most heavily trafficked, were Black. The county's three existing landfills were sited in predominantly Black areas. The Mascot Landfill was sited in 1969. The Escobrook Baptist Church was within two miles of the site, and 100% of the residents living within a mile of the landfill were Black. The Dahlgren Landfill was sited in 1971. Roughly 95% of the people living in the vicinity of this landfill were Black. The story is similar for the Owenton Landfill, sited in 1977. At the time of siting, all the residents living within a half mile of the landfill were Black. A Black church— the First Mount Olive Baptist Church—was also located within a mile of the landfill. A fourth landfill, privately owned and operated by the King Land Corporation, was developed on a 120-acre site in King and Queen County in 1986 in a predominantly White area. There were serious problems at the King Land facility from the outset. Dumping commenced at the site before the necessary soil tests were performed. Tests later revealed that incinerator ash was buried in groundwater, and there was no clay soil to prevent seepage and subsequent groundwater contamination. The county sought an injunction and in January 1987 prohibited landfill operation on the site. The King Land Corporation appealed the injunction, but the Board of Zoning Appeals upheld the injunction on March 16 on the grounds that King Land had ignored environmental, health, and safety concerns and that the operation of the landfill would reduce property values (*R.I.S.E. v. Kay*, 1991).

THE DECISION

District Judge Richard Williams found that the siting of landfills in King and Queen County from 1969 to 1991 disproportionately impacted Blacks. However, Judge Williams cited *East Bibb Twiggs v. Macon-Bibb Planning and Zoning Commission* (1989) in arguing that racially disproportionate impact alone is not sufficient to find that there was a violation of the equal protection clause. That is, the plaintiffs must

prove intentional discrimination to make their case. Though the historical placement of landfills in Black communities in the county was
"an important starting point" to determine whether there was discriminatory intent (see *Village of Arlington Heights v. Metropolitan Housing
Department*, 1977), the plaintiffs had not provided the statistical evidence to prove that the County Board of Supervisors' actions amounted
to intentional discrimination. Judge Williams also argued that the closure of the King Land landfill could not be construed as favoritism; it
was closed because the site was geologically unfit to operate a landfill
on. Ergo, the judge ruled in favor of the County Board of Supervisors
(*R.I.S.E. v. Kay*, 1991). R.I.S.E. appealed the ruling. The case was heard
in the U.S. Court of Appeals Fourth Circuit in March 1992. On October
15, 1992, the appeals court—finding no error in the trial court ruling—
upheld the decision of the district court (*R.I.S.E. v. Kay*, 1992).

Boyd v. Browner

A case involving compensation for families being relocated from a
contaminated neighborhood was brought before the U.S. District
Court in the District of Columbia on the grounds that federal agencies violated the due process clause of the Fifth Amendment and the
equal protection clause of the Fourteenth Amendment. In 1992, about
85 Black homeowners living in the Carver Terrace subdivision of Texarkana, Texas, sold their homes to the U.S. Army Corps of Engineers,
which was acting on behalf of the EPA. The buyout of Carver Terrace
occurred because the subdivision, which was constructed on land formerly used as a wood treatment facility, was contaminated. The Carver
Terrace residents (Boyd et al.) relied on market-dynamics arguments—
particularly the discrimination thesis—in bringing their case. They
brought suit against the EPA (Browner) alleging that they were coerced
into selling their properties for below-market prices because they were
threatened by the Corps of Engineers and EPA. They also contended
that their relocation compensation was inadequate. The plaintiffs compared their treatment to that of seven White communities relocated by
the EPA and argued that they were discriminated against. The plaintiffs
sought a rescission of their sales agreements and additional compensation (*Boyd v. Browner*, 1995).

BACKGROUND

The Carver Terrace subdivision was developed in the 1960s when 79 homes and a church were built on the former wood treatment site. In 1980, the Texas Department of Water Resources discovered that the soil and groundwater in the subdivision was contaminated with chemicals used to preserve wood. The Carver Terrace site was placed on the NPL and declared a Superfund site in 1984. At first, the EPA wanted to treat the soil and groundwater while the residents continued living on the site. However, when Congress reviewed the EPA's proposed remedy in 1990, it appropriated $5 million to buy out the homes and relocate the residents. The EPA contracted with the Corps of Engineers to appraise and acquire the homes in Carver Terrace and to arrange for residents' relocation. The Corps of Engineers was directed by the EPA to appraise the properties as if they were uncontaminated and pay *"clean value,"* or precontamination value, for each property. The Corps of Engineers hand delivered letters to each Carver Terrace landowner with notification that the property was appraised and the appraisal value (*Boyd v. Browner*, 1995, 1996). Each letter also contained the following notification: "If we are unable to negotiate a direct purchase from you, it will be necessary to acquire the property through condemnation proceedings" (*Boyd v. Browner*, 1995: 592).

By the end of 1992, all the Carver Terrace property owners had signed contracts selling their homes to the Corps of Engineers. The plaintiffs also applied for and received relocation benefits. However, Carver Terrace residents complained that they thought the quoted notification language was a threat, and they argued that White communities that were bought out by the EPA were treated differently. Between 1978 and 1994, seven White communities were bought out and relocated by the agency: Love Canal, New York; Times Beach, Missouri; Forest Glen, New York; Uniontown, Ohio; Montclair, New Jersey; United Creosoting, Texas; and Lansdowne, Pennsylvania. The offer letters sent to residents of the seven White communities were similar to that sent to Carver Terrace residents with the exception of one element. The letters sent to residents of the White communities did not contain language advising homeowners that if negotiations failed, their properties would be condemned and the price paid for the property would be based on the *contaminated value* of the property. The Federal Emergency

Management Agency oversaw the buyout of three of the White communities, while the Corps of Engineers managed the other four (*Boyd v. Browner*, 1995, 1996).

THE DECISION

District Judge James Robertson argued that in order to get a favorable ruling, the plaintiffs needed to show that the offer letters violated Congress's intent that the property owners of Carver Terrace receive "clean value" for their homes. To do this, the Carver Terrace residents needed to show some "final agency action" that prevented them from receiving precontamination value for their property. The judge argued that the plaintiffs failed to do so. Judge Robertson indicated that agency action is defined as "the whole or a part of an agency rule, order, license, sanction, relief, or the equivalent or denial thereof, or failure to act" (*Boyd v. Browner*, 1995: 593), as established in *Industrial Safety Equipment Assoc., Inc. v. EPA* (1988) and *American Trucking Assoc., Inc. v. United States* (1985). The judge argued further that the Corps of Engineers' letters were appropriate. The letters were informational; they did not announce any rule of law, imposed no obligation, determined no right or liability, and fixed no legal relationship. The fact that Carver Terrace residents perceived the letters as threatening did not make them "threats" or make them final agency action (*Boyd v. Browner*, 1995).

Under the Uniform Relocation Assistance and Real Property Acquisition Policies Act (42 U.S.C. §§ 4621, 4623), plaintiffs should receive replacement housing payments that, when added to the cost of acquiring their new dwelling, should be equal to the cost of comparable replacement dwelling. Carver Terrace property owners were notified of their relocation assistance payments by letter; the letters also informed them of their right to appeal the amount of those payments. None of the plaintiffs appealed the relocation assistance that was initially offered (*Boyd v. Browner*, 1995).

The Carver Terrace residents claimed they were discriminated against because they were threatened and such threats were not made against Whites in communities being relocated. The due process clause of the Fifth Amendment requires that the plaintiffs compare their treatment to people who are *similarly situated*, as established in *City of Cleburne v. Cleburne Living Center* (1985) and *Plyler v. Doe* (1982). Judge Robertson felt that the Carver Terrace residents did not establish that there were similar circumstances between themselves and the residents of other communities that were relocated. The plaintiffs also conceded that there were differences in relocation offers and acquisition practices in the seven White communities that were relocated. The judge went on to say that even if Carver Terrace residents could show that they were similarly situated to residents of the other communities that were relocated, they would have to show that there was intent to discriminate against them for there to be a violation of the equal protection clause (*Boyd v. Browner*, 1995).

Carver Terrace residents appealed the ruling, and the case was heard before the U.S. Court of Appeals in the District of Columbia Circuit in 1996. The appeals court upheld the district court ruling (*Boyd v. Browner*, 1996).

Title VI

EJ cases have also been filed under Title VI of the 1964 Civil Rights Act. Legal scholars argue that Title VI provides the best opportunity for private parties to bring EJ suits against state and local agencies. This is the case because most state and local environmental agencies receive federal funding; consequently, almost all permitting decisions are potentially subject to Title VI rules (Cole, 1994; Mank, 1999; Weinberg, 1999; Cory, 2008).

Title VI prohibits any entity receiving federal funding from discriminating on the basis of race, color, national origin, and the like (Civil Rights Act, 1964). Cole and Farrell argue that since the passage of the act, the U.S. Supreme Court "has systematically eviscerated the statute, stripping the concept of *discriminatory impact* from Title VI itself and holding in a series of decisions that one must prove *intentional* discrimination in order to establish a violation of section 601 of the statute" (2006: 271). This means that while communities such as Camden, New Jersey, can prove in court that Blacks in the state are twice as likely as Whites to live near a polluting facility and that this amounts to a *disparate impact*, this argument alone does not suffice to win a Title VI case. This happened in Camden. In 1999, the St. Lawrence Cement Company announced plans to construct a large cement-grinding facility in the Waterfront South community. The community, which already hosted numerous industrial facilities, mobilized to prevent the cement company from being built in the neighborhood. Nonetheless, construction began on the plant in November 1999. On April 19, 2001, Judge Stephen Orlofsky of the federal district court in Camden ruled in favor of Camden residents that there were disparate impacts from polluting facilities and issued an injunction against the cement plant, prohibiting it from operating (*South Camden Citizens in Action v. New Jersey Department of Environmental Protection*, 2001a; Cole and Farrell, 2006).

However, this was an ephemeral victory, as a few days later—on April 24—the U.S. Supreme Court ruled on a case arising in Alabama that there was no private right to action to enforce the disparate-impact regulations articulated in section 602 of Title VI (*Alexander v. Sandoval*, 2001). Upon appeal, the Third Circuit overturned Judge Orlofsky's ruling and, citing the *Alexander v. Sandoval* case, argued that the Camden plaintiffs could not use the disparate-impact argument as a basis for their suit (*South Camden Citizens in Action v. New Jersey Department of Environmental Protection*, 2001b). Light and Rand (1996) argue that Title VI litigation in EJ cases is limited because of the political nature of environmental racism.

EPA's Title VI Complaints

The mission of the EPA's Title VI (external compliance) program is to ascertain whether the recipients of federal funding comply with relevant nondiscrimination requirements as stipulated by federal law. The case-management process has three distinct phases: (a) jurisdictional review, (b) investigation, and (c) final agency decision. The first two stages have a strict time frame. That is, the jurisdictional review must be completed within 20 days of receiving the complaint, and the investigation must be completed within 180 days of receiving the complaint (Deloitte Consulting, 2011; LaRoss and Reeves, 2012; Huang, 2012).

Beginning in the early 1990s, EJ activists started using Title VI of the Civil Rights Act as a mechanism to address racial discrimination in the siting and permitting of hazardous facilities. Activists have used Title

VI in two ways: (a) suing recipients of federal funding in federal and state courts and (b) filing administrative complaints with the EPA and other agencies (Huang, 2012).

However, filing Title VI administrative complaints with the EPA and the Office of Civil Rights has been an ineffective way for EJ activists to challenge permits granted to facilities. The evidentiary bar is set so high in the courts that EJ communities have difficulty meeting it. In addition, the EPA has been very slow in responding to Title VI complaints (Cory, 2008; Neal, Famira, Miller-Travis, 2010; Huang, 2012). It became evident early on that only a relatively small percentage of the complaints submitted to the EPA would be accepted. My analysis of the outcome of Title VI complaints shows that between 1993 and 2002, less than 36% of the complaints filed were accepted each year.

An external audit of the handling of Title VI complaints by the EPA's Office of Civil Rights was conducted in 2011. The report found that the agency had not adequately responded to the Title VI complaints alleging discriminatory impacts of environmental rules. More specifically, the review identified a "record of poor performance" related to the administration of these complaints (Deloitte Consulting, 2011: 2). For example, only 6% of the 247 Title VI complaints filed between 1993 and 2010 were either accepted or dismissed in the agency's 20-day time limit. Indeed, the backlog of cases in limbo stretches back to 2001. Many cases were found to be awaiting action for as much as four years. Two complaints were awaiting a decision for more than eight years; one case was accepted nine years and another ten years after they were filed. Roughly half the petitions took a year or more to be processed. Between 2006 and 2007, the agency did not process a single Title VI petition, and there is a backlog of 32 cases filed since 2009 (Deloitte Consulting, 2011; Huang, 2012). In addition, the Office of Civil Rights has rejected many complaints, finding that no discrimination occurred. The EPA has come under increasing pressure to deal with Title VI cases more efficiently since the release of the auditor's report (LaRoss and Reeves, 2012).

In response, the EPA is revising its Civil Rights Act rules—a move that critics say will severely curtail the filing of new Title VI petitions that allege discrimination (Reeves, 2012). EJ groups are also responding to the delay in processing petitions by suing the EPA. In 2009, the

Rosemere Neighborhood Association filed suit against the agency. The Ninth Circuit District Court, under which the suit was brought, roundly criticized the EPA for its lax approach to responding to petitions. Two years later, the Center for Race, Poverty & Environment sued the agency for failing to act on a petition that was submitted in 1994 (Reeves, 2011, 2012; *Rosemere Neighborhood Association v. EPA*, 2009; *Padres Hacia Una Vida Mejor v. Jackson*, 2011).

One outcome of the *Rosemere Neighborhood Association v. EPA* (2009) case is that the EPA agreed to process all future Title VI complaints in the regulatory time frames stipulated and to produce a quarterly report of the inventory cases and their status. Because of the community lawsuits and the intense scrutiny the EPA has been under regarding its handling of Title VI cases, the agency is trying to clear the backlog.

Executive Order 12898

EJ supporters hailed President Clinton's signing of Executive Order 12898. The order directed federal agencies to identify and mitigate the negative environmental impacts that their policies might have on minority and low-income communities. However, scholars point out that the federal agencies, especially the EPA, have been inconsistent in their attempts to comply with Executive Order 12898 (Waterhouse, 2009; Trifun, 2009). Neal, Famira, and Miller-Travis (2010) argue that though EJ has made headway in some federal and state agencies, the letter and spirit of the executive order has not been achieved. They argue further that the executive order lays the foundation for federal EJ policies, but the Clinton administration was not consistent in its support for EJ; it failed to use existing environmental laws to achieve the goals of the executive order. The Bush administration neglected the order at times, weakened rules, and failed to enforce environmental and civil rights laws. Neal, Famira, and Miller-Travis (2010) point to the lack of enforcement of the Title VI of the Civil Rights Act as one of the major shortcomings of the government's response to the executive order. The analysts suggest that each agency covered by the executive order should be required to report its progress on compliance at regular intervals (Waterhouse, 2009; Trifun, 2009). It remains to be seen how well the proposed legislation aimed at codifying the executive order will ameliorate compliance levels.

Permitting

At the root of many EJ struggles is the issuance of permits to operate noxious facilities that are likely to expose people to hazardous conditions. Hence, Neal, Famira, and Miller-Travis recommend that before "undertaking any environmental permitting or other federal action that may adversely affect human health or the environment the lead federal agency should be required to conduct an EJ analysis to determine whether significant disproportionate adverse effects would be caused by the action and to the maximum extent feasible avoid, minimize or mitigate the adverse environmental justice impact" (2010: 4).

The EPA has responded to concerns about permits by making permitting the centerpiece of its *Plan EJ 2014* (U.S. EPA, 2011c). The goal of the *permitting initiative* is to ensure that EJ concerns are considered fully in the permitting process under existing federal environmental laws. This entails providing communities that are overburdened with hazards opportunities to have "full and meaningful access" to the permitting process.

Early EJ research on environmental regulation focused on racial and class differences in fines and the pace of cleaning up hazardous sites. Recent scholarship has demonstrated the importance of examining how factors such as the type of industry, the safety and compliance history of firms, and the type of settlement that violators negotiate affect fines. This chapter has also examined the challenges people exposed to industrial hazards face in the courts when they try to convince judges that there is discriminatory intent in cases where disproportionate impact is evident. Generally speaking, the legal, regulatory, and administrative dimensions of EJ problems need greater scholarly attention, as plaintiffs bringing EJ cases in the courts have found little success and filing Title VI complaints has been an ineffective strategy for halting or reducing the exposure to environmental hazards.

6

The Siting Process

Manipulation, Environmental Blackmail, and Enticement

This chapter examines five additional factors that can help account for the prevalence of hazardous facilities in minority communities:

1. Unique physical characteristics of the landscape of host communities
2. Manipulation of residents of host communities
3. Environmental blackmail
4. Enticement of host communities
5. Host communities inviting hazardous facilities in

The Unique Physical Characteristics Thesis

The geomorphology of a site is an important consideration in the siting of landfills and other industrial facilities. To counter the charge of discrimination, government agencies, politicians, and waste management industries sometimes contend that sites were chosen not because of the racial composition of the community but because of the sites' *geological formations*.

Warren County, North Carolina, Revisited

The use of the argument regarding physical characteristics of the landscape can get murky when it comes to the siting of landfills in predominantly Black communities. The case of three small, rural, Black communities in the South demonstrates this. In Warren County (discussed in chapter 1), there were clear specifications from the EPA as to the type of soil formation and the depth the water table should be in land on which landfills could be placed. When residents opposing the PCB landfill argued that the proposed site did not have the requisite soil formation and that the landfill bottom would be 7 feet above the water table rather than the EPA's minimum specification of 50 feet, the EPA waived its own requirements and gave permission for the landfill to be built and operated (LaBalme, 1987; Exchange Project, 2006; *Warren County v. North Carolina*, 1981; *Twitty v. North Carolina*, 1987).

In two other Black communities (Emelle, Alabama, and Noxubee, Mississippi) where plans were being made to site megalandfills in the late 1970s, proponents of the landfills argued that the sites were chosen because of their unique geological formations that made the sites ideal for the construction of dumps. Landfill supporters argued that race had nothing to do with the choice of these sites.

Emelle, Alabama

A hazardous waste landfill has dominated the landscape of Emelle, Alabama, since 1977. The small, predominantly Black hamlet of Emelle appeared on the radar screen as a possible landfill site in 1973 when the EPA published a report listing 74 potential sites throughout the United States for large-scale hazardous landfill development. Underlying Emelle is a 700-feet-thick layer of Demopolis chalk (sometimes referred to as Selma chalk) that is impermeable, a factor that makes the site attractive to hazardous waste management corporations. The EPA estimates it would take about 300 years for any chemicals in the landfill to migrate through the chalk to underground aquifers; Waste Management, Inc., estimates it would take about 10,000 years for chemicals to reach the aquifers (*Gregory v. Chemical Waste Management*, 1996; *National Solid Wastes Management v. Alabama Department of Environmental Protection*, 1990a; *State of Alabama v. EPA*, 1990; *Hunt v. Chemical Waste Management*, 1991). The geological integrity of the chalk is influenced by the presence of faults, fractures, and other discontinuities. Faults and fractures exist through the Selma chalk at Emelle, and this could increase the speed at which materials move through the chalk. The Emelle landfill is also located in an earthquake risk zone. An 1886 earthquake in Sumter County caused a one-half-foot movement of the ground. It is possible that earthquakes could create cracks in the chalk that could hasten the migration of leachate and hazardous wastes through the chalk (*Hunt v. Chemical Waste Management*, 1991).

Nonetheless, within four years of the publication of the EPA report, a group of ten investors known as Resource Industries of Alabama (RIA) was formed to develop a commercial hazardous waste disposal facility in Sumter County. RIA purchased 340 acres of land about five miles north of Emelle in 1977 and then applied for an interim permit from the state of Alabama to operate the site. One of the partners in RIA, James Parsons, the son-in-law of former governor George Wallace, was instrumental in getting the interim permit from Alabama's Department of Public Health. The Emelle site began operations shortly after the land was purchased (*Gregory v. Chemical Waste Management*, 1996; Gunter and Williams, 1984; Alabama Department of Environmental Management, 2011).

Local residents and surrounding communities have not prospered during the time the landfill has been operating in their midst. Sumter County (in which Emelle is located) had 16,908 people in 1980; the population fell to 13,763 in 2010. Blacks constituted 69% of the population of the county in 1980 and 75% of its population in 2010. In 1980, a third of the county's residents lived below the poverty level; more than 90% of those living below the poverty level were Black. The median household income for Blacks in the county was $11,015 in 1980 (U.S. Census Bureau, 1990, 1995, 2010; U.S. GAO, 1983; Bullard, 1993b). The 2006–2010 American Community Survey shows that the unemployment rate in Sumter County was 9.7% over this period. Only 6.3% of the residents of the county worked in professional, scientific, management, and administrative and waste management services. The median household income in Sumter County was $25,338. The median household income was $40,474 in Alabama and $50,046 in the U.S. Twenty-five percent of the households in the county received food stamps (the Supplemental Nutrition Assistance Program). In all, 32.8% of the families lived below the poverty level (U.S. Census Bureau, 2006–2010, 2010).

More than three decades after the landfill was built, Emelle itself remains a very small community, occupying two-tenths of a square mile. It had a population of 53 in 2010, 94.3% of whom were Black. Females constitute 62.3% of the population. The median age of residents of the town is 50.3 years (U.S. Census Bureau, 2010). Though the focus has been on Emelle, the predominantly Black town of Geiger—with a population of 170—lies just four miles north of the landfill complex. Geiger is 73.5% Black. Gainesville, with a population of 208, is located nine miles east of the landfill; 82.2% of its population is Black. Livingston, which lies 20 miles southeast of the facility, has a population of 3,485. Blacks constitute 63.9% of Livingston's population (Chemical Waste Management, 2005; U.S. Census Bureau, 2010).

WMX AND TAXES

About four months after the RIA began operating the landfill, it was approached by Waste Management's acquisition managers. Waste Management was interested in a joint venture with RIA or outright acquisition of the company. If RIA did not accept either option, then Waste Management planned to set up a competing facility. RIA responded by selling its operation to Waste Management's subsidiary Alabama Solid Waste Systems in February 1978 (the subsidiary was later merged with Waste Management). Chem Waste, which also operated the Emelle facility, is wholly owned by Waste Management. Waste Management is now known as WMX Technologies (hereinafter WMX). When WMX bought the property from RIA, it agreed "to operate a hazardous waste disposal facility . . . to its maximum capacity during the full economically feasible life of such facility." However, in 1996, RIA sued WMX for not operating the facility to its maximum capacity, hiding revenues generated at Emelle, and cheating RIA out of royalty payments. The court sided with RIA and ruled against WMX (*Gregory v. Chemical Waste Management*, 1996: 608). The Emelle site—which the company refers to as the "Cadillac" of landfills—accepts toxic wastes from 45 states, Puerto Rico, and Canada (Gunter and Williams, 1984).

In 1979, Sumter County granted WMX a five-year tax exemption. However, when the county denied WMX another tax exemption in 1984, WMX took the county to court. The county had a tax code that granted tax exemptions to facilities constructed primarily to control, reduce, or eliminate air or water pollution. WMX argued that hazardous waste management was a form of air and water pollution control and that the Emelle landfill was constructed primarily for that purpose. Hence, WMX contended that it deserved the air and water pollution control tax break. The court ruled against WMX, arguing that the

Emelle facility was not built primarily for the purposes of controlling air and water pollution. The court also noted that WMX does not use the vast majority of its property or equipment to clean the air or water; therefore, it does not deserve a property tax exemption (*Chemical Waste Management v. State of Alabama*, 1987). The tax receipts were important to the county, and they were part of the reason key local leaders supported the landfill. That is, the county received five dollars for every ton of waste buried in the landfill (*Anniston Star*, 1990)

INCINERATION AT EMELLE

From the outset, RIA envisioned Emelle as a full-service hazardous waste disposal facility with an incinerator. In fact, when WMX bought the facility, RIA had already made a down payment on an incinerator. The incinerator was constructed, and it operated briefly in 1982. After that incinerator was closed, WMX proposed constructing a chalk-drying PCB incinerator (even before the company had a permit to handle PCBs). In March 1984, WMX did a feasibility study of the proposed PCB incinerator and found that the incinerator could generate between $20 million and $30 million in revenues annually (*Gregory v. Chemical Waste Management*, 1996). During this time, WMX had large quantities of PCBs already stored at the Emelle facility. In July 1984, WMX was ordered by the EPA and the Eleventh Circuit Court of Appeals to remove the 2.8 million gallons of PCBs from the Emelle facility. It was not until December of that year that the EPA authorized WMX to handle PCBs at the Emelle facility. The public was notified about the authorization to handle PCBs in 1985 (*State of Alabama v. EPA*, 1989; *Chemical Waste Management v. Broadwater*, 1985). WMX made proposals to develop incineration capacity at Emelle again in 1985 and 1986, but its efforts failed (*Gregory v. Chemical Waste Management*, 1996).

WMX was exploring incineration at Emelle at a time when changes in the waste disposal regulations made incineration a more lucrative option for waste management companies. In 1984, Congress passed the Hazardous and Solid Waste Amendments, which applied stringent rules to the land disposal of hazardous wastes. In May 1985, a nationwide ban prohibiting the burial of liquids in hazardous waste landfills went into effect. These rules had a noticeable impact on the volume of hazardous waste disposed of at Emelle. Beginning in 1985, there was a

Table 6.1. Amount of Wastes Shipped to Emelle

Year	Total shipment (in tons)
1978	100,000
1985	341,000
1986	456,000
1987	564,000
1988	549,000
1989	788,000
1990	290,000

Sources: National Solid Wastes Management v. Alabama Department of Environmental Management, 1990a; Hunt v. Chemical Waste Management, 1991.

significant increase in the amount of hazardous wastes being shipped to Emelle (see table 6.1). The facility accepts wastes from virtually every manufacturing sector. The wastes include more than 100 volatile, corrosive, poisonous, or cancer-causing chemicals (*National Solid Wastes Management v. Alabama Department of Environmental Management*, 1990a; Alabama Department of Environmental Management, 2011).

HAZARDOUS WASTE PERMIT

When WMX bought the Emelle facility in 1978, the company was not required to possess a federal or state hazardous waste permit because the Resource Conservation and Recovery Act (RCRA) regulations requiring permits had not gone into effect yet. WMX applied for the permits in 1983 and was allowed to operate on an interim status till final approval of the permits. However, by 1987, local residents began questioning more openly the operations of WMX and the landfill. They urged the EPA to reject WMX's application for a final operating permit. In 1987, four environmental organizations (Alabamians for a Clean Environment [ACE], the Sierra Club, the Alabama Conservancy, and Greenpeace) filed suit against the EPA and the Alabama Department of Environmental Management, challenging WMX's application for a hazardous waste permit seeking permission to expand the facility, to dig additional disposal trenches, to build an incinerator, and to waive groundwater monitoring requirements. The environmental groups argued that the permit sought by WMX would allow the corporation to expand the size and capabilities of the facility significantly, and that would harm the environment and the people living close by. The environmental groups challenged the plans for the incinerator also. WMX finally dropped plans to build an incinerator at Emelle in 1987 (building instead a facility in Port Arthur, Texas, that could handle 150 million British thermal units of waste per hour) because of an ongoing dispute with RIA over royalty payments. Though the court dismissed the suit brought by the environmental groups, the challenge from environmental groups and local activists raised people's awareness of the operations of the facility; this made it more difficult to build an incinerator after 1987 (*Alabamians for a Clean Environment v. Thomas and Pegues*, 1987; *Gregory v. Chemical Waste Management*, 1996).

After WMX dropped plans to build an incinerator, the EPA modified the permit to terminate approval for the incinerator. The state of Alabama and the environmental groups challenged the procedures the EPA followed in issuing the final operating permit for Emelle, but the court affirmed the EPA's decision to grant the permit (*State of Alabama v. EPA*, 1990).

IMPORTING PCBS FROM TEXAS

Emelle was in the news again in 1988 when the EPA agreed to allow WMX to dump 47,000 tons of PCB-contaminated soil from Geneva Industries in South Houston in the landfill. Geneva Industries, a former petrochemical plant, was a Superfund site contaminated with toxic chemicals. After a remedial investigation and feasibility study were conducted, off-site disposal was the remediation option selected (*State of Alabama v. EPA*, 1989).

Alabama was not notified about the shipment until shortly before the wastes were scheduled to arrive in Emelle. Alabama officials were chagrined that wastes from another state were being shipped to the landfill without earlier notification and sued to delay the shipments (*Chemical Waste Management v. Broadwater*, 1985). Early in the summer of 1988, the Texas Water Commission and WMX (with the knowledge of the EPA) entered into an agreement to ship PCB-tainted soil to Emelle. WMX put in a bid to dispose of the contaminated soil at the Emelle landfill in January 1988 and was awarded a contract by the Texas Water Commission. WMX did not notify Alabama authorities at the time its bid was approved (*State of Alabama v. EPA*, 1989).

Alabama legislators first heard about the PCB-tainted soil shipments in June 1988. The governor and attorney general wrote to the EPA administrator requesting a delay in the shipments; the EPA did delay the shipments in order to respond to the letters. The final hazardous waste permit for Emelle that WMX had applied for was granted and became effective in July 1988. On September 29 of that year, the EPA notified Alabama officials that waste shipments would begin on October 7. Alabama brought suit against the EPA for not providing proper notification, and shipments were delayed till the hearings were completed. The courts ruled in favor of Alabama, granting a temporary injunction against the shipment of PCB-tainted soil to Emelle. The courts also ordered the EPA to reopen the record of decision for the Geneva, Texas, site and to explore alternative forms of soil remediation. The district court decision was appealed. In April 1989, the Eleventh Circuit Court of Appeals, noting that that the plaintiffs were not objecting to the burial of the PCB-tainted soil at the Emelle facility but only to the fact that they were notified late in the process, lifted the temporary injunction, thereby paving the way for the wastes to be disposed of in the landfill (*State of Alabama v. EPA*, 1988a, 1988b, 1989).

OUT-OF-STATE WASTES AND THE HOLLEY BILL

Most of the wastes buried at Emelle are not generated in Alabama. By 1990, about 85% of the wastes buried at the facility were from out of state (*National Solid Wastes Management v. Alabama Department of Environmental Management*, 1990b). As the volume of wastes handled by the facilities increased during the 1980s, state officials questioned whether Alabama should continue to be the repository of wastes from other states and tried to find a way to resolve the issue. In response, they enacted the Holley Bill, which prohibited commercial hazardous waste treatment or disposal facilities located in Alabama "from accepting hazardous wastes generated in another state which prohibits the treatment, storage, or disposal of hazardous wastes within its own borders, or which refuses or fails to comply with [CERCLA]" (*National Solid Wastes Management v. Alabama Department of Environmental Management*, 1990a).

Among other things, Alabama argued that it lacked the financial resources and trained personnel necessary to deal with the risks and hazards posed by transporting the voluminous amounts of hazardous wastes pouring into the state. The National Solid Wastes Management Association and WMX were not sympathetic to Alabama's position; they challenged the Holley Bill in court, arguing that the bill violated the Constitution because it restricted the movement of interstate commerce (the commerce clause). Because Alabama's Holley Bill did not close the state's borders to all out-of-state wastes, only wastes originating from states that were not in compliance with federal waste laws (and when they complied with federal laws, their wastes could be handled in Alabama again), the courts ruled that the Holley Bill did not violate the commerce clause (*National Solid Wastes Management v. Alabama Department of Environmental Management*, 1990a). This ruling meant that Alabama could reject wastes from 22 states and the District of Columbia (*National Solid Wastes Management v. Alabama Department of Environmental Management*, 1990b).

The National Solid Wastes Management Association and WMX appealed the district court ruling. Relying on the precedent established in Warren County and similar cases, the appeals court ruled in favor of WMX, arguing that "even if Alabama's purpose in enacting the Holley Bill was to protect human health and the environment in Alabama, that purpose 'may not be accomplished by discriminating against articles of commerce coming from outside the State unless there is some reason, apart from their origin, to treat them differently'" (*National Solid Wastes Management v. Alabama Department of Environmental Management*, 1990b: 811). The appeals court perceived the Holley Bill as "a protectionist measure not based adequately on legitimate local concerns" (*National Solid Wastes Management v. Alabama Department of Environmental Management*, 1990b: 809).

Less than a year after the Holley Bill was penned, Alabama passed another law that dramatically affected the shipment of out-of-state wastes to Emelle. The law was passed in April 1990 and became effective in July of that year. It instituted a "base fee" of $25.60 per ton on all wastes disposed of at commercial facilities in Alabama and an "additional fee" of $72 per ton on all wastes generated outside the state and disposed of in Alabama waste facilities. The law also had a "cap" provision that limited the amount of wastes that could be disposed of in Alabama facilities in a given year. WMX filed suit before the act went into effect. Once again, the company argued that the law was unconstitutional because it violated the commerce clause. However, the Supreme Court of Alabama upheld the base fee, the additional fee, and the cap instituted by Alabama. The court argued that the base fee and the cap were evenhandedly applied and did not discriminate against wastes from any particular source. The court also argued that Alabama had a right to institute an additional fee on out-of-state wastes to compensate for the fact that Alabama was serving as a dumping ground for some states and Alabamans had to bear the additional risks of the hazardous wastes buried in the state (*Hunt v. Chemical Waste Management*, 1991).

WMX appealed the Alabama supreme court ruling, and the case was heard before the U.S. Supreme Court in 1992. In addition to the argument that the fees and cap provision violated the commerce clause, WMX argued that the fees discouraged full use of the landfill. The fees had a dramatic effect on the amount of wastes transported to the landfill. The amount of wastes disposed of at the landfill dropped from 788,000 tons in 1989 to 290,000 tons the year after the ordinance was passed. The U.S. Supreme Court ruled in favor of WMX. Justices argued that the differential treatment of in-state and out-of-state wastes by charging an additional fee for out-of-state wastes violated the commerce clause (*Chemical Waste Management v. Hunt*, 1992).

THE FACILITY

The Emelle facility expanded to cover 2,730 acres of land by the early 1990s. There are 22 disposal trenches, waste lagoons, a waste drum storage area, a liquid waste tank storage area, a liquid waste solidification unit, and a solvent and fuel recovery area on the property. The facility is permitted to store up to 2,922,836 gallons of hazardous wastes in containers on the property. The landfill complex also has a tank storage capacity of 5,250,531 gallons. Millions of cubic yards of garbage are buried in closed trenches on the property. The trench that is currently accepting wastes has a disposal capacity of 5,259,358 cubic yards (Alabama Department of Environmental Management, 2010, 2011).

Emelle receives almost every type of hazardous waste identified in the RCRA regulations. The facility is estimated to have an operating life of about 100 years. Though the site has to be monitored, regulated, and maintained forever, WMX is financially obliged to pay the costs of such monitoring and maintenance for only 30 years after the facility is closed

(*State of Alabama v. EPA*, 1990; *Gregory v. Chemical Waste Management*, 1996; *Hunt v. Chemical Waste Management*, 1991).

Though local residents were assured that liquids would not penetrate or leak from the landfill, tests conducted by WMX analysts showed as early as 1983 that water was seeping into the closed trenches, creating a toxic leachate. Between 10 million and 15 million gallons of leachate are being collected annually and stored in aboveground tanks. There was also evidence that leachate seeped into the Selma chalk (*Hunt v. Chemical Waste Management*, 1991). In 1987 and 1993, low levels of volatile organic compounds were detected in some of the wells sampled. Between 1995 and 1997, TCE, chloroethane, vinyl chloride, and other compounds were detected in sample wells (Chemical Waste Management, 2005).

FRAGILE COALITION

Black residents, some of whom worked at the landfill, were hesitant to oppose the facility at first. However, by the early 1980s, they began to more openly express their concerns about the health of nearby residents, occupational hazards, and the environmental violations of the corporation (Bailey, Faupel, and Gundlach, 1993; Richards, 1988). Blacks were the first to call attention to the Emelle facility. In 1981, a group of activists from the Minority People's Council demonstrated at WMX's main gate. The group, led by Wendell Paris, protested unsafe working conditions in the plant (Bailey, Faupel, and Gundlach, 1993). Paris later argued that the volume of wastes coming to the Emelle landfill was "turning Sumter County into the pay toilet of America and local residents into hazardous waste junkies" (qtd. in Bullard, 1990: 72).

Paris expressed the ambivalence Blacks felt toward the Emelle landfill complex. On the one hand, they were worried about their health and the environment; on the other, they sought employment at WMX's facility and bristled at the minuscule number of Blacks employed there. Such ambivalence was not at issue in the group Sumter Countians Organized for the Protection of the Environment (SCOPE). SCOPE, composed of White residents of the county, took a reformist approach. It focused on monitoring landfill operations, ensuring public access to reliable information, and holding the management of WMX accountable to the public. Instead of demonstrations, SCOPE held public meetings. Some of SCOPE's members wanted to take a more direct-action approach; hence, a dissident group split off from SCOPE to form ACE. ACE remained a largely White organization with a membership of about 300. Its goal was to shut down the Emelle facility. It organized rallies and demonstrations (Bailey, Faupel, and Gundlach, 1993; Bailey, Faupel, and Holland, 1992; Gunter and Williams, 1984).

Up until 1987, Black and White activists organized separately and did not really support each other's efforts. Years of racial tensions and mistrust in the community made it difficult for the groups to collaborate. Furthermore, competing frames and goals hindered the formation of a coalition. While SCOPE wanted to work within the status quo and monitor the plant, Blacks in the Minority People's Council wanted to develop a social justice agenda that examined the relationship between occupational hazards, environmental inequality, and economic security. ACE wanted to close the landfill, a position that not all Blacks supported since some worked at the facility and employment opportunities were scarce elsewhere. At the time, neither SCOPE nor ACE embraced the approach favored by Blacks, which was to blend environmental, racial, and social justice concerns into one activist agenda. However, in 1987, ACE made a breakthrough. It worked with Greenpeace and Citizens Clearinghouse for Hazardous Wastes to organize a rally in Montgomery, followed by a caravan that led to the gates of WMX. The rally was called the "Toxic Trail of Tears." This attempt to enlist the participation of African Americans and Native Americans was more successful since the theme and the activities evoked powerful symbols that motivated minority activists to participate. Sumter County was one of the assembly points in the 1830s for the Trail of Tears, the forced relocations of southeastern Native American tribes from their homelands to Oklahoma. Montgomery, the starting point of the rally, was significant in the civil rights movement. However, the alliance between Black and White activists remained tenuous (Bailey, Faupel, and Gundlach, 1993; Bailey, Faupel, and Holland, 1992; Nabokov, 1991).

Noxubee County, Mississippi

Noxubee County made headlines when corporations and venture capitalists battled each other to place an enormous landfill near the tiny settlement of Shuqualak in the 1980s and 1990s. Shuqualak is only about 15 miles from the Emelle landfill. Though there were no hazardous waste sites in Mississippi, the companies sought permits to dump hazardous wastes in Noxubee County. The proposed landfill would have had the capacity to process 200,000 tons of wastes annually. The ensuing controversy lasted several years. To put this in perspective, in 1990, the entire state of Mississippi produced only 45,000 tons of hazardous wastes. The 1990 census showed that roughly 35% of the residents of Mississippi were Black, but 68.1% of the 12,604 people living in the hypersegregated county of Noxubee were Black. At the time of the controversy, Shuqualak had 570 people, 60.2% of whom were Black. In the three census tracts that compose Noxubee County, between 39.9% and 45.2% of the residents live below the poverty level. Most people in the county did not complete high school; 26.1% had less than a ninth-grade education, and another 24.3% did not graduate from high school. Only 6.1% had a bachelor's degree and 1.9% a graduate degree (Melvin, 1994; U.S. Census Bureau, 1990; Alabama Department of Environmental Management, 2011; Crawford, 1996b). The county had an unemployment rate of about 12% (Dewitt, 1991).

The story of hazardous wastes in Noxubee County is complicated. It involves a Native American tribe (the Choctaws), Blacks, and Whites. The story also involves powerful corporations, venture capitalists, politicians, policymakers, several nonprofits, and the media. Local Native American and Black elites acted in ways that showed their interests were more aligned with the corporations and venture capitalists than with their neighbors. Consequently, before it was all over, Blacks, Whites, and Native Americans were arrayed on each side of the conflict (Crawford, 1996b).

AN ALTERNATIVE TO EMELLE

Like Sumter County, Noxubee County is located in what is known as the Black Prairie Belt. This is a reference to the thick black soil that covers the area. Selma chalk also underlies the county. There are other connections to Emelle too. As the opposition to the Emelle site grew, WMX searched for alternative locations to do business. The company explored the possibility of building a waste treatment facility in Shuqualak in 1982. In June of that year, about 225 people attended a town meeting about the proposed Noxubee Treatment Center, and in August, the town's board of aldermen endorsed the project. Some residents who opposed the plan formed a group called Protect the Environment of Noxubee (PEON) in late 1983 to campaign against the facility. In late spring 1985, PEON's indefatigable organizers managed to push a bill through the legislature that put a five-and-a-half-year moratorium on the siting of any commercial hazardous waste facilities in Mississippi. This effectively blocked WMX's bid. Though Ike Brown, the county's most notable Black politician and vice president of the local chapter of the NAACP, supported the project, some Blacks such as retired schoolteacher Essie Spencer were outspoken members of PEON who opposed the facility. However, Brown and some Blacks in Shuqualak expressed the view that the predominantly White members of PEON opposed WMX because they wanted Blacks to remain economically disadvantaged and in their control (Crawford, 1996b).

THE CHOCTAWS' INVOLVEMENT

PEON's strategy offered only a temporary respite as companies made plans, bided their time, and waited for the moratorium to expire. Thus, in 1988, a new group of developers entered the fray. National Disposal Systems, a Florence, Mississippi, company, also wanted to do business in Noxubee County. National Disposal Systems took a creative approach. It enlisted the help of Philip Martin, chief of the Mississippi Band of Choctaws. Martin was known for his aggressive courtship of companies to build facilities on the reservation. Under Martin's leadership, General Motors, Ford, Xerox, AT&T, and Navistar signed agreements with the tribe to build plants and produce goods on the reservation. Nevertheless, tribal members were not united behind Martin's economic development plans. Opponents were critical of the way the tribal council was run, the high wages Martin received, and the budget deficit the tribe ran. When National Disposal Systems approached the tribe in 1988, it made a proposal to purchase land and give it to Chief Martin and the tribe. In return, National Disposal Systems would lease the land from the tribe for 25 years to operate a hazardous waste disposal site. The Choctaws were also promised half a million dollars for the right to operate the facility, 10% of gross receipts from the facility, and a five-year rental fee of $125,000. Estimates were that the Choctaws could earn about $1 million per month from the facility. But there was a wrinkle—the land on which all of this would occur was located about 15 miles away from the reservation. Hence, the tribe and National Disposal Systems hatched an ingenious plan. The Choctaws would seek permission from the Department of the Interior to declare as trust lands the 483-acre parcel that National Disposal Systems purchased in 1990 and planned to hand over to the tribe. That way, that land would be governed by reservation rules (Crawford, 1996b; DeWitt, 1991).

Members of the tribe wanted to learn more about the waste disposal business, so they took a tour of the Emelle facility. When they arrived in Emelle, they were met by a group of ACE protestors. ACE activists feared the visit was a prelude to development of hazardous waste landfills in Noxubee County. The Choctaw reservation is in Neshoba County and is separated from Noxubee County by another county. The tribe had requested a tour of the Emelle landfill complex to get a better idea of how such a facility operated. Robert Benn, the Bureau of Indian Affairs' Choctaw Indian superintendent, said that tribal lands were subject to federal environmental regulations but exempt from state regulations. Linda Campbell, spokeswoman for ACE, charged that Choctaw Chief Philip Martin had received $500,000 from National Disposal Systems, but it is unclear what the money was for and what had been done with it (DeWitt, 1991).

Martin signed a contract (which was kept secret) with National Disposal Systems in July 1990; the tribe received a $300,000 signing bonus. The contract contained a pledge for the company to hire Choctaw workers and to establish a "host county/community" fund that would amount to 2% of gross revenues. However, the contract did not have any language that would hold National Disposal Systems responsible for liabilities that could arise in the new venture, a significant omission since National Disposal Systems was actually a shell company with limited assets. This meant the tribe would have been responsible for liabilities. There was also a possibility that the tribe could be left with a hazardous waste disposal facility on its hands if National Disposal Systems pulled out of the agreement after their 25-year lease was up. Details of the contract were leaked in November and December 1990. On December 21, the BIA representative to the Choctaw tribe recommended that the National Disposal Systems land be denied Indian trust land status.

The BIA representative noted that residents of Noxubee County were not notified of the plan for the site and might object to it; he also noted that members of the tribe were not fully apprised of the plans either. He indicated that the liability was also too high for the tribe to take on. On February 14, 1991, a group of Choctaws opposed to Martin's plans signed a petition to rescind the contract with National Disposal Systems. On April 19, the tribe voted 786 to 525 to reject the deal with National Disposal Systems (Crawford, 1996b).

COMPETING PROSPECTS

National Disposal Systems was not the only venture capitalists interested in Noxubee County as the possible site of a waste disposal facility. Ed Netherland and a group of venture capitalists began plans to build a waste disposal facility in the southeastern U.S. in 1988. He secured the backing of Gary Neal, chief operating officer of the Danner Company (which runs a chain of Shoney's and Captain D restaurants in the Southeast). The Danner Company committed $1 million to the venture. Out of this alliance, Federal Technologies, Incorporated (FTI), was born in 1989. FTI tried to place a facility in Marion County, Tennessee, but strong public opposition foiled its efforts. FTI tried again—this time in Giles County—but the opposition in this part of Tennessee was ferocious; hence, the consortium failed to construct an incinerator there also (Crawford, 1996b).

Wearied by the battles in Tennessee, in 1990, Ed Netherland and FTI began looking farther afield to Mississippi. By this time, Mississippi was interested in building a waste disposal facility because the legal tug-of-war over waste disposal at Emelle made Mississippi's governor and other politicians in the state feel as if they could no longer assume that they could simply ship their wastes across the border to Alabama. In 1990, FTI initiated plans to purchase a 6,000-acre ranch in Noxubee County from Martin Conrad for $3.5 million. The ranch actually belonged to the Indiana University Foundation (it was given to the foundation as a gift from Conrad in 1975 on condition that when it was sold, it would not be subdivided). In FTI's effort to get an upper hand on its competitors, it tried to get the Noxubee Board of Supervisors to pass a resolution stating that only one hazardous waste disposal facility could be built in the county. The resolution also promised not to consider any

other applications to build such a facility in the county until the Board of Supervisors had either issued a permit to FTI or denied its application. As opposition to FTI's plans increased, the company offered Noxubee County $1 million for the opportunity to construct the facility. It also offered to build a community center in the county. Some board members were eager to strike a deal with FTI even though FTI had not disclosed its financial assets to them. Like National Disposal Systems, there was no evidence that FTI could underwrite the liability that such a venture could pose. One board member urged caution and pushed others to ask FTI to build a school in the community also. The board voted on December 3 to endorse the FTI proposal. Three months later, in March 1991, FTI announced it was partnering with a Hughes Aircraft subsidiary (Hughes Environmental Systems) in the venture to build a $70 million waste facility in the county (the estimate for the facility rose to $80 million as competitors upped the ante). This consortium also planned to build a Center for Environmental Optimization to build and operate an incinerator and a landfill and to sponsor research. The consortium provided a $75,000 grant to Mississippi State University to study effective methods for handling wastes (Crawford, 1996b).

Union Pacific also sought to build a hazardous waste disposal facility in Noxubee County. Railroads transport large quantities of hazardous chemicals, so the rail industry expanded into the waste disposal business in the 1970s. Union Pacific's subsidiary United States Pollution Control, Incorporated (USPCI), handled the waste business. Venture capitalists operating under the name of Mississippi Farms began making inquiries about developing a waste disposal site in Noxubee County in 1989. They convinced Houston-based USPCI to explore the venture with them. By 1991, USPCI was making a concerted effort to build a hazardous waste facility in the county (Crawford, 1996b).

The local branch of the NAACP supported the FTI–Hughes Aircraft bid to build the landfill-incinerator complex in Shuqualak while opposing a USPCI proposal. While FTI had expended much time and effort garnering support in the Black community, USPCI virtually ignored this constituency. Ike Brown was a paid consultant to Hughes. He was a vocal supporter of the Hughes bid and got the local NAACP to pass a resolution supporting the project (Crawford, 1996b).

Since there were two rivals still vying to build a waste disposal facility in Noxubee County, by 1993, FTI-Hughes promised a capital investment of $150 million, garbage service, a "Good Neighbor" fund, and new uniforms for the girls' basketball team. FTI-Hughes also offered to pay the minimum wage of $7 per hour at a time when most people in the surrounding area made $6 per hour. In turn, USPCI promised to build a community center for the county, to construct a municipal landfill, to establish a trust fund to finance community development projects, and to sponsor the girls' basketball team. The county board eventually hired a consulting firm to evaluate the deals, and the firm reported that neither of the offers was a good deal in terms of *compensating the host community*—Noxubee County. There were several suggestions in the report for counteroffers that the county should make that would provide funds to the county before construction began and during the operation of the facility (Crawford, 1996b).

PEON was back in the thick of things during the 1990s. The group was a vocal critic of the plans to site a waste disposal facility in the county; it organized community opposition to all the proposals. Prominent national Black EJ activists such as Damu Smith of Greenpeace visited Noxubee County and collaborated with the opposition. In addition, local Black opponents of the waste facility plan emerged and provided an alternative voice to Ike Brown and the NAACP. Nonetheless, the NAACP continued to support the FTI-Hughes proposal. It pointed out that only FTI-Hughes had consulted the Black community and involved it in any of the discussions regarding the proposed waste facility. The NAACP's stance prompted a group of Blacks—led by John Gibson and Essie Spencer—to form African Americans for Environmental Justice (AAEJ) to oppose the landfill. AAEJ asked the EPA to investigate whether the state violated Title VI of the Civil Rights Act in permitting the dump. The state's Department of Environmental Quality and Office of Pollution Control took umbrage at the charge of environmental racism. Charles Chisolm of the Office of Pollution Control asserted that the requirements were racially neutral. Other state officials argued that they did not pick the site; a private company did (Melvin, 1994; Crawford, 1996b).

In January 1993, PEON sued the governor of the state, challenging the legality of the Environmental Protection Council, which was charged with overseeing the process. The circuit court judge, James E. Graves

Jr., ruled in favor of PEON. Opposition to the waste disposal proposals continued to mount, and in April 1993, FTI-Hughes announced that it had not exercised its option on the Conrad ranch, while the Indiana University Foundation announced that the land was up for sale. In May, all but one of the FTI-Hughes boosters had lost their seats in the Macon and Brooksville city elections and were replaced with anti-waste-dump advocates. Much to the surprise of many locals, FTI-Hughes and USPCI merged. However, by the end of 1993, the FTI-Hughes office in the county was closed and all the staff dismissed. USPCI sought the support of the NAACP but in May 1994 decided to close its Macon and Shuqualak offices. The company was put up for sale in October; at this time, the company also announced that it would no longer try to build a hazardous waste facility in Noxubee County (Crawford, 1996b).

Examining the Unique Physical Characteristics Thesis

Crawford (1996a) examined whether the unique geological formation of the Selma chalk was responsible for which community was chosen to host landfills in Mississippi. Waste company executives insisted that the Noxubee County site was chosen because of its geological characteristics—the Selma chalk. Crawford studied Noxubee and six adjoining counties of similar geological characteristics. He found that Noxubee County had the lowest per-capita income, the highest percentage of food stamp and welfare recipients, the highest rates of live births to unmarried women, the highest unemployment, and a high rate of illiteracy and infant mortality. Baden and Coursey (2002) also examined the unique physical characteristics thesis in their longitudinal study of hazardous waste facilities in Chicago. They found that proximity to waterways was positively related to the siting of such facilities. Zahran, Hastings, and Brody (2008) also examined this thesis and found that the siting of TSDFs in the southeastern United States was influenced by hydrological suitability.

C. Smith's (2007) study of the placement of landfill sites in Detroit found that these sites were significantly more likely to be located in census tracts with navigable waterways, in tracts where a landfill or Superfund site previously existed, or adjacent to such tracts. Smith also studied the location of seven Superfund sites in Detroit and found that they were most likely to be sited in census tracts with navigable waterways, adjacent to expressways, and in census tracts with a lower percentage of owner-occupied units.

Manipulation, Enticement, and Environmental Blackmail

Bullard (1990) details how African American communities in the Southeast were coerced into making *trade-offs* between health risks, jobs, and other economic incentives such as better schools and recreational amenities when they chose to host hazardous facilities. Researchers have also documented the political machinations and enticements that poor Blacks and Native Americans were offered to host hazardous landfills (Crawford, 1996b; Schneider, 1993; Nossiter, 1991; Bailey and Faupel, 1992a, 1992b; Bailey, Faupel, and Gundlach, 1993; Boerner and Lambert, 1995). Similar processes have been described in Hispanic and Black communities in South Central Los Angeles (Blumberg and Gottlieb, 1989) and Robbins, Illinois (Pellow, 2002). Though researchers such as Boerner and Lambert (1995) argue that the *economic benefits* of poor, minority communities hosting hazardous facilities outweigh the *costs*, they provide sketchy evidence to support this claim—they list perceived benefits but not the costs of hosting such facilities.

As the preceding discussions about attempts to site hazardous facilities on Native American reservations and in other minority communities show, companies trying to site such facilities stress the economic benefits (such as jobs and increased tax revenues) of the facilities when dealing with low-income and minority communities. Economic benefits are more influential in swaying poor communities to accept hazardous facilities than they are in affluent communities (Higgins, 1993; Crawford, 1996b; Ishiyama and TallBear, 2001; Thorpe, 1996; J. Weaver, 1997; Churchill and LaDuke, 1992; Brugge, Benally, and Yazzie-Lewis, 2006).

Long after noxious facilities are sited and the environment degraded, companies still tout their charitable contributions to communities. For instance, the Alcoa Foundation reported giving $301,000 to seven local organizations in 2012. This included $53,000 to Jefferson Elementary School for smart boards, $120,000 to Clarkson University for the Mytholympic Games, $38,500 to the St. Lawrence County Community Development program to develop a tracking system for food pantry users, $18,047 to the Friends of the Robert Moses State Park Nature Center, and $15,000 to support the FISHCAP economic development program. The remainder of the funds went to area hospitals (ALCOA, 2012a).

Compensating Host Communities

Boerner and Lambert argue that "prohibitions on siting . . . in minority and low-income neighborhoods are likely to economically harm the residents of those neighborhoods. Essentially, proposals to prohibit, limit, or discourage polluting facilities from locating in minority and low-income communities deny those areas the economic benefits associated with hosting industrial and waste plants" (1995: 90). The scholars argue further that the "benefits far outweigh the cost of hosting such facilities" (90). The researchers suggest that minority and low-income communities be allowed to make trade-offs and decide whether to host such facilities. That is, TSDF operators can obtain approval for their proposals from regulators and targeted communities by offering direct payments and agreeing to tonnage taxes.

Others such as David Taylor (1999), Jenkins, Maguire, and Morgan (2004), and Been (1994a), have also argued that host-community compensation can benefit communities in which hazardous facilities are sited. However, the preceding discussions highlight the challenges that minority and low-income communities face in negotiating compensation. As the cases involving Native reservations and Black communities in the South show, one cannot fully negotiate compensation if one does not know *what* can be negotiated for and *with whom* to negotiate. In the case studies discussed earlier, waste disposal companies were quick to dangle the promise of jobs before communities; they were also willing to fund local clubs and organizations or build a community center when pressed. However, these "benefits" only scratch the surface. Compensation did not include health care. When the Diamond community in Norco demanded health coverage, Shell flatly denied such compensation. The compensation packages do not include strict environmental protection for current and future generations. Housing and property values seem not to be up for discussion either. Yet numerous studies such as those discussed earlier indicate that property values suffer from being in close proximity to hazardous facilities or what is left behind after the companies pull up stakes. Even the question of jobs is nebulous. In the case of Norco and Emelle, jobs for host-community residents were few. Even though Native American reservations host hazardous facilities, the unemployment rates are still high and wages low in these communities.

Boerner and Lambert (1995) report that residents of Emelle are "happy" to host the landfill; however, despite the benefits these authors claim will accrue to communities hosting hazardous facilities, the town and county are still poor. Though the Emelle facility generated more than a billion dollars in revenues from 1981 to 1995, little of that income trickled down to local residents (*State of Alabama v. EPA*, 1990; *Gregory v. Chemical Waste Management*, 1996; *Hunt v. Chemical Waste Management*, 1991). The latest census data show that poverty levels are still high in Emelle and Sumter County, and incomes in the area still lag behind the rest of the state and the country as a whole (U.S. Census Bureau, 2010). But do communities such as Emelle get the benefits of added environmental protection from the state? In 1980, the Conservation Foundation released a study in which it found that Alabama spent $39 per person on pollution control, while the national average was $71 per person (Crawford, 1996b).

As the preceding discussion shows, states such as Louisiana, Mississippi, and Alabama structure their taxes and environmental policies to benefit industries. They offer up to ten years of local property tax relief (Roberts and Toffolon-Weiss, 2001; B. Wright, 2005; Louisiana Economic Development, 2012; Mississippi Development Authority, 2012; *Chemical Waste Management v. State of Alabama*, 1987). An example of Louisiana's business-friendly environmental policies can be seen in the regulation of oil-field waste. In 1980, Congress gave states control over the regulation of such wastes. Louisiana decided to classify its oil-field waste as nonhazardous; these wastes—which contain carcinogens and radioactive materials—are injected into pits without any additional regulation or remediation (Roberts and Toffolon-Weiss, 2001; Koeppel, 1999).

Bullard and Wright (2012) suggest a *fenceline-community performance bond*. They argue that before companies are issued an operating permit, they should establish a buffer that requires a safe distance between the facility and residential communities. This idea was also suggested in the *Toxic Wastes and Race at Twenty* report (Bullard, Mohai, Saha, and Wright, 2007).

Inviting Facilities In

Low-income and ethnic-minority communities sometimes play a role in inviting hazardous facilities and land uses into their communities. This is the case with the storage of nuclear wastes on Native reservations (Clarke, 2002). Robbins, Illinois, is another case in point. The cash-starved, poverty-stricken town tried for years to attract a waste company. In 1986, Robbins, the Reading Energy Company, and Foster Wheeler, Inc., struck a deal to build a $23 million incinerator that would generate $2 million a year in rental fees for the town. The state of Illinois subsidized the construction of the facility. That was a controversial plan that had Black supporters and opponents on both sides of the issue. Despite fervent opposition, the incinerator—graced by a 37-storey-tall white smokestack—opened in 1997. However, Foster Wheeler lost about $1 million per month on the incinerator; hence, it offered Robbins $600,000 less than promised. The incinerator had numerous environmental violations in the short time it operated. The facility was shuttered in 1999 (Pellow, 2002).

Though there are instances when minorities invite hazardous facilities into their communities, this is the exception rather than the rule. This practice does not account for the thousands of hazardous facilities that are sited in minority communities around the country.

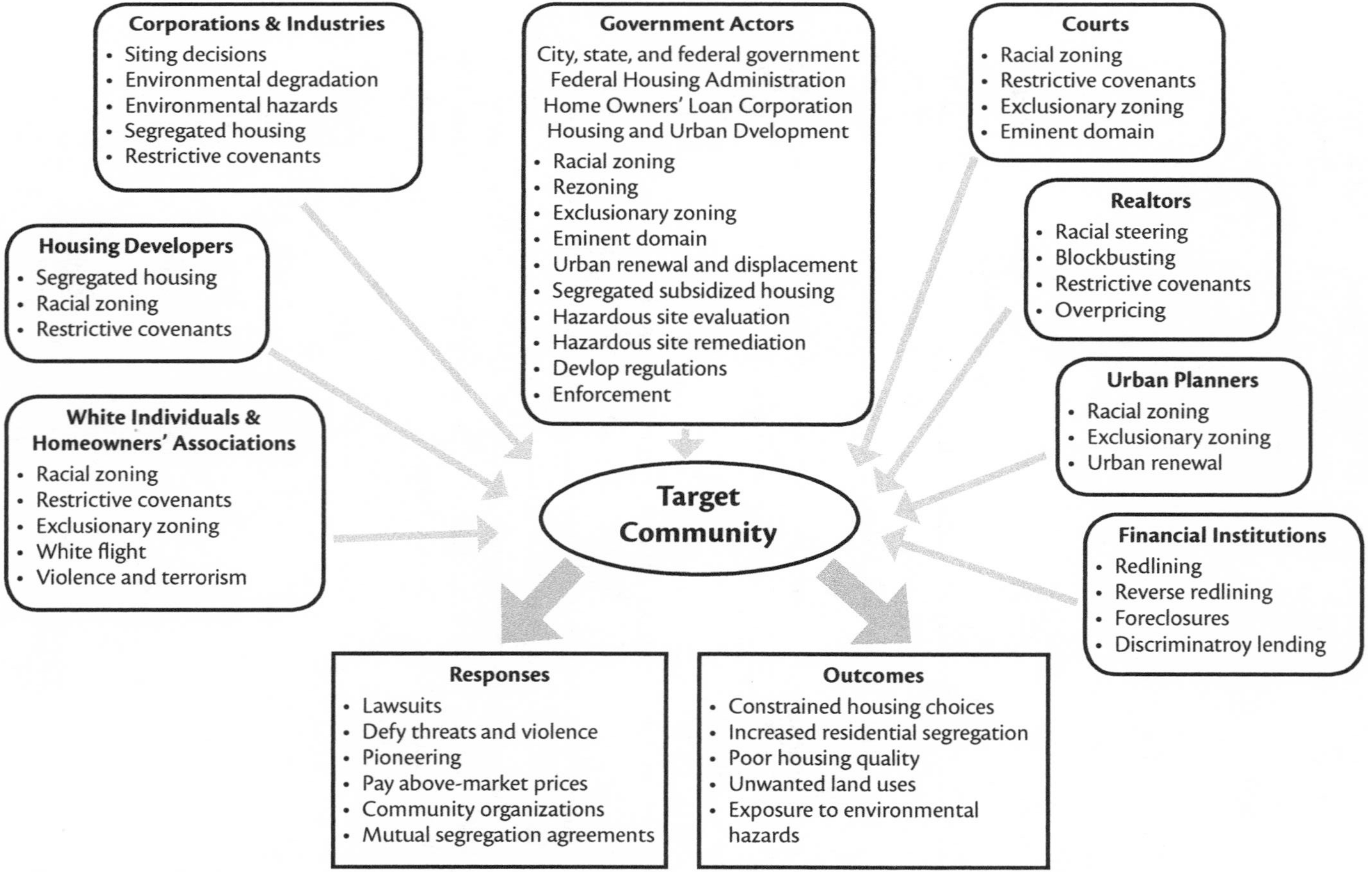

Courts
- Racial zoning
- Restrictive covenants
- Exclusionary zoning
- Eminent domain

Realtors
- Racial steering
- Blockbusting
- Restrictive covenants
- Overpricing

Urban Planners
- Racial zoning
- Exclusionary zoning
- Urban renewal

Financial Institutions
- Redlining
- Reverse redlining
- Foreclosures
- Discriminatroy lending

Government Actors
City, state, and federal government
Federal Housing Administration
Home Owners' Loan Corporation
Housing and Urban Dvelopment
- Racial zoning
- Rezoning
- Exclusionary zoning
- Eminent domain
- Urban renewal and displacement
- Segregated subsidized housing
- Hazardous site evaluation
- Hazardous site remediation
- Develop regulations
- Enforcement

Corporations & Industries
- Siting decisions
- Environmental degradation
- Environmental hazards
- Segregated housing
- Restrictive covenants

Housing Developers
- Segregated housing
- Racial zoning
- Restrictive covenants

White Individuals & Homeowners' Associations
- Racial zoning
- Restrictive covenants
- Exclusionary zoning
- White flight
- Violence and terrorism

Target Community

Outcomes
- Constrained housing choices
- Increased residential segregation
- Poor housing quality
- Unwanted land uses
- Exposure to environmental hazards

Responses
- Lawsuits
- Defy threats and violence
- Pioneering
- Pay above-market prices
- Community organizations
- Mutual segregation agreements

Figure 7.1. Urban racial containment: actors, actions, and constraints on housing choices

7

The Rise of Racial Zoning

Residential Segregation

Much of the existing EJ research identifies aspects of but does not fully explicate the complex patterns of residential inequalities that character-ize urban and rural areas. This is the case because regression models and spatial analyses, particularly those conducted at large scales (national and regional), are limited in their ability to unmask the complex factors that influence population shifts in particular cities and towns. The EJ research is also limited by the questions that scholars ask and explore. That is, if one simply asks the question, *Who came first*, the noxious facility or the minorities? one gets an answer that indicates whether a facility was built first or if a community existed before a facility was constructed. However, this answer does nothing to elucidate the *process* by which the past or present-day population came to live adjacent to that facility. Though scholars have tried to answer the question of who or what came first, a more pressing question—and one that is not often explored in the EJ literature—is, *Who or what keeps* people living adja-cent to noxious facilities and undesirable land uses?

Figure 7.1 is a schematic depiction of the major actors and actions that help to account for who or what keeps people living in undesirable locales or in particular sections of cities and towns. As the figure shows, the EJ literature has focused heavily on a subset of corporate (siting, environmental degradation, and hazards) and government actions (regulation, enforcement, and hazardous site evaluation and remedia-tion) but has paid little attention to a myriad of other factors that influ-ence where minorities and low-income people live in cities and why they continue to inhabit those places.

Though figure 7.1 identifies only the major actors, actions, and impacts, this is done solely for the sake of clarity and simplicity. The remaining chapters of this book contain detailed discussions of the complex relationships between the actors, the ways in which actions are coordinated, and the ways in which outcomes are predetermined. The chapters also analyze the complex relationship between minority communities and the various actors interested in controlling residential patterns. Though the arrows are depicted as unidirectional, those representations reflect the dominant force of the influence. In many cases, the actions and impacts have been recursive. That is, the target communities responded to actions directed at them, and those who were targeting them made counter-responses. The ensuing discussion demonstrates the need for greater understanding of the historical and contemporary processes that impact residential patterns in communities of interest.

The Traditional Ecological Model and the Dual Housing Model

The EJ literature examines the impacts of environmental hazards on Black, Asian, Hispanic, and Native American communities because such minority neighborhoods are readily identifiable. Predominantly minority neighborhoods persist because residential segregation is a pervasive feature of American society. Understanding residential segregation is important in the context of this discussion, as studies find that residential segregation is related to exposure to environmental hazards. For Blacks and Hispanics in particular, high incomes *do not protect* them from segregation (Logan, 2001; de Leeuw et al., 2007). Ard (2013) has found that high incomes do not protect Blacks from exposure to pollution either.

Though scholars agree that segregated housing patterns still exist in municipalities across the U.S., they disagree on the origins of these patterns and why they persist. There are competing theoretical explanations for why this is the case. Some scholars espouse a traditional ecological model that posits that segregation is a *natural process* that arises from competition for housing between different racial and ethnic groups (Kasarda, 1972; Berry and Kasarda, 1977). However, proponents of a rival theory—the dual housing model—believe that segregation ensues because Whites not only *preempt* the best housing in urban centers but *monopolize* new construction in suburbia too. Consequently, minorities are left with inferior housing and restricted choices (Sterns and Logan, 1986).

This process is facilitated by realtors and financial institutions whose practices help to limit minorities to housing no longer desirable by Whites. Because realtors can control the flow of information about housing and financial institutions control funds, these two groups can effectively define and maintain the existence of "minority" and "White" communities. They can also stymie the growth of racially mixed neighborhoods by redlining them or declaring them blighted (Taggart and Smith, 1981; Lake, 1981; Leahy, 1985). Local governments also play a role in segregation, in that they sometimes use racially restrictive, exclusionary, and expulsive zoning laws that promote racially homogeneous neighborhoods and limit where minorities can live (Rabin, 1990; Young, 2005; D.E. Taylor, 2009).

Scholars also point to a practice in the South in which small towns that are expanding their borders and annexing nearby communities tend to exclude communities of color on their fringes from the annexation process. This usually results in minority enclaves that have access to no or inferior public services. In some cases, the expanding towns exercise regulatory power over the excluded enclaves—the residents of which cannot vote in municipal elections (de Leeuw et al., 2007; Aiken, 1987; Lichter, 2007; University of North Carolina Center for Civil Rights, 2006). Lichter (2007) found that White towns were less likely to annex Black communities, regardless of size.

Racialization of Zoning

Zoning and housing segregation play important roles in dictating historical and contemporary residential patterns. Unfortunately, the chicken-or-egg debate obscures the fact that even if one proves that a hazardous facility was operational before minorities began residing in surrounding neighborhoods, discriminatory zoning laws and housing practices intended to constrain the residential options of minorities help to account for the presence of minorities around these facilities. As scholars such as Maantay (2002) argue, zoning laws have far-reaching effects on where noxious land uses are located and the environmental and health impacts that arise from such uses. She contends that this is the case because zoning acts as a *driver* of where noxious land uses can be legally located within a municipality. Boone (2005) makes a similar argument.

In America, the use of zoning laws to *promote and enforce* segregation is ubiquitous. Initially, zoning laws were developed and used as a mechanism to separate land uses, to regulate building heights, and to protect the aesthetic character of neighborhoods. However, during the early twentieth century, zoning ordinances evolved, and many cities used them to separate Blacks and other minorities from White residents (D.E. Taylor, 2009). H.L. Pollard, a notable attorney for the Los Angeles Realty Board and the California Real Estate Association, claims that "racial hatred played no small part in bringing to the front some of the early districting ordinances that were sustained by the United States Supreme Court, thus giving us our first important zoning decisions" (qtd. in Weiss, 1987: 83–84).

Though the last of the racially restrictive zoning laws were struck down by the courts decades ago, the lingering effects of racial zoning are still evident. This is the case because zoning laws stipulating where people of different races or ethnic groups could live were coupled with powerful *institutional tools and practices* aimed at controlling residential and industrial land uses and fostering segregation. These were buttressed by deep-rooted prejudice and the individual and collective discriminatory behavior of ordinary citizens.

As this chapter shows, historical discriminatory zoning laws have lingering impacts on residential patterns. This chapter discusses a variety of zoning laws and the myriad of ways in which they were used to restrict Blacks' and other minorities' residence and movement in cities. Racial zoning laws—which were more commonly used in southern and western cities than in northern ones—were enacted for the following purposes:

1. To designate separate city blocks on which Whites lived and ones on which Blacks and other people of color lived

2. To withhold building permits from people trying to build in areas where the majority of the residents were of a different racial group than the applicant
3. To make it illegal for people to live on a street where the majority of the residents were of a racial group they were forbidden by law to marry (antimiscegenation)
4. To create buffer strips to separate Blacks and Whites
5. To create agreements between Whites and Blacks about racial districts each would inhabit
6. To invoke executive military segregation orders
7. To designate Black and other minority neighborhoods as commercial, industrial, or manufacturing districts

Widespread violence, threats, and intimidation accompanied the institution of these ordinances. In addition, walls, fences, and other physical barriers were constructed to hinder the movement of Blacks and to enforce segregation. The ensuing racial conflicts spilled into the courts, where litigation was frequent, tactical, and long running.

Anti-Chinese Restrictive Zoning Ordinances

As the case of Yick Wo v. Hopkins (1886) indicates, the Chinese were the target of early discriminatory land-use ordinances. They were also the target of the earliest racially restrictive zoning ordinances. In 1890, Chinese residents of San Francisco were arrested for violating Order No. 2190. The so-called Bingham Ordinance stipulated the location and district in which the more than 20,000 Chinese residents of the city could reside and conduct business. The ordinance, which went into effect on February 17 of that year, stated, "It is hereby declared to be unlawful for any Chinese to locate, reside, or carry on a business within the limits of the city and county of San Francisco, except in that district of said city and county hereinafter prescribed for their location." The ordinance also stipulated the length of time (60 days) that Chinese residents had to comply with the new ordinance. Any Chinese who did not comply was found guilty of a misdemeanor and jailed for up to six months (In re Lee Sing, 1890: 4; Federal Reporter, 1890: 359).

The ordinance passed despite the fact that the 1868 Burlingame

Treaty between the U.S. and China stated that "Chinese subjects, visiting or residing in the United States, shall enjoy the same privileges, immunities and exemptions in respect to travel or residence, as there may be enjoyed by the citizens or subjects of the most favored nation" (Burlingame Treaty, 1868). In deciding the case, Circuit Court Judge Lorenzo Sawyer argued that "the gross inequality of the operation of this ordinance upon Chinese, as compared with others, in violation of the constitutional, treaty, and statutory provisions cited, are so manifest upon its face, that I am unable to comprehend how this discrimination . . . can fail to be apparent to the mind of every intelligent person" (*In re Lee Sing*, 1890: 3; *Federal Reporter*, 1890: 360).

Black Migration—The Impetus for the Spread of Racial Zoning

By the second decade of the twentieth century, the courts signaled that they would uphold municipal ordinances that partitioned cities into commercial and residential zones or restricted how tall buildings could be. Around the time municipalities in the North were developing and passing zoning laws to protect property values and the aesthetic appeal of neighborhoods, southern city councils began passing ordinances to test their effectiveness at enforcing racial segregation (D.E. Taylor, 2009).

Though the Chinese were the first targets of racially restrictive ordinances, Blacks were the most frequent targets. Southern cities were the first to enact anti-Black zoning ordinances. This is the case because the Great Northern Migration of Blacks really began as a southern phenomenon. Between 1870 and 1900, many Blacks moved from one part of the South to the next and to points westward. They also moved from rural to urban areas of the South to take advantage of job opportunities and to follow the expanding cotton cultivation. In 1879, for instance, Blacks began moving from Mississippi and Louisiana to Kansas. One activist, Henry Adams of Louisiana, organized about 98,000 Blacks for this exodus. Hence, by 1920, a fourth of southern Blacks lived in urban centers (Fligstein, 1981; Tolnay and Beck, 1991; Weise, 2004).

To understand Black migration patterns, I analyzed the demographic characteristics of 32 cities that had a Black population of 80,000 or

more in 1970. Table 7.1 shows that with the exception of Jacksonville, the percentage of Blacks in southern cities in 1860 was between 10% and 38%. Blacks made up more than a fourth of the population in three cities—Jacksonville, Norfolk, and Richmond. The most dramatic rise in the Black population occurred in Memphis, where the percentage of Blacks increased from 17.2% in 1860 to 40% in 1910. The Black population rose rapidly in Norfolk, Atlanta, and Nashville over the same period also. By 1910, the Black population exceeded 25% of the population in ten southern cities.

As later discussions will show, the Black population did not have to be particularly large for the increase to trigger racial zoning, restrictive covenants, anti-Black violence, and other attempts to control the size of said population as well as the residential patterns of the urban areas. These responses occurred all over the country even when the proportion of Blacks in particular cities remained relatively stable.

The increasing number of Blacks residing in southern cities alarmed Whites. This concern was magnified after the 1906 race riot in Atlanta (Crowe, 1969; Burlein, 2001; Godshalk, 2005; Mixom, 2005). Race riots broke out in other southern cities between 1917 and 1921. The riots occurred in Houston, Winston-Salem, Millen (Georgia), Charleston, Washington, D.C., Knoxville, Elaine (Arkansas), Tulsa, and Augusta (Jones-Correa, 2000–2001).

Whites also responded to the burgeoning Black population by using intimidation tactics and coercion, increasing rents, enlisting realtors to limit the sections of the cities in which Blacks were allowed to rent or purchase property, and working with urban planners to devise racially restrictive zoning ordinances. Whites also entered into private agreements that used restrictive covenants to limit which neighborhoods Blacks could settle in (Silver, 1997; D.E. Taylor, 2009). For instance, a study of racial differences in rental costs found that in St. Louis, Blacks paid about 15% more than Whites for similar housing in the same neighborhood. The study also found that, overall, housing costs were more than 25% higher in Black neighborhoods than in White neighborhoods (Yinger, Galster, Smith, and Eggers, 1978). Realtors played an important role in facilitating segregation efforts. For example, the St. Louis Real Estate Board prohibited its realtors from selling or renting

Table 7.1. Number and Percentage of Blacks in Selected Cities with 80,000 or More Blacks in 1970: 1910–1970

Selected cities	% Black in 1860	1910 No. Blacks	1910 %	1920 No. Blacks	1920 %	1930 No. Blacks	1930 %	1940 No. Blacks	1940 %	1950 No. Blacks	1950 %	1960 No. Blacks	1960 %	1970 No. Blacks	1970 %	Increase in no. of Blacks
Jacksonville, FL	46.5	29,293	50.8	41,520	45.3	48,196	37.2	61,782	35.7	72,450	35.4	82,525	41.1	118,158	22.3	76,638
Memphis, TN	17.2	52,441	40.0	61,181	37.7	96,550	38.1	121,498	41.5	147,141	37.2	184,320	37.0	242,513	38.9	181,332
Birmingham, AL		52,305	39.4	70,230	39.3	99,077	38.2	108,938	40.7	130,025	39.9	135,113	39.6	126,388	42.0	56,158
Norfolk, VA	29.6	25,039	37.1	43,392	37.5	43,942	33.9	45,893	31.8	62,826	29.4	78,806	25.8	87,261	28.3	43,869
Richmond, VA	37.7	46,733	36.6	54,041	31.5	52,988	29.0	61,251	31.7	72,996	31.7	91,972	41.8	104,766	42.0	50,725
Atlanta, GA	20.3	51,902	33.5	62,796	31.3	90,075	33.3	104,533	34.6	121,285	36.6	186,464	38.3	255,051	51.3	192,255
Nashville, TN	23.2	36,523	33.1	35,633	30.1	42,836	27.8	47,318	28.3	54,696	31.4	64,570	37.8	87,851	19.6	52,218
Houston, TX	22.2	23,929	30.4	33,960	24.6	63,337	21.7	86,302	22.4	124,766	20.9	215,037	22.9	316,551	25.7	282,591
Washington, D.C.	18.0	94,446	28.5	109,966	25.1	132,068	27.1	187,266	28.2	280,803	35.0	411,737	53.9	537,712	71.1	427,746
New Orleans, LA	14.3	89,262	26.3	100,930	26.1	129,632	28.3	149,034	30.1	181,775	31.9	233,514	37.2	267,308	45.0	166,378
Dallas, TX		18,024	19.6	24,023	15.1	38,742	14.9	50,047	17.1	56,958	13.1	129,242	19.0	210,238	24.9	186,215
Louisville, KY	10.0	40,522	18.1	40,087	17.1	47,354	15.4	47,158	14.8	57,657	15.6	70,075	17.9	86,040	23.8	45,953
Baltimore, MD	13.1	84,749	14.2	108,322	14.8	142,106	17.7	165,843	19.3	225,099	23.7	325,589	34.7	420,210	46.4	311,888
Kansas City, MO	4.3	23,566	9.5	30,719	9.5	38,574	9.6	41,574	10.4	55,682	12.2	83,146	17.5	112,005	22.1	81,286
Indianapolis, IN	2.7	21,816	9.3	34,678	11.0	43,967	12.1	51,142	13.2	63,867	15.0	98,049	20.6	134,320	18.0	99,642
Columbus, OH	5.4	12,739	7.0	22,181	9.4	32,774	11.3	35,765	11.7	46,692	12.4	77,140	16.4	99,627	18.5	77,446
St. Louis, MO	2.1	43,960	6.4	69,854	9.0	93,580	11.4	108,765	13.3	153,766	17.9	214,377	28.6	254,191	40.9	184,337
Philadelphia, PA	3.9	84,459	5.5	134,229	7.4	219,599	11.3	250,880	13.0	376,041	18.2	529,240	26.4	653,791	33.6	519,562
Cincinnati, OH	2.3	19,639	5.4	30,079	7.5	47,818	10.6	55,593	12.2	78,196	15.5	108,754	21.6	125,070	27.6	94,991
Pittsburgh, PA	2.3	25,623	4.8	37,725	6.4	54,983	8.2	62,216	9.3	82,453	12.2	100,692	16.7	104,904	20.2	67,179
Newark, NJ	1.8	9,475	2.7	16,977	4.1	38,880	8.8	45,760	10.6	74,965	17.1	138,035	34.1	207,458	54.2	190,481
Los Angeles, CA	1.5	7,599	2.4	15,579	2.7	38,894	3.1	63,774	4.2	171,209	8.7	334,916	13.5	503,606	17.9	488,027
Gary, IN		383	2.3	5,299	9.6	17,922	17.8	20,394	18.3	39,253	29.3	69,123	38.8	92,695	52.8	87,396
Chicago, IL	0.9	44,103	2.0	109,458	4.1	233,903	6.9	277,731	8.2	492,265	13.6	812,637	22.9	1,102,620	32.7	993,162
Oakland, CA	1.2	3,055	2.0	5,489	2.5	7,503	2.6	8,462	2.8	47,562	12.4	83,618	22.8	124,710	34.5	119,221
Boston, MA	1.3	13,564	2.0	16,350	2.2	20,574	2.6	23,679	3.1	40,057	5.0	63,165	9.1	104,707	16.3	88,357
New York, NY	1.5	91,709	1.9	152,467	2.7	327,706	4.7	458,444	6.1	747,608	9.5	1,087,931	14.0	1,668,115	21.1	1,515,648
Cleveland, OH	1.8	8,448	1.5	34,451	4.3	71,899	8.0	84,504	9.6	147,847	16.2	250,818	28.6	287,841	38.3	253,390
Detroit, MI	3.1	5,741	1.2	40,838	4.1	120,066	7.7	149,119	9.2	300,506	16.2	482,223	28.9	660,428	43.7	619,590
Buffalo, NY	1.0	1,773	0.4	4,511	0.9	13,563	2.4	17,694	3.1	36,645	6.3	70,904	13.3	94,329	20.4	89,818
San Francisco, CA	2.1	1,642	0.4	2,414	0.5	3,803	0.6	4,846	0.8	43,502	5.6	74,383	10.0	96,078	13.4	93,664
Milwaukee, WI	0.2	980	0.3	2,229	0.5	7,501	1.3	8,821	1.5	21,772	3.4	62,458	8.4	105,088	14.7	102,859

Source: Gibson and Jung, 2005.

property located in White neighborhoods to Blacks in 1923 (Real Estate Board of Chicago, 1917; *St. Louis Real Estate Bulletin*, 1923).

Though southern cities experienced a rise in the Black population first, Blacks also began moving to the North because they were drawn by economic opportunities and a less hostile racial climate. The rate of Black migration was slow yet steady before 1910 but increased dramatically after that. As table 7.1 shows, the Black population exceeded 5% of the population in only one northern city in 1860; that was Columbus, Ohio, where they made up 5.4% of the population. Up until the first decade of the twentieth century, the Black population grew slowly in northern cities. In fact only Indianapolis, Columbus, Philadelphia, and Cincinnati had Black populations that exceeded 5% as late as 1910. Between 1870 and 1910, about 535,000 Blacks left the South for the North. However, in the next four decades, around 3.5 million followed suit (Collins, 1997; C. Brown, 1998). Scholars such as James Grossman extend the period of migration to 1970. Estimates are that from 1916 to 1970, approximately seven million Blacks left the South for the North (Grossman, 1989, 2005).

Racial Zoning in Southern and Western Cities

Baltimore—Color Blocks

Southern cities explored zoning as a form of *land-use regulation* and as a *mechanism to facilitate residential segregation* simultaneously. Baltimore was at the vanguard of these efforts. Black Baltimoreans did not live in segregated neighborhoods as late as the 1860s, but as the Black population grew, the city's neighborhoods became increasingly segregated (Power, 1983). In the early 1900s, Baltimore's leaders argued over and passed legislation to limit the height of buildings to 70 feet in localities that had monuments, churches, public buildings, and upscale residences (Power, 1984). The Maryland court decision followed others upholding building height restrictions in New York in 1888 and Boston in 1906 (*New York Times*, 1913; D.E. Taylor, 2009).

However, while northern cities continued to focus on zoning as a mechanism to regulate building height and commercial districts, southern cities began using zoning as a tool to *impose racial order* on cities. Baltimore is an example of this. Though the racial climate in the city was tense and there were minor incidents of violence and vandalism, these factors in and of themselves did not trigger anti-Black zoning ordinances. The city's White residents decided to put a racially restrictive ordinance in place only after a prominent Black attorney, W. Ashbie Hawkins, purchased a house at 1834 McCulloh Street in May 1910. George McMechen, another prominent Black attorney and graduate of the Yale Law School, leased the property from Hawkins and moved in with his wife (Anna, a schoolteacher) in June. The police were summoned to protect the house from vigilantes who hurled stones and bricks through the windows and threatened to blow up the house. Despite the uproar, three other Black families moved onto the same block shortly after the McMechens did. Whites convened a mass meeting on July 5, and attendees prepared a petition demanding that the mayor and city council stop the incursion of Blacks into the neighborhood (*New York Times*, 1910; Hawkins, 1911; Carle, 2002). The petition asked the mayor and city council to "take some measures to restrain the colored people from locating in a White community, and proscribe a limit beyond which it shall be unlawful for them to go" (Petition, 1910). The fear of Blacks moving into White neighborhoods prompted the drafting of a racially restrictive ordinance. Indeed, the mayor—J. Barry Mahool—explained that "this so-called segregation ordinance" arose because "the first negro[es] began to have a desire to push up into the neighborhood of the White resident" (*New York Times*, 1910: 10).

Baltimore's first racially restrictive ordinance was drafted by an attorney, Milton Dashiell, who lived at 1110 McCulloh Street—just one block from the Black neighborhood of Biddle Alley. Despite the objections of Blacks and with no Republicans on the council voting for it, the ordinance passed. The ordinance made it illegal for any Blacks to move onto a block where more than half the residents were White, and vice versa. Blacks were also prohibited from using any residences on White blocks as places of public assembly, and vice versa. Violators could be fined up to $30 and imprisoned for 30 days to a year. The city solicitor, Edgar Allan Poe (lawyer and grandnephew of the famous poet), declared the ordinance constitutional on December 17, and Mayor Mahool signed it into law on December 20, 1910 (*New York Times*, 1910; Power, 1983; Silver, 1997).

Blacks were not the only ones who objected to the ordinance; White property owners living in racially mixed neighborhoods and realtors believing the law would dampen business objected to it also. Within a month of its passage, 26 criminal cases against violators were sent to trial. The ordinance was declared ineffective and void in the first case tried. That decision prompted segregationists to try harder to craft an ordinance that could withstand legal challenges. Councilman Samuel West—who had sponsored the first racially restrictive ordinance in the council—decided to engage William Marbury to draft a revised ordinance. Marbury made sure that the prohibitions on Blacks moving onto White blocks and vice versa did not apply to mixed-race blocks. That removed one of the objections to the ordinance. Mahool signed the new ordinance on April 7, 1911. However, about a month after its passage, the city council repealed it. In the third iteration of the ordinance, the council added an amendment stipulating that neither Black schools nor Black churches could be established on White blocks, and vice versa. As his last official act as mayor, Mahool signed the racially restrictive ordinance on May 15, 1911 (Power, 1983). Its stated goal was to ensure "the preservation of peace, the prevention of conflict and ill-feeling, between the white and colored persons in Baltimore City, and for promoting the general welfare of the City" (*State of Maryland v. John H. Gurry*, 1913: 540).

At the time Baltimore passed its Segregation Ordinance, about 85,000 Blacks lived in the city; Blacks constituted roughly 14.2% of its population (*State of Maryland v. John H. Gurry*, 1913; Du Bois, 1972; Gibson and Jung, 2005; Pietila, 2010). Mayor Mahool, an avowed Progressive and social justice advocate who supported the ordinance, espoused the view that "Blacks should be quarantined in isolated slums in order to reduce the incidents of civil disturbance, to prevent the spread of communicable disease into the nearby White neighborhoods, and to protect property values among the White majority" (qtd. in Power, 1983: 301).

It should be noted that there was a connection between Progressivism and racism, and by the start of the twentieth century, Progressivism was an influential dogma in American intellectual and political thought. As a result, during the time that ordinances such as these were being developed, many of the Progressive thinkers and activists from both North and South ascribed to the racist views of the times and even promoted the pseudoscientific White-supremacist theories of Black racial inferiority and White racial superiority (Power, 1983; Bernstein, 1998).

* * *

The Baltimore ordinance and all the others it inspired appeared to be *race neutral* on the surface to comport with the *separate but equal* doctrine of *Plessy v. Ferguson* (1896) (Carle, 2002). Proponents of these statutes said the statutes were race neutral because they made a "distinction" between the races that did not amount to "discrimination." A *distinction* implies a difference, while *discrimination* implies favoritism or partiality. According to this line of argument, segregation statutes were not discriminatory since they restricted both races equally (Bernstein, 1998).

Nevertheless, Blacks did not think the Baltimore ordinance made a fair and equal distinction between the races; consequently, they challenged it two years after it was adopted. John Gurry, a person of color, was indicted for violating the ordinance. William Ashbie Hawkins, Gurry's lawyer, was the founder of the Baltimore branch of the NAACP and a law partner of McMechen (Hawkins, 1911; Carle, 2002). When the ordinance was challenged in 1913, the Maryland Court of Appeals contended that some aspects of the ordinance were valid and that it was within the purview of the city to pass such a law. The court argued that since each racial group had similar restrictions, the ordinance was valid. Furthermore, it was the duty of the city to protect the general welfare of city residents. Since animosity might arise and violence might erupt between Whites and Blacks if they lived side by side, cities had the power to take action to forestall conflicts and violence. Consequently, it was appropriate to use an ordinance to separate the races (Hawkins, 1911; *State of Maryland v. Gurry*, 1913).

However, the court did rule that one aspect of the ordinance was unconstitutional. Judges argued that the ordinance ignored the property rights of some residents. For instance, if a Black person had purchased property in a block that was declared a White block, once the ordinance was passed, he or she would not be allowed to take possession of the property. It would be unlikely that a Black person would be able to sell the property to a White person. The property could not be sold to another person of color. In effect, the Black person would be left with property he or she could not use or sell. Though a White person with property in a minority neighborhood could not take possession of it and could not sell or rent to other Whites, he or she might be able to sell or rent it to people of color. In addition, if either racial group inherited property in blocks in which they were prohibited to live, they could not take possession of their property. Under such conditions, the ordinance was declared unconstitutional because it was tantamount to the taking of property (*State of Maryland v. Gurry*, 1913).

A week before the Maryland Court of Appeals returned the verdict that struck down the third segregation ordinance, the Baltimore city council enacted a fourth. The fourth racially restrictive ordinance tried to correct a flaw in the third by making its application prospective. Hence, it grandfathered living arrangements in place at the time of passage and applied the new ordinance only to new moves onto White and Black blocks (Power, 1983).

Despite revisions, Baltimore's racially restrictive ordinance was struck down in the case of *Jackson v. State* (1918). The case challenged the validity of Ordinance No. 339, which was enacted on September 25, 1913. The Court of Appeals of Maryland found the ordinance to be unconstitutional in the *Jackson* case. Nevertheless, several other cities followed in Baltimore's footsteps and enacted racial zoning ordinances (Massey and Denton, 1993; Silver, 1997).

Winston-Salem — Color Blocks and Racial Districts

A case involving a Baltimore-style racially restrictive ordinance, *State v. Darnell* (1914), was heard by the Supreme Court of North Carolina. On July 5, 1912, the board of aldermen of Winston passed an ordinance that made it illegal for Whites to live on blocks where the majority of the residents were people of color and for Blacks to live on blocks where a majority of the residents were White. The 7,828 Blacks living in Winston in 1910 accounted for 46% of the population (Gibson and Jung, 2005). In 1913, William Darnell, a person of color, moved into a house on a street where the majority of the residents were White. Darnell was charged and fined for violating the ordinance. The court dismissed the case against Darnell, arguing that "an act of this broad scope, so entirely without precedent in the public policy of the State and so revolutionary in its nature, cannot be deemed to have been within the purview of the legislature." The court did not believe that the General Assembly intended to confer such "broad and arbitrary a power" on the aldermen. The judges argued that though the aldermen claimed to act in the general welfare of the city, the ordinance was arbitrary. It opened the door to making laws prohibiting people of different political parties or religious groups from living on the same street. The court also thought the ordinance prevented property owners from selling or renting their property to whomever they pleased. The court felt that such an ordinance could result in an exodus of the most enterprising Blacks from the city, leaving it with "the unthrifty and less desirable element" of the race (*State v. Darnell*, 1914: 339–340).

Years later, in 1930, the Board of Aldermen of the City of Winston-Salem passed a comprehensive zoning ordinance that partitioned the city into zones or racial districts. Blacks were prohibited from living in districts designated A-1, B-1, and C-1. Whites were prohibited from living in A-2, B-2, and C-2 districts. The zoning ordinances were revised on March 10, 1939. In the revision, the boundaries of some of the districts were changed such that houses owned or rented by Blacks on Greenwood Avenue were transferred from a Black-designated district to a White-designated district. Blacks were ordered to vacate their houses once the ordinance was revised. Affected property owners brought suit against the city in the case of *Clinard v. City of Winston-Salem* (1940). The Supreme Court of North Carolina ruled the ordinance unconstitutional in 1940 and placed a permanent injunction on the city's attempts to expel Blacks from their homes.

Louisville—Color Blocks and a Landmark Case

A residential segregation case that was heard by the U.S. Supreme Court was *Buchanan v. Warley* (1917). The case originated in Louisville, which passed a racially restrictive segregation ordinance despite the fact that between 1865 and 1930 the city was spared the race riots and lynchings that occurred elsewhere. Nonetheless, segregationists used bombs to threaten Blacks purchasing property in White neighborhoods. For instance, when White activists Anne and Carl Braden purchased a home for a Black man in a White Louisville suburb, vigilantes promptly bombed the home (Braden, [1958] 1999).

Concern began to rise around 1908 when Louisville's prosperous Black entrepreneurs and professionals started purchasing homes in White neighborhoods. This led to great unease among Whites, some of whom responded by renting out their homes to avoid living close to Blacks (G. Wright, 1980, 1985; Bernstein, 1998). In November 1913, in a speech before the Real Estate Exchange, W.D. Binford of the *Louisville Courier-Journal* and *Louisville Times*, called for the passage of a racially restrictive zoning ordinance. He argued that such an ordinance was necessary to protect "the property owners of Louisville who have sacrificed so much in the past from the effects of the negro's presence" (*Louisville Courier-Journal*, 1913). While the *Courier-Journal* remained neutral on the topic, the *Louisville Times* advocated for an ordinance. The *Louisville Times* went so far as to report that property values had fallen by about 50% in neighborhoods that Blacks had moved into. Whites who lived adjacent to Black neighborhoods were swayed by Binford's speech, so they began lobbying their councilmen to pass a racially restrictive zoning ordinance. The councilmen responded quickly, and in January 1914, a racial zoning bill was introduced in the city council. In the meantime, prominent Blacks mobilized to form a branch of the NAACP to challenge the ordinance (G. Wright, 1980, 1985; Bernstein, 1998).

In March 1914, the Louisville city council passed an ordinance to segregate the city into White and color blocks. Anyone violating the ordinance could be fined between $5 and $50 per day. At the time, the 40,522 Blacks living in the city constituted 18.1% of its population. The ordinance prohibited Whites from living on blocks where the majority of the residents were people of color and Blacks from living on blocks that were predominantly White. The NAACP moved swiftly to develop a test case to challenge the ordinance. William Warley, an African American, was a member of the Louisville chapter of the NAACP, and Charles Buchanan was a White realtor who objected to the limitations the ordinance placed on his business. Both collaborated with the NAACP in its campaign to overturn the ordinance. Buchanan sold Warley property on a block designated for Whites. The contract—drafted by NAACP lawyers—had a clause in it that stated that the agreement was not valid unless Warley could take occupancy of the property legally. This sale was orchestrated to provide a direct challenge to the Louisville statute. Hence, a lawyer representing Buchanan (but paid for by the NAACP) filed suit to challenge the ordinance. Warley sought and got the city attorney's office to represent him. In reversing the judgment of the Kentucky Court of Appeals, the U.S. Supreme Court justices argued that the denial of a person of color the right to occupy property he or she owns because it is in a White neighborhood amounts to a taking of property and is not a legitimate use of the *police powers* of the state. It violates the Fourteenth Amendment. The justices pointed out that "the constitutional guaranty of equal protection, without discrimination on account of color, race, religion, etc., includes 'the right to acquire and possess property of every kind.'" In effect, the Louisville ordinance destroyed rights which were vested before the ordinance took effect without compensating residents (*Buchanan v. Warley*, 1917; Bernstein, 1998; Carle, 2002; Gibson and Jung, 2005).

Klarman (2004) argues that though *Buchanan v. Warley* is often seen as a case in which the courts affirmed the civil rights of Blacks, the case was mostly about property rights, and the courts decided primarily on those grounds. However, Bernstein and Somin (2004) argue that the case was decided on both property rights and civil rights grounds. Vose (1959) argues that after the *Warley* decision, Whites switched tactics and focused more attention on engineering private racially restrictive covenants. Schmidt (1982) has argued that *Buchanan v. Warley* was an important case because it acted as a deterrent to the passage of more repugnant state-sponsored residential segregation ordinances. Other scholars such as Fischel (1998) also agree with Schmidt.

Atlanta—Racial Districts, Buffer Strips, and the Peyton Wall

The race riot that erupted in Atlanta in 1906 helped to shape the city's racial zoning policies. Several factors contributed to the violent episode that occurred on September 22–24. The city's Black population was rising rapidly—almost doubling between 1890 and 1910. In 1910, the 51,902 Black residents constituted a third of Atlanta's population. The White population was also growing rapidly during this period—almost tripling —but that still did not ease the apprehension Whites felt about Blacks.

Other factors contributed to the outbreak of violence—the emergence of a Black economic elite that Whites resented and felt threatened by, White politicians stoking anti-Black sentiments during the gubernatorial election campaign and vowing to keep Blacks "in their place," and newspaper articles that frequently reported—without corroboration—that Black males were attacking and assaulting White females. On the day the riot broke out, four such "assaults" were reported in the newspapers. A White mob formed spontaneously and began attacking Black residents and Black establishments. The militia was summoned, but by the time the rioting ceased, between 25 and 40 Blacks and two Whites were dead. African Americans armed themselves for protection, but 250 of them were arrested and their weapons seized (Crowe, 1969; Burlein, 2001; Godshalk, 2005; Mixom, 2005; Gibson and Jung, 2005).

Atlanta passed a racial zoning ordinance seven years after the riot. The Supreme Court of Georgia, in overturning a lower court decision, ruled in 1915 that the city ordinance adopted in November 1913 denied "the inherent right of a person to acquire, enjoy, and dispose of property." The *Carey v. Atlanta* (1915: 456) ruling said that there were inadequate protections of rights of property acquired before the ordinance passed; hence, it violated the due process clause. In response, Atlanta revised the ordinance to exempt properties acquired before its passage. However, as soon as the ordinance was revised, opponents challenged it in court. Hence, the case of *Harden v. City of Atlanta* (1917) came before the Fulton County Superior Court in 1916. Frank Harden, an African American, sued the city for prosecuting him when he rented a house located at the corner of Linden and Myrtle Streets in an area zoned for White occupancy. The court found that the ordinance was not unreasonable and ruled against Harden. In 1917, the Supreme Court of Georgia upheld the lower court ruling.

Atlanta's restrictive zoning ordinance was similar to the Louisville statute, so after the *Buchanan v. Warley* (1917) decision, the Atlanta ordinance was challenged again in court. In the case of *Glover v. City of Atlanta* (1918), the Fulton County Superior Court found that the statute was not in violation of the Fourteenth Amendment. The case went to the state supreme court. Citing the *Buchanan v. Warley* decision, the Supreme Court of Georgia reversed the lower court ruling and found the Atlanta ordinance to be unconstitutional in 1918.

After Atlanta's racially restricted zoning ordinances were struck down, city planners drafted a plan that designated unofficial districts defined by race (Bernstein, 1998). Robert Whitten, a Progressive city planner, submitted a draft to partition the city into three districts— Whites in R1, Blacks in R2, and mixed districts in R3. Whitten defended the plan by arguing that "race zoning is essential in the interest of the public peace, order and security and will promote the welfare and prosperity of both the White and colored race" (Atlanta City Planning Commission, 1922). The legality of the plan was questioned, and the Supreme Court of Georgia ruled it unconstitutional in 1926 in the case of *Smith v. City of Atlanta* (1926). The Atlanta city council responded by passing a zoning ordinance based on Richmond's statute in 1929. The mayor vetoed it. Undeterred, the city passed a similar statute in 1931 (S. Meyer, 2001).

During Mayor William Hartsfield's time in office (1937–41, 1942–62), *buffer strips* were used as a planning and zoning device to maintain segregated neighborhoods. That is, strips of major thoroughfares were zoned "for commercial uses" on both sides of the streets for considerable distances. Such strips acted as *barriers to population movement*; they were effective in keeping Blacks from spilling into White neighborhoods. Residential construction was prohibited in such zones even when there was no commercial or industrial development in an area zoned as commercial. Highways, cemeteries, industrial tracts, rail lines, and second-growth forests were also used to create *buffer strips* between the city's Black and White neighborhoods. In addition, streets such as Willis Mill Road were dead-ended deliberately to obstruct passage from the Black to the White neighborhoods (Blumberg, 1964; Bayor, 2001; Avila and Rose, 2009).

Nevertheless, by the late 1940s, Blacks began moving into Mozley Park at rates that alarmed Whites. Mozley Park residents had been particularly resistant to neighborhood integration. Blacks moving into the neighborhood were threatened, and Whites began selling and moving away. In 1949, a group of 100 White residents of the neighborhood visited city hall and presented a petition asking for protection against the incursion of Blacks. Mayor Hartsfield orchestrated a compromise that allowed Blacks to move into a section of the neighborhood. The West Side Mutual Development Committee was created in 1952 to facilitate agreements between Blacks and Whites to abide by *selective racial change* in the neighborhood (Silver and Moeser, 1995; Connerly, 2005).

The purpose of the West Side Mutual Development Committee was to provide a forum for Black and White leaders to manage and negotiate the residential districts in which Blacks and Whites would reside while respecting the buffer strips. The committee made arrangements for Whites to list their homes with Black realtors, to move out of neighborhoods en masse, and to get market prices for their homes, while Blacks were able to purchase the homes without racial violence and inflated prices. Black realtors also agreed to participate in *racial steering*. That is, they agreed that they would not show Black home buyers property in White neighborhoods that were not undergoing racial transition. Through this process, Whites in Mozley Park sold 737 homes to Blacks between 1954 and 1955. Though committee members agreed that Blacks would not reside beyond the agreed-on buffer zone, by 1962, Blacks had jumped the West Side buffer zone and were living beyond the pine forest that was intended to prevent such movement (Blumberg, 1964; Silver and Moeser, 1995; Harmon, 1996; Kruse, 2005).

Atlanta was one southern city that escaped the bombings that accompanied Blacks moving into predominantly White neighborhoods. Scholars argue that this occurred because Black and White leaders collaborated to provide segregated housing for the growing Black middle class. Hence, 8,500 housing units were made available to Blacks between 1945 and 1965 in Atlanta. However, critics argue that the city's Black leaders focused on improving housing opportunities rather than challenging White separatists, the protection of their market position, and the institution of racially restrictive zoning (Schutze, 1986; Eskew, 1997).

The *negotiated racial districts* were not enough to allay the fears of White Atlantans. Hence, in 1962, city construction crews built roadblocks on Peyton and Harlan Roads after a Black doctor tried to purchase a home in Peyton Forest. The board of aldermen responded to White residents' complaints by constructing the barricades. The wooden barricades—painted black and white—were intended to separate the middle-class subdivision nestled amid loblolly pines, called Peyton Forest, from the Black section of the city. The Peyton Wall, as the barricades were called, drew the ire of Blacks, who surrounded the barriers with picket lines. Civil rights activists announced a boycott of area merchants, and two lawsuits were filed. Nearby White residents loved the wall; they wrapped it in Christmas paper and adorned it with ribbons. Late one Friday night, shortly after the barriers were erected, the I-beams supporting the structure were yanked out of the ground, the timber was sawed, and bits were tossed into a nearby creek. On Saturday morning, Peyton Forest residents responded by chopping down trees and shrubs, piling them into the street, and weighting down the materials with stones. That night, opponents of the barricade burned the new makeshift barrier. Mayor Ivan Allen announced that the city would rebuild the barricades, and construction crews began work on a new barricade by Monday morning. Robed Klansmen patrolled the street and guarded the new barricade. Nevertheless, the Peyton Wall did not survive for long. The district court ruled that the wall was illegal, and the barricade was destroyed. This prompted an exodus of Whites from the neighborhood. Within a month of the removal of the barricade, most of the homes in Peyton Forest were put up for sale with Black realtors. By 1963, all but 15 White homeowners had sold their homes to Blacks and moved out of Peyton Forest (Bayor, 2001; Kruse, 2005).

Richmond—Linking Restrictive Zoning and Antimiscegenation Laws

The Supreme Court of Virginia upheld the racial segregation ordinances passed in Richmond in 1911. Mary Hopkins, an African American woman, and John Coleman, an African American man, were charged with moving onto White blocks after ordinances were passed designating White and color blocks in Richmond and Ashland, respectively. In 1910, the 46,733 Blacks living in Richmond made up 37% of the population. The Supreme Court of Virginia upheld two lower court decisions that questioned the validity of both ordinances. The judges ruled that the ordinances were valid and exemplified a reasonable use of the police powers of the municipalities in question (*Hopkins v. City of Richmond* and *Coleman v. Town of Ashland*, 1915; Gibson and Jung, 2005). The Richmond case is interesting because planners first tried their hand at comprehensive city zoning before attempting racial zoning. Richmond passed an ordinance in 1908 regulating the heights and arrangements of buildings; that ordinance was upheld by the Virginia Supreme Court of Appeals in 1910. This paved the way for the promulgation of a racial segregation ordinance that passed a year later. The Richmond ordinance and similar ones passed in the Virginia towns of Norfolk, Portsmouth, Roanoke, and Ashland were modified versions of the Baltimore ordinance (Silver, 1997).

However, Richmond went a step further than other cities when it linked racial zoning with antimiscegenation laws. That is, a person could not live on a street if the law did not permit him or her to marry people of the predominant racial group on that street. The *Richmond v. Deans* case challenged a city ordinance that was approved in February 1929 that prohibited anyone from occupying a residence on a street where the majority of the residences were occupied by people an individual moving onto the street was prohibited by law from marrying. Here the framers of the ordinance attempted to tie racially restrictive ordinances to antimiscegenation laws. The NAACP sued to prevent the city from enforcing the ordinance. The city argued that zoning, intended to stave off racial conflict and immorality that would arise from integration, was a legitimate use of police powers. It also argued that the ordinance was fair since it treated Blacks and Whites equally. Judge D. Lawrence Groner ruled in favor of the NAACP and concluded that the ordinance was invalid. The case was appealed, and in January 1930, the circuit court upheld the lower court ruling. In May 1930, the U.S. Supreme Court declined to hear the city's final appeal of the case. If *Richmond v. Deans* had withstood the challenge, segregation would have been achieved by the enforcement of antimiscegenation laws. In the wake of *Buchanan v. Warley*, cities such as Richmond tried to find other ways of using racial ordinances to achieve residential segregation. Hence, this shift in the use racially restrictive ordinances represented an attempt to use more indirect methods to restrict residency (Council of the City of Richmond, 1929; *City of Richmond v. Deans*, 1930a, 1930b; S. Meyer, 2001).

St. Louis—Color Blocks

Blacks have been living in St. Louis since its founding in 1764. One neighborhood, the Ville, emerged as the center of Black culture and a haven for middle-class Blacks. Blacks constituted 2.1% of the city's population in 1860. However, in 1910, the 43,960 Blacks in St. Louis constituted 6.4% of the population. The Black population continued to increase and in 1920 constituted 9% of the city's population. As the city's Black population increased, Blacks were increasingly segregated in a few sections of the city. Efforts to draft a segregation ordinance began in 1911, but it took five years to pass. Neighborhood associations were formed in support of the ordinance; it also had the firm backing of the St. Louis Real Estate Exchange and the United Welfare Association. In 1916, by a margin of three to one, residents of St. Louis voted to enact a racially restrictive segregation ordinance that stipulated that one could not occupy a residence on a block on which more than 75% of the residents were from another racial group. However, the NAACP succeeded in getting the ordinance overturned a year later. In response, Whites living in neighborhoods close to the Ville formed the Marcus Avenue Improvement Association and others like it to focus on getting Whites to sign private racially restrictive covenants (Kelleher, 1970; City of St. Louis, 1996; National Register of Historic Places, 1999; Gibson and Jung, 2005).

New Orleans—Racial Districts and the Withholding of Building Permits

Despite the 1917 *Buchanan v. Warley* decision, cities tinkered with and passed racial segregation ordinances that deviated slightly from ones already struck down by the courts. In this vein, New Orleans passed two ordinances in 1912 and 1924 that segregated the residences of Whites and people of color. Though the city's Black population had risen from 89,262 in 1910 to 100,930 in 1920, the percentage of Blacks remained at roughly 26% (Gibson and Jung, 2005). The 1912 act was passed to segregate the city "in the interest of peace and welfare." To this end, civic leaders thought it prudent to "foster the separation of White and negro residential communities" (*Land Development Company v. City of New Orleans*, 1926: 1). As a result, in 1912 and 1924, ordinances were passed that prohibited Blacks from establishing residences in White neighborhoods, and vice versa. The city engineer was authorized to deny building permits to Whites wanting to build in Black neighborhoods or Blacks wanting to build in White neighborhoods. Violators could be fined up to $25 and/or imprisoned for up to 30 days. These ordinances were challenged in court by the Land Development Company of Louisiana in 1926. The company argued that it was being denied the right to rent its property to Blacks, and that constituted a taking of the property without due process or compensation. The district court in which the case was heard dismissed the case, arguing that the plaintiff, the Land Development Company, made only vague suggestions about the potential of the statute to harm its business; it had not shown how it was being harmed in a direct and clear way. The ordinances stood till the case went to the Fifth Circuit Court of Appeals in 1927. In April of that year, the Court of Appeals reversed the district court decision and struck down the prohibition on racially mixed neighborhoods (*Land Development Company v. City of New Orleans*, 1926, 1927; Colten, 2002).

The New Orleans ordinances were also challenged in the case of *Tyler v. Harmon*. In 1925, Joseph Tyler sought to prevent Benjamin Harmon from modifying his cottage to create an additional apartment that Tyler believed Harmon intended to rent to Blacks. The Supreme Court of Louisiana ruled that the racially restrictive ordinance was valid. The court also issued an injunction against Harmon, barring him from renting his cottage to Blacks (*Tyler v. Harmon*, 1925, 1926; *Benjamin Harmon v. Tyler*, 1927). The Court of Appeals reversed the lower court decision and struck down the ordinances (*Land Development Company v. City of New Orleans*, 1926, 1927; Colten, 2002).

Dallas—Mutual Segregation Agreement

In August 1916, Dallas approved a racially restrictive law (Ordinance No. 195) that designated blocks on which Blacks and people of color could live (the ordinance made reference to the "colored race" but later defined "colored" to mean people of African descent). A second racially restrictive decree was approved in January 1924 by the city. This second ordinance reflected a segregation agreement reached through negotiations between White and Black representatives that identified sections of the city to be occupied by each racial group (*City of Dallas v. Liberty Annex*, 1927). In March 1927, the state of Texas took the experiment with racially restrictive zoning ordinances a step further than other states when the Fortieth Legislature passed a law authorizing municipalities to develop ordinances to segregate Blacks and Whites.

Cities were authorized to withhold permits from Whites and Blacks constructing homes in districts they were prohibited from building in by the ordinances. The statute also stipulated that Blacks and Whites should enter into mutual covenants or agreements regarding the designation of White and Black districts within each municipality. To comply with these guidelines, Dallas held an election and formally adopted the two aforementioned racially restrictive zoning ordinances as part of its charter in December 1927 (Tex. Rev. Civ. Stat., 1927; *City of Dallas v. Liberty Annex*, 1927).

Dallas's racial zoning ordinances were challenged even before they were formally adopted as part of the city's charter. A real estate development company that had been selling lots in a subdivision to Blacks sued in court in 1926. Liberty Annex Corporation sued the city commissioners and the Lagow Improvement Association for enforcing an ordinance that prevented Blacks from occupying the properties they purchased. Liberty had constructed homes on 52 lots, while 32 remained unsold at the time the ordinance passed. The company feared it would be left with lots it could not sell if Blacks could not take occupancy of their property. The suit was dismissed by the trial court, but the Court of Appeals of Texas heard the case of *Liberty Annex v. City of Dallas* and decided on December 4, 1926, that the zoning ordinance was unconstitutional (*Liberty Annex v. City of Dallas*, 1926). The next year, the Supreme Court of Texas ruled that the Liberty Annex subdivision was not included in the area covered by the mutual segregation agreement ordinance and, therefore, was not covered by the ordinance (*City of Dallas v. Liberty Annex*, 1927). The litigants were back in court in 1929. On May 27, the Court of Appeals of Texas ruled that the city's segregation ordinances were unconstitutional (*City of Dallas v. Liberty Annex*, 1929).

Miami—A Wall and a County-Wide Ordinance

Though Blacks lived in Miami since its founding, they were concentrated in two enclaves. Hence, in 1930, Miami's roughly 29,000 Black residents lived in Overtown (formerly known as Colored Town), a neighborhood of 105 city blocks, and West Coconut Grove, located a few miles south of the city's business district (Mohl, 1995). In 1936, Miami and the Dade County Planning Board outlined a plan to *remove*

Black residents from the central city and *resettle* them in three Black towns that would be constructed outside Miami proper. In 1937, federal funds were used to construct the Liberty Square public housing project to implement part of the plan (Mohl, 1995; Bayor, 2001).

The city's Black population continued to grow—from 49,518 in 1940 to 137,299 in 1960. Three new Black enclaves (Liberty City, Brownsville, and Opa-locka) were created in the 1940s (Mohl, 1995). On August 14, 1945, Dade County commissioners passed an ordinance that attempted to segregate Miami and the rest of the county using a racially restrictive ordinance. Two Black families who purchased property beyond the "red line" in a White residential area near Brownsville were arrested and charged with violating the ordinance. When the actions of the county were challenged in court, the Supreme Court of Florida ruled in 1946 that the county had no authority to pass the racially restrictive ordinance or to bar Blacks from taking occupancy of their property (*State of Florida v. Wilson*, 1946; Mohl, 1995).

Other mechanisms were also used to separate Black and White residents in the Coconut Grove section of Miami. Coconut Grove came into being in 1925 when Miami annexed the area. Black immigrants from the Bahamas had always lived in close proximity to Whites (their employers) in Coconut Grove. However, as the Black population rose and the need to improve housing conditions in West Coconut Grove became more urgent, White Coconut Grove residents objected to the construction of new housing for Blacks close to their section of town. Consequently, in the 1940s, a 1,300-foot wall was constructed to separate the all-Black West Coconut Grove (also known as Bahamian Grove or the Black Grove) from the all-White section of Coconut Grove (Mohl, 1987; Dunn, 1997; Nielsen, 1998; Bayor, 2001; Plasencia, 2011).

Oklahoma City—Executive Military Segregation Order and a "Non-Trespass" Buffer

Oklahoma City was a place in which racially restrictive covenants were upheld long after they were struck down elsewhere. In January 1933, there were numerous protests following an attempt by Blacks to move onto blocks where White residents lived. Believing that a race riot was imminent, Governor William Murray issued an executive military order that established racially segregated zones in the city. The zones for Blacks and Whites were separated by a neutral "Non-Trespass" buffer zone. The city council passed an ordinance that formalized the governor's act (S. Meyer, 2001). The NAACP challenged the ordinance in court in 1935 and finally defeated it in 1936 in the case of *Allen v. Oklahoma City* (1936).

Birmingham—Bricks, Bombs, and Buffer Strips

Birmingham, Alabama, used a complex system of segregationist tools to control where Blacks could live in the city. First and foremost, the city was an agglomeration of segregated company towns. In addition, it relied on the southern phenomenon of achieving Black and White "streets" by relegating alley dwelling to Blacks and reserving dwelling on the main thoroughfares for Whites. Moreover, the city enacted zoning ordinances and buffer strips to curtail Black movement.

THE RACIALIZATION OF SPACE IN A SOUTHERN INDUSTRIAL COMPANY TOWN

Incorporated in 1871 by the Elyton Land Company, Birmingham was a planned city that sprung up on the 4,500 acres of Jones Valley farmland around rich deposits of iron and coal. Blacks were incorporated into the labor force from the outset, as the industrialists establishing the town saw Blacks as a vital source of cheap labor who were relegated to the most dangerous jobs in the mines and mills. The town was segregated from the beginning. Blacks and Whites lived on separate blocks and largely on different sides of the railroad tracks. Blacks also lived in the alleys on the Southside as well as adjacent to the Alice Furnace on the Westside and the Sloss Furnaces on the Eastside. Workers lived in "quarters" or company-built towns or camps. Relatively few Whites lived in the quarters. Instead, they lived in houses separated from the smaller, more cheaply constructed wooden shacks that Blacks inhabited (Connerly, 2005).

An 1886 report indicated that about 40% of the city's population was Black, but by 1890, Blacks constituted 43% of the population (Connerly, 2005). The growth in the Black population led to increased demand for housing in Birmingham. Though the number of Blacks increased from

16,575 in 1900 to 130,025 in 1950, the percentage of Blacks in the city did not exceed 43.1% in that period (Gibson and Jung, 2005).

CITYWIDE RACIAL ZONING

The belief that the Black population was growing too rapidly led Birmingham's civic leaders to develop a general zoning code in 1915; the code was revised in 1926 to form a comprehensive racially restrictive zoning ordinance. While civic leaders were convinced that the zoning restrictions were acceptable to both races, Blacks desired unrestricted housing opportunities (Eskew, 1997; Connerly, 2005). The least desirable and most *hazard-prone* land in the city was zoned for Black residence. That is, Blacks were forced to live along Village Creek, which flooded often. Blacks began establishing communities in Tuxedo Park, Moro Park, Ensley, and East Birmingham before World War I. However, because Moro Park and East Birmingham were close to Village Creek, these neighborhoods also flooded frequently. As Emory Jackson, editor of the city's Black newspaper the *Birmingham World*, wrote in 1949, "Negroes in Birmingham are zoned near the railroad tracks, near the over-flowing creeks, near the shops" (qtd. in Eskew, 1997: 63; Connerly, 2005: 20). The city was so committed to containing Blacks in this neighborhood that when John Charles and Frederick Law Olmsted Jr. (son of the codesigner of New York's Central Park) planned the park system in 1925 and proposed the conversion of Village Creek into a linear park system akin to Boston's famed Emerald Necklace, civic leaders balked at the plan (Connerly, 2005). It should be noted that it was illegal in Birmingham for Blacks to use any city-owned parks at the time of Olmsted's proposal and for some time after that.

The burgeoning Black population, coupled with industrial incursion into the areas of the city where Blacks lived, made it difficult for Blacks to find housing. The housing in Black neighborhoods was so inadequate that by the 1830s more than 97% of the dwellings in "Old Birmingham" were declared substandard. In all the census tracts in which Blacks resided, the housing was deemed substandard by the Birmingham District Housing Authority (S. Meyer, 2001).

Racial tensions ran high in Birmingham as Whites openly expressed their fears of Blacks. Concomitantly, White supremacists became increasingly aggressive in their dealings with Blacks. In the meantime, the city's racially restrictive zoning ordinance continued to evolve. The 1944 General City Code of Birmingham and a supplementary ordinance made it unlawful for Blacks to live in areas zoned A-1 or White residential. The ordinance also made it illegal for Whites to live in areas zoned B-1 or Black residential (*City of Birmingham v. Monk*, 1950).

The situation became more volatile in 1945 when Alice Allen, secretary to the president of historically Black Miles College, purchased a home on 11th Avenue North near the corner of 16th Street on November 8. The property was zoned commercial, meaning that it was available for White and Black occupancy. Desperate to escape the atrocious housing conditions in Black neighborhoods, Blacks had developed a habit of buying and living in commercial buildings in restricted zones, and the city had ignored the practice. Center Street was the dividing line between the Black and White sections of town. Lower-middle-class Whites lived in the North Smithfield section of the Graymont subdivision west of Center Street. A White public housing project, Elyton Gardens, was built in Graymont. However, Smithfield was surrounded on three sides by the Black neighborhood of East Thomas and the Smithfield Court housing project that housed Blacks. Realtors had trouble finding White buyers for property on streets bordering Black neighborhoods, so they began to advertise and sell to Blacks. Allen's house was on the north side of the street, the side occupied by Whites. Hence, one week after she purchased the property, the Birmingham City Commission changed the classification of the property from commercial and designated it as multifamily housing for Whites only (Eskew, 1997; S. Meyer, 2001; Connerly, 2005).

Allen's procurement of property that was close to the White community of Graymont–College Hills drew instantaneous protests from Graymont residents. Whites warned Allen not to move in, while vigilantes smashed the windows of the house. The city's zoning ordinance stipulated that Blacks were not allowed to live west of Center Street. When Allen was forbidden to move into her house, she retained the services of Black NAACP attorney Arthur Shores, who filed suit against the city on August 6, 1946. Hoping to preempt a legal challenge to the city's racial zoning ordinance (since courts elsewhere had already struck down similar ordinances), the city commission declared the November 1945 rezoning of Allen's property "null and void." This cleared the way for Allen to take occupancy of her property. The city commission's change of heart occurred on August 22, 1946—two weeks after Shores filed the lawsuit (Eskew, 1997; S. Meyer, 2001; Connerly, 2005). But instead of rezoning the entire Graymont–College Hills community to allow for Black occupancy, the city rezoned only one property at a time for Black occupancy when a lawsuit was filed (Kruse, 2005).

Birmingham's White residents and civic leaders studied how other southern cities dealt with residential segregation and copied Atlanta's approach. They thought buffer strips could provide an effective barrier to Black movement into White neighborhoods. Consequently, members of the Graymont–College Hills Civic Association lobbied the city to designate a 150-foot-wide commercial buffer strip to separate their homes from Black residences. However, Blacks countered by organizing a civic association—the Birmingham Protective Property Association— to deal with housing issues and voice the concerns of the city's Black residents. The Birmingham Protective Property Association objected to the buffer strip on the grounds that the creation of such a strip in an area formerly designated for Black occupancy would further restrict Blacks attempting to find decent housing or taking occupancy of their properties. The city commission settled the impasse by voting for a 50-foot commercial buffer zone. More than 140 Black property owners in the proposed buffer zone protested the plan (Connerly, 2005).

In 1947, Samuel Matthews, a drill operator, decided to build a home at 120 11th Court North. Mathews purchased the lot in 1946 from a White realtor who had acquired 50 lots which he intended to sell to Black home builders. The realtor bought the lots in anticipation of the neighborhood being rezoned for Black occupancy. Matthews, who believed he had purchased property in a section zoned for Black occupancy, constructed a six-room frame house on the property. However, he was informed by the building inspector that he could not occupy his home because the lot was zoned for White occupancy only. Arthur Shores took Matthews's case and sued the city. The city offered to rezone the property so that Matthews could occupy it if the lawsuit was dropped, but Matthews and Shores rejected the offer and went to court. The federal district court judge, Clarence Mullins, ruled on July 31, 1947, that the zoning restrictions were unconstitutional. Vigilantes responded to the court decision by defacing the house with warnings that Matthews should not move in. Matthews tried to rent or sell the home to Whites but had no takers because of the close proximity to the Black neighborhood. On August 18, Matthews's home was dynamited and completely destroyed. Matthews was uninsured, so he could not afford to rebuild. Moreover, the city ignored the court's ruling, and the ordinance remained in place (S. Meyer, 2001; Eskew, 1997).

The story of restrictive zoning in Birmingham did not end with the bombing of Samuel Matthews's home. In March 1949, the NAACP convened a housing summit at which attendees expressed their dissatisfaction about the state of housing in the city. Days after the conference, Bishop S. Greene of the African Methodist Episcopalian Church and chancellor of Daniel Payne College, moved into the disputed White section of the city. He had purchased two homes on 11th Avenue West in December 1948. Johnnie and Emily Madison also purchased a home on 11th Avenue West in February 1949; the homes had been on the market for a long time because Whites would not buy them. The Graymont–College Hills Civic Association protested Bishop Greene's actions to the city commissioners. City commissioners were urged to "move the Negroes out, or arrest everyone of them for violating the zoning ordinance." The public improvements commissioner, James Morgan, believed the zoning code was unenforceable but had no appetite for integration. He was in a quandary and discussed his predicament with other commissioners. Calling the code "weak and illegal," he said, "I am not in favor of them moving in with us, but where are they going [to live]?" The commissioner of public safety, T. Eugene "Bull" Connor, argued that racial integration would result in "breaches of the peace, riots, and destruction of property and life" (S. Meyer, 2001: 26).

As the commissioners weighed their options, Bishop Greene's and the Madisons' homes were bombed. The bombings occurred on March 24, and no one was arrested. When William German—a Black insurance salesman—purchased a house at 1100 Center Street North, Klansman and auto mechanic Robert E. Chambliss ("Dynamite Bob"), who was later convicted of the 1963 bombing of the 16th Street Baptist Church that killed four young Black girls, warned German not to move in because he would suffer the same fate as Bishop Greene. Bombings of Black residences, churches, and other institutions became a regular occurrence in Birmingham. Thus, on August 17, 1949, about 2,000

Blacks held a mass protest at Smithfield Court to demand an end to the bombings and terrorism being directed at them. Nonetheless, between 1947 and 1965, there were about 50 bombings targeting Black homes and institutions; some reports indicate that as many as 100 bombs were detonated in the city between 1955 and 1965. Arthur Shores's home was bombed twice in 1963. Bombings were so commonplace that Birmingham became known as "Bombingham," and the Center Street neighborhood was called "Dynamite Hill." In the absence of adequate police protection, Blacks defended themselves and their property by taking up arms, firing at vigilantes crowding around their homes, setting up countersurveillance around the homes of Blacks living in White neighborhoods, recording the license-plate numbers of cars from which bombs and bricks were hurled, and giving chase to such vehicles (Shores, 1974; Eskew, 1997; Temple and Hansen, 2000; S. Meyer, 2001; National Register of Historic Places, 2004; Connerly, 2005; *Birmingham News*, 2006; Wheeler, 2009).

The bombs did not deter Blacks from purchasing property in the contested area of North Smithfield. Thus, in June 1949, Mary Means Monk, a schoolteacher, bought a lot at 950 Center Street—a location she thought was zoned for Black occupancy. Monk was well into the construction of her house when she was denied a permit to complete it on the grounds that it was in an area zoned for Whites. In September 1949, Shores filed suit on behalf of Monk and 15 other Black plaintiffs who owned a total of 47 lots in the North Smithfield neighborhood that they were not allowed to take occupancy of. In the case of *City of Birmingham v. Monk* (1950), Judge Clarence Mullins declared that Birmingham's racially restrictive zoning ordinance was unconstitutional on December 16, 1949. The city filed an appeal in January 1950, arguing that the zoning ordinances constituted a legitimate use of police powers. Thurgood Marshall, Peter Hall, and David Hood joined Shores in arguing the case. On December 19, 1950, the Fifth Circuit Court upheld the lower court ruling. The city granted Mary Monk permission to occupy her property a day later. The house was dynamited on December 21 (Eskew, 1997).

In studying Atlanta's handling of racial zoning issues, George Byrum Jr. (chair of Birmingham's Zoning Board of Adjustment) reported that Atlanta had no racial zoning ordinances after 1926. Instead, Atlanta

used realtors quite effectively to *achieve and maintain* residential segregation. That is, the real estate industry used *professional codes* and
sanctions to monitor and control the movement of Blacks into White
neighborhoods. Atlanta also formed an ad hoc committee of Blacks
and Whites to forge an agreement about neighborhood boundaries for
racial groups to inhabit. Birmingham's North Smithfield neighborhood
was undergoing a demographic transition at the same time that Atlanta's
Mozley Park neighborhood was getting an influx of Blacks. Hence, Birmingham formed a biracial committee similar to Atlanta's. The committee met in private during the summer of 1949. Committee members
decided that Center Street was the *racial divide* and that there would be
no commercial buffer strips east of it. The committee also proposed that
a 30–40-acre area north of 11th Avenue be zoned for Black occupancy.
The group also recommended that the city purchase Black-owned lots
that were west of Center Street. The compromise hatched by the committee was opposed by the Graymont–College Hills Civic Association
as well as by Black community leaders. Prominent Black activists who
rejected this and similar proposals insisted that the city's racial zoning
ordinance was illegal and that they would not compromise in order to
maintain it (Kruse, 2005).

Commenting on the state of housing segregation, Los Angeles Municipal Judge Loren Miller contends that the 1917 *Buchanan v. Warley*
decision came after a decade of legal enforcement of racially discriminatory zoning laws and was followed by "informal, but effectual and
unconstitutional enforcement for many years" (1965: 74). He cites Birmingham as an example of a city that continued enforcing its racial
zoning ordinance till around 1950.

Bombs, Fences, and Highway Buffers in Other Southern Cities

Bombs were used to destroy the homes and institutions of Blacks in
other southern and southwestern cities such as Nashville and Dallas
in an effort to deter Blacks from moving into White neighborhoods
(Thometz, 1963; D. Doyle, 1985; Schutze, 1986; Eskew, 1997). During the
1950s, the city commission required that developers erect a steel fence to
separate Black and White neighborhoods in North Memphis. Interstate
highways were also planned to serve as barriers to Black movement in

Memphis, Richmond, Kansas City (Missouri), Atlanta, Tulsa (Oklahoma), and Charleston (West Virginia) (Bayor, 2001).

Racial Zoning in Northern Cities

What began as a southern interregional migration of Blacks in the late nineteenth century transitioned to a primarily South-to-North migration in the early twentieth century. As the Great Northern Migration intensified, housing shortages became commonplace in northern cities. In many cities, warehouses, store rooms, railroad cars, churches, boat houses, and tents were used to house the new arrivals. The rooming houses and tenements were so packed that many people crowded into one room, and as many as four or five people slept on one bed in shifts. Overcrowding was so intense in Pittsburgh that Black settlements began to spring up in vulnerable, hazard-prone areas such as the hollows and ravines, on hillsides, along the river banks, alongside the railroad tracks, and in the milk yards (Hirsch, [1983] 1998; Trotter and Day, 2010).

Famed author Langston Hughes described the overcrowding he grew up with on Cleveland's east side during the migration:

> Rents were very high for the colored people in Cleveland, and the Negro district was extremely crowded because of the great migration. It was difficult to find a place to live. We always lived . . . either in an attic or a basement and paid quite a lot for such inconvenient quarters. White people on the east side of the city were moving out of their frame homes and renting them to Negroes at double and triple the rents they could receive from others. . . . As always, the white neighborhoods resented Negroes moving closer and closer—but when the whites did give way, they gave way at very profitable rentals. (1940: 27)

Race riots broke out in northern border cities between 1903 and 1908 as the Black population grew. Riots occurred in Evansville and Greensburg (Indiana), Springfield (Ohio), and Springfield (Illinois) (Massey and Denton, 1993; Brady, 1996). Another series of race riots occurred in more northerly cities from 1917 to 1921. They occurred in East St. Louis (Illinois), Chester (Pennsylvania), New York City, Chicago, and Omaha

(Nebraska) (Jones-Correa, 2000–2001). As a result, northern cities contemplated and instituted racially restrictive zoning ordinances.

Indianapolis—Spite Fences and Restrictive Zoning

In 1851, the Indiana Supreme Court added an article to the state's constitution that prohibited Blacks from living in the state. The article was expunged in 1866, and by the late nineteenth century, Blacks were elected to the city council. However, as the city's Black population grew from 15,931 in 1900 to 34,678 in 1920, Whites expressed discomfort with what they perceived as too many Blacks in the parks, on the streets, and on public transportation. This was evident in 1901 when a mob of young White men, armed with clubs and rocks and calling themselves the bungaloos, attacked and chased Blacks out of Fairview Park in suburban Indianapolis. About a dozen Blacks were injured, and the police had difficulty controlling the melee. Neighborhoods that were racially mixed in 1900 became segregated as Whites either moved from such neighborhoods or took actions to prevent Blacks from moving into predominantly White neighborhoods. Hence, in 1920, the city enacted a law that prevented Blacks from purchasing homes in White neighborhoods. Yet Blacks constituted only 11% of the city's population in 1920. The ordinance was successfully challenged by the Indianapolis branch of the NAACP (Little, 1994; Thornbrough, [1957] 1993, 2000; Brady, 1996; Gibson and Jung, 2005).

The restrictions on where Blacks could settle in the city resulted in increasingly crowded Black wards that contained dilapidated housing. Consequently, about 48% of the population in Ward Five was Black in 1920 (Thornbrough, 1961; Brady, 1996). Blacks were also overcharged for rent in the city. Dwellings that were rented to Whites for $18 per month were rented to Blacks for $25 per month (Brady, 1996). Blacks were also barred from living in suburban subdivisions developed on the fringes of the city. For instance, in 1910, when Emerson Heights was developed, a clause in the deeds read, "The grantee . . . agrees for himself, his heirs and assigns, not to sell or lease to colored people" (qtd. in Brady, 1996).

Whites were apprehensive of the growing Black population and sought to intimidate and isolate Blacks who moved into White neighborhoods. Thus, when an African American dentist, Lucein Meriwether, moved onto the 2200 block of North Capitol Avenue in 1920, the Capitol Avenue Protective Association erected 12-foot-high "spite fences" on either side of his residence. The case went to court, and in 1921, a Superior Court judge ruled that the fences should either be removed or replaced with fences that could be no more than six feet high. Whites also resorted to violence. In 1924, a hand grenade was thrown into the house of a Black family. Handbills with derogatory, anti-Black statements were also circulated. A group, the White Supremacy League, was formed to prevent Blacks from moving into White neighborhoods or securing employment in the city. Other groups such as the Mapleton Civic Association claimed that their main goal was to prevent people of color from living among them because such an occurrence would lower their property values (*Indianapolis Freeman*, 1924a, 1924b; Thornbrough, 1961; Brady, 1996). They argued, "One of our chief concerns is to prevent members of the colored race from moving into our midst, thereby depreciating property values" (*Indianapolis World*, 1921).

Tensions continued to rise, and in March 1926, the city council passed a zoning ordinance proclaiming that "in the interest of public peace, good order and the general welfare, it is advisable to foster the separation of white and negro communities" (*Journal of the Common Council*, 1926: 54). The ordinance prohibited Whites from living in Black neighborhoods and Blacks from living in White neighborhoods. The authors of this ordinance were well aware of the *Buchanan v. Warley* (1917) ruling but wanted to devise a statute that could serve as a test case to force the U.S. Supreme Court to render a different ruling. The framers of the Indianapolis ordinance were also buoyed by the ruling of the Supreme Court of Louisiana that upheld the constitutionality of a racial zoning ordinance in the city of New Orleans in 1926. The Indianapolis ordinance was framed similarly to the New Orleans statute—neither prohibited the buying or selling of property; instead, the ordinances prohibited people purchasing property in restricted zones from occupying it if they were of the wrong race (*Buchanan v. Warley*, 1917; *Indianapolis Recorder*, 1926; *Tyler v. Harmon*, 1925, 1926; Thornbrough, 1961).

However, by 1926, there was vigorous opposition to racially restrictive ordinances, and the NAACP continued to challenge their legality. An African American doctor working in collaboration with the NAACP contested the Indianapolis ordinance, which prevented him from taking occupancy of his property. The Indianapolis ordinance was ruled unconstitutional by the Marion County Superior Court on November 23, 1926. When the New Orleans statute was struck down in 1927, it put an end to the idea of devising racially restrictive ordinances to get a decision that differed from the one reached in *Buchanan v. Warley* (1917) (*Benjamin Harmon v. Tyler*, 1927; NAACP, 1927; Thornbrough, 1961).

Industrial Order and Northern Racialized Company Towns

The chicken-or-egg and the minority move-in hypotheses are predicated on the assumption that minorities move to live adjacent to hazardous facilities and that they are the only ones doing so. The following discussion of company towns not only dispels this myth; it establishes the fact that both White and non-White workers have moved to live close to industrial facilities at times. Company towns are relevant to this discussion as they were private entities that were developed with residential "zones" organized by race, gender, class, and immigrant status. The discussion also shows that White and non-White workers had different *opportunities* and *options* to flee polluted neighborhoods when they wished to.

Beginning in the early nineteenth century, industrialists took deliberate actions to socially engineer their workforce and the living arrangements of workers. Samuel Slater pioneered this trend when he constructed mill villages around his New England textile factories (Cameron, 1960; D.E. Taylor, 2009). Francis Cabot Lowell and his partners constructed company towns in Waltham in 1813 and Lowell in 1826, composed primarily of unmarried, native-born, young, farm women and girls from northern New England (Ware, 1931). Industrialists such as George Pullman built complete towns around their industrial facilities. Pullman built the town of Pullman around his Pullman Palace Car Company (Ely, 1885; Greer, 1979). The company town of Gary (Indiana) shows how race, ethnicity, and class played a role in segregation efforts.

Gary

The lakeshore town of Gary, Indiana, was once one of the most important centers of steel production in the country. Gary is home to U.S. Steel.

The company was formed in 1901 when J.P. Morgan purchased the Carnegie holdings in steel. In 1906, U.S. Steel began building its integrated plant to produce coke, iron, and steel and a town to house its workers (Greer, 1979; C. Brown, 2000; Brady and Wallace, 2001). U.S. Steel, one of the world's largest steel mills, occupied thousands of acres of Gary's lakeshore (*United States Steel v. Russell Train*, 1977; Greer, 1979).

Gary was originally laid out to replicate the bureaucratic hierarchy of the mill and to reflect the ideological thinking of its owner. The best houses were reserved for the managers and supervisors—all were native born and of western European ancestry. Their houses were built closest to the plant so that they could walk to work easily. Unfortunately for these employees, their close proximity to the mill meant they got the worst pollution. Hence, the workers exposed to the least pollution inside the factory were subject to the worst pollution at home. As one moved down the hierarchy, workers were housed in smaller, less well-built homes farther away from the mill. When the workforce was all White, eastern European immigrants lived in the worst housing on the southern fringe of the city. Just after World War I, when Blacks and a small number of Hispanics first moved to the city, they lived among the Whites. Blacks lived in the worst housing on the Southside. As better housing opportunities materialized, Whites moved to all-White neighborhoods, leaving Blacks—who could not get housing elsewhere—in the southern section of the city. In 1950, 97% of Gary's Black population lived in Midtown—a two-square-mile area. Realtors refused to show Blacks homes in other neighborhoods, and city authorities rejected African American applications for public housing in neighborhoods outside Midtown (Greer, 1979; Hurley, 1995; D.E. Taylor, 2009).

Blacks found it difficult to move out of the decrepit homes in Midtown. Blacks wanting to flee Midtown ended up settling in homes in other parts of the city that Whites abandoned. Realtors used the technique of "blockbusting" to exploit racial tensions and to scare Whites into selling their homes en masse. Blockbusters usually bought a home on a block, sold it to a Black family, and then contacted the remaining Whites on the block to warn them of an impending Black "invasion" and depressed property values. Whites usually panicked and sold their homes cheaply. These homes were quickly resold to Blacks at much higher prices (Hurley, 1995).

Some Whites used racially restrictive covenants to forbid the sale of their homes to Blacks. Others put signs in their yards reading, "For Whites Only." However, realtors were successful in their blockbusting efforts by targeting older residents, and some neighborhoods such as Tolleston changed to a predominantly Black neighborhood rapidly. However, in Miller and Glen Park—suburbs on Gary's eastern and southern borders—affluent Whites who cherished the rolling sand dunes, easy access to Lake Michigan, and relatively pristine environment did not want to vacate these communities. They did not want to have Black residents in these neighborhoods either. Consequently, Whites responded by banning the posting of "For Sale" signs on lawns, and Glen Park residents resorted to blatant intimidation tactics. The result was that Blacks remained trapped in Gary's polluted neighborhoods, as it was very difficult to acquire property in the suburbs (Hurley, 1995; D.E. Taylor, 2009).

Exclusionary Zoning

Though the use of racially restrictive zoning laws has all but disappeared and the use of racially restrictive covenants has declined over time, zoning laws are still being used to limit minority housing options. That is, zoning can be used in *indirect ways* to promote residential segregation without specifically naming a particular racial or ethnic group as the target. One tactic has involved the creation of rigid zoning laws that are either relaxed or not enforced for Whites but are strictly enforced for Blacks and other minorities. Another tactic is to encapsulate Black communities in commercial and industrial zones. For instance, when Ford Motor Company moved its plant to Milpitas, California, and the labor union attempted to construct housing for Black workers, the city rezoned the site for industrial use (Abrams 1966).

Exclusionary zoning is another practice that can be used to *manipulate* the racial composition of a community. Exclusionary zoning practices are pervasive and persistent. They represent a *subtle use of zoning* to achieve *discriminatory ends*. Rather than devise ordinances stipulating which people can live and build where, exclusionary zoning achieves segregation by focusing on *the regulation of housing units and lots*.

Exclusionary zoning typically involves practices that result in the exclusion of certain types of residents from a particular area by control-ling the type of residential development that occurs there. This involves zoning for large lots, low-density development, growth-management strategies such as moratoria on the construction of new housing, huge exaction fees for new development, a ban or limit on the development of multifamily housing units, a ban on mobile homes and prefabricated (factory-built) dwellings, architectural design specifications, and deep setback requirements. Such exclusionary zoning has the effect of keep-ing poor people, large families, older residents, single individuals, and racial and ethnic minorities out of particular areas (*Britton v. Town of Chester*, 1991; Collin, 1992; Ritzdorf, 1997; Maantay, 2002; Clinger-mayer, 2004; Fischel, 2004; Connerly, 2005; C. Arnold, 2007; Park and Pellow, 2011).

A case in point is Blackjack, Missouri. In 1970, this predominantly White suburb of St. Louis was chosen as the site on which a nonprofit organization affiliated with the Methodist Church planned to build fed-erally subsidized townhouses on 25 acres for low- and moderate-income Black and White families. Within nine months of the announcement, Blackjack was incorporated, and the community passed a zoning ordi-nance that limited development to three homes per acre. This ordinance effectively squashed plans for subsidized housing. The Department of Justice filed suit, and the lower court upheld the zoning ordinance. However, the circuit court overturned the lower court ruling in 1974. The U.S. Supreme Court let the circuit court ruling stand (*United States v. City of Blackjack*, 1974; King, 1978).

The zoning ordinance specifying large lot development in Arlington Heights (a suburb of Chicago) was challenged in court by the Metro-politan Housing Development Corporation in 1972. The lower court ruled in favor of the city in 1974, but the court of appeals, arguing that the zoning ordinance would have a discriminatory effect, overturned the ruling. The U.S. Supreme Court sided with the city in reversing the decision of the court of appeals. Supreme Court justices argued that even if an ordinance had a *racially disproportionate impact*, that was not sufficient grounds to strike it down. The Supreme Court did remand the case to the court of appeals to examine whether the ordinance vio-lated the Fair Housing Act (*Village of Arlington Heights v. Metropolitan Housing*, 1977).

The State of the EJ Research

Expulsive and Intensive Zoning

Researchers have studied the impacts of expulsive zoning on minority and low-income communities. Rabin's (1990) study of 12 communities documented how minority and low-income neighborhoods have been rezoned to accommodate *unwanted land uses* and environmental hazards. Rabin refers to this practice as "expulsive zoning," as it has the effect of *driving out* both residents and land uses that can afford to move.

Municipalities often manipulate zoning so that minority and low-income neighborhoods are included in or abut industrial zones. A 1998 study examined zoning patterns in 31 census tracts in seven cities (Anaheim, Costa Mesa, Orange, and Santa Ana in California; Pittsburgh; San Antonio; and Wichita). In all the cities studied, census tracts that had high concentrations of minorities and were low income were subject to more *intensive zoning* (industrial and commercial) than were tracts that were high income and had low concentrations of minorities. The study found that 13 of the 19 low-income, high-minority census tracts had some industrial zoning, and in seven of the tracts, more than 20% of the tract was zoned for industrial uses. In comparison, of the 12 high-income, low-minority tracts, only one was zoned industrial. The study also found that commercial land uses were also more likely to be concentrated in low-income, high-minority tracts than in other tracts (C. Arnold, 1998, 2007).

Maantay studied how changing the zoning designation of portions of a municipality impacted residents. She examined the expansion and contraction of *M zones* (manufacturing zones) in New York City from 1961 to 1998. In New York City, M zones tend to host facilities such as waste transfer stations, medical waste treatment facilities, sludge pelletization plants, waste water treatment plants, recycling facilities, construction and demolition debris processing plants, combined sewer overflow outfalls, junkyards, and marine transfer stations. Maantay's research found that the people living in or directly adjacent to major M zones were predominantly minority and poor. More specifically, minorities constituted 77.1% of the residents of the Bronx in 1990 but 87.4% of those living in M zones in the borough. In Brooklyn, where minorities constituted 59.7% of the borough's population in 1990, they constituted 63.6% of the residents living in M zones. Similarly, minorities constituted 19.8% of the residents of Staten Island but 33.1% of those living in the borough's M zones. Overall, minorities constituted 56.6% of New York City's residents in 1990 but 60.7% of those living in M zones in the metropolis. Maantay also found that the Bronx, the least affluent borough in the city, had the most major increases in M zones from 1961 to 1998; Manhattan had the most significant decreases in M zones in that period (Maantay, 2002).

Downey (2005) came to an opposite conclusion after studying Detroit. He argues that Detroit's Black community expanded along its fringes rather than along the city's manufacturing corridors. Hence, Blacks were not found disproportionately in manufacturing neighborhoods and corridors. However, historical context is important in studying cities such as Detroit. Depending on the time period examined, one may or may not find Blacks and other minorities living in close proximity to industrial facilities. For instance, up until the late nineteenth century, Detroit was a walking city without public transportation. Consequently, White ethnic neighborhoods sprang up around the factories, as workers lived close to their workplace (Farley, Danziger, and Holzer, 2000). In 1910, Blacks constituted a mere 1.2% of the city's population, and as late as 1940, only 9.2% of the residents of the city were Black (Gibson and Jung, 2005). However, when the Black population began to increase rapidly during the 1940s, many of the White ethnic neighborhoods resorted to violence and the use of restrictive covenants to deter Blacks from moving in. Hurley (1997a, 1997b) argues that this was the case in St. Louis and East St. Louis, where working-class Whites lived close to the factories and restrictive covenants and other discriminatory real estate practices prevented Blacks from living close to industrial districts.

Heresthetics and the Structuring of Options

Clingermayer argues that heresthetics (the *structuring of arguments and options* to determine who wins) is an important dimension of exclusionary zoning and the planning process. He argues that exclusionary zoning ordinances are often couched in language that deflects attention away from the *intended or unintended disparate impacts* on the poor and ethnic minorities (Clingermayer, 2004). This is done by framing regulation in value-laden terms such as environmental protection, neighborhood protection, neighborhood improvement, historic preservation, creation of open space, control of sprawl, alleviation of traffic congestion, growth management, smart growth, and other planning principles intended for the good of the people (Clingermayer, 2004; Fischel, 2004). This tactic can be seen as a continuation of a tactic used in the first half of the twentieth century, when neighborhood associations and other civic groups opposed to neighborhood racial integration claimed they were acting in the interest of "preservation" and "protection" (D.E. Taylor, 2009).

When the manipulation of the arguments and process is deliberate, it can be considered as heresthetics. If the process occurs by chance, it is happenstance. Clingermayer argues that small municipalities with homogeneous populations tend to be more exclusionary than are large jurisdictions with heterogeneous populations (Clingermayer, 2004). In an earlier study published in 1996, Clingermayer found that exclusionary zoning was associated with a high rate of homeownership. Other factors that had significant positive associations with exclusionary zoning were home values, income levels, and the percentage of the White population (Clingermayer, 1996).

A Return to the Past?

Some scholars argue that a new wave of housing ordinances aimed at restricting the housing options of immigrants is taking hold in the U.S. The new legislation targets undocumented immigrants, preventing them from renting housing in cities that adopt such ordinances. The ordinances also levy fines of up to $1,000 a day on property owners and tenants who violate the ordinances. In the wake of the immigration-reform protests that took place around the country in 2006, more than 40 municipalities proposed anti-immigrant restrictive ordinances (Bono, 2007; Oliveri, 2009).

The first of the contemporary anti-undocumented-immigrant housing ordinances was proposed in San Bernardino, California, in April 2006. San Bernardino's Illegal Immigration Relief Act says, "Illegal

aliens are prohibited from leasing or renting property. Any property owner/renter/tenant/lessee in control of property, who allows an illegal alien to use, rent, or lease their property shall be in violation of this section, irrespective of such person's intent, knowledge or negligence" (qtd. in Oliveri, 2009: 59). The San Bernardino measure failed to get the city council's approval, and backers failed to place it on the ballot for a popular vote. However, a few months later, the former coal-mining town of Hazleton—located about 97 miles northwest of Philadelphia—became the first city to pass such an ordinance. The Hazleton ordinance also placed restrictions on the hiring of undocumented workers. When the ordinance passed in July 2006, Hazleton had a population of roughly 30,000, and about a third was Hispanic. Anti-immigrant ordinances were also crafted in other cities experiencing growth in the Latino population. Within three years, 105 municipalities in 29 states considered Hazleton-style anti-immigrant ordinances, and 42 passed them. Several of these ordinances have been challenged in court. Among them are Hazleton; Farmers Branch, Texas; Escondido, California; Cherokee County, Georgia; Topeka, Kansas; Valley Park, Missouri; and Riverside, New Jersey (Bono, 2007; *Pedro Lozano et al. v. City of Hazleton*, 2007; Oliveri, 2009). In 2009 alone, more than 1,500 bills aimed at immigration enforcement were introduced at the local and state level. Of those, 222 became law and 131 were adopted as resolutions (Richey, 2011).

Soon after the Hazleton ordinance passed, LatinoJustice–Puerto Rican Legal Defense and Education Fund (PRLDEF), the American Civil Liberties Union (ACLU)–Pennsylvania, ACLU–Immigrant Rights Project, the Community Justice Project of Harrisburg, and local attorneys filed a complaint in the U.S. District Court for the Middle District of Pennsylvania challenging it. Hazleton responded by repealing its ordinance and passing an amended version to take its place in December 2006. The litigants filed an amended complaint and obtained a temporary restraining order blocking the city from enforcing the ordinance. In July 2007, Judge James Munley struck down the Hazleton ordinance. The city of Hazleton appealed the decision (*Pedro Lozano et al. v. City of Hazleton*, 2007; LatinoJustice, 2008). In September, 2010, the U.S. Court of Appeals upheld the lower court ruling. The appeals court argued that Hazleton had overstepped its bounds in passing the ordinance. The mayor of Hazleton, Lou Barletta, vowed to take the case to the U.S. Supreme Court. By 2010, Hazleton's population had dwindled to 25,350, and 37.3% of the residents were Hispanics (Preston, 2010; *Pedro Lozano et al. v. City of Hazleton*, 2010; U.S. Census Bureau, 2010). In 2011, the U.S. Supreme Court vacated the decision of the U.S. Court of Appeals in Philadelphia (*City of Hazleton v. Pedro Lozano et al.*, 2011; *Pedro Lozano et al. v. City of Hazleton*, 2011) and ordered it to reexamine the Hazleton case in light of the high court's decision on May 26 to uphold an ordinance in Arizona by which a business owner's operating license could be revoked if he or she knowingly or intentionally employs an undocumented worker (*Chamber of Commerce v. Whiting*, 2011). However, in 2012, in the case of *Arizona v. United States*, the U.S. Supreme Court struck down key provisions of the Arizona immigration law by ruling that it was illegal for police officers to check the legal status of any person suspected of being undocumented. On July 26, 2013, the U.S. Court of Appeals in Philadelphia ruled that the Hazleton ordinances that prohibited the employment of undocumented workers and prevented them from renting housing in the city were unconstitutional (*Pedro Lozano et al. v. City of Hazleton*, 2013).

EJ scholars Park and Pellow (2011) studied Aspen, Colorado, and found a rise in anti-immigrant sentiments and conflicts around housing as the city's very rich struggle with the paradox of wanting low-wage Hispanic service workers to do their bidding but not wanting to live among them.

Nothing Random

The foregoing discussion demonstrates that residential patterns in many cities are not random. Neither did they arise from natural evolutionary processes. The discussion shows that a variety of institutions and people invested significant time and energy in devising instruments to keep the races separate and to segregate cities. The discussion puts into question the economic rationality and chicken-or-egg theses that presume that minorities have free choice in where they can move to or live. The discussion shows that the housing choices of Blacks and other minorities are *more constrained* than those of Whites; hence, minorities might not be able to move to avoid environmental hazards even if they want to.

Though researchers are beginning to examine the relationship between zoning and proximity to environmental hazards, much more research is needed in this area. Though EJ scholars often cite zoning as an explanation for why minorities are found closer to hazardous facilities or experience greater exposures to air pollution and the like, they have not invested much time in actually investigating this argument fully. They usually do not include any variables in their studies to examine the impact of zoning. Not only are more studies along the lines of Maantay (2002), C. Arnold (1998, 2007), and Rabin (1990) needed, EJ researchers should be examining how the use of racial districts, commercial and industrial buffer strips, and other racial zoning laws are related to the siting patterns of hazardous facilities and exposure to toxins. So it is not just a question of what year a particular facility was built and what the demographic characteristics of the neighborhood were at the time of construction (and how it changed later on); researchers should also be examining what zoning laws were in effect at the time of siting and how those changed over time. That is, who or what kept people living adjacent to noxious facilities once they were built? Such research could elucidate the extent to which historical racial zoning impacted the siting patterns of hazardous facilities and whether there are lingering effects arising from siting and residential segregation.

8

The Rise of Racially Restrictive Covenants

Guarding against Infiltration

Restrictive covenants are used by developers and individual property owners to control land uses and occupancy. Among other things, they have been used to segregate communities and forestall the siting of commercial and industrial facilities in upscale residential neighborhoods. Despite their widespread use and importance, EJ scholars have ignored the impact these instruments have on residential patterns, the siting of industrial and manufacturing facilities, and the exposure to environmental hazards in cities.

Despite the many judicial rulings against racial segregation ordinances, these decisions did not affect the *private agreements* that homeowners entered into among themselves to create and preserve racially homogeneous neighborhoods. In deciding private racial covenants cases, three fundamental questions were before the courts: Were racially restrictive covenants valid? Was it legal for municipalities and states to use their judicial and other police powers to enforce racial covenants between private parties? Were racially restrictive covenants enforceable when the neighborhoods they were intended to protect had undergone substantial demographic changes?

Restrictive covenants are clauses inserted in property deeds that specify and delimit what property owners can do with their land and the buildings they construct on them. Clauses can specify under what conditions the property can be sold, how and to whom, the height of buildings, the materials they can or cannot be constructed of, how far from the street the buildings may be set, the size of the lot, the percentage of the lot that can be built on, and the use to which the property can be put. At first, the covenants were used to enhance the aesthetic appeal of neighborhoods by specifying that open space should be left in front of buildings; some stipulated that structures should be set back from the sidewalk. Restrictive covenants were also used to create residential enclaves by stipulating that commercial activities could not occur on properties encumbered by the covenants. Other covenants were concerned with creating upscale communities, so they prohibited multiple dwelling units (D.E. Taylor, 2009).

However, restrictive covenants were used during the first half of the twentieth century as tools to segregate cities and prohibit Blacks and other minorities from moving into sections of cities (J. Farrell, 2002). The racially restrictive covenants began appearing in the late nineteenth century, and by 1900, developers began inserting them into the deeds of homes built in new subdivisions. The covenants targeted Blacks most frequently, but other ethnic minorities, Jews, and eastern Europeans were also the targets of these clauses. Racially restrictive covenants were used *in tandem with* racial zoning laws in some cities, while they were used *in lieu of* racially restrictive zoning in others.

The federal government encouraged the use of racially restrictive covenants to create and maintain racially homogeneous neighborhoods. The Federal Housing Administration (FHA)—established in 1934—produced an *Underwriting Manual* with guidelines for preserving property values and desirable community characteristics; it stated, "If a neighborhood is to retain stability, it is necessary that properties shall continue to be occupied by the same social and racial classes." Ergo, the *Manual* instructed appraisers to guard against the "infiltration" of "inharmonious racial or nationality groups" into neighborhoods. The *Manual* urged the use of "subdivision regulations and suitable restrictive covenants" as mechanisms to maintain neighborhood exclusivity (Federal Housing Administration, 1938). The U.S. Commission on Civil Rights argues that real estate companies, builders, and financial institutions act in ways that translate the *prejudice of property owners* into *discriminatory action*. The commission also argued that these actors are "aided and abetted" by the government, and these parties bear the primary responsibility for housing segregation (1973: 3). Consequently, as late as 1959, less than 2% of the FHA-insured housing built was available to ethnic minorities. A 1967 study showed that of 400,000 housing units in FHA-insured subdivisions, only 3.3% had been sold to minorities (U.S. Commission on Civil Rights, 1973).

Despite the widespread use of private racially restrictive covenants during the first half of the twentieth century, they were expensive to effectuate and enforce. For the covenant to be enforceable, the signers had to account for a specified percentage (usually 75% or more) of the residents of the street, neighborhood, or subdivision being covered. It was costly to acquire the necessary signatures and to incorporate the restrictions into existing deeds. There were also costs associated with enforcing the covenants once they were in place. As later discussion shows, the NAACP hedged its bet that frequent legal challenges to the covenants would prove costly to signers, and that, in turn, would reduce their popularity. The covenants were more expensive to put in place in existing neighborhoods than in new housing developments (Vose, 1959; Brooks, 2002).

There was a class dimension to the use of these covenants that is often overlooked. Plotkin's (1999) study of Chicago found that affluent White communities used covenants most heavily. Brooks's (2002) analysis also bears this out. Brooks found in his study of covenant and noncovenant areas of the city that the covenant areas were less densely populated and had a higher percentage of Whites, a lower percentage of immigrants, a lower percentage of Blacks, a higher percentage of white-collar workers, higher median home prices, and a lower percentage of substandard housing (see table 8.1). White working-class neighborhoods

Table 8.1. Comparison of Extensively Covenanted and Noncovenanted Areas of Chicago in 1940

Characteristics	Covenant areas	Noncovenant areas
Average population	38,725	47,364
Percentage native Whites	79.20%	71.60%
Percentage foreign born	15.70%	20.20%
Percentage Black	5.0%	6.8%
Percentage white collar	49.50%	38.10%
Median housing value	$4,966	$3,652
Percentage substandard housing	14.80%	18.30%
Number of persons per room	0.74	0.75

Source: Brooks, 2002.

tended to use a combination of violence and covenants to deter Blacks from moving in. Plotkin also found that neighborhood associations in wealthy White neighborhoods encouraged residents of White working-class neighborhoods contiguous to Black communities to use restrictive covenants. The goal was to create a stronger buffer between Black and wealthy White communities.

Racially Restrictive Covenants in Southern and Western Cities

Anti-Asian Restrictive Covenants in San Buena Ventura and the Imperial Valley

The earliest racially restrictive covenants were directed against Chinese residents living in California. One early case, *Gandolfo v. Hartman*, was decided in 1892. It involved the violation of a covenant that was signed in 1886 regarding a lot on East Main Street in San Buena Ventura, California. The covenant specified that the parties, their heirs, and assigns could not rent any buildings or grounds "to a Chinaman or Chinamen" without the consent of the parties to the agreement. The defendant in this case, Hartman, purchased the property from one of the original signers of the covenant and then leased the property to two Chinese men, Fong Yet and Sam Choy. A lawsuit was brought against Hartman for violating the terms of the covenant. Judge Erskine Ross decided that the covenant violated the Fourteenth Amendment as well as the 1880 treaty with China that offered Chinese residents in America the protections afforded those from a "most favored nation" (*Gandolfo v. Hartman*, 1892: 181; Ming, 1949; Groves, 1950–1951). Later courts ignored this ruling.

Punjabi immigrants were also targeted by racially restrictive covenants in the early part of the twentieth century. An influx of Punjabi farmers into California's Imperial Valley resulted in the passage of an ordinance barring the sale of land to "Hindoos." The Punjabi farmers— who were mostly male—circumvented the restrictions by marrying Mexican women living in the area, as these women were not prohibited by law from taking possession of land. More than 500 such marriages are recorded (Leonard, 1994; Majumdar, 2006–2007).

Charlotte—Racial Districts

In 1875, Charlotte, North Carolina, was a city in which rich and poor, Black and White, merchants and laborers intermingled and resided on the same blocks and in the same neighborhoods. However, in the late nineteenth and early twentieth century, a group of powerful business-men spearheaded a reorganization of the ideological and physical land-scape of the city. These men set out to control what they saw as unruly Blacks and unreliable White working-class mill workers. Some of the ways in which they sought to impose order on the city was to create racially and socioeconomically exclusive neighborhoods and to rede-fine people's understanding of desirable landscapes (Hanchett, 1993; Morrill, 2004).

Charlotte's leaders considered the use of racially restrictive zoning ordinances to impose segregation on the city but opted not to use them (Silver, 1997). Instead, private racially restrictive covenants that barred the sale of property to Blacks were widely used to segregate the city. Piedmont Park, a subdivision developed by F. Abbott and George Ste-phens shortly after 1900, served as a model for neighborhoods seeking to redefine residential space. Not only was it the first neighborhood to jettison the city's grid street system, but developers and residents in the neighborhood focused on keeping "undesirables" out. The deed restric-tions called for a purely residential neighborhood. The covenants also barred Blacks from owning or renting property in the subdivision. There was also a class dimension to the covenants—they stipulated that homes built in the community should be at least $1,500. This was a princely sum in the early 1900s, when most of the homes were being built. Though the covenants did not bar poor Whites outright, the price tag on the homes served as an effective mechanism to keep working-class Whites out of the neighborhood (Hanchett, 1993; Morrill, 2004).

Between 1900 and 1930, several other subdivisions were developed with restrictive covenants modeled after Piedmont Park's. Conse-quently, Elizabeth, Myers Park, Chatam Estates, Wilmore, Dilworth, and Eastover developed as purely residential, racially and socioeco-nomically exclusive communities in and around the city. The busi-ness elites hastened to build mansions in these new subdivisions as soon as they were opened up for development. For instance, Edward Dilworth Latta built a Colonial Revival–style mansion on East Boulevard in Dilworth, while cotton magnate Ralph VanLandingham built a bungalow-style house on the Plaza in Chatham Estates. Other elites moved their mansions from downtown neighborhoods to the new exclusive enclaves, and Myers Park was the most coveted destination. Myers Park was developed by George Stephens, codeveloper of Piedmont Park, on land he purchased from his father-in-law (John Myers) after marrying into the wealthy family. So coveted was a Myers Park address that Dr. Charles McManaway moved his stylish Italianate mansion from West Trade Street to Queens Road in Myers Park after that subdivision opened in 1912. Prominent merchant Benjamin Withers also moved his mansion from its downtown East Trade Street location to Selwyn Avenue in Myers Park. Other merchants such as department-store magnate J. Ivey built impressive homes with expansive gardens in Myers Park too. Famed industrialist and philanthropist James Duke also lived in an imposing Colonial Revival–style mansion in Myers Park. Duke's Lynnwood mansion was built on 15 acres; it had 45 rooms and 12 bathrooms (Hanchett, 1993; Kratt and Hanchett, 2009; Douglas, 1994, 1995; Morrill, 2004).

While the city's businessmen carved out upscale enclaves for themselves, middle-class Whites lived in Wesley Heights, and White mill workers lived in Villa Heights, Belmont, and Optimist Park. Black middle-class residents lived in Biddleville and Washington Heights. Brooklyn was another Black neighborhood (Hanchett, 1993; Douglas, 1994).

The story of Charlotte illustrates the extent to which business and political elites were willing to organize the neighborhoods in which they lived to exclude people and land uses they perceived as undesirable. At the same time, they orchestrated the land uses of other neighborhoods to determine how residential, commercial, and industrial land uses would evolve. The North Carolina courts upheld the racially restrictive covenants for decades (for example, see *Eason v. Buffaloe*, 1930; *St. Louis Union Trust v. Foster*, 1937; *Sheets v. Dillon*, 1942; *Vernon v. R.J. Reynolds Realty*, 1945; *Phillips v. Wearn*, 1946). However, the 1948 *Shelley v. Kraemer* U.S. Supreme Court decision (discussed later in this chapter) made it illegal to use the police powers of the city or state to *enforce* the covenants (Hanchett, 1993; Douglas, 1994, 1995). The decision did *not* make the covenants illegal; private parties could continue to use and enforce the covenants among themselves.

Contemporary Myers Park reflects the tenacity of prosegregationist and elitist forces. Today the neighborhood is dotted with multimillion-dollar mansions perched on spacious lots adorning wide, tree-lined streets (J. Rose, 2010). While the city of Charlotte is 27% Black, Myers Park is only 5% Black. Communities such as Myers Park are able to maintain their racial exclusivity because the deeds are often monitored and enforced by home-owner associations. Myers Park residents were thrust into the spotlight in 2009 when the NAACP filed a complaint against the Myers Park Housing Association (MPHA). At issue was a sample deed posted on the association's website that listed ten restrictions that covered the community's 3,300 homes. The first restriction stated, "The lot hereby conveyed shall be used for residential purposes only and shall be owned and occupied by people of Caucasian race only." Though the MPHA's president, Pamela May, argued that the posting of the restrictive covenant with the racially exclusionary language on the association's website was "completely unintentional" and that "the whole situation is regrettable," the MPHA website indicated that the covenants were judiciously enforced. The MPHA has also funded strategic lawsuits to maintain "community character"; none of these involved racial restrictions (Singleton, 2009).

Since the courts cannot be used to enforce racial exclusion in communities such as Myers Park, it is understandable why none of the lawsuits involved the racial restrictions in the deed. Charlotte's Community Relations Committee ruled in favor of the NAACP; it argued that the racially restrictive covenant violated the Federal Fair Housing Act of 1968 and the city's Fair Housing Ordinance (Singleton, 2009). The NAACP was not content with this decision and is seeking to get the racially restrictive clause expunged from the Myers Park covenants. However, Ken Davies, the attorney for the MPHA, argues that the racially restrictive clause "is a completed legal recording": "We have no authority to go back and tell the register of deeds to eliminate this or that from whatever deed we don't like. And everyone knows that it's something that is a historic relic" (Rose, 2010).

Kansas City—Restrictive Covenants Used in Tandem with Racial Zoning

Kansas City, Missouri, has used both racial zoning and restrictive covenants to achieve residential segregation. From 1908 through the 1940s, one developer—the J.C. Nichols Company—built dozens of subdivisions in and around the city and added racially restrictive clauses to the homes that barred sale of the properties to or their occupancy by Blacks, Armenians, Jews, Turks, Persians, Syrians, and Arabs (J. Thomas, 2005). The Missouri courts upheld racially restrictive covenants for decades. In 1918, the Supreme Court of Missouri found that a covenant covering property on Wirtman Place in Kansas City was valid and that Elizabeth and August Koehler had violated the covenant by renting their property to Blacks (*Elizabeth Koehler v. Rowland*, 1918). Though the number of Blacks in the city had increased from 23,566 in 1910 to 30,719 in 1920, they constituted only 9.5% of the population (Gibson and Jung, 2005).

Washington, D.C.—Creating Barriers to Movement

The Court of Appeals of the District of Columbia and the U.S. Supreme Court found valid a covenant that covered 25 parcels, was signed by 30 Whites living in the 18th Street and New Hampshire Avenue neighborhood in 1921, and barred Blacks from occupying property in the neighborhood (*Corrigan v. Buckley*, 1924, 1926). The 109,966 Blacks living in the city in 1920 constituted 25.1% of the city's population (Gibson and Jung, 2005). Another racially restrictive covenant was also upheld in the case of *Grady v. Garland* in 1937 in Washington, D.C. Grady brought suit on behalf of himself and five other lot owners seeking to get the restrictive covenants binding their lots to be declared as "clouds upon the titles of the owners thereof, impeding the free use and enjoyment of their properties." Grady wanted the covenant to be canceled since minority families were already living to the west of the properties bound by the covenant. The covenants were placed on the lots between 1901 and 1905, when they were built by the real estate firm Middaugh & Shannon. This was done years before cities began passing anti-Black racial zoning ordinances. In upholding the covenant, the U.S. Court of Appeals for the District of Columbia argued that the covenant was intended to prevent people of color from living in the eight lots in the square. The covenant "furnishes a complete barrier against the eastward movement of colored population into the restricted area—a dividing line." Given the vague arguments made by the plaintiff, the court refused to strike down the covenant because the justices thought such action would destroy the value of the defendants' property (*Grady v. Garland*, 1937: 819).

Private-party racially restrictive covenants were also challenged under the aegis of neighborhood change. In cases where dramatic neighborhood changes had occurred, the courts were willing to nullify the covenants, but where such changes were not apparent, the covenants were enforced by the courts. For instance, in the case of *Hundley v. Gorewitz* (1942), six homes on the west side of 13th Street had a restrictive covenant (dating back to 1910) that prohibited property owners from renting, selling, or leasing their property to Blacks or other people of color. Frederick Hundley and his wife, Mary Hundley, bought one of these properties in 1941. Neighbors Gorewitz and Bogikes filed suit against the Hundleys. In 1941, the district court found the Hundleys in violation of the covenant and canceled their deed. The case went to the court of appeals, which reversed the lower court ruling on the grounds that the neighborhood had changed so that enforcement of the covenant was not beneficial. The court of appeals argued that "when it is shown that the neighborhood in question has so changed in its character and environment and in the uses to which the property therein may be put that the purpose of the covenant cannot be carried out, or that its enforcement would substantially lessen the value of the property, or, in short, that injunctive relief would not give a benefit but rather impose a hardship, the rule will not be enforced" (*Hundley v. Gorewitz*, 1942: 24).

Other cases in Washington, D.C., questioned the validity of the covenants in neighborhoods where the racial characteristics were purported to have changed substantially since the time the covenant was enacted. In 1906, 20 of 30 lots on Bryant Street were sold with deeds prohibiting Blacks from occupying the properties. James and Mary Hurd, African Americans, bought a house in the restricted area in 1945, as did three other African Americans. At the time of the sales, 11 lots were already owned by Blacks. The district court ruled that the deeds of the African American petitioners were null and void and ordered them to vacate their property within 60 days of the decision. Hurd appealed the case, but the court of appeals upheld the district court ruling. In the *Hurd v. Hodge* case, plaintiffs tried to argue that the neighborhood had undergone a racial transformation—enough to void the restrictive covenant. However, the court of appeals was not convinced by this argument and ruled to enforce the covenant (*Hurd v. Hodge*, 1947, 1948). The case was coupled with others and heard by the U.S. Supreme Court; the decision is discussed later in this chapter. Similarly, in the case of *Mays v. Burgess* (1945), the court of appeals also ruled that it would enforce the restrictive covenant because the neighborhood had not undergone significant changes.

St. Louis—Restrictive Covenants as a Counterpart to Restrictive Zoning

The case of *Shelley v. Kraemer* originated in St. Louis. The use of private racially restrictive covenants preceded attempts to develop racially restrictive zoning ordinances in the city. In 1911, property owners on Labadie Avenue signed a restrictive covenant stating that no one who is not Caucasian could use or occupy the properties for 50 years. The covenant specifically mentioned that "people of the negro or Mongolian Race" should not occupy the properties covered by the deed. There were a total of 57 parcels in the subdivision, and the 30 property owners who signed the covenant held titles to 47 parcels. At the time the agreement was signed, five parcels were owned by Blacks (one parcel had been occupied by Blacks since 1882). On August 11, 1945, J.D. Shelley and his wife, Ethel, who were African Americans, bought property in the restricted area. The Shelleys did not know that the property was covered by a racially restrictive covenant. The house was bought by a real estate company and placed in the name of Josephine Fitzgerald (also a defendant), a White individual acting as a "straw party." The Shelleys then bought the house from the real estate company. In October of that year, Louis and Fern Kraemer sued to prevent the Shelleys from moving in. The Shelleys questioned whether all the signatures needed to make the covenant effective were obtained. The trial court dismissed the petition because all the property owners had not signed the covenant. The case was appealed to the Supreme Court of Missouri. That court reversed the lower court ruling, finding instead that the covenant was valid and that its enforcement by the court did not violate the Fourteenth Amendment (*Louis Kraemer v. Shelley*, 1946, 1948; *Shelley v. Kraemer*, 1948). This case was coupled with others and eventually heard before the U.S. Supreme Court; the decision is discussed later in this chapter.

Los Angeles—Caucasians Only

Racially restrictive covenants were common in Los Angeles. In 1919, the Supreme Court of California ruled in the case of the *Los Angeles Investment Company v. Gary* that a covenant stating that "no person or persons other than those of the Caucasian race shall be permitted to occupy the property" was valid. Alfred Gary and his wife, both African Americans, acquired a property covered by this deed restriction. The courts declared that the covenant was enforceable (*Los Angeles Investment Company v. Gary*, 1919). Though the number of Blacks living in Los Angeles had more than doubled between 1910 and 1920, Blacks constituted only 2.4% of the city's population in 1910 and 2.7% in 1920 (Gibson and Jung, 2005). Yet about 80% of Los Angeles was covered by racially restrictive covenants (U.S. Commission on Civil Rights, 1973; Abrams, 1966).

Seattle—Targeting Blacks, Asians, and Jews

Private racially restrictive covenants were also widely used in Seattle. Many still appear in the deeds to homes. Consequently, the King County Recorder's Office holds 416 racially restrictive deeds and covenants, covering roughly 95 neighborhoods and tens of thousands of homes in Seattle and suburban King County. The first of these covenants was penned in 1924 by the Goodwin Company; it covered three tracts of land in the Victory Heights neighborhood in North Seattle (Silva, 2009). From the 1920s through the 1940s, neighborhoods in North Seattle, West Seattle, South Seattle, and the suburbs across Lake Washington had deed restrictions on the homes that barred Ethiopians, Africans, and other Blacks; Mongolians, Chinese, Japanese, Malays, and other Asians; and Jews from acquiring or residing in homes in these areas. The restrictive covenants also targeted Native Americans, Pacific Islanders, and people of Mexican ancestry. Neighborhoods covered by racially restrictive covenants were also developed by the South Seattle Land Company, the Seattle Trust Company, the Puget Mill Company, the Crawford & Canover Real Estate Partnership, and the Boeing Aircraft Company (Pettus, 1948; Majumdar, 2006–2007; Silva, 2009).

W.E. Boeing, founder of the Boeing Aircraft Company, led efforts to blanket the city and its fledgling suburbs with racially restrictive covenants. Bill and Bertha Boeing developed vast tracts of land in North Seattle, including Richmond Beach, Richmond Heights, Blue Ridge, Shoreview, and Innis Arden in Shoreline (Silva, 2009; Majumdar, 2006–2007). A typical Boeing racially restrictive clause reads,

> No property in said addition shall at any time be sold, conveyed, rented, or leased in whole or in part to any person or persons not of the White or Caucasian race. No person other than one of the White or Caucasian race shall be permitted to occupy any property in said addition of portion thereof or building thereon except a domestic servant actually employed by a person of the White or Caucasian race where the latter is an occupant of such property. (Innis Arden Covenant, 1941)

Others of the aforementioned developers also used racially restrictive clauses similar to Boeing's. Homeowners in neighborhoods built before 1920 also organized themselves into associations and drafted racially restrictive covenants to cover their properties. For instance, White homeowners in the Capitol Hill neighborhood were worried that Blacks would purchase houses in the area. Horace Cayton's family was one of the first to move into the neighborhood; they did so in 1903. Cayton was a prominent Black journalist, author, and politician. In 1909, a White realtor went to court to try to oust the Caytons on the grounds that they caused property values in Capitol Hill to decline. The Caytons won the case but had to move from the neighborhood five months after the decision because defending their right to live in their own home bankrupted them. Neighborhood Whites began campaigning in 1927 to add a racially restrictive clause to the deeds of 964 homes in a 183-block area. The campaign, orchestrated through the Capitol Hill Community

Club, took three years to complete. Other older Seattle neighborhoods such as Montlake, Madrona, Queen Anne, and Squire Park also organized similar campaigns (Silva, 2009; Q. Taylor, 2003).

Eventually, the covenanted areas created a ring that left people of color and Jews crammed into an L-shaped part of Seattle's inner city and effectively excluded them from residences in other parts of it. The case of Richard Ornstein, a Jewish refugee from Austria, made headlines in 1952 when he tried to purchase a home in the Sand Point Country Club area of the city (Silva, 2009; Turnbull, 2005). Upon hearing about the pending purchase, Daniel Allison, head of the Sand Point Country Club Commission, declared, "the community will not have Jews as residents." Citing the restrictive covenant that barred the sale of homes in the neighborhood to Jews and ethnic minorities, Allison launched a campaign to prevent Ornstein and his realtor from completing the purchase (Heitzman, 1953).

Racially Restrictive Covenants in Northern Cities

By the time some northern cities began to consider zoning as a mechanism to foster residential segregation, the courts had already struck down racial zoning ordinances in southern cities. Consequently, private racially restrictive covenants—intending to achieve the same aims— were popularized in lieu of racial zoning ordinances. However, the following discussion shows that White residents of northern cities were just as alarmed as their southern counterparts about racial mixing and began taking steps early on to limit where Blacks could live in cities.

The Chicago Plan—Bombs, Realtors, and Restrictive Covenants

THE EVOLUTION OF THE PLAN

In 1900, White Chicagoans began to collaborate with each other in order to control who lived in particular neighborhoods after three Blacks moved onto Vernon Avenue. Five years later, White residents of Forrestville Avenue became more aggressive and tried to force Blacks from the street; the case was taken to court. The violence against Black families moving into White Chicago neighborhoods also started early in the twentieth century. In 1911, the home of a Black family who had

moved onto Champlain Avenue was pelted with bricks. When harass-
ment and intimidation failed, some Blacks were coerced into selling
their property to neighborhood "improvement" associations wanting
them to move (Spear, 1967).

Though the practice of city councils passing zoning ordinances to
segregate municipalities by blocks or districts was not widespread in
northern cities, the idea was contemplated and in the case of Chicago
practiced informally through the customs of the neighborhood improvement associations and board of realtors. Neighborhood associations
began appearing in Chicago around 1908, and these groups openly
campaigned for the *separation of the races.* The Hyde Park Improvement Club, organized in the fall of 1908, had 350 members. Hyde Park,
a neighborhood flanking the University of Chicago, was not incorporated into Chicago till 1892. In 1909, the Hyde Park Improvement Club
circulated a manifesto declaring that "Blacks had to confine themselves
to the 'so-called Districts,' real estate agents must refuse to sell property in White blocks to Blacks [or run the risk of being blacklisted], and
landlords must hire only White janitors" (*Record-Herald*, 1909). In the
absence of a racially restrictive city ordinance, the Hyde Park Improvement Club established a committee to purchase properties owned by
Blacks that were located in blocks where the majority of the residents
were White and to offer bonuses to Black renters to break their leases
and move out of White neighborhoods (Spear, 1967).

Hyde Park residents used the community newspaper as a mouth-
piece to publicize their segregationist agenda. However, the genteel
residents of Hyde Park were not above using violence to achieve their
goal of a racially exclusive neighborhood. When a Black family was not
persuaded to move out of the neighborhood voluntarily, vandals broke
into their home on Greenwood Avenue and shattered all the windows.
The frightened family moved the following day. Hyde Park residents
also used *economic sanctions* to get their point across. They boycotted
merchants who sold goods to Blacks living in White neighborhoods.
Hyde Park residents also urged the segregation of public parks, recreation areas, and schools (Spear, 1967).

Lack of housing exacerbated matters, and World War I aggravated
the housing shortage. When the U.S. entered the war, construction of
new housing ceased, as resources were diverted to help the war effort.

By the summer of 1919, as southern Blacks streamed into the city, Chicago was short about 50,000 housing units; this affected about 200,000 people. Between 1920 and 1930, 65,355 Black migrants settled in the city, and rents skyrocketed—doubling in some instances. White realtors and landlords were not the only ones exploiting Black tenants and home buyers. Black landlords such as Jesse Binga benefited financially by overcharging Black tenants also. Despite the fact that Blacks were aware that they were being gouged by realtors and landlords, they paid the higher prices—which they referred to as the "color tax"—in order to secure housing (Tuttle, 1970; Drake and Cayton, [1945] 1993; Hirsch, 1998; Cooley, 2010). Blacks found it increasingly difficult to find housing because of a convergence of factors: the increasing migration of Blacks into the city, the limited number of units available for occupancy, rising anti-Black sentiments, and the shrinkage in the areas of the city where Blacks could live without objections from Whites.

As a result, by the second decade of the twentieth century, some property owners' associations, initially organized as part of the City Beautiful Movement to undertake community beautification projects, turned their attention to driving Blacks out of their neighborhoods and preventing others from moving in. For instance, the Community Property Owners' Protective Association (founded in 1917) openly promoted segregation. In addition, mass meetings were held and inflammatory publications were circulated that riled up residents. The seven-member Chicago Real Estate Board (CREB) stoked the flames of anti-Black sentiments by announcing that sales of homes to Blacks on previously all-White blocks caused precipitous declines in property values of $5,000 or more per block. CREB suggested that neighbors pressure each other to prevent the sale of homes to Blacks. It also suggested that Blacks should consider block-by-block segregation and called on Black realtors to stop selling homes in White neighborhoods to Blacks. It also tried to get the city council to enact legislation to prevent more Blacks from moving to Chicago (Tuttle, 1970).

Blacks responded by founding their own neighborhood associations that focused on neighborhood stability and beautification. Despite the ubiquitous perception that Blacks degraded pristine White neighborhoods when they moved in and that Black communities were reservoirs of perpetual squalor, Blacks living in the Michigan Boulevard Garden

Apartments took great pride in the landscaped gardens surround-
ing the buildings. They decried unkempt lawns and shabby buildings.
The block groups or neighborhood associations used communal tools
to maintain their gardens and hired gardeners to landscape vacant lots
(*Chicago Daily News*, 1953; *Chicago Defender*, 1920, 1921; Graham, 1921;
Half-Century Magazine, 1924; R. Taylor, 1948; Cooley, 2010).

In response to Chicago's housing shortage and the difficulty Blacks
faced in securing housing, philanthropist Julius Rosenwald of Sears,
Roebuck, built the Michigan Boulevard Garden Apartments to house
Blacks in the 1920s. The development had 421 units built around a large
landscaped courtyard. There were also stores—some Black owned—in
the development. Rosenwald invested about $2.7 million in the project,
which returned about 2.4% profit in the first seven years of operation
(Devereux, 1978, 2005; Radford, 2005). Though there was a building
boom in Chicago in the 1920s, it ground to a halt during the Depression
and did not keep pace with the city's growth and demand for housing.
More than 287,000 dwelling units were constructed in the city during
the 1920s; however, only about 15,500 units were constructed during the
1930s. Only 137 units were built in 1933—the nadir of building for the
period (Hirsch, [1983] 1998).

Realtors were staunch advocates of segregation and housing discrimination. The National Association of Real Estate Boards (NAREB), an
organization founded in 1908 and representing 83,000 real estate brokers, promoted segregation at every turn. A 1923 NAREB textbook for
realtors argued that "the purchase of property by certain racial types is
very likely to diminish the value of other property" (E. Fisher, 1923: 116).
Additional NAREB textbooks published in 1923 asserted that Blacks
were a threat to property values and that immigrants were also undesirable residents (Benson and North, 1922; U.S. Commission on Civil
Rights, 1973). As late as 1966, the NAREB opposed fair-housing legislation (Bonastia, 2000).

Chicago's segregationists also used fire bombs to scare Blacks away
from White neighborhoods. The bombings increased as the housing
shortage intensified, and Blacks were forced to look for housing outside
the Black Belt. The Black Belt, also known as Bronzeville or the Black
Metropolis, was a South Side neighborhood in which most of Chicago's
African American residents lived. Increasingly, White neighborhood

associations such as the Hyde Park–Kenwood Association promoted the use of bombs and bullets to preserve the racial homogeneity of their neighborhood. The Hyde Park–Kenwood Association was so intent on preventing Blacks from breaching the Cottage Grove Avenue divide that it employed gangsters to enforce the line in the 1920s and 1930s (Illinois Association for Criminal Justice, 1929; Tuttle, 1970; Drake and Cayton, [1945] 1993; Cooley, 2010). Hyde Park's *Property Owners' Journal* summed up residents' sentiments when it proclaimed in 1920, "There is nothing in the make-up of a Negro, physically or mentally, which should induce anyone to welcome him as a neighbor" (qtd. in Chicago Commission on Race Relations, 1922: 116–122).

A wave of bombings engulfed Chicago between 1917 and 1921. During that period, 58 Black residences were bombed, and two Blacks were killed as a result of the bombing. Jesse Binga's home—purchased for $30,000 in an exclusive White neighborhood—was bombed six times. Binga helped to secure mortgages for Blacks; hence, his office and the apartment buildings he owned were bombed too. The homes of other Black pioneers who moved into White neighborhoods, apartment buildings housing Blacks, African American churches, and the homes of Black and White realtors selling to Blacks were also bombed. The police did not make any arrests, even when Blacks phoned in bomb threats and buildings were staked out before the bombings (Tuttle, 1970; Drake and Cayton, [1945] 1993; Cooley, 2010).

Racial tensions between Blacks and Whites were high; thus, the race riot that broke out in the city in 1919 did little to quiet the anxieties that Whites had about Blacks and racial mixing. After the riot, homeowner associations intensified their efforts to prevent Blacks from moving into neighborhoods bordering the Black Belt. There was also increased Ku Klux Klan activity—particularly in neighborhoods that bordered the Black Belt. Nevertheless, in the 1940s and 1950s, Blacks began moving into neighborhoods such as Oakland, Kenwood, Woodlawn, Hyde Park, Park Manor, Englewood, North Lawndale, and Morgan Park. They also built homes along Wabash, Michigan, and South Park Avenues as well as Grand Boulevard. The wealthiest Blacks also lived in the southern part of the Black Belt. Even though the Black Belt expanded, Blacks were increasingly segregated. This was evidenced by data showing that 49.7% of Blacks lived in exclusively Black census tracts in 1940.

A decade later, 53% of Blacks lived in such tracts (K. Jackson, [1967] 1992; Hirsch, [1983] 1998; Cooley, 2010).

Racially restrictive covenants became more commonplace after the courts began striking down the racially restrictive zoning ordinances. Chicago abandoned efforts to develop racially restrictive zoning after the *Buchanan v. Warley* (1917) ruling, so White residents began relying even more heavily on restrictive covenants to keep neighborhoods segregated. Once the use of covenants became widespread, the anti-Black bombing campaigns dissipated. The city's newspapers kept residents apprised of the efficacy of the covenants. In 1920, racially restrictive covenants crafted by the Hyde Park–Kenwood Property Owners' Association had prevented 57 Blacks from buying homes in the neighborhood in a 60-day period. By 1930, between 75% and 85% of all residential property in the city was bound by restrictive covenants barring owners from selling or renting to Blacks. In neighborhoods close to the Black Belt, such as Washington Park and the communities surrounding the University of Chicago, over 95% of the properties were bound by these covenants (Tuttle, 1970; *Buchanan v. Warley*, 1917; *Harvard Law Review*, 1918; Drake and Cayton, [1945] 1993; Brooks, 2002; Plotkin, 1999).

CREB, which felt that neighborhood racial homogeneity was essential to the protection of property values, announced it would expel realtors who sold property to Blacks. CREB's goal was to cover the city with racially restrictive covenants. Consequently, the organization recommended that residents form homeowner associations to prevent Blacks from moving in and supplied a model contract—drafted by Nathan William MacChesney of the Chicago Planning Commission—to those who wished to use them. CREB also collected signatures of the people signing covenants and sponsored speakers to travel around the city to campaign for the use of covenants. The campaign was so effective that the *Hyde Park Herald* gloated that the covenants covered the city "like a marvelous delicately woven chain of armor" stretching from "the northern gates of Hyde Park at 35th and Drexel Boulevard to Woodlawn, Park Manor, South Shore, Windsor Park, and all the far-flung White communities of the South Side" (qtd. in Philpott, [1978] 1991: 195). The campaigns were effective. In Park Manor, the improvement association got almost all of the property owners in the 104 blocks it oversaw to sign covenants (R. Weaver, 1944).

The efforts to build low-income public housing in Chicago also re-sulted in increased use of restrictive covenants. As the Metropolitan Housing Council of Chicago (1935) reported, "Areas where there was a small percentage of Negroes and areas adjacent to these scattered Negro sections entered upon vigorous drives on deed restriction" (qtd. in Nes-bitt, 1949: 278).

The Chicago model was propagated around the country. Between 1923 and 1924, real estate boards in Milwaukee, Detroit, Kansas City, Los Angeles, and other cities also prohibited their realtors from sell-ing or renting property located in White neighborhoods to Blacks (Real Estate Board of Chicago, 1917; *St. Louis Real Estate Bulletin*, 1923). So pervasive was this sentiment that in 1924 NAREB adopted a code of ethics proclaiming that "a Realtor should never be instrumental in introducing into a neighborhood a character of property or occupancy, members of any race or nationality, or any individuals whose presence will clearly be detrimental to property values in that neighborhood" (*Oregon Real Estate News*, 1956).

CHALLENGING THE COVENANTS
In 1927, about 500 homeowners in Chicago's Washington Park sub-division signed a restrictive covenant that barred property owners from leasing, selling, or having any part of their premises occupied by peo-ple of color except janitors, chauffeurs, or servants. The neighborhood contained 583 parcels covering 27 city blocks. In 1934, Olive Burke filed suit against Isaac Kleiman for leasing an apartment to James Hall, an African American. At the time of the suit, three other properties were in violation of the covenant. Three buildings located within 650 feet of Olive Burke's property housed 96 minority tenants. The defendant, Kleiman, argued that the character of the neighborhood had changed so dramatically that the covenant should no longer be enforced. The Court of Appeals of Illinois disagreed. The justices argued that since only a few of the 583 parcels had violated the covenant, the violations did not constitute a change big enough to warrant voiding the cove-nant. Moreover, there was action pending against the other violators to stop them from violating the covenant (*Burke v. Kleiman*, 1934a, 1934b)

Residents of the Washington Park subdivision were back in court in 1937. By then, they had formed the Woodlawn Property Owners'

Association to help enforce the restrictive covenant. Carl Hansberry, an African American and father of the renowned playwright Lorraine Hansberry, acquired a property in the area covered by the covenant through a third-party White individual who bought the property with the intention of passing it on to a holding institution or reselling directly to a person of color. Hansberry, who was already leasing an apartment in the restricted area, was ordered to vacate that premises by the courts. He moved into the Rhodes Avenue property, at which point Anna Lee filed suit against him. Hansberry was prevented from collecting rent from the two White tenants in his building. In the event that the White tenants moved, Hansberry was also prohibited from renting to Black tenants. Hansberry was given 90 days to vacate the property (*Lee v. Hansberry*, 1937).

While the case wended its way through the courts, Carl's wife, Nannie, armed herself with a loaded German luger and patrolled her house as she tried to safeguard her four children within (Hansberry, 1969; Cooley, 2010). In the meantime, Hansberry argued in court that the covenant was not valid because 95% of the property owners in the restricted area had to sign the agreement for it to take effect. The defendant claimed that 95% of the owners had not signed the covenant. Relying on the findings in *Burke v. Kleiman* that asserted that 95% of the property owners had signed the covenant, the appeals court did not probe Hansberry's claim. Moreover, the Appellate Court of Illinois argued that Hansberry had entered into a conspiracy with Burke to take possession of the property even though he knew the property was covered by a restrictive covenant. Hence, the judges concluded that Hansberry acquired the property illegally (*Lee v. Hansberry*, 1937; *Burke v. Kleiman*, 1934a, 1934b).

Hansberry appealed the ruling to the Supreme Court of Illinois and again argued that the restrictive covenant was not valid. Investigation into Hansberry's claim found him to be correct. It turned out that only about 54% of the property owners had signed the covenant. Despite the appeals court's error, the Supreme Court of Illinois upheld the lower court ruling (*Lee v. Hansberry*, 1939). Hansberry's case went to the U.S. Supreme Court. In 1940, the U.S. Supreme Court ruled that the Supreme Court of Illinois decision denied Hansberry the due process guaranteed by the Fourteenth Amendment. Moreover, the condition that 95% of the property owners sign the restrictive covenant for it to go into effect was not met. Consequently, the decision of the Supreme Court of Illinois was reversed (*Hansberry v. Lee*, 1940).

Detroit and Its Suburbs—Bombs, Restrictive Covenants, and Walls

Violence in the form of vandalism and bombings was also used to enforce segregation in Detroit. It should be noted that in many cities, the anti-Black violence was *organized* and *gendered*. During the daytime, women patrolled the neighborhoods that Blacks had moved into and participated in the picket lines. Young boys were recruited to hurl objects at homes and vandalize them because they were unlikely to be arrested by the police. At night, the men took over the patrols, pickets, bombings, and other acts of terrorism and violence (Sugrue, 1996; J.M. Thomas, 1997).

BLACKS DEFEND THEIR HOMES
As was the case in Chicago, White Detroiters adopted a plan of using bombs, Ku Klux Klan activity, realtors in the Detroit Real Estate Board, and racially restrictive covenants to control where Blacks lived. From the outset, Blacks challenged these measures—sometimes with deadly outcomes. David Freund (2007) documents how suburban Whites organized to prevent Blacks from moving into their neighborhoods. In Dearborn, for instance, realtors served only White clients, and any Blacks who moved into the suburb were visited by the police and asked to move out (Farley and Frey, 1994).

Inside the city of Detroit, a pitched battle raged for decades as Whites fought to prevent neighborhood integration. In 1917, a White property owner began renting his apartment building—located at 202 Harper Avenue—to Blacks. Soon after the new renters moved in, neighborhood Whites entered the building and threw out the possessions of the Black families. A nearby police officer refused to help when Blacks sought assistance. Instead, he instructed the renters to leave the neighborhood for their own safety (Levine, 1976; Zunz, 1982).

The case of Ossian Sweet gained notoriety in the battle over *neighborhood change* and the right to live in a home one purchased. Dr.

Sweet graduated from Wilberforce College and then earned a medical degree from Howard University. He did his postgraduate training in Europe, where he studied in Vienna and at Madame Curie's Institute in Paris. He learned how to use radium to treat cancer (Farley, Danziger, and Holzer, 2000). Dr. Sweet and his family wanted to move from the crowded Black Bottom neighborhood, so in June 1925, he and his wife, Gladys, purchased a home at 2905 Garland Avenue on Detroit's East Side. The Sweets purchased the house from Edward Smith and his wife, an interracial couple. Residents of the working-class White immigrant community had assumed the Smiths were White, so they had not bothered the couple. Upon learning that the house had been sold to African Americans, White residents hastily formed the Waterworks Improvement Association. The association was formed on July 14 by 700 neighborhood residents who attended a meeting at the Howe School auditorium to discuss the rumors that a Black family had purchased a home in the area. Residents got help in organizing their association from the leader of the Tireman Improvement Association (a hastily organized Klan-backed group), which had successfully orchestrated the ouster of Dr. Alexander Turner and his family from the house they purchased on Spokane Avenue in the Tireman Avenue neighborhood. When the Turners tried to move into their home in June 1925, a screaming, stone-throwing mob of about 5,000 Whites gathered at the house and vandalized it. A few hours after the Turners moved in, two White men representing the Tireman Improvement Association entered the house and asked to buy the property. Under duress, the Turners agreed to sell, and the police escorted them out of the neighborhood. A few weeks later, a Black undertaker, Vollington Bristol, was forced by a mob out of the home he built in a White neighborhood. John Fletcher and his family met a similar fate when they purchased a home on Stoepel Avenue. As the Fletchers sat down to dinner in their new home, neighbors discovered the family was Black, and a crowd of around 4,000 quickly gathered outside. Bricks hurled at the house shattered the windows. The Fletchers fired into the crowd, striking a teenager in the thigh. The family was arrested; they also moved out of their home the next day (Conot, 1973; Levine, 1976; Wolcott, 1993; Linder, 2000; Vine 2004).

The Sweet family originally planned to move into their new home in July but delayed the move in the hope that racial animus would

subside. They moved into their home on September 8, 1925, and prepared for trouble. Ossian's brothers—Otis, a dentist, and Henry, a stu-
dent—joined three friends and the Sweets in their home that day. The
group had a large supply of food as well as nine guns and ammunition.
A crowd formed near the house, but nothing transpired the first day
and night. However, on the second day, when the crowd grew larger
and more unruly, the Sweets asked four more friends to join them.
The crowd outside—estimated to be as large as 2,000—began hurling
rocks at the house on the evening of day two. As windows were shattered, shots rang out when the police stationed outside the house and
the people inside began shooting. One person in the crowd was killed
and another injured. The six policemen on the scene stormed the house
and arrested all 11 occupants for murder. The NAACP retained famed
attorney Clarence Darrow to defend the Sweets in court in 1925, while
Black communities around the country held fund-raisers in support
of the family. After 46 hours of deliberation, the trial ended in a hung
jury. The defendants were released on bail to await a second trial, which
began in April 1926. This time the court decided to try each defendant
separately, beginning with Henry Sweet, the only person inside the
house who admitted to firing his gun. Darrow focused his arguments
on the civil rights and property rights of Blacks. He contended that
they were unable to exercise these rights and were being discriminated
against in the Detroit housing market. He also noted that the police did
not protect Blacks when they were threatened or assaulted by Whites.
After four hours of deliberation, the jury returned with a not-guilty verdict in May. The charges were dropped for the remaining defendants
(Conot, 1973; Levine, 1976; Capeci, 1984; Wolcott, 1993; Linder, 2000;
Farley, Danziger, and Holzer, 2000; Vine 2004).

A year after the Sweets' trial, one of their attorneys, Julian Perry,
purchased a home on the border of Detroit and the suburb of Grosse
Pointe Park. The house was promptly bombed, and Perry moved back
to a Black neighborhood (Levine, 1976).

THE SPREAD OF RESTRICTIVE COVENANTS
Private parties turned to restrictive covenants to prevent Blacks from
moving into White neighborhoods in Detroit and its suburbs. Racially
restrictive covenants made their first appearance in Detroit in 1910 and

by the late 1940s covered about 80% of the residential property in the city that was located beyond Grand Boulevard (Sugrue, 1996). Historically, the Michigan courts upheld these agreements. The Michigan Supreme Court found racially restrictive covenants between private homeowners valid and enforceable in the case of *Parmalee v. Morris* (1922). When Anna Morris and her husband—both of whom were Black—bought property in the Ferry Farm subdivision of Pontiac (a Detroit suburb), residents of the community filed suit against them. In 1922, the court ruled that the covenant—which read, "Said lot shall not be occupied by a colored person"—was valid and enforceable (*Parmalee v. Morris*, 1922).

In 1925, Mr. Starks—a parlor-car conductor—and his wife purchased a lot on Lakewood Avenue in the Oneida Park subdivision of Detroit. Mrs. Starks—who had the phenotypic features of a Caucasian—conducted all matters related to the sale of the lot. The Starkses, who owned a home on Beniteau Street, also owned a second rental property. After buying the Lakewood Avenue lot for $3,800, the Starkses built a $14,000 house on it. When subdivision residents found out that the Starkses were Black, they tried to prevent them from occupying their house. White property owners in the subdivision had signed a restrictive covenant that read that lots should not be "sold, rented or leased to any person or class of persons whose ownership or occupancy would be injurious to the locality" (*Schulte v. Starks*, 1927: 102). The Starkses offered to sell their property to subdivision residents for $25,000. The property of Schulte (the neighbor who filed suit against the Starkses to prevent occupancy) was worth $21,500. In the case of *Schulte v. Starks*, the Michigan Supreme Court upheld the lower court decision and ruled in favor of the Schultes in April 1927 (*Schulte v. Starks*, 1927).

In 1944, Dr. Albert Kathan and other residents in the Arden Park subdivision of Detroit brought suit against Alfred Williams, claiming that he violated a private racially restrictive covenant when he purchased property in the neighborhood that barred Blacks from living therein. There were 92 homes in the subdivision. The Michigan Supreme Court dismissed the suit in the case of *Kathan v. Williams* (1944) on the grounds that there was no common agreement (restrictive covenant) among the property owners of the subdivision to forbid the sale of property to Blacks.

When the Security Land Company developed a subdivision in Detroit with 338 lots in 1913, most of the lots—310 of them—were covered by a racially restrictive covenant that barred Blacks from purchasing lots or living in the subdivision. In 1945, Otis Sheldon, his wife (Louise), and her parents purchased a lot at 5325 Seebaldt Avenue. The transactions required to purchase the property were carried out by Louise Sheldon and her parents—all of whom "appear[ed] to be of the Caucasian race," according to court documents. Prior to the purchase of the property, the Sheldons were informed of the covenant restricting occupancy to Whites only. Otis Sheldon was Black; therefore, neighborhood residents who were members of the Northwest Civic Association filed suit against the Sheldons to force them to vacate their property. In April 1947, the Michigan Supreme Court ruled in the case of *Northwest Civic Association v. Sheldon* that Otis Sheldon could not occupy the property; he was given 90 days to vacate the property.

The case of *Sipes v. McGhee* (1947) also originated in the subdivision on Seebaldt Avenue. Between 1934 and 1935, homeowners on Seebaldt Avenue signed an agreement stating that the lots should not be occupied by people of color. The agreement also specified that 80% of the property owners must sign it for it to become effective. Orsel and Minnie McGhee, African Americans, purchased a house at 4626 Seebaldt Street in 1944. Benjamin Sipes and other property owners brought suit against the McGhees to force them to vacate their property. The Circuit Court of Wayne County found that the covenant was valid and ordered the McGhees to vacate their house in 90 days and to refrain from living in it in the future. The McGhees argued that the covenant was not signed by 80% of the property owners and was therefore not valid, but the Michigan Supreme Court found the covenant to be properly executed and enforceable. Detroit-area neighborhood associations paid careful attention to this case. In fact, 26 of them filed amicus briefs (*Sipes v. McGhee*, 1947; *McGhee v. Sipes*, 1947). This case was coupled with others and heard before the U.S. Supreme Court. The decision is discussed later in this chapter.

The case of *Mrsa v. Reynolds*, involving a racially restrictive covenant, was also decided in 1947. Katherine Mrsa and her neighbors filed suit against Collins Reynolds and his family after the Reynoldses purchased a lot at 17927 St. Aubin Avenue in the Oakdale subdivision of

Detroit. Lots in the subdivision had a covenant on them that prevented occupancy by "people of the African race." The lower court ruled in 1945 that the Reynoldses should vacate their premises within 60 days of the ruling. On appeal, the Reynoldses argued that the phrase "people of the African race" did not necessarily mean Black or Negro; therefore, the restrictions did not apply to them. In 1947, the Michigan Supreme Court upheld the lower court ruling and ordered the Reynoldses to vacate their property (*Mrsa v. Reynolds*, 1947).

In 1952, the Michigan Supreme Court upheld the trial court ruling in the case of *Phillips v. Naff* and dismissed the case, which alleged that the owner of a property in Highland Park (one of two small cities encircled by Detroit) that was covered by a restrictive covenant sold it to Blacks and was, therefore, liable to pay the plaintiffs damages for harming their property (*Phillips v. Naff*, 1952).

The U.S. Supreme Court and Private Racially Restrictive Covenants

As the foregoing discussion shows, a number of private racially restrictive covenant cases were making their way through the court system all over the country. Though the U.S. Supreme Court had found racial zoning ordinances invalid in 1917, the Court had not ruled on the validity of the private covenants. The cases in the court system questioned whether police powers could be used to enforce these private agreements. Cases from southern and northern cities were heard by the Court simultaneously. In 1948, four such cases were argued before the Supreme Court. Three of the Supreme Court justices recused themselves from the case because they owned houses covered by racially restrictive covenants. The cases of *Shelley v. Kraemer* (1948) from St. Louis, *Sipes v. McGhee* (1947) from Detroit, and *Hurd v. Hodge* (1948) and *Uricolo v. Hodge* (1947) from Washington, D.C., were linked together.

In reversing the rulings of the Missouri and Michigan supreme courts, the U.S. Supreme Court argued that "the restrictive agreements standing alone cannot be regarded as a violation of any rights guaranteed to petitioners by the Fourteenth Amendment. So long as the purposes of those agreements are effectuated by voluntary adherence to their terms, it would appear clear that there has been no action by

the State and the provisions of the Amendment have not been violated"
(*Shelley. v. Kraemer*, 1948: 334). However, the Court also argued that
once the covenant goes beyond the realm of *voluntary compliance* and
the judicial system is used to enforce it, such actions are unconstitutional (*Shelley. v. Kraemer*, 1948; *Sipes v. McGhee*, 1947). The lower court
rulings in *Hurd v. Hodge* and *Uricolo v. Hodge* were also overturned
(*Hurd v. Hodge*, 1948).

Despite these rulings, restrictive covenant cases in which Blacks
were barred from taking occupancy of property they acquired in White
neighborhoods kept coming before the courts. See for example the case
of *Phillips v. Naff*, which was decided in 1952. Moreover, the federal government did not stop supporting the use of restrictive covenants immediately after the 1948 U.S. Supreme Court ruling. It was not until 1950
that the Federal Housing Administration stopped insuring new developments covered by restrictive covenants (Grier, 1967).

Rising Segregation and the Efficacy of Racially
Restrictive Covenants

One fact is indisputable—cities became more segregated from the
1890s through 1970 (see Cutler, Glaeser, and Vigdor, 1999). This coincided with the rapid increase in the urban Black population. The U.S.
Census Bureau analyzes five indicators of segregation: the *dissimilarity
index*—how evenly spread population subgroups are in a given area;
the *isolation index*—to what extent members of a particular population subgroup share common neighborhoods; the *delta index*—how
concentrated members of a particular population subgroup is in dense
areas; the *absolute centralization index*—the degree of centrality of a
particular population subgroup; and the *spatial proximity index*—the
likelihood of members of a particular population subgroup living near
members of that same subgroup (U.S. Census Bureau, 2004). This analysis focuses on the most commonly used measure of segregation—the
dissimilarity index. A study of the dissimilarity indices of several cities from 1890 to 1930 found that levels of segregation were highest in
the Midwest and Northeast (Brooks, 2002; Cutler, Glaeser, and Vigdor,
1999). As table 8.2 shows, by 1930, Chicago had the highest dissimilarity index, which means it was the most segregated of the cities studied.

Table 8.2. Index of Dissimilarity for Level of Black-White Segregation in Cities, 1890–1930

Cities	Year				
	1890	1900	1910	1920	1930
Northern cities					
Chicago	64	58	69	77	85
Cleveland	61	62	60	69	80
Detroit	57	61	64	57	60
Indianapolis	42	38	44	42	40
Boston	57	56	63	65	68
New Haven	57	53	53	54	66
New York	43	46	48	58	64
Philadelphia	43	38	46	47	51
Southern cities					
St. Louis	34	41	54	61	76
Louisville	30	29	34	41	38
Memphis	19	20	28	34	46
Nashville	29	34	38	42	54
New Orleans	17	18	15	18	22
Atlanta	18	24	34	41	44
Baltimore	29	37	40	44	54
Charleston	15	18	17	17	20
Richmond	34	42	30	20	19
Western cities					
Los Angeles	21	26	28	48	68
San Francisco	42	40	35	42	44

Source: Brooks, 2002; Cutler, Glaeser, and Vigdor, 1999.

With the exception of St. Louis, which had a dissimilarity index of 76 in 1930, the southern cities had dissimilarity indices ranging from 19 to 54.

One should be cautious about interpreting the dissimilarity indices. Though southern cities might appear less segregated, that would be true if only *spatial segregation* was being considered. In some southern cities, Blacks lived in the back alleys, side streets, and servants' quarters of their White employers' homes, making the cities appear less spatially segregated. However, an elaborate system of social norms (such as segregated facilities, drinking fountains, and transportation) kept Blacks and Whites *socially isolated*. At the outset, southern cities relied on social norms to keep the races apart. In the North, where there was less of a history of social norms geared toward isolating Blacks, segregationists resorted to *spatial isolation* to keep the races apart in the cities (Myrdal, 1944; Spear, 1967).

Opinions vary on whether racially restrictive covenants were effective in facilitating residential segregation. One thing is clear: they grew so popular that in 1937 a leading national magazine awarded ten communities a "shield of honor" for adopting restrictive covenants that guarded against "the wrong kind of people" inhabiting those communities (qtd. in U.S. Commission on Civil Rights, 1973: 4). Racially restrictive covenants were enforced by the courts for more than three decades. Legal challenges were mounted against these covenants in 19 states, and the courts in these states held them valid and enforceable.

Hirsch ([1983] 1998) argues that the racially restrictive covenants had little impact on the maintenance of racial barriers in Chicago. He contends that covenants were not effective because they were violated regularly by landlords, who could make more money by renting their property to Blacks. According to Hirsch, the courts undermined the effectiveness of the covenants by remaining unresponsive to complaints against parties who violated them. He also argues that some of Chicago's municipal court judges did not uphold the covenants, many cases were withdrawn, and even the ones that were tried successfully were not enforced. Consequently, Hirsch claims that Black housing opportunities were constrained by the housing shortage and anti-Black violence—not the racially restrictive covenants.

Bernstein (1998) argues that restrictive covenants played a role in residential segregation in Chicago but did not play as large a role as is commonly assumed. However, Brooks's (2002) study of the effects of restrictive covenants in Chicago found that the instruments played a key role in maintaining residential segregation in the city. He argues that the covenants served as a mechanism to coordinate the activities of various institutions (such as banks, boards of realtors, and neighborhood associations) that were interested in promoting segregation.

An indication of the effectiveness of the racially restrictive covenants can be seen in the suburbs of Chicago. At the same time that the Black population of Chicago was growing rapidly—going from 492,265 in 1950 to 812,637 in 1960—the suburbs (particularly those in the northwest) were virtually all White. A 1958 census of 17 of Chicago's suburbs found that there were 266,000 people living in them, yet Evanston was the only one that had a few hundred Blacks living (in segregated

enclaves) in its confines. The non-White population of Chicago's suburbs grew slowly; non-Whites constituted 2.9% of the suburban population in 1950 and only 3.1% of the population in 1960. During this time,
the Catholic Council for Working Life reported that around 35,000
Black families in Chicago were eager and able to purchase suburban
homes if provided the opportunity (Dulaney, 1962). A similar pattern
can be seen in the Detroit suburbs. An assessment of 31 suburbs shows
that Blacks constituted less than 1% of the population in 26 of them in
1970 (U.S. Census Bureau, 1973).

R. Weaver (1953) argues that the racially restrictive covenants were
effective. He provides compelling data that show that over a 15-year
period—from 1935 to 1950—minorities were able to take occupancy of
only about 1.1% of the new homes constructed in the U.S. This was a time
period when racially restrictive covenants were widely used to bar Blacks
and other minorities from occupying homes in new developments.

Breaking the Stranglehold of the Covenants

Chicago is a good place to see how the high demand for housing, limited
supply, the presence of Blacks who could afford to pay above-market
prices for housing, the NAACP ready to challenge housing discrimination, property owners desirous of maximizing profits, and realtors willing to manipulate the system facilitated White flight while still maintaining control over where Blacks could live in the city. Realtors played
no small role in triggering demographic changes in neighborhoods.

These factors worked together to undercut the aims of the restrictive covenants. That is, Blacks—desperate to leave the Black Belt—were
able to convince property owners to sell to them. At the same time, real
estate companies rented their properties to Blacks at 20%–50% higher
rent than they did to Whites. As a result, property owners encouraged
White renters to move so that they could rent their property at much
higher rates to Blacks. This enticed White property owners to break
the restrictive covenants. White property owners also complained that
they were being denied the right to sell or rent their property at market
value. Another factor came into play: as soon as Blacks started moving
into previously all-White neighborhoods, White homeowners tried to

sell quickly and move away. Afraid of being stranded in Black neighborhoods or being forced to sell at below-market prices (when the neighborhood became predominantly Black), Whites jumped on the bandwagon and tried to sell at high prices so they could move out of the neighborhoods with their profits intact. Although the property owners' associations challenged the sales, refused to give titles to Blacks, and filed injunctions restraining Blacks from moving into their newly purchased homes, the rate of sales was brisk. This occurred because there was a huge pent-up demand for housing among Blacks, and some could afford to pay for housing outside Black neighborhoods. Consequently, it was not difficult to find Black buyers and renters (Tuttle, 1970; Drake and Cayton, [1945] 1993). For instance, a construction company building 65 units got 12,000 applications from residents in the Black Belt despite the fact that they needed to pay a deposit of $850. In another instance, 52 homes being constructed in the West Chesterfield neighborhood for Blacks sold even before the blueprints were completed (Hirsch, [1983] 1998).

Thus, there was a collective-action problem with the institution and maintenance of private racially restrictive covenants, and the practice of blockbusting exploited a loophole in the agreements. In contemplating or entering into these agreements, Whites had an incentive to hold out and not sign covenants or to sign and then break them, since taking either path allowed them to sell or rent their property to the highest bidder. Whites were also fearful of finding themselves locked into agreements that made it more difficult for them to rent or sell their property when others were exercising their right to use or dispose of their property as they pleased. Hence, the desire to maximize financial gains and market opportunities helped to weaken the effects of the covenants (Bernstein and Somin, 2004; Bernstein, 1998).

NAREB tried to respond to the changing times. Consequently, after the *Shelley v. Kraemer* decision, NAREB reworded its code of ethics to remove direct references to race and to include more vague language. The new code of ethics penned in 1950 read, "A Realtor should not be instrumental in introducing into a neighborhood a character of property or use which will clearly be detrimental to property values in that neighborhood" (*Shelley v. Kraemer*, 1948; *Oregon Real Estate News*, 1956).

Racially Restrictive Covenants Today—Old Habits Die Hard

Some people might argue that racially restrictive covenants are a thing of the past that has no bearing on neighborhood demographic characteristics today. But these instruments are not historical relics to be ignored. They still influence the landscape of American cities and towns. Despite the fact that in the 1980s the U.S. Department of Housing and Urban Development (HUD) began requiring title companies to *redact racially restrictive clauses* from covenants or to make a notation in the margins that the provisions were to be considered deleted, racially restrictive covenants still appear in many deeds today (J. Thomas, 2005). In 2010, readers of the *New Bedford Standard-Times* (in Massachusetts) were surprised to see an advertisement for the sale of land in Fairhaven that was accompanied by the passage, "The said land shall not be sold, leased or rented to any person other than of the Caucasian race or to any entity of which any person other than that of said race shall be a member, stockholder, officer or director." The Fairhaven records office shows that the deed restriction was placed on the property in 1946. The Massachusetts Commission Against Discrimination described the restrictive clause as "unlawful and unenforceable" (CBS News, 2010).

In some cases, subdivisions are still enforcing racially restrictive covenants. As mentioned before, this is the case in Myers Park (Charlotte), where residents are still upholding the covenants. Myers Park residents drew attention to themselves because they brazenly flaunted the covenants on their website and only removed the document because there was a public outcry and the NAACP filed a complaint against the MPHA (Singleton, 2009; J. Rose, 2010). The MPHA still has not indicated that it will not continue to enforce the racially restrictive covenant.

However, Myers Park is not as unusual as one may think. Racially restrictive covenants reach all the way to the American presidency. John F. Kennedy lived in a neighborhood with a racially restrictive covenant before he became president; so did Ronald Reagan (Turnbull, 2005; J. Thomas, 2005). In 1999, George W. Bush found himself trying to explain the racially restrictive covenant that covered his home in the Northwood section of North Dallas as he campaigned for the presidency. He purchased the home in 1988 and sold it in 1995 to move into the governor's mansion in Austin. The deed limited occupancy of the premises to Whites only; non-White servants could also live on the property of their employers. The covenant was placed on the property in 1939. Bush's presidential campaign spokesperson, Mindy Tucker, hastened to inform the public that the president was not aware of the covenant. She argued that Texas banned such covenants in 1984 and that Bush was never told that the property was encumbered with the deed restriction (Hutcheson, 1999; Kranish, 1999).

Bush made headlines again in 2008 when he purchased a house on Daria Place in the James Meaders Estates section of Preston Hollows in North Dallas. Preston Hollows—developed in the 1930s by Ira De-Loache and Al Joyce, was covered by a racially restrictive covenant limiting occupancy to Whites only; servants who were non-White could also occupy properties in the community. The restrictive covenant was placed on the properties in 1956, and the neighborhood association enforced it till 2000, when it was amended to expunge the racially restrictive clause. The amendments took effect in 2001 (Hafertepe, 2001; Wilonsky, 2008; Jacobs, 2009).

Innis Arden in Seattle is another community that succeeded in removing a racially restrictive clause from its covenant. After years of collecting signatures, in 2006, community residents amassed enough (360 signatures in all) to strike the clause from the covenant (Wash. Sess. Laws, 2006; Turnbull, 2005; Majumdar, 2006–2007). The state of Washington took steps to make it easier for community residents to remove racially restrictive clauses from their deeds. In March 2006, Governor Christine Gregoire signed a bill that made it easier for homeowner associations to expunge such clauses from the covenants (Engrossed Senate Bill, 2006).

Kansas City is another place in which racially restrictive covenants are still commonly found in homeowner association deeds that cover many neighborhoods built by J.C. Nichols. Some residents of some of these subdivisions still stick to the letter of the covenants even in contemporary times. Kim Wrench encountered this when he purchased a house in Greenway Fields in 1989. He did not meet the seller till the home inspection, at which point she made a fuss and informed the realtor that she would not have sold her home to Wrench had she known he was Black. However, residents of Red Bridge Estates had the racially restrictive clauses removed from the deeds of their homes in 2001 (J. Thomas, 2005).

NAREB is recognizing the repugnance of the racially restrictive clauses. In 1999, the organization launched a campaign to expunge racially restrictive clauses nationwide. It had some success in California, where a law went into effect in 2000 ordering homeowner associations to strike the clauses from their covenants. The law also enabled individual homeowners to remove the racially restrictive clauses from their deeds. In 2004, the law was amended to allow individual homeowners to go directly to the county recorder and expunge the clauses from their deeds. NAREB's president, Ron Branch, said of the racially restrictive clauses, "It's a very insensitive message, one that says although we acknowledge that black Americans can own real estate, we won't go to the energy and the effort to have everything removed so they can feel better about it" (J. Thomas, 2005).

Racially restrictive covenants matter. If covenants were not effective, as Hirsch ([1993] 1998) claims, one wonders why Preston Hollows residents would go to the trouble and expense of placing covenants on their homes in 1956. These instruments are still being used in places such as Myers Park to maintain racially homogeneous neighborhoods.

No Swarthiness Allowed—The Point System

The Grosse Pointes—five elegant waterfront suburbs of Detroit—developed another way to keep "undesirables" out of their towns. The property owners' associations collaborated with realtors and detectives to develop a point system that was used to determine who could purchase property or build in the area. The point system was secretly adopted in 1945 by the Grosse Pointe Brokers Association, which developed a "Prospect Protection Book" containing a checklist on which potential home buyers earned or lost points for being swarthy in appearance, having a religious background, having an accent, having a club membership, being neat, or appearing to be "typically American." To be allowed to live in the Pointes, people of northern European descent needed to earn 50 points; Polish, 55 points; southern and eastern

Europeans, 65 points; Syrians, Lebanese, and Maltese, 65 points; and Jews, 85 points (later raised to 90 points). Blacks, Asians, and Mexicans were barred from living in the towns. The "Prospect Protection Book" also contained the names and reports of prospective property owners who received a negative evaluation. Of the 1,597 prospects investigated between 1945 and 1960, 939 amassed enough points to be allowed to purchase property in the Pointes; however, 658 prospective buyers failed to do so. Brokers selling property to ineligible prospects had to forfeit all the commission of the sale to the Grosse Pointe Brokers Association. Brokers who demurred on forfeiting commissions were expelled from the association (*Grosse Pointe News*, 1961; Conot, 1973; Sugrue, 1996; Fine, 1997; Rothstein and Santow, 2012).

After being labeled "swarthy" and barred from purchasing property in Grosse Pointe in January 1960, William Bufalino Jr., president of Teamsters Local 985, sued the Grosse Pointe Brokers Association, the Grosse Pointe Property Owners' Association, and Maxon Brothers, Inc., for $1 million. The libel suit was brought before the Wayne County Circuit Court. In it, Bufalino argued that he was being discriminated against because he was Italian. Bufalino lost the case (*Grosse Pointe News*, 1961; Fine, 1997).

The point system gained international notoriety when John Maxwell filed a lawsuit in the St. Clair County Circuit Court because he was labeled "undesirable" and was being prevented from completing the mansion he was building in the Pointes. Maxwell alleged that he earned the label because the Grosse Point Brokers Association and the Grosse Pointe Property Owners' Association wanted to prevent him from selling his property to a Black buyer. The Michigan chapter of the Anti-Defamation League of B'nai B'rith got a copy of the form used to rank prospective home buyers and publicized it. This led to worldwide coverage about the system. The public hearings that were held in Detroit were covered by the international media. Though the state of Michigan ordered the towns to stop using the point system in 1960, the *Detroit Free Press* reported that the system was still being used in 1961 (Fine, 1997; *Grosse Pointe News*, 1961). The Pointes also took other steps to make their towns insular. To reduce the connections to Detroit, streets were blocked with a wall on the Detroit border. This is the case with Goethe and Wayburn Streets (Derringer, 2011).

The State of EJ Research

EJ researchers have ignored the impact of restrictive covenants on cities and suburbs. Though many scholars have studied the exposure to hazards in cities such as Chicago, Detroit, Los Angeles, Seattle, and others that were blanketed with restrictive covenants, none of these studies assess the impacts the covenants might have on the demographic characteristics of the metropolitan areas. In the analysis of siting patterns, restrictive covenants remain one of the most underresearched and undertheorized aspects of this type of research.

9

Racializing Blight

Urban Renewal, Eminent Domain, and Expulsive Zoning

Eminent domain is often used in tandem with rezoning, urban renewal, and other economic development initiatives to reshape cities and influence residential patterns. Its use has significant influence on determining who lives where in cities. Indeed, the use of eminent domain can result in the expulsion of minorities and low-income residents from communities. Though the use of eminent domain has great implications for EJ research and activism—in terms of how its use impacts minorities and low-income residents—little attention has been paid to this process by EJ researchers.

In America, government's use of eminent domain to take private property for public use is a longstanding tradition. The Fifth Amendment of the Constitution places two limitations on the exercise of eminent domain: that property taken must be put to public use and that the individual from whom the property is taken must receive *just compensation* (Sharp and Haider-Markel, 2008). Before World War II, the power of eminent domain was limited to the taking of private property by government for "public use" such as the building of schools, roads, and so on. However, since the 1950s, the courts have upheld the use of eminent domain in the taking of private property for "public purposes" such as developing urban renewal projects, slum clearance, and the elimination of blight. Increasingly, the courts have interpreted *public use* to be synonymous with *public purpose* (Pritchett, 2003; *Susette Kelo v. City of New London*, 2005; Kmiec, 2007; Carpenter and Ross, 2009). As later discussions will show, this shift has important EJ implications.

Pritchett (2003) argues that powerful, elite interest groups and institutions came together to construct a discourse around blight, to push for its eradication, to lobby for government funds to do so, and to promote the use of eminent domain to transfer cleared land to private developers. Hence, urban planners in groups such as the American Institute of Planners and the American Society of Planning Officials (merged as the American Planning Association in 1978), the Committee on Blighted Areas and Slums, the National Resources Planning Board, and NAREB and its research arm—the Urban Land Institute—supported the use of eminent domain to hasten private development of land. Teaford (1990) has made a similar argument.

The sentiment expressed by Justice Leonard Crouch in *New York City Housing Authority v. Mueller* (1936) was shared by other elites of the time. In deciding against a plaintiff who challenged the condemnation of his property, Crouch declared, "The menace of the slums in New York City has been long recognized as serious enough to warrant public action. . . . The slums still stand, the menace still exists" (341). William Burk painted a bleak picture of the slums in a 1937 report also. He argued that living in poor housing leads to delinquency and a breakdown of the family structure. Burk argued that "under slum living conditions, the family as a social unit practically ceases to exist" (1937: 10).

It is widely documented that urban renewal projects condemned and leveled many minority and poor communities that were labeled as "blighted" or "slums" to make way for commercial development, upscale residences, and public housing (Darden, Hill, Thomas, and Thomas, 1987; Sugrue, 1996; Goodman and Monti, 1999; Gotham, 2001; Pritchett, 2003; Maskovsky, 2006; Blais, 2007).

Historically, Black communities have often been described as slums regardless of the quality of the housing. For example, during the mid-nineteenth century, Black communities in Manhattan, such as Yorkville and Seneca Village, were described as slums (despite the existence of substantial houses, churches, and schools in the communities) and cleared to make way for Central Park (D.E. Taylor 2009). Comstock's (1912) study of housing conditions in Black neighborhoods in Chicago described the communities as slums, despite the fact that 72% of the housing was in good or fair repair and only 28% was in bad repair. Rice described an Atlanta Black neighborhood he labeled as a slum: "The housing conditions in 'Vine City' reflect a continuum of possibilities in housing. Most of the property is absentee-owned, run-down and even dilapidated. At the other extreme, there are some well-kept homes that are owner-occupied" (1966: 8).

D. Meyer (1973) argues that Black housing—regardless of quality—is often conceived of and described as slum or ghetto housing. He maintains that the two terms are used synonymously and that researchers ignore their own data in their haste or predisposition to label Black housing as slum housing. If all Black housing were slum housing, one place where one would expect to find substandard housing in the entire stock would be in all-Black towns. Yet H. Rose's (1965) study of the housing quality in ten all-Black towns found four (Brooklyn, Illinois; Kinloch, Missouri; Glenarden, Maryland; and Urbancrest, Ohio) in which between 52% and 82% of the housing stock was substandard in 1960. In contrast, 1% of the housing stock in Richmond Heights (Florida) was substandard; so were 27% of the houses in Lincoln Heights (Ohio), 34% of those in Lawnside (New Jersey), 43% of those in Robbins (Illinois), 44% of those in Fairmount Heights (Maryland), and 49% of those in North Shreveport (Louisiana).

Though the percentage of non-Whites who lived in dilapidated homes in 1950 was five times higher than it was for Whites, nationwide only 27% of non-Whites and 5.4% of Whites lived in dilapidated homes. In 1950, minorities made up 10.3% of the U.S. population, and Blacks constituted more than 95% of those minorities (Housing and Home Finance Agency, 1952; R. Weaver, 1953). Hence, the pervasive use of terms such as "slum" or "ghetto" to describe Black communities has rendered them vulnerable to being declared blighted and earmarked for clearance. This perception still persists today, as Black communities are frequently described as slums in the scholarly literature.

Pritchett (2003) contends that the term "blight" was used to describe the perceived negative impacts of some residents of city neighborhoods. He argues that the diagnosis of "urban decline" was used to justify the *removal* of large numbers of Blacks and other minorities from neighborhoods. Poor Whites were also displaced in urban renewal projects (T. Hines, 1982; Hirsch, [1983] 1998; Massey and Denton, 1993; Sugrue, 1996; Goodman and Monti, 1999; Goetz, 2000; Gotham, 2001; Kraus, 2004).

Over time, cities came to rely heavily on the use of eminent domain to acquire private property. Though low-income White neighborhoods were deemed blighted and eminent domain used to facilitate clearance, Black and Hispanic communities bore the brunt of the clearances. For instance, when the Los Angeles City Planning Commission identified 11 blighted areas and made plans to clear them, all but one were predominantly Mexican American or African American neighborhoods (*Chicago Defender*, 1949; Hirsch, [1983] 1998; Pritchett, 2003; U.S. Commission on Civil Rights, 1973). In southwest Washington, D.C., 97.5% of the residents of the area slated for demolition in the early 1950s were poor Blacks (*Berman v. Parker*, 1954).

Rae (2003) and M. Jackson (2008) document how one predominantly Black neighborhood in New Haven (Connecticut), the Hill, was fractured to construct a highway spur—the Oak Street Connector. Displaced Blacks moved to the Dixwell Avenue area—another Black neighborhood that was later threatened by urban renewal projects. In a similar vein, Highsmith (2009) analyzes the impact of freeway construction on the predominantly Black St. John neighborhood of Flint, Michigan. Some academics such as Wayne State University's Eleanor Wolf and Charles Lebeaux gave their nod of approval for slum clearance projects aimed at changing the demographic characteristics of communities adjacent to universities and hospitals. In their study of the impact of slum clearance on a poor census tract in Detroit, they argued, "There are even instances when important social institutions may be justified in displacing poor residents to modify the character of the immediate environment, e.g., universities and hospitals menaced by nearby populations with high crime rates" (1967: 8; Wayne State University used slum clearance to acquire land for expansion).

The controversy over the use of eminent to take private property for commercial development erupted again in the 1980s with a Michigan Supreme Court decision. In 1981, the court upheld Detroit's use of eminent domain to condemn an entire neighborhood of over 1,000 homes and numerous small businesses so that the site could be developed to entice General Motors to remain in the city (*Poletown Neighborhood Council v. City of Detroit*, 1981; see also Wilder and Stigter, 1989; Sharp and Haider-Markel, 2008).

Eminent Domain Today

Eminent domain is still being widely used to facilitate the private-to-private transfer of property. In late 2000, the Institute of Justice filed a lawsuit on behalf of Susan Kelo and her neighbors in the Fort Trumbull neighborhood of New London, Connecticut. The plaintiffs objected to the city's action in condemning their properties so that the land could be turned over to a private corporation wanting to construct offices and residences (Sharp and Haider-Markel, 2008). In 2005, the U.S. Supreme Court made an important decision in upholding the lower court's ruling in *Kelo v. City of New London*. The Supreme Court signaled that the government could use eminent domain to take private property from owners and transfer it to another private party for public purposes such as economic development. The Court argued that the economic development project constituted a "public use"; therefore, using eminent domain to acquire property of owners refusing to sell was appropriate. The court also contended that New London's use of eminent domain to acquire property for development was appropriate, as "economic development is a traditional and long accepted governmental function" (*Susette Kelo v. City of New London*, 2005). Justices Sandra Day O'Connor and Clarence Thomas dissented. In the dissent, Thomas argued that in allowing the government to take private property by "extending the concept of public purpose to encompass any economically beneficial goal guarantees that these losses will fall disproportionately on poor communities" (*Susette Kelo v. City of New London*, 2005: 486). Is there a basis for this claim?

Between 1998 and 2002, eminent domain was used more than 10,000 times to facilitate the private-to-private transfer of property (Berliner, 2003; Carpenter and Ross, 2010a). Accordino and Johnson's (2000) study of the 200 largest central cities found that 42% of them used the eminent domain process to acquire vacant and abandoned properties. Cypher and Forgey (2003) also studied cities' use of eminent domain. They studied 145 cities with a population of 100,000 or more and found that after obtaining private property, 49% of the time cities conveyed the acquired property to real estate developers, a third of the time the city retained ownership of the property, 13% of the time the property was conveyed to nonprofits, and the property was disposed of in other ways 12% of the time.

Dreher and Echeverria (2006) contend that there is no relationship between the use of eminent domain and the racial characteristics of neighborhoods in which the instrument is used. Byrne (2011) agrees with Dreher and Echeverria. Regarding claims stating that eminent domain disproportionately harms racial and ethnic minorities, Byrne says, "Such concerns in our time are seriously misplaced." He continues, "Redevelopment projects using eminent domain continue to be an invaluable tool for maintaining the economic competitiveness and livability of urban areas. . . . The discriminatory elements of older urban renewal reflect the racism generally prevalent in political life in the 1940's and 50's, and have been largely eliminated by the growth of political power by African Americans and other urban minorities" (2011: 1).

However, Fillilove (2007) studied 2,532 eminent domain projects in 992 cities and found that between 1949 and 1973, these projects displaced a million people. Two-thirds of those who were displaced were Black. Carpenter and Ross (2009) also examined the use of eminent domain to see whether cases involving private-to-private transfer of property disproportionately affected the poor, as Justice Thomas suggested. Analysis of the demographic characteristics of the Kelo neighborhood at issue in the eminent domain case found that the percentage of minorities was 42%. In comparison, minorities constitute 22% of the state of Connecticut. The Kelo neighborhood also had a higher percentage of residents with less than a high school diploma, with only a high school diploma, and living in poverty than the rest of Connecticut. Two-thirds of the Kelo neighborhood had renters, while a third of Connecticut residents are renters. Income levels were also substantially lower in the Kelo neighborhood than in the rest of Connecticut.

To understand whether the Kelo neighborhood was an anomaly or not, Carpenter and Ross (2009) also studied 184 project areas in 25 states and the District of Columbia where local governments planned to use eminent domain to acquire private property with the intent of transferring it to developers for private projects. The study found that the project areas targeted for eminent domain use had a higher percentage of minorities than did the surrounding communities that were not targeted for eminent domain. That is, while the mean minority composition for project areas was 58%, the mean minority composition of the surrounding communities was 45%. The project areas targeted for eminent domain use also had lower incomes, higher rates of poverty, and a higher percentage of renters than did surrounding communities. This study supports Thomas's assertion that eminent domain is disproportionately used in poor neighborhoods.

In the wake of the *Kelo* decision, 43 states passed laws that increased protection for property owners (Carpenter and Ross, 2010b). Hence, Carpenter and Ross (2010b) examined the demographic characteristics of neighborhoods in which eminent domain was at issue in New York City; New York is one of the states that did not pass new legislation protecting property owners against the use of eminent domain. The researchers found several cases, including the Atlantic Yards project (which proposed to build 16 skyscrapers surrounding a basketball arena), in which eminent was used to condemn private property to facilitate private development projects. In New York, neighborhoods can be deemed blighted and become slated for redevelopment if they are of "outmoded design," do not have adequate off-street parking, or are at risk of becoming an insanitary area. Carpenter and Ross studied 11 eminent domain projects in New York City and Long Island that had the potential to displace hundreds of residents and small business owners. They found that minorities and the poor were disproportionately impacted by these projects. Minorities constituted 92% of the residents in project areas, compared to 57% of surrounding communities that were not in the project areas. The project communities also had lower income than did nonproject communities ($21,323 compared to $29,880). The project communities also had a higher percentage of renters, higher rates of poverty, and lower education levels than did nonproject communities. This study also supports Thomas's thesis.

Federal Home Financing, Displacement, and Segregation

During the 1930s, real estate developers and civic leaders began pressuring the federal government to do something to reverse the course of urban decay that was readily apparent in many American cities.

Consequently, the Hoover administration established the Limited Dividend Housing Program as part of the Emergency Relief Act of 1932. The program was intended to use government funds and private capital to clear slums and construct low- and middle-income housing. Government financed 85% of the projects, and the limited-dividend corporations formed to build housing were limited to 4% return on their investment (Keating and Flores, 2000; P. Arnold, 1968). In these early years, federal housing programs were as much about job creation as they were about attending to the nation's housing needs. Hence, in 1933, Congress passed the National Industrial Recovery Act, which provided employment and authorized the use of federal funds for the purposes of slum clearance and the construction of low-cost housing (K. Jackson, 1985). Some of these programs were short-lived. This was the case with the Limited Dividend Housing Program; the Roosevelt administration canceled it in 1934 (Keating and Flores, 2000).

Other programs were developed to encourage the public acquisition of lands in blighted areas for clearance and resale to private developers. Federal funds were made available to finance slum clearance and urban renewal projects. For example, Title I provided funds to cities to acquire blighted property for redevelopment; the federal government paid two-thirds of the cost of land acquisition, while local governments were responsible for a third of the "write down" cost of the land. Many of these programs resulted in the eviction of Blacks from their homes, the bulldozing of Black communities to make way for new development, and the replacement of Black residents with Whites once new housing was constructed. Federal funds were also used to segregate Black and White residents in towns and cities by constructing separate public housing for each group (Gotham, 2001; Barron, 2004; Avila and Rose, 2009). Freund argues that the federal interventions into the housing market "did more than simply structure opportunity"; the actions "also helped popularize the idea that government interventions were *not* providing considerable benefits to white people" and "that urban and suburban outcomes resulted solely from impersonal market forces" (2007: 9; my emphasis).

The housing problem that affected much of the country went beyond blight. By 1930, the U.S. had other significant problems with housing that were exacerbated by the Great Depression—the rate of foreclosures was high, and housing starts were low. In 1926, a typical year, there were 68,000 foreclosures; however, when Roosevelt took office in 1933, there were 252,400 foreclosures, and housing starts were less than a tenth of the usual amount. Between 1928 and 1933, new construction of homes fell by 95%, and expenditures on homes fell by 90% in that same period. This made for a very tight housing market that was compounded by another problem—much of the existing housing was dilapidated (Federal Housing Administration, 1959; K. Jackson, 1985).

Hence, the Home Owners' Loan Corporation (HOLC) was created in 1933 to invigorate the housing market by helping homeowners finance their homes. Tens of thousands of mortgages in danger of default or foreclosure were refinanced through HOLC. Low-interest loans were also issued to help homeowners recover homes that were already foreclosed. These new mortgages were fully amortized, and the repayment period was extended to 20 years (instead of the five- to seven-year renewable mortgages that were common before HOLC was formed). HOLC had an immediate impact—between July 1933 and June 1935, the institution provided over $3 billion to finance more than a million mortgages (Federal Housing Administration, 1959; K. Jackson, 1985).

In deciding the credit worthiness of mortgage seekers, HOLC assessed the blocks and neighborhoods in which they lived and the likelihood of obtaining financing. A four-point classification system was used in the assessment. The highest classification value, "A," was assigned to blocks in neighborhoods that were new, all White, and racially homogeneous; these were shaded in green. Stable, outlying, Jewish and White working-class neighborhoods were ranked second, "B," and shaded in blue. Inner-city neighborhoods bordering predominantly Black communities or neighborhoods that already had a small number of Blacks living in them were ranked "C" and shaded yellow. The lowest category, "D," was reserved for all-Black neighborhoods. These neighborhoods were shaded red—hence the term "redlining." Neighborhoods with high crime or old and dilapidated housing were also redlined. The four categories were further subdivided into zones such as A1, A2, and so on. Realtors, bankers, and HOLC used this system to assign a score to each city block (K. Jackson, 1985). Ducre and Moore (2011) studied how the age of the housing stock was associated with the neighborhood rating and found that the average age of homes was 16 years in A zones,

23 years in B zones, 31 years in C zones, and 45 years in D zones. The percentage of owner-occupied homes was also highest in A zones and lowest in D zones.

To systematize the classification scheme, HOLC surveyed 239 mid-sized cities between 1939 and 1945 to determine mortgage risk. HOLC then used the data to develop a series of urban "Residential Security Maps" for the entire country; neighborhoods that had beautiful, well-kept homes were shaded green, and those with old or poorly maintained housing and evidence of vandalism were colored in red. Inner-city neighborhoods that had Black residents or were perceived to be at risk of Blacks or Jews moving in (i.e., becoming racially mixed) were automatically colored red regardless of the quality of the homes. The practice resulted in a *systematic institutionalized devaluation* of Black, racially mixed, and old inner-city neighborhoods across the country. The system made it difficult for residents of redlined neighborhoods to obtain funding to build new homes or to renovate existing ones (K. Jackson, 1985; Gotham, 2001; Hillier, 2003; Ducre and Moore, 2011).

HOLC was following a decades-old practice (by realtors, developers, planners, and civic leaders) of making race and ethnicity a part of the real estate appraisal process and propagating the idea that Blacks and other ethnic-minority groups caused property values to fall. For instance, NAREB made this argument in its 1922 manual (Benson and North, 1922). McMichael (1931) made a similar argument in his appraisers manual. Babcock—author of the 1939 FHA *Underwriting Manual*—also alluded to this argument in his influential book *The Valuation of Real Estate* (Babcock, 1932). K. Jackson (1985) argues that HOLC played a critical role in signaling the federal government's approval and support of the practice and idea. HOLC was also instrumental in the widespread adaptation of the practice. Though HOLC's Residential Security Maps and the coding of neighborhoods were supposed to be secret, these maps were widely used by financial institutions, realtors, developers, and the like. In fact, bankers and realtors helped to construct the Residential Security Maps.

Hillier (2003) contends that the practice of denying loans to residents in high-risk areas predated the construction of HOLC maps. She points to the Chicago Commission on Race Relations' report that was drafted in the wake of the 1919 race riots, which stated that some lending institutions completely avoided making loans in areas where Blacks lived (Chicago Commission on Race Relations, 1922). Hillier also points to a "Mortgage Conference" held in New York in 1932, where participants shared block-level maps and encouraged member banks to avoid making loans in neighborhoods with high concentrations of Blacks. Researchers are beginning to study the impact of redlining on segregation.

Hillier (2003) also examined how HOLC's redlining grade affected lending patterns in Philadelphia, finding that the grades on the HOLC redlining maps did not explain differences in lending patterns and that the relationships were insignificant. She reports that HOLC made 60% of its loans in areas shaded red and another 20% in areas shaded yellow. However, she also found that residents in neighborhoods that were redlined were charged higher interest rates. She concludes that financial institutions were avoiding redlined neighborhoods before HOLC redlined them on the maps and that HOLC's maps were not widely distributed. That is, financial institutions were using independent sources of information to make lending decisions. Hillier identifies independent sources of redlining information were in use before the advent of the HOLC maps.

Moreover, Hillier argues that the HOLC maps were not as widely distributed as Jackson (1985) suggests. She agrees that "some private lenders and the Federal Housing Administration (FHA) definitely did have access to the HOLC maps" but that "access was not nearly as widespread as prior historical narratives have assumed" (2003: 399). Summaries of the report on each city were distributed beginning in 1938. Hillier concedes that HOLC reinforced residential segregation in some cases. When the agency foreclosed on property, HOLC allowed brokers selling off the property to abide by local segregation practices. Hillier argues that this practice constitutes racial steering, not redlining, because the discrimination is targeted at individuals, not at a particular area per se.

A study of the lending patterns of insurance companies—which invested heavily in housing construction and mortgages after World War II—found that these companies did not issue any mortgages in 23% of urban census tracts from 1945 to 1954. Between 1955 and 1964, insurance companies did not issue any mortgages to 38% of urban census tracts, and between 1966 and 1967, they did not issue any mortgages to 67.7% of urban census tracts (Hanchett, 2000). The Veterans Administration also systematically excluded Blacks from its GI Bill loan programs, which guaranteed approximately 5 million mortgages throughout the country. The Veterans Administration endorsed the use of racially restrictive covenants till 1950 and refused to underwrite mortgages it thought would introduce perceived inharmonious or incompatible racial groups into White neighborhoods (Freund, 2006). In 1949, both the FHA and the Veterans Administration announced they would cease insuring housing that had racially restrictive clauses in the deeds, effective February 15, 1950. Despite the pronouncement, the FHA and Veterans Administration continued to insure loans on properties they knew were encumbered by restrictive covenants that barred sale or rental of the property to Blacks and other minorities (Miller, 1965).

Greenlining the Suburbs

Suburban communities such as Ladue, Missouri, were rated favorably by HOLC. Ladue, a suburb of St. Louis, was dotted with rolling hills, woodlands crisscrossed by streams, spacious estates, and 40 miles of bridle paths that horses and riders cantered along. In 1940, the area was given an "A" rating and shaded green because, as HOLC describes it, the community was "highly restricted" and was the abode of "capitalists and other wealthy families." The report also noted that not "a single foreigner or negro" dwelled in the community (K. Jackson, 1985). Today, Ladue is a community with mansions worth $10 million or more, 70-foot-tall trees, and six country clubs (Bry, 2011). The latest census shows that though it is an inner-ring suburb, the median home price in Ladue is $773,000, and 36.5% of the homes are worth $1 million or more. Ladue has a population of 8,521 that is 94.1% White, 1% Black, 3% Asian, and 1.4% Hispanic. In contrast, St. Louis is 42.2% White, 49.2% Black, 3.5% Hispanic, and 2.9% Asian. The median home price in St. Louis is $122,200 (U.S. Census Bureau, 2006–2010, 2010).

Hazardous Ranking and a Wailing Wall

HOLC's antipathy to Black neighborhoods is evident in the ranking it gave Lincoln Terrace (in St. Louis County) in 1937. Lincoln Terrace, a small enclave of four- and five-room bungalows that were constructed in 1927, was originally intended for White, middle-class occupancy. However, when that venture did not succeed, the enclave was transformed into a Black residential district. Despite the fact that the homes were relatively new and in good condition, HOLC gave the enclave the lowest possible ranking of D-12 in 1937 and D-8 in 1940. HOLC rationalized its classification by arguing that the homes had "little or no value, . . . having suffered a tremendous decline in values due to the colored element now controlling the district" (qtd. in K. Jackson, 1985: 200).

The construction of the "wailing wall" in Detroit is another example of the extent to which HOLC pushed its agenda of separating Black communities from new, all-White subdivisions. By 1940, well-established Black neighborhoods could be found in Detroit on the West Side, in Paradise Valley, and in Conant Gardens. There was a fourth small Black community on the northwestern edge of the city at Eight Mile and Wyoming. The half-a-square-mile, three-by-fourteen-block Black enclave in the Eight Mile–Wyoming area was located in a part of the city that was predominantly White. However, the area was being eyed for development, as more than 72% of the lots were vacant. Many of the plots were owned by Blacks who purchased them with the hope of building their homes on them in the future, but others plots were owned by banks and real estate companies that foreclosed on them. Other plots had reverted to the city or state when owners could not pay their taxes (Detroit Housing Commission, 1939; Daines, 1940; Sugrue, 1996).

The housing crisis evident in the Eight Mile–Wyoming Black enclave was part of a national trend of high foreclosures and repossession of property by banks (Federal Housing Administration, 1959). There were competing ideas about what to do about the neighborhood. Some people wanted to clear the area and build public housing on it, while others wanted to see single-family homes constructed in this and surrounding areas. The Eight Mile–Wyoming section of the city was characterized by homes scattered amid farms and woodlands. So the city of Detroit, desperate to expand its tax base, sought to redevelop the area (Sugrue, 1996).

New, exclusive middle-class, White communities were being developed around the Eight Mile–Wyoming Black enclave as well. A quarter mile to the south was the West Outer Drive neighborhood, which was separated from the Black community by a buffer of undeveloped land and a sand quarry. A mile to the east lay the Palmer Woods and Sherwood Forest neighborhoods, which were adorned with large homes on winding tree-lined streets. The Eight Mile–Wyoming Black community was thrust into the spotlight when a developer proposed an exclusive all-White subdivision immediately to the west of it. HOLC gave the Eight Mile–Wyoming neighborhood a "D" or hazardous rating, and the FHA refused to fund the new subdivision because of its proximity to the redlined Black neighborhood (Sugrue, 1996; K. Jackson, 1985). Since the FHA's creation in 1934, it required the insertion of a racially restrictive clause in the deeds of homes and took steps to ensure this happened by providing a model contract to developers. The FHA continued this practice till 1947 (Miller, 1965).

The developer was able to secure loans and mortgages from the FHA only after agreeing to build a one-foot-thick, six-foot-high, half-a-mile-long wall on the property line that separated the subdivision from the Black community. The wall—which is still in existence today—was constructed in 1940. It became known as the Birwood Wall, "wailing wall," or "dividing wall." At the time the wall was built and for several years after, Black residents tried unsuccessfully to get HOLC and the FHA to provide funding to help with home construction in the Eight Mile–Wyoming enclave (Sugrue, 1996; Buss, 2008).

The National Picture

Between 1935 and 1950, roughly 9 million new homes were constructed by private developers in the U.S. However, minorities gained occupancy to only about 100,000, or 1.1%, of these. During this same period, 2,761,000 homes were administered by the FHA. Of these, only about 50,000 were made available to non-Whites. The majority of the new homes occupied by minorities were in segregated enclaves (R. Weaver, 1953).

Federally Subsidized Public Housing—Separate and Unequal

The story of public housing in America highlights the vulnerability of place for Blacks on several dimensions. Yet despite the gross inequities that are apparent, it is an area of research that has received little attention from EJ scholars. Black communities located in or near the core of cities or in sight of corporate offices were systematically razed and either relocated on the periphery of cities or displaced permanently. A colonial mentality also dominated the thinking, as Blacks were not perceived as the appropriate residents for the core of cities; the elites in charge of city planning dictated where in the cities Blacks could reside. Hence, while much of the EJ research has examined the siting of facilities (i.e., adding structures to an area), EJ scholars have not recognized the extent to which the obliteration (removal and destruction) of Black and other minority communities has played a role in dictating who lives where in cities.

Public housing has been another instrument used to dictate where Blacks and other minorities could live in cities. Bickford and Massey (1991) argue that a number of factors converged to result in the concentration of Blacks in public housing projects. They contend that the migration of Blacks coincided with White suburbanization, increased concern about urban blight, and inner-city decay. Urban elites were concerned about these trends because they believed these conditions were harmful to business interests and important civic institutions. These elites mobilized and took advantage of federal funding and urban renewal legislation to undertake massive *slum clearance* in burgeoning Black neighborhoods that were located close to business districts and key institutions. Public housing was used to house Blacks displaced by slum clearance projects. A constellation of actors orchestrated the movement of urban residents, decided who would live where, and used federal funds to facilitate their activities.

Limited-Dividend Public Housing

New York first sought to deal with inadequate and dilapidated housing by undertaking slum clearance in order to construct limited-dividend low-income housing. The 1926 State Housing Law allowed for the creation of limited-dividend corporations (whose profits could not exceed 6% return on investment) to build housing. Between 1926 and 1933, a dozen such corporations constructed 5,890 housing units in the city. However, despite these efforts, New York still had a massive housing shortage, and large sections of the city were described as slums (Karlin, 1937).

The Roosevelt administration also built low-income houses, and here too residency in the units and the siting of them quickly became racialized. As de Leeuw et al. argue, from the outset, federally funded low-income housing has "contributed significantly to the establishment and entrenchment of residential segregation and concentrated poverty throughout the United States" (2007: 4). The authors argue that this is the case because "most public housing built . . . was comprised of large, densely populated 'projects,' often consisting of high-rise buildings, located in poor, racially segregated communities" (4).

A Housing Division was created in the Public Works Administration (PWA), and this unit dispensed $125 million in federal funds to clear slums and construct low-income housing. Twelve proposals originated in Philadelphia alone, as planners, architects, and housing advocates hastened to reshape urban housing (Bauman, 1977).

One of the early public housing projects to be constructed—and the only limited-dividend one constructed in Philadelphia—was the Carl Mackley Houses, which overlooked Juniata Park (the complex was sometimes called Juniata Park Housing). It was funded by the PWA and built on 5.4 acres during 1933 and 1934; the 284-unit complex, which opened in 1935, grew out of a partnership with a labor union—the American Federation of Labor–Congress of Industrial Organizations (AFL-CIO)—and the federal government. The AFL-CIO's Housing Investment Trust lent over $26 million in union pension funds to the project to cover construction costs and to provide rent subsidies. This was an unusual arrangement. In fact, when union members first proposed the project, Philadelphia's Mayor Hampton Moore branded it a communist idea and tried to block it. Once the PWA eliminated the limited-dividend housing program, the focus shifted to slum clearance and the construction of public housing that was dominated by private corporate development interests. In 1934, $144 million was released to selected cities primarily for slum clearance and secondarily for the construction of demonstration projects (Bauman, 1977; Borski, 1999; Stoiber, 1999). Philadelphia set things in motion by using $4.5 million to clear a 22-acre section of Southwark that was declared a slum and constructing a 700-unit demonstration project on it for White residents. The city wrestled with where to locate a housing project for Blacks (Bauman, 1977).

Separate and Unequal Public Housing

ATLANTA

Atlanta is another good example of a place where the discourse about blight, eminent domain, and urban renewal converged to have differential impacts on Blacks and Whites. In 1933, a group of prominent businessmen and city residents, led by real estate developer Charles Forrest Palmer, were funded by the PWA to build two public housing projects—Techwood Homes for Whites and University Homes for Blacks. These projects were originally funded under the limited-dividend program, but because of delays, the developers received final approval and funding through the PWA. Housing for Whites took priority; hence, Techwood Homes was constructed and completed first. Techwood Homes was built on what used to be known as Techwood Flats—a fourteen-block, racially mixed neighborhood located just northwest of downtown Atlanta and sandwiched between the headquarters of Coca-Cola and the all-White Georgia Institute of Technology (Georgia Tech) campus. To build the project, Techwood Flats was condemned and cleared, and 1,611 families were displaced. Prior to clearance, 28% of the residents of Techwood Flats were Black (Ruechel, 1997; Keating and Flores, 2000; Barron, 2004; Holliman, 2008).

The city's business elites and planners saw Techwood Flats as a pariah to be eviscerated (Keating and Flores, 2000). Techwood Flats was described as a slum growing "glacier-like toward high priced business property, carrying depression of values with it steadily and surely" (Public Works Administration, 1935: 208). Palmer opined, "Why such an untended abscess should fester between the lovely campus of our proudest school and the office buildings in the heart of our city" is unfathomable (Palmer, 1955: 7). The president of Georgia Tech, Marion Brittain, also campaigned to clear Techwood Flats (Brittain, 1948) because, as Palmer noted, "Students of Georgia Tech could look out the college windows and be close enough to count most of the miserable shacks huddled in the valley below them. That was all they could see on 24 acres of Negro and poor white habitation" (qtd. in Keating and Flores, 2000: 278).

When the Techwood Homes project was built, it had 604 units to house White families only. The first building that was completed was the 189-unit Techwood Dormitory, designed to house 300 Georgia Tech students. The buildings—nestled amid grassy courtyards—occupied less than a fourth of the hilly, twenty-two-acre site. The ample open space was elaborately landscaped. The grounds had clay tennis courts, fenced playgrounds, a wading pool, parks, and benches. The complex also had eight retail stores, five free laundries, commercial equipment, a library, an auditorium, medical and administrative offices, storage space, and garages. These projects were large job-creation undertakings too; more than 2,000 men were employed to build the Techwood Homes complex (Keating and Flores, 2000; Barron, 2004; Holliman, 2008).

With the clearing of Techwood Flats and the rebuilding of dorms and public housing units, Atlanta practiced what Marcuse (1986) refers to as *exclusionary displacement*. The new housing that replaced the original Techwood Flats housing was priced too high for displaced residents— Black and White—to afford. Rents at Techwood ranged from $23.47 to $46.45 per month; hence, tenants had to earn between $700 and $1,800 per year to qualify to live in the complex. When the complex was fully occupied, the average annual income of the residents was $1,008. This ranked in the 70th percentile among Atlanta residents (Keating and Flores, 2000).

Some Blacks who used to live around Georgia Tech were placed in University Homes, which was built adjacent to the all-Black Clark-Atlanta University. However, University Homes was not completed till 1937. Many of the former Techwood Flats residents were never rehoused (National Park Service, 1993; Ruechel, 1997; Keating and Flores, 2000; Barron, 2004; Holliman, 2008).

Clark Howell Homes was constructed adjacent to Techwood Homes. Clark Howell consisted of 630 semidetached townhouses in 58 two-story buildings. Each unit had individual entrances, a gabled roof, and private yard space. The complex was built with a park, a library, and a community center. A 250-unit, 17-story complex, Palmer House, was constructed adjacent to Techwood and Clark Howell for elderly residents in 1966 (Keating and Flores, 2000).

Techwood, Clark Howell, and Palmer House remained all-White housing projects till they were integrated in 1968. Within six years of integration, 50% of the residents were Black. Believing that the crime rate would increase as more Blacks moved into the projects, Coca-Cola's chief executive officer, Paul Austin, proposed that Techwood be cleared and residents relocated on the outskirts of the city (Holliman, 2008; Keating and Flores, 2000). In a 1971 memo to Robert Woodruff, former chief executive officer of Coca-Cola, Austin suggested that once razed, Techwood should be replaced with "an ultra-modern middle income apartment complex with its own shopping mall, theatre, recreation area and park" (Austin, 1971).

During the 1960s, Austin, Woodruff, and other business elites spearheaded projects that used federal urban renewal funds to remove Blacks from neighborhoods close to downtown. For instance, between 1963 and 1970, more than 1,800 low-income Black families were also displaced from Bedford Pines, a neighborhood that was located just east of Atlanta's central business district (Keating and Flores, 2000). This left Techwood, Clark Howell, and Palmer House in the crosshairs of businessmen desirous of having upscale residential neighborhoods flanking their corporate headquarters.

The 1996 Centennial Olympic Games provided an opportunity to displace Blacks from the area a second time. By then, 92% of Atlanta's public housing residents were Black. Most of Techwood and Clark Howell were bulldozed to make way for luxury apartments to house athletes participating in the Olympics. Since Techwood was listed on the National Register of Historic Places in 1976, some of the original buildings were spared. In all, 1,195 units of low-income housing was replaced by 800 luxury units intended for mixed-income residents (who took occupancy after the Olympics). After the Olympics, only 78 of the Techwood Homes residents returned to live at Centennial Place (Techwood's new name) (National Park Service, 1993; Holliman, 2008; Keating and Flores, 2000; McNulty and Holloway, 2000).

MARIETTA

Marietta, Georgia, also used federal funds to develop segregated housing. Though Marietta had been a small town of about 8,000, its population grew rapidly in the 1930s, thereby creating a housing shortage. The city's leaders responded by creating the Marietta Housing Authority, applying for federal funds, and using the money to build two housing projects—one for Whites and one for Blacks. The city's poorest neighborhood, Hollandtown, had Blacks living on the west side and Whites on the east. Hollandtown was located just two blocks from Marietta's downtown district. Marietta received an $800,000 federal grant in 1939 and set about building the two "equal equity" housing projects. Though the two projects were constructed of similar size and with similar building materials, they were unequal in a number of ways that had detrimental impacts on Blacks (*Cobb County Times*, 1941; Barron, 2004).

Hollandtown was slated for urban renewal, and one of the new housing projects—Clay Homes—was planned for the neighborhood. To build Clay Homes, the western section of the neighborhood was condemned as a health hazard, and no transitional housing was provided for the Black residents, who were forced to move. Blacks were the only ones evicted since Whites were allowed to continue living in the eastern portion of the neighborhood while the construction of Clay was under way. When completed, Clay Homes housed only White residents. Fort Hill Homes was built for Blacks on the northeastern fringe of the city. Instead of living a few blocks from the city center, poor Blacks were housed to the edge of the city. Residents of Clay Homes benefited from city services such as the trolley; they also had access to a Whites-only public school. In contrast, the main road to Fort Hill Homes was one of the last in the city to be paved, and the area surrounding the project lacked basic infrastructure. The project was surrounded by open fields, dusty areas, and patches of woodlands. Residents did not have easy access to commercial or retail institutions. They also lacked public transportation—the closest stop on the segregated trolley line was five blocks away. To get to the trolley, Fort Hill residents had to traverse a wooden footbridge and walk down an unpaved road. The inequities did not stop there. While the Clay project was built with a playground and spray pool, such amenities were not provided at Fort Hill (Barron, 2004).

DALLAS

Dallas was another city that developed separate public housing projects for Whites and Blacks. Despite the mandates issued in the 1960s to desegregate public housing, the public housing in many cities remained segregated for decades more (Goering, 1986). In a 1989 decision, a federal district court ruled that the "primary purpose of [the Dallas] public housing program was to prevent blacks from moving into white areas of th[e] city." The justices also found that the city took deliberate measures to create and maintain segregation through public housing (*Walker v. HUD*, 1989: 1293).

BALTIMORE

Baltimore also assessed its housing stock in the 1930s and began to construct public housing. In 1933, Maryland's Joint Committee on Housing conducted a study that found that Blacks lived in the worst housing in Baltimore. However, the report also concluded that blight was a "problem of the Negro race." The committee recommended that three Black neighborhoods be redeveloped for White residents. The report said of one of the neighborhoods, it "should be developed as a fairly good class White residential area. There is no reason except obsolescence of buildings for it to be inhabited by colored people" (qtd. in Williams, 2004: 32).

Despite the involvement of a large number of Black social reformers and institutions in lobbying for public housing for Baltimore's Black residents, the construction of public housing also resulted in the displacement of Black families and institutions and the transformation of racially mixed neighborhoods into segregated ones. Slum clearance and the construction of public housing also resulted in a reduction in the number of housing units available to Blacks. Though Blacks constituted two-thirds of the residents living in neighborhoods described as blighted, 45% of the public housing units were built in White neighborhoods (Williams, 2004).

BIRMINGHAM

Urban renewal projects destroyed Black neighborhoods in Birmingham, Alabama, too. In 1937, Birmingham described 22 neighborhoods as blighted; 13 of these were predominantly Black. Overall, 70% of the dwelling units considered blighted were located in predominantly Black neighborhoods. During the 1930s, Black-owned homes were slated for clearance in order to build the Smithfield Court public housing project.

When Blacks complained that the city's racially restrictive zoning law made it very difficult to find replacement homes, the city redrew the racial zoning line so that the homeowners could move their homes to lots just west of their former location. Black activists in the NAACP also traveled to Washington, D.C., to ensure that Smithfield Court was built with the same amenities found in White public housing projects. During the 1950s, an entire Southside Black neighborhood was cleared to make way for the construction of the University of Alabama at Birmingham's medical center. Blacks—who already had a difficult time finding housing in the city—were not relocated (Connerly, 2005; National Register of Historic Places, 2004).

CHICAGO

Areas designated as blighted in Chicago mapped onto the contours of the Black Belt and on rapidly changing, racially mixed Westside neighborhoods (*Chicago Defender*, 1949; Hirsch, [1983] 1998; Pritchett, 2003). Massive public housing projects were also constructed in Chicago. Beginning in 1934, Chicago destroyed 21,000 housing units deemed substandard. About a third of the housing destroyed was located in Black neighborhoods. Overcrowding was so severe in Black neighborhoods that a census conducted in 1934 found that the average Black household contained 6.8 persons, compared to 4.7 persons in the average White household (Hirsch, [1983] 1998). Some low-income White neighborhoods were experiencing population declines at a time when the population of Black neighborhoods was skyrocketing. For instance, the population of a four-square-mile blighted White area declined from 186,639 residents in 1920 to 121,036 residents in 1940. In contrast, the population of a similarly sized blighted Black community in the city had 152,413 residents in 1920 and 191,861 in 1940 (Nesbitt, 1949).

The Chicago Housing Authority (CHA) was founded in 1937 with the express purpose of clearing the city of slums and rebuilding neighborhoods with large-scale public housing projects. Huge portions of the inner city, including the entire Black Belt, were slated for slum clearance. Much of the housing in the Black Belt consisted of two- and three-flat apartments built before 1900. Many lacked private bathrooms at the time they were earmarked for slum clearance. As early as 1940, the site for the 4,400-unit Robert Taylor Homes was selected. Built as part of a four-mile-long cluster of high-rise housing projects that was the largest in the country, this behemoth stretched for miles and housed about 27,000 people at its peak occupancy. Shortly after the site for the Taylor homes was identified, city engineers chose to run the Dan Ryan superhighway right through the neighborhood; railroad tracks ran on the other side of the expressway. This meant that the five gargantuan housing projects built in the cluster were physically cut off from the rest of the city and surrounding neighborhoods (Hunt, 2001).

Working- and middle-class Whites objected to the placement of public housing projects in their neighborhoods. When the Chicago Housing Authority proposed the construction of a 250-unit public housing project for low-income defense workers in 1944, Whites living east of Cottage Grove opposed the plans. They succeeded in keeping the project out of a White community. However, when the upper-class Black community of West Chesterfield formed a Citizens Committee and objected to the project being placed in their neighborhood, they failed to stop it (Cooley, 2008; P. Smith, 2000; Nesbitt, 1949; *Chicago Bee*, 1943; Lancaster, 1944). At the time, West Chesterfield was an enclave in which Black professionals built homes. The *Chicago Bee* (1944) described the neighborhood as "the nation's only exclusive residential community of wealthy Negro home owners."

Nonblighted Black neighborhoods were also cleared in urban renewal projects. This occurred in 1947 when Chicago made a deal with the New York Life Insurance Company to develop the Lake Meadows community on the South Side. The developers cleared several blocks of well-maintained homes so that residents of Lake Meadows could get an unobstructed view of the lake. Critics argued that the development ignored actual slums and demolished well-kept Black neighborhoods where most of the properties were Black owned. Though most of the residents of Lake Meadows were Black, the project replaced only a small percentage of the units demolished and allowed for the expansion of the Illinois Institute of Technology campus (*Chicago Defender*, 1949; Hirsch, [1983] 1998; Pritchett, 2003).

Most of the people displaced by slum clearance in Chicago between 1948 and 1956 were Black. An Urban League report revealed that 86,000 people were displaced in that period; of that number, roughly two-thirds, or 57,000, were Black. During this period, Blacks constituted around 20% of the city's population (Dulaney, 1962). Slum clearance converted some Black homeowners into public housing tenants.

DETROIT

White Detroiters also objected vociferously to proposals to build public housing projects in their neighborhoods. Things came to a head in 1941 when it was announced that a 200-unit public housing project for Blacks would be built at the corner of Nevada and Fenelon in a neighborhood that already had a substantial Black population. Whites formed the Seven Mile–Fenelon Improvement Association to coordinate opposition to the project. For a short while, middle-class Blacks living in nearby Conant Gardens joined the coalition. Whites were not only disturbed about the placement of the project in the racially mixed neighborhood; they were also angered by the FHA's decision to refuse to insure any more mortgage loans in the Seven Mile–Fenelon area. Despite opposition, the project—named Sojourner Truth after the famous African American poet and speaker—was completed in 1941. At the time, only one other project in the city housed Blacks. Nonetheless, White residents in the surrounding area as well as Congressman Rudolph Tenerowicz, the pastor of St. Louis the King Church (Rev. Constantine Dzink), and Joseph Bulla (head of the Seven Mile–Fenelon Neighborhood Improvement Association) insisted that the project should be a Whites-only residence. The Detroit Housing Commission and the FHA flip-flopped on which racial group should inhabit the project. In January 1941, it was designated as Whites-only housing, but two weeks later, the housing was promised to Black war workers. This led to protests from Whites. The first Black families were not allowed to move into Sojourner Truth till the next year. On February 28, 1942, a small number of Black families tried to move into the units they had been paying rent on since the beginning of the year. Black supporters gathered, but so did local White residents and militants, who surrounded the project and hurled objects at the people trying to move in. About 200 police were on hand, yet the violence escalated. Shots rang out, and about 40 people were injured. In addition, 220 people were arrested; of the 109 held for trial, 106 were Black. Tensions boiled for several months. At the end of April, 1,100 city and state police officers as well as 1,600 Michigan National Guard troops were called in to quell the violence and protect the 168 Black families who had moved into Sojourner Truth (Capeci, 1984; Sugrue, 1996; Farley, Danziger, Holzer, 2000).

The Sojourner Truth controversy made federal officials look for vacant lots in the suburbs to build housing for Black defense workers. The FHA purchased 170 acres in nearby Dearborn to build 1,400 temporary homes. However, fearing that Blacks would be allowed to live in such housing, the mayor of the city, Orville Hubbard, led an all-out battle against the plan. Dearborn's civic leaders filed injunctions in the courts and succeeded in getting them. They blocked the project long enough so that when the war was over, housing for war workers became a moot issue (Sugrue, 1996).

Detroit and its suburbs undertook urban renewal projects that displaced many Black families. Hamtramck, a predominantly Polish American municipality completely surrounded by Detroit, used federal funds to raze its black residential neighborhoods in 1962 to allow the Chrysler plant there to expand. Federal funds were also used to raze additional homes to construct an expressway to the plant; most of the homes bulldozed for this project were also Black owned or occupied (Rothstein and Santow, 2012).

NEW YORK

In New York City, more than 250,000 people were dislocated by urban renewal projects between 1946 and 1953 (Caro, 1974). Relocation was not always a priority for the urban renewal projects. Mushkatel and Nakhleh (1978) studied projects that displaced about 177,000 families and an additional 66,000 individuals between 1949 and 1963. Only about 118,128 families were relocated in that period. Eminent domain played a critical role in this process. Shoup argues that urban renewal programs "relied heavily—sometimes callously—on eminent domain" (2008: 1).

WASHINGTON, D.C.

Washington, D.C., also used eminent domain to undertake an extensive slum clearance project in 1952. The District of Columbia Redevelopment Land Agency oversaw the project, which cleared most of the southwest quadrant of the city. In the process, more than 20,000 poor Blacks were dislocated, and their homes and businesses were replaced with office buildings, stores, and middle-class housing (*Schneider v. D.C. Redevelopment Land Agency*, 1953; *Berman v. Parker*, 1954; Pritchett, 2003).

KANSAS CITY

Though Kansas City, Missouri, began its slum clearance projects in the 1950s, it followed the pattern established by municipalities that began their projects two decades earlier. In so doing, the city demolished the 54.2-acre neighborhood of Attucks located near downtown, displacing 478 Blacks. A total of 1,783 Blacks and 1,960 Whites were displaced by Kansas City's slum clearance and urban renewal projects spanning the period 1953 to 1978. Blacks were displaced in disproportionate numbers; 48% of those who were displaced were Black, yet Blacks were only a small portion of the city's population during this period (Gotham, 2001). Blacks constituted 12.2% of the population in 1950, 17.5% in 1960, and 27.6% in 1970 (Gibson and Jung, 2005).

When Kansas City constructed its public housing in the 1950s, the projects were segregated, and the first complex constructed in 1952 housed White families. Five housing projects—ranging in size from the 139-unit West Bluff to the 454-unit Guinotte Manor—housed Whites. Blacks were concentrated in two large projects—the 462-unit T.B. Watkins Homes and the 738-unit Wayne Miner Court. Despite objections from the city's African American newspaper—the *Kansas City Call*—and the Urban League, the housing projects were segregated and those for Blacks clustered in one part of the city (*Kansas City Call*, 1954; Mincer, 1987; Gotham, 2001).

ST. LOUIS

St. Louis also undertook extensive slum clearance projects. The efforts were spearheaded by the League of Women Voters, the Citizens' Council on Housing and Community Planning, the Civic Committee on Conservation and Rehabilitation, the building trade unions and labor council, the leading newspapers, planners, business executives, and politicians. As early as 1938, the League of Women Voters began campaigning for slum clearance with radio ads urging the construction of public housing and carefully orchestrated "slum tours." Unionists in the building trades who saw the job-creation potential of public housing construction began advocating for the construction of housing projects in St. Louis in the 1930s also (Heathcott, 2008; Teaford, 1990). When the city chose a site for slum clearance, 96% of the residents in the area were Black. When Blacks objected to the clearance, pointing out that the neighborhood was not the most dilapidated in the city, the Citizens' Council defended the choice of site by arguing, "No more dramatic example may be found than these 54 blocks located in *the very center of our city*. . . . People going and coming from work through this district are offended by the state of decay they witness on all sides. Unfortunately, too, every visitor who arrives in our city by train is given a poor impression of St. Louis as he or she is transported immediately through such dismal districts" (qtd. in Nesbitt, 1949: 275).

In 1942, the St. Louis Housing Authority opened its two first housing projects to 1,200 families. White families moved into Clinton-Peabody in the southern portion of the city, while Black families were placed in Carr Square Village in the northern part of the city. Clearance of a site for a third housing project began that same year (Heathcott, 2008). In 1959, sections of Mill Creek Valley—an African American neighborhood—were cleared to make way for Laclede Town, Grand Towers, U.S. 40 (the Ozark Expressway), and an expansion for St. Louis University. Not all displaced residents were rehoused; public housing was constructed to house the poorest Black residents (City of St. Louis, 1996; Goodman and Monti, 1999).

Challenging Segregated Public Housing

As the preceding discussion indicates, segregation was a hallmark of public housing development from its inception. Before World War II, 236 of the 261 projects funded by the U.S. Housing Authority and 43 of the 49 projects funded by the PWA were segregated (Popkin et al., 2003). By 1962, more than two million people were housed in roughly half a million units of public housing that had been constructed with federal funds (K. Jackson, 1985).

Housing segregation became an issue during the 1960 presidential campaign, and John F. Kennedy made a campaign promise to eliminate it in all federal agencies. On November 20, 1962, President Kennedy issued an executive order forbidding discrimination in the sale or rental of federally subsidized, insured, or administered housing. The executive order also mandated the desegregation of the nation's public housing projects (Executive Order 11063, 1962). It authorized the FHA to withhold funding from developers who discriminate. However, the order did not cover housing *already built* before its effective date; neither did it cover housing that *did not* receive any federal subsidies. Hence, the order covered only about 15% of new housing and between 2% and 3% of the total housing stock. Moreover, the executive order did not immediately result in significant policy shifts. Five years after its passage, there was still no supporting legislation to strengthen it (Grier, 1967; Miller, 1965). Title VI of the Civil Rights Act of 1964 officially outlawed discrimination in the administration of federally subsidized public housing. This was followed by the passage of the Fair Housing Act in 1968 (Title VIII of the Civil Rights Act of 1968). Despite these government mandates, desegregation of public housing (both in terms of where they were built and the demographic composition of the population housed within them) moved at a snail's pace (Keating and Flores, 2000; Popkin et al. 2003).

Though many EJ advocates argue that low-income housing is built on land adjacent to noxious facilities or hazardous sites because such land is the cheapest, such arguments miss the point that during the height of the period when public housing was being constructed, there was ample vacant land in and around cities that was cheap and free of industrial hazards. However, many suburban communities—not wanting to have low-income or minority dwellers in their midst—opted not to apply for federal funds or to build any public housing.

The Gautreaux Case

A landmark legal challenge to the practice of segregating public housing occurred in Chicago. The city's public housing development followed a familiar pattern: build public housing for Whites first, segregate the developments, concentrate Blacks in projects built in poor Black neighborhoods, build larger complexes to house Blacks, and construct projects housing Blacks with inferior amenities. In 1938, the year after the CHA was formed, three projects to house White residents were opened. They were the 1,027-unit Jane Addams Houses, the 925-unit Julia Lathrop Homes, and the 426-unit Trumbull Park Homes. A small fraction of the units (2.5%) in the Jane Addams Homes were reserved for Blacks. These complexes were scattered on the Near West Side, the North Side, and the South Side of the city, respectively. A much larger project, the 1,662-unit Ida B. Wells Homes, was constructed on the South Side for Blacks in 1941. Chicago and other cities built these segregated developments according to federal guidelines. They were adhering to the government's "Neighborhood Composition Rule," which stipulated that residents of public housing projects should be the same race as the people in the neighborhood in which the housing project is located. Over time, Chicago's housing projects designated for Blacks got larger and larger. Wells Homes was expanded to 2,293 units in 1955. Cabrini—which opened as a 586-unit complex in 1942—was expanded to 3,607 units by 1962. When Robert Taylor Homes opened in 1962, it was the largest housing project constructed in the United States. The 4,415-unit development had 28 identical 16-story buildings built on superblocks adjacent to the Dan Ryan Expressway on the South Side of the city (Choldin, 2005). Between 1950 and the mid 1960s, the CHA applied for and got approval to build 33 housing projects; 98% of these were located in Black neighborhoods (Hirsch, [1983] 1998; Wyly and Hammel, 2000).

Chicago's Black public housing residents challenged the segregation policies of the CHA and HUD in the courts. In 1966, Dorothy Gautreaux and around 43,000 other Black public housing tenants and people on the waiting list for public housing in Chicago brought two lawsuits against the CHA and HUD. Though Gautreaux, a resident of Altgeld Gardens on the city's Far South Side, died of cancer in 1968, the class-action suit continued in her name. Plaintiffs alleged that between 1950 and 1965, the CHA, aided and abetted by HUD, deliberately placed Blacks in Black housing projects and that public housing for Blacks was sited only in Black neighborhoods. The litigants contended that the CHA deliberately chose public housing sites so that they could avoid placing Black families in units in White neighborhoods. They argued that this violated their Fourteenth Amendment rights (equal protection clause). Blacks pointed to four White housing projects in White neighborhoods in which Blacks were typically denied residence. As far back as 1954, the CHA frequently refused to allow Blacks to live in these projects. Consequently, in December 1967, Blacks constituted between

1% and 7% of the residents of the projects. Yet they constituted about 90% of the residents of CHA's public housing projects as well as roughly 90% of the 13,000 people on the waiting list (*Gautreaux v. Chicago Housing Authority*, 1969a, 1969b; 1974; *Hills v. Gautreaux*, 1976; *Gautreaux v. Pierce*, 1982).

The court case also revealed that projects intended to house Blacks were not built in predominantly White neighborhoods because the CHA had a preclearance system that thwarted the development of projects. That is, aldermen from White neighborhoods chosen as potential sites for housing projects were apprised of the plan and asked whether they approved it. The aldermen vetoed 99.5% of the units proposed in White neighborhoods and only 10% of those proposed in Black neighborhoods. The CHA did not proceed with projects that the aldermen disapproved of. The aldermanic preclearance procedure was used to circumvent the city council (*Gautreaux v. Chicago Housing Authority*, 1969a, 1974).

The court ruled in *Gautreaux v. Chicago Housing Authority* in 1969 that the CHA discriminated against Blacks in both its tenant-assignment and site-selection procedures. The judge argued that the CHA's practices maintained the separation of the races in Chicago. The judge—noting that there was negligible racial violence documented in the housing projects—dismissed the CHA's claim that segregated public housing was necessary to reduce racial tensions. Consequently, the CHA was ordered to modify its tenant-assignment procedures. It was also ordered to build three public housing developments in neighborhoods in the metropolitan area in which less than 30% of the residents were minority for every project built in neighborhoods where the non-White population exceeded 30% (the ratio was later reduced to one-to-one). HUD was sued because the plaintiffs alleged that the agency was culpable for sanctioning and assisting the CHA in executing its discriminatory policies and practices by funding the organization and condoning its practices. From 1950 to 1966, HUD provided the CHA with almost $350 million in funding. The HUD case was initially dismissed primarily for failure to state a claim. The decision was appealed and brought before the Seventh Circuit Court. The court argued that HUD was also responsible for the discriminatory site-selection and tenant-placement policies practiced by the CHA. Both cases were consolidated from then on (*Gautreaux v. Chicago Housing Authority*, 1969b, 1999, 2007; *Gautreaux v. Romney*, 1971, 1972; *Hills v. Gautreaux*, 1976).

The city's public housing tenants formed residents' councils in each project and a Central Advisory Council (CAC) to monitor the CHA's compliance with the court rulings. Since the CHA was painfully slow in complying with the court order, the rancorous relationship between the CHA and the CAC resulted in numerous court battles. Chicago ignored the court order to build scattered-site public housing. Though the CHA built public housing for the elderly, it did not construct any additional kinds of public housing till the 1990s (*Gautreaux v. Chicago Housing Authority*, 1974, 1999, 2007; *Gautreaux v. Pierce*, 1982). Similar challenges to discriminatory policies in public housing were brought in other cities such as Boston (*NAACP v. HUD*, 1987), Dallas (*Walker v. HUD*, 1989), Minneapolis (*Hollman v. Cisneros*, 1995), and Baltimore (*Thompson v. HUD*, 2005).

The 1976 U.S. Supreme Court decision (*Hills v. Gautreaux*) ushered in Section 8 vouchers. This is a national program, aimed at *dispersing the poor* in urban and suburban communities, that issues subsidized rent vouchers to public housing residents to obtain lodging on the open market. The model for this program was the Gautreaux program that started in Chicago. Initially the program was small. Only about 400 of the Gautreaux litigants had the opportunity to participate in the program, which allowed public housing residents to use rent vouchers to move to suburban communities. The program expanded as the Gautreaux model and Section 8 vouchers were adopted all over the country as mechanisms for reducing the concentration of tenants in public housing and providing housing opportunities outside the projects. When the Gautreaux program ended in 1998, 7,100 families had participated in it (*Hills v. Gautreaux*, 1976; P. Fisher, 2005).

The State of EJ Research

C. Smith (2007) has studied the effects of redlining on the location of Superfund sites in Detroit. Smith found that Superfund sites are clustered in the central city in areas there were not redlined by HOLC. Smith argues that though Blacks were living in Detroit's central city, the Superfund sites appear in areas of high economic deprivation close to where

Blacks lived but not directly in Black neighborhoods. Though Smith's research tells us about redlining in Detroit, an important component of the racial geography of the city—the widespread use of racially restrictive covenants—was not examined in this study. That is, were the core parts of the city that have Superfund sites covered by racially restrictive covenants or not? What was the relationship between the location of Superfund sites and the location of covenanted neighborhoods?

Hernandez (2009) has studied the effect of redlining on property values in Sacramento from 1930 to 2004. The researcher found that between 1938 and 1949, when the HOLC maps were produced for Sacramento, property values decreased by 30% in the redlined areas, while they increased by 46% in the city as a whole. Hence, HOLC maps appear to have had a dampening effect on property values in redlined districts.

Studies exploring the link between residential segregation and health outcomes are relatively new. Environmental justice researchers are among the pioneers in this emerging field. They are examining the connection between residential segregation and exposure to environmental hazards. Morello-Frosch and Lopez's (2006) article provides an overview of the research on residential segregation and health disparities and the connections between the two. Environmental justice researchers are looking more specifically at the relationship between exposure to air pollution from stationary and mobile sources, the siting pattern of hazardous facilities, and segregation. For instance, Lopez (2002) studied the relationship between outdoor air pollution and residential segregation in 44 metropolitan areas with populations of more than a million. He found that Blacks were more likely than Whites to be living in census tracts with higher concentrations of air toxins.

Morello-Frosch and Jesdale (2006) examined the links between exposure to toxins in the air, cancer risk, and racial residential segregation in 309 metropolitan areas in the U.S. Like Lopez (2002), Morello-Frosch and Jesdale used the 1990 census in their analysis. Morello-Frosch and Jesdale found that as racial and ethnic residential segregation increased, so did the cancer risk associated with exposure to ambient air toxins. That is, the estimated cancer risks associated with air toxins were highest in census tracts in metropolitan areas that were *hypersegregated*. The researchers used multivariate models to demonstrate that the segregation effects were strongest for Hispanics. When poverty was examined, the researchers found that cancer risk did not increase with increasing poverty. Their findings suggest that the impact of segregation on cancer risk is independent of poverty levels.

Apelberg, Buckley, and White (2005) conducted a similar study in Maryland using 2000 census data. Their results differed somewhat from those of Morello-Frosch and Jesdale (2006). Instead of examining the level of segregation in areas being studied, Apelberg, Buckley, and White examined the proportion of racial groups within the area. They found that census tracts with the highest quartile of African Americans were three times more likely to be high risk for cancer than were those in which the percentage of African Americans was in the lowest quartile. Concomitantly, cancer risk decreased as the percentage of Whites in the census tracts increased. Cancer risk also declined as the percentage of Hispanic residents increased. There was also a strong relationship between social class and cancer risk; the risk increased as poverty increased.

Lee and Ferraro (2007) examined the relationship between segregation and health disparities among Puerto Ricans and Mexican Americans in Chicago and found differences in the two groups of Hispanics. The study found that segregation was associated with poorer health among Puerto Ricans; however, this was not the case for Mexican Americans. Moreover, second- and later-generation Mexican Americans living in hypersegregated neighborhoods had better health status than did first-generation Mexican American living in such neighborhoods.

Chakraborty and Armstrong (1997) studied the relationship between segregation and proximity to noxious facilities. They found a slight negative association between segregation and facility proximity for minority communities. Their findings run counter to those of the aforementioned studies. Downey (2005) has also conducted a study of segregation and proximity to manufacturing facilities in Detroit. He argues that segregation has reduced Blacks' exposure to pollution from industrial facilities.

Downey, Dubois, Hawkins, and Walker (2008) used the EPA's RSEI data to study 329 metropolitan areas in the continental United States to study racial and ethnic differences in environmental inequality. The RSEI data contain toxicity-weighted air-pollution concentrations. The study found that environmental inequalities varied widely from one metropolitan area to another. The study used logistic regression models to examine how residential segregation and income inequality is related to environmental inequality. The researchers found that residential segregation and racial income inequality are poor predictors of environmental inequality outcomes.

There are still gaps in the EJ research on segregation that needs to be filled. EJ studies should examine how historical residential segregation patterns are related to exposure to hazards. This relationship should be made explicit in the research, and scholars should include variables to test the impact of this factor on exposure. Similarly, more work should be done on urban renewal activities and the use of eminent domain to understand how these processes influence population dynamics in cities and whether they have disproportionate negative impacts on any particular group. EJ scholars should also investigate how contemporary urban revitalization programs are affecting access to housing, gentrification, displacement of vulnerable populations, and exposure to hazards.

10

Contemporary Housing Discrimination

Does It Still Happen?

In a 1972 study of segregation of African Americans in Pittsburgh, Darden concluded that regardless of income, Blacks experienced great difficulty renting or buying homes in nonsegregated areas. Is this still the case? The Black population is still rising, and Blacks continue to be primarily urban dwellers. The Hispanic population is rising rapidly. Though smaller than the aforementioned groups, the Asian and Native American populations are rising too. Although residential segregation is declining, Blacks still live in highly segregated communities in many cities (U.S. Census Bureau, 2004). But has the *level of residential segregation* changed? Studies of residential segregation have found that since the 1970s, it has been more prevalent in large northern cities than in southern ones (Sterns and Logan, 1986). The Census Bureau's analysis of 220 metropolitan areas that had 20,000 or more Black residents in 1980 shows that there has been a reduction in the residential segregation of Blacks between 1980 and 2000 (U.S. Census Bureau, 2004).

Overall, there was a 12% decrease in White-Black segregation in the 220 metro areas between 1980 and 2000 (see table 10.1). However, there were some regional variations—the West and the South had the lowest levels of segregation; these two regions also had the largest decrease in residential segregation in the time period studied. Both the Northeast and the Midwest had a dissimilarity index of .74 in 2000; the White-Black level of segregation dropped more in the Midwest than in the Northeast during this time. The size of the metro area also mattered in the level of segregation seen. That is, the smaller the size of the metro area, the lower the dissimilarity index. The size of the Black population in the metro area also mattered. The level of segregation increases as

Table 10.1. Dissimilarity Index and Residential Segregation of Blacks: 1980–2000

Characteristics	Number of metro areas	Dissimilarity index			Percentage change 1980–2000
		1980	1990	2000	
Weighted average of metro areas	220	0.73	0.68	0.64	−12
Region					
Northeast	31	0.78	0.77	0.74	−5
Midwest	53	0.82	0.79	0.74	−10
South	114	0.66	0.61	0.58	−12
West	22	0.71	0.63	0.56	−22
Size of metro areas					
One million or more	43	0.78	0.73	0.69	−11
500,000–999,999	33	0.69	0.63	0.60	−13
Under 500,000	144	0.60	0.56	0.53	−12
Percentage of Blacks in metro areas					
Less than 6.2%	55	0.64	0.57	0.53	−17
6.2%–10.5%	55	0.72	0.66	0.61	−14
10.5%–19.1%	55	0.75	0.69	0.65	−14
Over 19.1%	55	0.73	0.70	0.67	−8
Rate of increase of Black population between 1980 and 2000					
Under 25.4%	55	0.79	0.76	0.72	−9
25.4%–41.7%	55	0.72	0.70	0.67	−6
41.7%–63.1%	55	0.67	0.62	0.59	−12
Over 63.1%	55	0.68	0.60	0.57	−17

Source: Compiled from U.S. Census Bureau, 2004.

the percentage of Blacks in the metropolitan increases. The five indicators of segregation reported by the census were studied, and all showed a reduction in segregation for the time period analyzed (U.S. Census Bureau, 2004).

Though many EJ studies explain the siting patterns of industrial facilities and exposure to hazards as being an outcome of segregation, these studies tend not to indicate what *measure of segregation* is being used to test the arguments. There is also a tendency in EJ studies to focus on White-Black segregation while ignoring other kinds of segregation. The dissimilarity index is the most widely used measure of segregation. However, as table 10.2 shows, the index varies dramatically depending on the racial and ethnic groups it is calculated for. The table shows that in Detroit, for instance, Black-Asian segregation is almost as high as White-Black segregation. In Chicago, Black-Asian segregation is higher that White-Black segregation. The table shows the dissimilarity index for Whites, Blacks, Hispanics, and Asians in 2000 for 40 of the metropolitan areas discussed in the book. It shows that it is not just Blacks and Whites who do not live in the same neighborhoods; in many cities, Hispanics and Blacks as well as Asians and Blacks *do not* live in the same neighborhoods. Blacks are the most segregated group, while the least segregation exists between Whites and Asians (U.S. Census Bureau, 2000). This is a phenomenon that is not well articulated or examined in EJ studies.

Have these trends continued into the twenty-first century? Economics professors Edward Glaeser of Harvard University and Jacob Vigdor of Duke University declared in a Manhattan Institute report of the most recent census data that "all-white neighborhoods are effectively extinct" (2012: 1). They argue that 50 years ago, 20% of urban neighborhoods had no Blacks living in them. However, in 2010, 199 out of every 200 neighborhoods have Black residents. But the story is more complicated than this. The researchers found that since 1970, the separation of Blacks from other racial groups has declined in all of the country's 85 largest metropolitan areas. Segregation is also lower in 657 of the 658 housing markets tracked by the Census Bureau. Since 2000, segregation has declined in 522 of those 658 housing markets (Glaeser and Vigdor, 2012).

Logan and Stults (2011) have also examined the 2005–2009 American Community Survey data and concur that the U.S. has become *more diverse*. White-Black segregation levels are declining—but very slowly. The researchers also found that despite great increases in the Hispanic and Asian populations, these two groups are as segregated as they were 30 years ago. Furthermore, Logan and Stults argue that the growth in the Hispanic and Asian populations has created more *concentrated ethnic enclaves* in many parts of the country. The researchers found that since 2000, the level of residential segregation between Whites and Blacks has continued to decline at roughly the same pace as the declines witnessed in the 1990s. Hispanics and Asians are much less segregated from Whites than Blacks are. The level of Hispanic and Asian segregation has remained relatively steady since 1980. Because of the rapid increase in the population of Hispanics and Asians, there is a tendency for their ethnic enclaves to become more homogeneous over time. Consequently, these two groups live in more *isolated* settings in 2005–2009 than they did in 2000.

Table 10.2. Dissimilarity Indices for 40 Metropolitan Areas in 2000

Metropolitan area	Dissimilarity Index					
	White-Black	White-Hispanic	White-Asian	Black-Hispanic	Black-Asian	Hispanic-Asian
Detroit, MI PMSA	85	46	46	78	81	59
Gary, IN PMSA	84	48	32	71	82	56
Milwaukee–Waukesha, WI PMSA	82	60	41	78	64	52
New York, NY PMSA	82	67	51	56	78	57
Chicago, IL PMSA	81	62	44	77	82	63
Newark, NJ PMSA	80	65	35	61	75	60
Cleveland–Lorain–Elyria, OH PMSA	77	58	38	75	75	61
Buffalo–Niagara Falls, NY MSA	77	56	47	63	68	55
Flint, MI PMSA	77	27	35	64	77	42
Cincinnati, OH–KY–IN PMSA	75	30	42	62	68	39
St. Louis, MO–IL MSA	74	29	42	63	70	38
Miami, FL PMSA	74	44	31	74	66	45
Birmingham, AL MSA	73	48	47	65	75	47
Philadelphia, PA–NJ PMSA	72	60	44	59	66	56
Indianapolis, IN MSA	71	44	39	52	60	43
New Orleans, LA MSA	69	36	48	59	67	40
Kansas City, MO-KS MSA	69	46	35	59	65	39
New Haven–Meriden, CT PMSA	69	60	34	43	59	56
Memphis, TN–AR–MS MSA	69	48	38	53	67	45
Baltimore, MD PMSA	68	36	39	56	64	34
Los Angeles–Long Beach, CA PMSA	68	63	48	54	66	55
Houston, TX PMSA	67	56	49	52	61	58
Pittsburgh, PA MSA	67	30	49	55	71	41
Baton Rouge, LA MSA	67	32	51	57	66	41
Boston, MA–NH PMSA	66	59	45	43	57	51
Atlanta, GA MSA	66	52	45	58	63	41
Louisville, KY–IN MSA	64	36	41	55	63	35
Washington, DC–MD–VA–WV PMSA	63	48	39	56	62	37
Denver, CO PMSA	62	50	30	56	51	45
San Francisco, CA PMSA	61	54	49	50	52	48
Dallas, TX PMSA	59	54	45	51	63	61
Greensboro–Winston-Salem–High Point, NC MSA	59	51	46	40	52	50
Tulsa, OK MSA	59	40	40	48	58	36
Charlotte, NC–Gastonia–Rock Hill, SC, MSA	55	50	43	41	45	43
Seattle–Bellevue–Everett, WA PMSA	50	31	35	33	32	30
Portland, OR–Vancouver, WA PMSA	48	35	32	47	45	40
Tacoma, WA PMSA	46	32	34	24	25	23
Texarkana, TX–Texarkana, AR MSA	45	42	30	43	38	44
Phoenix–Mesa, AZ MSA	44	52	28	31	39	51
Tucson, AZ MSA	39	50	26	38	31	51

Source: Compiled from U.S. Census Bureau, 2000.

Logan and Stults examined 367 metropolitan areas and found that in 2005–2009 the average White individual lived in a neighborhood that was 75% White, 8% Black, 11% Hispanic, and 5% Asian. Two decades earlier, in 1990, the average White person lived in a neighborhood in which 83% of the households were also White. In contrast, in 2005–2009, the average Black person lived in a neighborhood that was 35% White, 45% Black, 15% Hispanic, and 4% Asian. The average Hispanic lived in a neighborhood that was 35% White, 11% Black, 46% Hispanic, and 7% Asian. In comparison, the typical Asian lived in a neighborhood that was 49% White, 9% Black, 19% Hispanic, and 22% Asian (Logan and Stults, 2011; Logan, 2011).

Racial segregation is still a very strong predictor of *unequal neighborhoods*. Affluent Blacks have only marginally higher contact with Whites than poor Blacks do. In fact, affluent Blacks and Hispanics tend to live in neighborhoods with fewer resources than poor Whites have. Logan argues, "Blacks' neighborhoods are separate and unequal not because blacks cannot afford homes in better neighborhoods, but because even when they achieve higher incomes they are unable to translate these into residential mobility" (2011: 15). With the exception of affluent Asians, minorities live in poorer neighborhoods than Whites with comparable incomes do (Logan, 2011).

Rethinking White Flight, Residential Sorting, Ethnic Churning, and Buffering

Sociologists have argued that the number of White census tracts is decreasing nationally, while the number of tracts with two or three minority groups is increasing (Denton and Massey, 1991). Farley and Frey (1994, 1996) and Logan and Zhang (2010, 2011) contend that in the residential sorting under way in neighborhoods, *buffering* is occurring. That is, high-status second- and third-generation Hispanics and Asians are integrating White communities. These Hispanics and Asians are less segregated from Whites than they are from Blacks. The buffer hypothesis argues that Whites remain in neighborhoods integrated by high-status Asians and Hispanics—even if Blacks also move into the neighborhoods (after Asians and Hispanics do). According to the buffer thesis, Asians and Hispanics live in an *intermediate zone* (physical buffer) within the same census tracts, and that provides a buffer between Blacks and Whites. The buffer can also be a social one that mediates the differences between Blacks and Whites.

Logan and Zhang's (2011) analysis of Census data in 20 metropolitan areas found that the percentage of census tracts that had Whites, Blacks, Hispanics, and Asians living in them has increased from 22.5% in 1980 to 38.2% in 2010. In contrast, the percentage of census tracts with only Whites, Hispanics, and Asians living in them has declined from 28.6% to 15.2% over the same period. There was an increase in the number of census tracts that had no Whites in them. That is, the number of all-minority tracts is increasing—the number of these has increased by 80% since 1980. Lee, Iceland, and Sharp (2012) and Farrell and Lee (2011) also make a similar argument that the burgeoning Hispanic and Asian populations have reduced the number of all-White neighborhoods and have increased the number of neighborhoods that Whites cohabit with minorities or that are all minority.

Contemporary Housing Discrimination

Can housing segregation be explained by factors such as differences in income? That is, if Whites have higher incomes than minorities do, then Whites will be able to purchase more expensive homes that minorities cannot afford, and that would result in segregated neighborhoods. Sociologists such as Massey and Denton (1993) have examined this possibility and have found that the high levels of racial segregation found in American metropolitan areas cannot be fully explained by racial *differences in income*. Logan (2011) also found that residential segregation is not fully explainable by differences in income between Whites and minorities. Farley, Danziger, and Holzer argue that "residential segregation is a matter of skin color, not income, occupation, or education" (2000: 165). The researchers argue that the Black-White segregation index in Detroit in 1990 was 88; however, if the segregation index were based on household income, it would be 15. The index would be 5 if it were based on householders' occupation and 6 if it were based on adults' educational attainment.

Is housing discrimination a thing of the past? Not by a long shot. There is still widespread discrimination in the housing markets that helps to trap minorities in undesirable neighborhoods. Recent studies find significant levels of discrimination in the home sales and rental markets. Racial steering and other forms of discrimination create significant barriers to about half of all Black and Hispanic home buyers. Even among equally qualified borrowers, Blacks were rejected 60% more frequently than Whites (Yinger, 1986, 1995; Chai and Kleiner, 2003). HUD's 2000 Housing Discrimination Study found that White home buyers were significantly more likely than comparable Black home buyers to be shown and recommended homes in predominantly White neighborhoods. Discrimination against Hispanic renters has increased since 1989 (de Leeuw et al., 2007). Yinger (1986) studied housing discrimination in Boston and found that Black testers were shown 36.3% fewer apartments than their White team members were.

Squires, Friedman, and Saidat (2002) studied housing discrimination among 921 adults in Washington, D.C., and the adjacent suburbs of Maryland and Virginia. They found that while 80.5% of Whites said they got their first choice when they moved into their current residence, only 67.4% of Blacks indicated they did. Blacks were more than four times as likely to report that they experienced discrimination in the quest to secure housing or financing. Blacks were also more than twice as likely as Whites to report knowing someone who had experienced discrimination while seeking to secure housing or financing. Whites and Blacks had very different perceptions of fairness in the housing market; 57.9% of Whites and 16.1% of Blacks felt the choices in the housing market were the same for Blacks and Whites.

Another indicator of contemporary housing discrimination is the fact that federal, state, and local housing officials get more than 10,000 complaints from minorities annually. A 2006 National Fair Housing Alliance report estimated that there are at least 3.7 million instances of housing discrimination each year, but less than 1% is reported (C. Clark, 1994; Dymi, 2007).

Choi, Ondrich, and Yinger (2005) and Zhao, Ondrich, and Yinger (2006) examined data from the 2000 Housing Discrimination Study and found that though there was evidence that the magnitude of discrimination in the rental housing market had declined since 1989, considerable discrimination still existed. They found frequent and statistically significant discrimination against Black and Hispanic renters.

The discrimination stemmed from realtors' own prejudice as well as the prejudice of their White clients.

Ross and Turner (2005) also compared discrimination in the rental housing market in 1989 and 2000 and found that though the rates at which White testers were shown preferential treatment over Black testers had declined during that time, Black testers were still being treated unfairly when they sought to rent housing. Black testers were treated less favorably than White testers on the availability of rental units, the ability to inspect units, the terms and conditions of the lease, and encouragement. The study also found that Blacks faced significant discriminatory hurdles when they sought to purchase a house. Black testers were treated less favorably than White testers on the availability of homes to purchase, the ability to inspect homes, geographic—racial—steering, assistance with financing, and encouragement. The study found that the incidence of racial steering had increased between 1989 and 2000. That is, there was a significant increase in the percentage of Blacks being steered to predominantly Black neighborhoods when looking for a home. The researchers also examined the extent of discrimination faced by Hispanics in the rental market. They found that Hispanic testers were treated less favorably than White testers in the rental market. When it comes to purchasing a home, Hispanics receive less favorable treatment than Whites in regard to receiving information about home financing. Weil (2009) also reports that Hispanics seeking housing on the Gulf Coast in the wake of Hurricane Katrina experienced discrimination.

Home Financing and Redlining

Forms of redlining are still being used by financial institutions. In recent years, several major banks have been investigated and fined for redlining minority communities and other discriminatory lending practices. The term "reverse redlining" has been used to describe the practice of targeting minority communities and issuing minority borrowers mortgage loans that have high interest rates and fees (*United States v. Countrywide*, 2011a, 2011b). Between 2007 and 2009, the NAACP sued 15 banks for offering high-interest loans to Blacks even when they qualified for low-interest loans. The banks include Wells Fargo, Citibank, and JPMorgan Chase, among others (Tedeschi, 2010). This is important because high-cost loans increase the likelihood of default and increase the chances that homes will be foreclosed on. It also means that home-owners are at risk of becoming renters or homeless in the process.

In 2011, the Department of Justice filed a complaint against Bank of America's subsidiary Countrywide for charging 200,000 Black and Hispanic borrowers higher interest rates and fees than White borrowers with similar qualifications and credit scores. Between 2004 and 2008, Countrywide did not offer minority homeowners conventional mortgages that had lower interest rates, though White homeowners were offered such mortgages. The complaint alleged that victims of Country-wide's practices were primarily of Hispanic ancestry in California, while they were primarily Black in the Midwest and the East. However, the discrimination occurred in 180 geographic markets in 41 states plus the District of Columbia. The higher interest rates and fees that were charged to Blacks and Hispanics were not based on their creditworthi-ness or any other objective criteria of risk; they were based on the bor-rowers' race and ethnicity. Bank of America agreed to pay $335 million in restitution and penalties to the victims (*United States v. Countrywide*, 2011a, 2011b; Rothstein, 2012; *USA Today*, 2012).

Lawsuits are under way in several cities. The city of Memphis brought suit against Wells Fargo in 2011 for issuing what bank employees referred to as "ghetto loans" to Blacks. Bank employees were instructed to target subprime loans (with high interest rates and fees) to zip codes in the city with a high percentage of Blacks, as residents of these areas "weren't savvy enough" to recognize they were being taken advantage of. Even though Wells Fargo made only 15.1% of its loans in predominantly Black neighborhoods, 41.1% of its foreclosures were in neighborhoods that were more than 80% Black. Only 23.6% of the bank's foreclosures were in neighborhoods that were less than 20% Black, yet 59.5% of the loans were in such neighborhoods (*City of Memphis v. Wells Fargo*, 2011).

Similar practices were instituted in Baltimore, where Wells Fargo established a special branch composed exclusively of Black employ-ees whose job it was to visit Black churches to advertise the subprime loans. Similar advertising did not occur through White church net-works. Loan officers also targeted predominantly Black zip codes for their lending (*Baltimore v. Wells Fargo*, 2011). Even before Wells Fargo's practices came to light, the inequities in lending were apparent. A study of lending patterns in Baltimore found that 73% of the predominantly White census tracts received a medium or high volume of single-family mortgage loans, while the same was true for only 5% of the predominantly Black census tracts (Shlay, 1987). The loans made to Blacks bore high interest rates and fees. In 2007, 43% of Black borrowers and only 9% of White borrowers were issued subprime mortgages. In 2006, 65% of Blacks and 15% of Whites were issued such loans. To exacerbate matters, Wells Fargo made large numbers of foreclosures in Black neighborhoods from 2000 on. As a result, between 2005 and 2009, 51% of the bank's foreclosures were in neighborhoods that were more than 80% Black, while only 12% of its foreclosures occurred in neighborhoods that were 20% or less Black (*Baltimore v. Wells Fargo*, 2011).

In 2012, Wells Fargo agreed to pay $125 million and establish a $50 million assistance fund to settle the suits brought against the company. Court documents show that between 2004 and 2007, roughly 34,000 creditworthy Hispanics and Blacks were given more expensive subprime loans and that through 2009, minority borrowers were charged higher fees and interest rates than comparable White borrowers were (*USA Today*, 2012).

Studies show that race was a significant factor in the type of loan homeowners got. In 2000, low-income Blacks were more than twice as likely as low-income Whites to have subprime loans, and high-income Blacks were about three times as likely as high-income Whites to have subprime loans. Yet a *Wall Street Journal* study found that in 2000, 41% of all borrowers qualified for conventional loans with lower rates. By 2006, research found that 61% of borrowers qualified for conventional loans (Bradford, 2002; Brooks and Simon, 2007; Rothstein, 2012). However, in 2006, 53.7% of Black, 46.6% of Hispanic, and 17.7% of White mortgage recipients received high-interest loans. It is evident that there was a *spatial pattern* to the lending also. In census tracts where 80% of more of the residents were minority, 46.6% of those residents received high-interest loans. In contrast, only 21.7% of the residents in census tracts where less than 10% of the residents were minorities received high-interest loans (Avery, Brevoort, and Canner, 2007). ACORN studied the issue in 172 metropolitan areas in 2007 and found that 27.5% of the residents had received high-cost loans. However, the racial disparities were stark: 55.3% of Blacks, 46.6% of Hispanics, and 20.4% of

Whites had received high-interest loans (ACORN Fair Housing, 2007). Bocian, Ernst, and Li (2008) have also found that the presence of high percentages of minorities in an area is associated with a higher proportion of high-cost loans being executed.

Holmes (2000) studied census tracts in nine metropolitan areas (Los Angeles, Atlanta, Chicago, Des Moines, Baton Rouge, Boston, Albuquerque, Pittsburgh, and Nashville) to see if there was a relationship between racial characteristics and the number and type of mortgage loans issued in 1991 and 1992. The analysis of conventional loans (those without government insurance) found that Hispanic neighborhoods received more loans than similar White neighborhoods did. However, the study found that Black neighborhoods received fewer loans than similar White neighborhoods did; this was particularly true of Chicago, Atlanta, and Pittsburgh. The study also found that minority neighborhoods were receiving larger quantities of insured loans (FHA, Veterans Administration [VA], and Farmers Home Administration [FmHA] insured). Holmes concludes that racial composition has only a marginal impact on the flow of conventional and insured mortgage loans in some regions.

In effect, the financial institutions have created a *dual mortgage market* that has detrimental impacts on minorities—particularly Blacks and Hispanics (U.S. HUD, 2000; Apgar and Calder, 2005; Trifun, 2009). The operation of a dual mortgage market within a *dual housing market* intensifies the impacts that housing discrimination has on those who are being discriminated against. Rugh and Massey argue that "residential segregation created a unique niche of minority clients who were differentially marketed risky subprime loans" (2010: 629). They found that residential segregation and race contributed to the rates of foreclosure. That is, the higher the degree of Black and Hispanic segregation, the higher the rate of foreclosure in a neighborhood.

Implications for EJ Research

Buffering

The EJ studies discussed in chapter 4 tend to characterize neighborhood change in terms of White flight (Whites fleeing neighborhoods as Blacks move in) and residential sorting or ethnic churning (one ethnic group replacing another). The EJ literature on neighborhood succession has cast Hispanics and Asians as groups *displacing* Blacks in neighborhoods. However, the census and the types of analysis discussed in this chapter point to emerging dynamics that EJ researchers have not articulated or investigated in their research. That is, instead of displacing Blacks, high-status Hispanics and Asians are *paving the way* for Blacks to enter predominantly White neighborhoods without triggering White flight. Hence, the understanding of the physical and social buffers that Asians and Hispanics provide is an important element of neighborhood change that is understudied in EJ research. Hence, the research discussed in this section calls for a rethinking of concepts such as ethnic churning and residential sorting as they have been described and operationalized in the EJ literature.

Residential Segregation and Reverse Redlining

The Fair Housing Act of 1968 outlawed housing discrimination, including the practice of redlining—that is, the denial of loans and mortgages on the basis of the racial composition of a neighborhood. Despite the existence of the Fair Housing Act, reverse redlining is being practiced by financial institutions. In effect, the racial composition of a neighborhood is being used as the basis to target residents and to offer them high-interest loans. Some researchers—believing that residential segregation makes it easier for financial institutions to identify the targets of subprime loans—are exploring the relationship between residential segregation and discriminatory lending practices. Relman argues that "the people who are most vulnerable to abusive lending practices are geographically concentrated and are, therefore, easily targeted by lenders" (2008: 637).

While studies have found that higher percentages of high-cost loans are executed in areas with high percentages of minorities (U.S. HUD, 2000; Avery, Brevoort, and Canner, 2006; Bocian and Zhai, 2005; ACORN Fair Housing, 2007; Bocian, Ernst, and Li, 2008), these studies do not tell us if the *concentration* of minorities (i.e., the level of residential segregation) is related to discriminatory lending practices. Researchers are beginning to examine the relationship between

Table 10.3. Relationship between Segregation and Subprime Lending

Metropolitan area	State	Dissimilarity index	% high-cost loans
Metropolitan areas with the ten highest Black-White dissimilarity indexes			
Detroit–Warren–Livonia	Michigan	84	34
Milwaukee–Waukesha–West Allis	Wisconsin	81	29
Chicago–Naperville–Joliet	Illinois	78	31
Cleveland–Elyria–Mentor	Ohio	77	28
Flint	Michigan	76	37
Muskegon–Norton Shores	Michigan	76	38
Buffalo–Niagara Falls	New York	76	25
Niles–Benton Harbor	Michigan	73	30
St. Louis	Missouri	73	31
Cincinnati–Middletown	Ohio	73	25
Average		77	25
Metropolitan areas with the ten lowest Black-White dissimilarity indexes			
Missoula	Montana	24	15
Santa Cruz–Watsonville	California	24	14
Blacksburg–Christiansburg–Radford	Virginia	24	20
Jacksonville	North Carolina	24	22
Boulder	Colorado	23	10
Bellingham	Washington	22	16
Prescott	Arizona	21	21
Santa Fe	New Mexico	21	17
Hinesville–Fort Stewart	Georgia	18	39
Coeur d'Alene	Idaho	16	25
Average		22	20

Source: Compiled from Squires, Hyra, and Renner, 2009.

residential segregation and discriminatory lending practices via subprime loans. Squires, Hyra, and Renner (2009) conducted a national study of segregation and subprime lending and found that the higher the segregation of Blacks and Hispanics in metropolitan areas, the higher the amount of subprime loans executed in those areas. Table 10.3 shows the relationship between the dissimilarity index and the rate of subprime lending in selected metropolitan areas. Generally speaking, the percentage of subprime lending was higher in metropolitan areas with higher levels of Black-White segregation.

The study also found that a 10% increase in the level of Black segregation was associated with a 1.4% increase in the number of high-

interest loans executed. A 10% increase in the level of Hispanic segregation was associated with a 0.6% increase in high-cost lending. In
the most highly segregated Black neighborhoods, the number of high-
interest loans executed increased by 7%; it increased by 4.2% in similar
Hispanic neighborhoods. In metropolitan areas with high educational
attainment, the proportion of high-interest loans executed tended to be
lower. Ordinary least squares regression analysis showed that racial segregation was a significant predictor of the proportion of loans that were
subprime. That is, the levels of segregation of Blacks and Hispanics
were significant predictors of subprime loans when poverty, percentage minority, median home value, creditworthiness, and educational
attainment were held constant (Squires, Hyra, and Renner, 2009).

Race, Home Equity, and Wealth

Though EJ researchers—whether skeptical or supportive of EJ claims—
make frequent references to property values as being important in
determining where minorities live or where noxious facilities are sited,
scholars have yet to elucidate the link between property ownership,
wealth inequality, and the impacts these factors have on the ability to
move to or reside in desirable locations. Yet racial differences in wealth
in America are well documented (Oliver and Shapiro, 1995; Kennickell,
Starr-McCluer, and Suden, 1997; Krivo and Kaufman, 2004). The largest source of wealth for most American households is the *equity in their
homes* (U.S. Census Bureau, 2001). This is critical, as the preceding discussion provides extensive documentation of the extent to which minorities—especially Blacks—are discriminated against at various stages in
the process of acquiring a home. In effect, housing discrimination can
reduce the ability of minorities to acquire wealth through homeownership (Yinger, 1995; Bradford, 2002; Krivo and Kaufman, 2004).

Research shows that Blacks and Hispanics own homes of lesser value
than do comparable Whites, even after housing characteristics are controlled for (Krivo and Kaufman, 2004). Krivo and Kaufman (2004)
analyzed the 2001 American Housing Survey and found that 73.3%
of Whites in the sample owned their homes. In comparison, 54.5% of
Asians, 49.2% of Hispanics, and 45.5% of Blacks were homeowners. But

how does homeownership translate into equity? The study found that Asians had the largest amount of equity accumulated in their homes and Blacks the least. On average, Asian homeowners had $185,368 in home equity, Whites had $126,773, Hispanics had $98,770, and Blacks had $81,533. Asians are in an advantageous position because 36.1% of them made large down payments on their homes and only 1.5% had high-interest loans (of 9% interest or greater), 9.5% had adjustable-rate mortgages, and 16.2% had FHA/VA/FmHA mortgages. Though the FHA/VA/FmHA loans require lower down payments, they cost more than conventional mortgages. Thirty percent of Whites made large down payments on their homes. Slightly higher percentages of Whites than Asians have high-interest and variable-rate mortgages; 4.3% of Whites have high-interest home loans, 14.5% have adjustable-rate mortgages, and 17.8% have FHA/VA/FmHA mortgages. Much lower percentages of Blacks and Hispanics made large down payments. Blacks and Hispanics also had markedly different mortgage packages than Asians and Whites did. On average, 23.5% of Hispanics made large down payments on their homes. While 6.8% of Hispanics had high-interest mortgages, 13.2% had variable-rate loans, and 32.7% had FHA/VA/FmHA mortgages. A fourth (24.9%) of Blacks made large down payments on their houses. However, 10.8% of them had high-interest mortgages, 15.4% had adjustable-rate mortgages, and 36% had FHA/VA/FmHA mortgages (Krivo and Kaufman, 2004). Oliver and Shapiro (1995) proffer a *sedimentation thesis* that can help us to understand these results. They argue that the pervasive barriers to homeownership that Blacks have faced in historical and contemporary times has a *cumulative impact* that continues to impede their ability to generate wealth.

How has the rate of homeownership changed, and how has it been affected by the housing crisis? Studies show that Blacks and native-born Hispanics experienced the largest absolute losses in homeownership between 2005 and 2008 (Kochhar, Gonzalez-Barrera, and Dockterman, 2009). Rosenbaum (2012) found that the least educated, least affluent, and Black households had the largest drops in homeownership in 2011. Between 2001 and 2011, Black homeownership dropped by 3.7%; homeownership by high school dropouts fell by 4.5% in the same period. To put this in context, homeownership dropped by about 1% nationally between 2001 and 2011.

Gentrification, Homeownership, Displacement, and Segregation

L. Freeman (2006) asserts that homeowners stand to benefit from gentrification. He demonstrates that some Black homeowners do benefit from gentrification. But is this a widespread phenomenon? Glick (2008) explored this question in his study of the impact of gentrification on wealth acquired through home equity in seven metropolitan areas (Denver, Miami, New Orleans, Oklahoma City, Phoenix, Portland, and Seattle) between 1994 and 2004. He used the American Housing Survey's Metropolitan Sample and found that the gentrifying areas of metropolises had high concentrations of Black and Hispanic owners at the onset of the gentrification process. The study found that the median home equity rose for Black and Hispanic homeowners at the onset of gentrification, but as gentrification takes hold in neighborhoods, Blacks and Hispanics move out of gentrifying neighborhoods to other parts of metropolitan areas, where home equity gains are lower. For instance, in Denver in 1994, 11% of Black and Hispanic homeowners lived in neighborhoods that were beginning to gentrify. However, by 2004, only 6% of Black and Hispanic homeowners lived in gentrifying neighborhoods.

Glick (2009) and Wyly, Atia, and Hammel (2004) also make a connection between gentrification and predatory lending. They argue that the two are likely to coincide as they tend to take place in neighborhoods traditionally underserved by mainstream financial institutions.

Mortgage Acquisition and Gentrification

Can minorities buy homes in already gentrified areas? Wyly and Hammel (2004) used Home Mortgage Disclosure data to examine the extent to which Blacks and Hispanic home buyers had access to gentrified neighborhoods in 23 cities. The researchers found that minority applicants seeking mortgages in gentrified neighborhoods were much more likely to have their applications rejected than White applicants were. That is, Blacks were 2.33 times more likely and Hispanics 1.44 times more likely to be rejected for mortgages in gentrified neighborhoods than were comparable White applicants. The borrowers whose applications were most likely to be approved were the high-income, single, White males.

Kirkland (2008) sees gentrification as a racial phenomenon and calls for greater understanding of how race and gentrification is related. Bostic and Martin (2003) also examined the relationship between race and gentrification. They focused on the question of whether Black homeowners act as a gentrifying force. In studying several cities, they found that Black homeowners contributed to gentrification in the 1970s but not in the 1980s.

These studies point the way to the kinds of EJ research that are needed in this field. There are relatively few EJ studies that analyze the relationship between home financing, financial institutions, and residential patterns. It is imperative that EJ researchers expand the scope of their work to examine these relationships in urban and rural settings, as discrimination in the financial sector can result in foreclosures, displacement, the conversion of homeowners to renters, loss of wealth or the inability to acquire it, and denial of access to property. In short, financing has a huge impact on the kind of housing one has access to and whether one can afford to move or where one can move to.

Conclusion

Future Directions of Environmental Justice Research

This book has examined the question of why minorities may not move from neighborhoods that host noxious facilities. In so doing, it has discussed several theories used to explain the prevalence of hazardous facilities in minority communities. It has also reviewed hundreds of studies that can help us understand this phenomenon. The foregoing discussions lead me to conclude that the aspects of EJ research dealing with noxious facilities and exposure to environmental hazards are robust and evolving rapidly. Nonetheless, there are many areas where this field of study needs to make adaptations.

There is no question that spatial analyses have been enormously important to EJ research, but the time is right for a new generation of spatial analysis that makes a more concerted effort to take history into consideration. The focus on national, regional, and metropolitan studies often misses important local phenomena that go unaccounted for. It is also time for the spatial analyses to move beyond the question of who lives beside what facilities; researchers should be willing to tackle the more difficult question of understanding what forces compel people to live beside such facilities.

EJ research has to pay more attention to the relative danger of facilities. A nuclear plant or a uranium dump is more dangerous than a municipal landfill taking only household trash is. More effort should be put into understanding the impact that different types of facilities have on health, property values, jobs, host-community compensation, and so on. The ownership structure of hazardous facilities also matters. EJ research should be more concerned with absentee ownership, multinationals headquartered overseas, branch facilities, subsidiaries, and other ownership structures that impact the operation of the facilities, accountability, and community relations.

Much of the EJ research has focused on large industrial facilities; however, there is a plethora of small facilities such as dry cleaners, gas stations, and garages that have impacts on nearby residents worth studying. More work should be done on these neighborhood businesses to help us understand the issues that arise with them more fully. More attention should also be paid to industrial sectors such as agriculture. Though smokestacks and flares might not be seen belching pollutants into the air, agricultural operations degrade the environment and have significant health impacts on workers and residents of surrounding communities.

This book draws on several strands of research relevant to EJ that EJ scholars are not well connected to. Though some economists have been skeptical and critical of EJ claims, not only do the hedonic models they use help to answer questions about what happens to property values when facilities are sited in communities, but the findings support EJ claims. Historically, realtors and urban planners have been strong proponents of segregation; however, research conducted by the real estate industry on factors affecting property values provides important techniques and results that should be of interest to EJ scholars. EJ researchers should also pay more attention to urban planning research for the same reasons.

Finally, EJ research has to become more theoretically focused. The studies should have explicit theoretical frames that are tested. This means scholars will have to break the habit of merely mentioning practices such as segregation or zoning as factors that lead to disproportionate exposure to hazards and actually examine these factors in a more systematic way. This would mean making a clear distinction between instruments such as racially restrictive covenants and racial zoning. It would also mean recognizing the impacts of other kinds of zoning such as expulsive, exclusionary, and intensive zoning. These ideas should be operationalized and tested in the research.

Though EJ scholars have examined demographic variables extensively in their research, newer approaches are needed here also, as sociologists have uncovered phenomena such as buffering that suggest a rethinking of EJ approaches to studying neighborhood demographic change. They also suggest a need to include a broader range of racial and ethnic groups in analyses.

It is clear from the foregoing discussion that EJ scholarship should adopt multimethod approaches that combine, for example, spatial, historical, economic, sociological, and planning techniques. Furthermore, EJ scholars should not be timid about developing multidisciplinary collaboratives to tackle more complex questions and to build more sophisticated models to explain processes and relationships such as those discussed here. Such collaboratives could also devise strategies to support EJ claims-making in the legal and policymaking arenas.

EJ scholarship has grown by leaps and bounds over the past three decades; hence, it is appropriate to pause and assess the state of the research. We are at an important juncture where it is also necessary to identify directions in which to proceed. It is my hope that the discussion in this book can provide some pointers on how to expand and improve this field of research.

REFERENCES

Abrams, C. 1966. "The Housing Problem of the Negro." *Daedalus* 95 (1): 64–76.

Accordino, J., and G. Johnson. 2000. "Addressing the Vacant and Abandoned Property Problem." *Journal of Urban Affairs* 22 (3): 301–315.

ACORN Fair Housing. 2007. *Foreclosure Exposure: A Study of Racial and Income Disparities in Home Mortgage Lending in 172 American Cities.* September 5.

Adeola, F.O. 2000. "Cross-National Environmental Injustice and Human Rights Issues: A Review of Evidence in the Developing World." *American Behavioral Scientist* 43 (4): 686–706.

Adeola, F.O. 1994. "Environmental Hazards, Health, and Racial Inequity in Hazardous Waste Distribution." *Environment and Behavior* 26 (1): 99–126.

Agyeman, J., R. Bullard, and B. Evans, eds. 2003. *Just Sustainabilities: Development in an Unequal World.* MIT Press.

Aiken, C.S. 1987. "Race as a Factor in Municipal Underbounding." *Annals of the Association of American Geographers* 77:564–579.

Alabama Department of Environmental Management. 2011. "Chemical Waste Management Emelle, Alabama: Fact Sheet."

Alabama Department of Environmental Management. 2010. "Hazardous Waste Facility Permit."

Alabama v. Olin. 1979. No. CA79 G 5174NE (N.D. Ala. September 10).

Alabamians for a Clean Environment et al. v. Thomas and Pegues. 1987. 26 ERC 2116 (N.D. Ala.).

ALCOA (Aluminum Company of America). 2012a. "Alcoa Foundation Awards over $300,000 to Local Organizations." October 1. Available at http://www.alcoa.com/ massena_operations/en/news/releases/news_detail.asp?xpath=2012_10_1MAS FoundationGrants.

ALCOA (Aluminum Company of America). 2012b. "Alcoa's Massena Operations." Available at http://www.alcoa.com/massena_operations/en/info_page/home.asp.

Alexander v. Sandoval. 2001. 532 U.S. 275.

Allen, D.W. 2001. "Social Class, Race, and Toxic Releases in American Counties, 1995." *Social Science Journal* 38:13–25.

Allen v. City of Oklahoma. 1936. 175 Okl. 421; 52 P.2d 1054.

Ambler, M. 1990. *Breaking the Iron Bonds: Indian Control of Energy Development.* University Press of Kansas.

American Trucking Assoc., Inc. v. United States. 1985. 755 F.2d 1292 (7th Cir. February 27).

Amott, T., and J. Matthaei. 1991. *Race, Gender, and Work: A Multicultural History of Women in the United States.* South End.

Anderson, A.B., D.L. Anderton, and J.M. Oakes. 1994. "Environmental Equity: Evaluating TSDF Siting over the Past Two Decades." *Waste Age,* July. Pp. 83–100.

Anderson, J.L., and E. Sass. 2004. "Is the Wheel Unbalanced? A Study of Bias on Zoning Boards." *Urban Lawyer* 36:447.

Anderton, D.L., A.B. Anderson, J.M. Oakes, and M.R. Fraser. 1994. "Environmental Equity: The Demographics of Dumping." *Demography* 31 (2): 229–248.

Anderton, D.L., A.B. Anderson, P.H. Rossi, J.M. Oakes, M.R. Fraser, E.W. Weber, and E.J. Calabrese. 1994. "Hazardous Waste Facilities: 'Environmental Equity,' Issues in Metropolitan Areas." *Evaluation Review* 18 (2): 123–140.

Anderton, D.L., J.M. Oakes, and K.L. Egan. 1997. "Environmental Equity in Superfund: Demographics of the Discovery and Prioritization of Abandoned Toxic Sites." *Evaluation Review* 21 (1): 3–26.

Angel, B. 1991. *The Toxic Threat to Indian Lands.* Greenpeace. June.

Anniston Star. 1990. "The Governor's Proposed Fee on Hazardous Waste Is Really— Political Pollution: This Time He's Doing—Environmental Demagoguery." January 17.

Apelberg, B.J., T.J. Buckley, and R.H. White. 2005. "Socioeconomic and Racial Disparities in Cancer Risk from Air Toxics in Maryland." *Environmental Health Perspectives* 113 (6): 693–699.

Apgar, W.C., and A. Calder. 2005. "The Dual Mortgage Market: The Persistence of Discrimination in Mortgage Lending." In *The Geography of Opportunity: Race and Housing Choice in Metropolitan America.* X. Briggs, ed. Brookings Institution Press. Pp. 101–124.

Ard, K.J. 2013. "Changing Exposures: Health Risk from Industrial Toxins in the United States from 1995 to 2004." Ph.D. dissertation, University of Michigan.

Arizona v. United States. 2012. 132 S. Ct. 2492 (June 25).

Arnold, C.A. 2007. *Fair and Healthy Land Use: Environmental Justice and Planning.* Planning Advisory Service Report. October.

Arnold, C.A. 1998. "Planning Milagros: Environmental Justice and Land-Use Regulation." *Denver University Law Review* 76 (1): 1–155.

Arnold, P.E. 1968. "Public Housing in Atlanta." *Atlanta Historical Society Journal* 13 (September): 11.

Ash, M., and T.R. Fetter. 2004. "Who Lives on the Wrong Side of the Environmental Tracks? Evidence from the EPA's Risk-Screening Environmental Indicators Model." *Social Science Quarterly* 85:441–462.

Associated Press. 2002. "Study Looks for Link between DDT and Breast Cancer." December 17.

Atlanta City Planning Commission. 1922. *The Atlanta Zone Plan: Report Outlining a Tentative Zone Plan for Atlanta.*

Atlas, M. 2002. "Few and Far Between? An Environmental Equity Analysis of the

Geographic Distribution of Hazardous Waste Generation." *Social Science Quarterly* 83:365–378.

Atlas, M. 2001. "Rush to Judgment: An Empirical Analysis of Environmental Equity in U.S. Environmental Protection Agency Enforcement Actions." *Law & Society Review* 35 (3): 633–682.

Austin, P. 1971. Memo to Robert W. Woodruff. Robert Woodruff Papers. Emory University Special Collections.

Avery, R.B., K.P. Brevoort, and G.B. Canner. 2007. "The 2006 HMDA Data." *Federal Reserve Bulletin* 93:73–109.

Avila, E., and M.H. Rose. 2009. "Race, Culture, Politics, and Urban Renewal: An Introduction." *Journal of Urban History* 35 (3): 335–347.

Aydin, R., and B.A. Smith. 2008. "Evidence of Dual Nature of Property Value Recovery Following Environmental Remediation." *Real Estate Economics* 34 (4): 777–812.

Babcock, F.M. 1932. *The Valuation of Real Estate*. McGraw-Hill.

Baden, B.M., and D.L. Coursey. 2002. "The Locality of Waste Sites within the City of Chicago: A Demographic, Social, and Economic Analysis." *Resource Energy Economics* 24:53–93.

Baden, B.M., and D.L. Coursey. 1997. *The Locality of Waste Sites within the City of Chicago: A Demographic, Social, and Economic Analysis*. School of Public Policy, University of Chicago.

Bailey, C., and C.E. Faupel. 1992a. "Environmentalism and Civil Rights in Sumter County, Alabama." In *Race and the Incidence of Environmental Hazards: A Time for Discourse*. B. Bryant and P. Mohai, eds. Westview. Pp. 140–152.

Bailey, C., and C.E. Faupel. 1992b. "Movers and Shakers and PCB Takers: Hazardous Waste and Community Power." *Sociological Spectrum* 13:89–115.

Bailey, C., C.E. Faupel, and J.H. Gundlach. 1993. "Environmental Politics in Alabama's Blackbelt." In *Confronting Environmental Racism: Voices from the Grassroots*. R.D. Bullard, ed. South End. Pp. 107–122.

Bailey, C., C.E. Faupel, and S.H. Holland. 1992. "Hazardous Wastes and Differing Perceptions of Risk in Sumter County, Alabama." *Society and Natural Resources* 6: 21–36.

Bailey, C., C.E. Faupel, S.H. Holland, and A. Warren. 1989. "Public Opinions and Attitudes Regarding Hazardous Waste in Alabama: Results from Three 1988 Surveys." Rural Sociology Series 14. Auburn University. September.

Baltimore v. Wells Fargo. 2011. Second Amended Complaint for Declaratory and Injunctive Relief and Damages. Document 153. Civil Case No. 1:08-cv-00062-JFM (D. Md. April 7). Available at http://www.relmanlaw.com/docs/BaltimoreWells FargoComplaint.pdf.

Banzhaf, H.S., and R.P. Walsh. 2008. "Do People Vote with Their Feet? An Empirical Test of Tiebout's Mechanism." *American Economic Review* 98 (3): 843–863.

Barron, M. 2004. "Adequately Re-housing Low Income Families: A Study of Class and Race in the Architecture of Public Housing, Marietta, Georgia, 1938–1941." *Perspectives in Vernacular Architecture* 11:54–70.

Bauman, J.F. 1977. "Safe and Sanitary without the Costly Frills: The Evolution of Public Housing in Philadelphia, 1929–1941." *Pennsylvania Magazine of History and Biography*, January. Pp. 114–128.

Bayor, R.H. 2001. "Racism as Public Policy in America's Cities in the Twentieth Century." In *Crossing Boundaries: The Exclusion and Inclusion of Minorities in Germany and America*. L.E. Jones, ed. Berghahn Books. Pp. 70–84.

Bazelon, E. 2003. "Bad Neighbors." *Legal Affairs*, May–June. Available at http://legal affairs.org/issues/May-June-2003/story_bazelon_mayjun03.msp.

Bean v. Southwestern Waste Management Corp. 1979. 482 F. Supp. 673 (S.D. Texas).

Been, V. 1995. "Analyzing Evidence of Environmental Injustice." *Journal of Land Use and Environmental Law* 11 (1): 1–28.

Been, V. 1994a. "Compensated Siting Proposals: Is it Time to Pay Attention?" *Fordham Urban Law Journal* 21 (3): 787–826.

Been, V. 1994b. "Locally Undesirable Land Uses in Minority Neighborhoods: Disproportionate Siting or Market Dynamics?" *Yale Law Journal* 103 (6): 1383–1422.

Been, V. 1993a. "Conceptions of Fairness in Proposals for Facility Siting." *Maryland Journal of Contemporary Legal Issues* 5 (1): 13–24.

Been, V. 1993b. "Siting of Locally Undesirable Land Uses: Directions for Further Research." *Maryland Journal of Contemporary Legal Issues* 5 (1): 105–113.

Been, V. 1993c. "What's Fairness Got to Do with It? Environmental Justice and the Siting of Locally Undesirable Land Uses." *Cornell Law Review* 78 (6): 1001–1085.

Been, V., and F. Gupta. 1997. "Coming to the Nuisance or Going to the Barrios? A Longitudinal Analysis of Environmental Justice Claims." *Ecology Law Quarterly* 24 (1): 1–56.

Belliveau, M., M. Kent, and G. Rosenblum. 1989. *Richmond at Risk: Community Demographics and Toxic Hazards from Industrial Polluters*. Citizens for a Better Environment.

Bello, W. 1994. *Dark Victory: The United States, Structural Adjustment and Global Poverty*. Pluto.

Benjamin or Ben Harmon v. Joseph W. Tyler. 1927. 273 U.S. 668; 47 S. Ct. 471; 71 L. Ed. 831 (March 14).

Benson, P.A., and N.L. North. 1922. *Real Estate Principles and Practices*. Prentice Hall.

Berliner, D. 2003. *Public Power, Private Gain*. Institute for Justice.

Berman v. Parker. 1954. 348 U.S. 26 (No. 476-53).

Bernstein, D.E. 1998. "Philip Sober Controlling Philip Drunk: *Buchanan v. Warley* in Historical Perspective." *Vanderbilt Law Review* 51:797–879.

Bernstein, D.E., and I. Somin. 2004. "Judicial Power and Civil Rights Reconsidered. *Yale Law Journal* 114 (3): 591–657.

Berry, B.J.L., L.S. Caris, D. Gaskill, C.P. Kaplan, J. Piccinini, N. Planert, J.H.J. Rendall III, and A. de Ste. Phalle. 1977. *The Social Burdens of Environmental Pollution: A Comparative Metropolitan Data Source*. Ballinger.

Berry, B.J.L., and J.D. Kasarda. 1977. *Contemporary Urban Ecology*. Macmillan.

Betancur, J. 2011. "Gentrification and Community Fabric in Chicago." *Urban Studies* 48 (2): 383–406.

Bickford, A., and D. Massey. 1991. "Segregation in the Second Ghetto: Racial and Ethnic Segregation in American Public Housing." *Social Forces* 69 (4, June): 1011–1036.

Birmingham News. 2006. "Difficult Lessons: Desegregating the Schools, 1962–1963." February 26.

Blair, J.P., and R. Premus. 1987. "Major Factors in Industrial Location: A Review." *Economic Development Quarterly* 1 (1): 72–85.

Blais, L.E. 2007. "Urban Revitalization in the Post-*Kelo* Era." *Fordham Urban Law Journal* 34 (May 31): 657–687.

Blauner, R. 1969. "Internal Colonialism and Ghetto Revolt." *Social Problems* 16 (Spring): 393–408.

Blumberg, L. 1964. "Segregated Housing, Marginal Location, and the Crisis of Confidence." *Phylon Quarterly* 25 (4): 321–330.

Blumberg, L., and R. Gottlieb. 1989. *War on Waste: Can America Win Its Battle with Garbage?* Island.

Bobo, L.D. 1997. "The Color Line, the Dilemma, and the Dream." In *Civil Rights and Social Wrongs.* J. Higham, ed. Pennsylvania State University Press. Pp. 31–58.

Bobo, L.D., and C. Zubrinsky. 1996. "Attitudes on Residential Integration: Perceived Status Differences, Mere In-Group Preference, or Racial Prejudice?" *Social Forces* 74:883–909.

Bocian, D.G., K.S. Ernst, and W. Li. 2008. "Race, Ethnicity and Subprime Home Loan Pricing." *Journal of Economics and Business* 60:110–124.

Bocian, D.G., and R. Zhai. 2005. *Borrowers in Higher Minority Areas More Likely to Receive Prepayment Penalties on Subprime Loans.* Center for Responsible Lending. Available at http://www.responsiblelending.org/mortgage-lending/research -analysis/rr004-PPP_Minority_Neighborhoods-0105.pdf.

Boer, J.T., M. Pastor Jr., J.L. Sadd, and L.D. Snyder. 1997. "Is There Environmental Racism? The Demographics of Hazardous Waste in Los Angeles County." *Social Science Quarterly* 78 (4): 793–810.

Boerner, C., and T. Lambert. 1995. "Environmental Justice Can Be Achieved through Negotiated Compensation." In *Environmental Justice.* J. Petrikin, ed. Greenhaven. Pp. 85–99.

Boffey, P.M. 1968. "Nerve Gas: Dugway Accident Linked to Utah Sheep Kill." *Science* 162 (3861, December 27): 1460–1464.

Bolin, B., A. Nelson, E.J. Hackett, K.D. Pijawka, C.S. Smith, D. Sicotte, E.K. Sadalla, E. Matran, and M. O'Donnell. 2002. "The Ecology of Technological Risk in a Sunbelt City." *Environment and Planning A* 34:317–339.

Bonacich, E.A. 1994. "Theory of Ethnic Antagonism: The Split Labor Market." In *Social Stratification: Class, Race, and Gender in Sociological Perspective.* D. Grusky, ed. Westview. Pp. 474–486.

Bonastia, C. 2000. "Why Did Affirmative Action in Housing Fail during the Nixon

Era? Exploring the 'Institutional Homes' of Social Policies." *Social Problems* 47 (4): 523–542.

Bono, M. 2007. "Don't You Be My Neighbor: Restrictive Housing Ordinances as the New Jim Crow." *Modern American* 3 (2): 29–38.

Boone, C.G. 2005. "Zoning and Environmental Inequality in the Industrial East Side." In *Land of Sunshine: An Environmental History of Metropolitan Los Angeles*. W. Deverell and G. Hise, eds. University of Pittsburgh Press. Pp. 167–178.

Boone, C.G., and A. Modarres. 1999. "Creating a Toxic Neighborhood in Los Angeles County: A Historical Examination of Environmental Inequity." *Urban Affairs Review* 35 (2): 163–187.

Borski, R.A. 1999. "In Recognition of the Dedication of the Carl Mackley Apartment Complex—Hon. Robert A. Borski." *Congressional Record*, 106th Congress (1999–2000). July 1. E1481–E1482.

Bostic, R.W., and R.W. Martin. 2003. "Black Home-Owners as a Gentrifying Force? Neighbourhood Dynamics in the Context of Minority Home-Ownership. *Urban Studies* 40 (12): 2427–2449.

Boston, J., L.C. Rigsby, and M.N. Zald. 1972. "The Impact of Race on Housing Markets: A Critical Review." *Social Problems* 19 (3): 382–393.

Bouvier, R.A., J.M. Halstead, K.S. Conway, and A.B. Malano. 2000. "The Effect of Landfills on Rural Residential Property Values: Some Empirical Analysis." *Journal of Regional Analysis and Policy* 30:23–37.

Bowen, W.M. 2002. "An Analytic Review of Environmental Justice Research: What Do We Really Know?" *Environmental Management* 29:3–15.

Bowen, W.M., M.J. Salling, K.E. Haynes, and E.J. Cyran. 1995. "Toward Environmental Justice: Spatial Equity in Ohio and Cleveland." *Annals of the Association of American Geographers* 85:641–663.

Boyd (Dorothy) et al. v. Browner (Carol M.). 1996. 107 F.3d 922; 323 U.S. App. D.C. 289.

Boyd (Dorothy) et al. v. Browner (Carol M.). 1995. 897 F. Supp. 590 (D.D.C.).

Boyle, M.A., and K.A. Kiel. 2001. "A Survey of House Price Hedonic Studies of the Impact of Environmental Externalities." *Journal of Real Estate Literature* 9:117–144.

Braden, A. [1958] 1999. *The Wall Between*. New update prepared by Julian Bond. University of Tennessee Press.

Bradford, C. 2002. *Risk or Race? Racial Disparities and the Subprime Refinance Market*. Center for Community Change. Available at http://www.knowledgeplex.org/kp/report/report/relfiles/ccc_0729_risk.pdf.

Brady, C.M. 1996. "Indianapolis at the Time of the Great Migration, 1900–1920." *Black History News and Notes* 65 (August): 12–36. Available at http://www.carolynbrady.com/indymigration.html.

Brady, D., and M. Wallace. 2001. "Deindustrialization and Poverty: Manufacturing Decline and AFDC Recipiency in Lake County, Indiana 1964–93." *Sociological Forum* 16 (2): 321–358.

Bristol, T. 1992. "First Environment." *Turtle Quarterly*, Fall. P. 29.

Brittain, M.L. 1948. *The Story of Georgia Tech*. University of North Carolina Press.

Britton v. Town of Chester. 1991. 595 A.2d 492 (N.H.).

Brook, D. 1998. "Environmental Genocide: Native Americans and Toxic Waste." *American Journal of Economics and Sociology* 57:105–113.

Brooks, R., and R. Simon. 2007. "Subprime Debacle Traps Even Very Credit-Worthy: As Housing Boomed, Industry Pushed Loans to a Broader Market." *Wall Street Journal*, December 3. Available at http://online.wsj.com/article/SB119662974358 911035.html.

Brooks, R.R.W. 2002. "Covenants and Conventions." Working paper. Northwestern University Law School. April.

Brown, C. 2000. "The Role of Employers in Split Labor Markets: An Event-Structure Analysis of Racial Conflict and AFL Organizing, 1917–1919." *Social Forces* 79 (2): 653–681.

Brown, C. 1998. "Racial Conflict and Split Labor Markets: The AFL Campaign to Organize Steelworkers, 1918–1919." *Social Science History* 23 (3): 319–347.

Brown, K. 1991. "Environmental Discrimination: Myth or Reality?" Unpublished paper. Washington University School of Law. March 29.

Brown, P., D. Ciambrone, and L. Hunter. 1997. "Does 'Green' Mask Grey? Environmental Equity Issues at the Metropolitan Level." *International Journal of Contemporary Sociology* 34:141–158.

Brugge, D. 2002. "The History of Uranium Mining and the Navajo People." *American Journal of Public Health* 92 (9): 1410–1419.

Brugge, D., T. Benally, and E. Yazzie-Lewis. 2006. *The Navajo People and Uranium Mining.* University of New Mexico Press.

Bry, C. 2011. *Ladue Found: Celebrating 100 Years of the City's Rural to Regal Past.* Virginia Publishing.

Bryant, M. 1993. "Unequal Justice? Lies, Damn Lies, and Statistics Revisited." *SONREEL News* 25 (September–October): 3–4.

Buchanan v. Warley. 1917. 245 U.S. 60; 38 S. Ct. 16; 62 L. Ed. 149 (November 5).

Bullard, R.D. 2005. "Foreword." In *Diamond: A Struggle for Environmental Justice in Louisiana's Chemical Corridor.* S. Lerner, author. MIT Press. Pp. xi–xii.

Bullard, R.D. 1994. *Unequal Protection: Environmental Justice and Communities of Color.* Sierra Club Books.

Bullard, R.D. 1993a. "Anatomy of Environmental Racism." In *Toxic Struggles: The Theory and Practice of Environmental Justice.* R. Hofrichter, ed. New Society. Pp. 25–35.

Bullard, R.D. 1993b. "Anatomy of Environmental Racism and the Environmental Justice Movement." In *Confronting Environmental Racism: Voices from the Grassroots.* R.D. Bullard, ed. South End. Pp. 15–40.

Bullard, R.D. 1990. *Dumping in Dixie: Race, Class, and Environmental Quality.* Westview.

Bullard, R.D. 1983. "Solid Waste Sites and the Black Houston Community." *Sociological Inquiry* 53 (2–3): 273–288.

Bullard, R.D., and G.S. Johnson. 2000. "Environmental Justice: Grassroots Activism and Its Impact on Public Policy Decision Making." *Journal of Social Issues* 56 (3): 555–578.

Bullard, R.D., P. Mohai, R. Saha, and B. Wright. 2008. "Toxic Wastes at Twenty: Why Race Still Matters after All of These Years." *Environmental Law* 38:371–411.

Bullard, R.D., P. Mohai, R. Saha, and B. Wright. 2007. *Toxic Wastes and Race at Twenty 1987–2007: Grassroots Struggles to Dismantle Environmental Racism in the United States*. United Church of Christ.

Bullard, R.D., and B.H. Wright. 2012. *The Wrong Complexion for Protection: How the Government Response to Disaster Endangers African American Communities*. NYU Press.

Bullard, R.D., and B.H. Wright, eds. 2009. *Race, Place, and Environmental Justice after Hurricane Katrina: Struggles to Reclaim, Rebuild, and Revitalize New Orleans and the Gulf Coast*. Westview.

Bullard, R.D., and B.H. Wright. 1987a. "Blacks and the Environment." *Humboldt Journal of Social Relations* 14:165–184.

Bullard, R.D., and B.H. Wright. 1987b. "Environmentalism and the Politics of Equity: Emergent Trends in the Black Community." *Mid-American Review of Sociology* 12 (2): 21–38.

Bullard, R.D., and B.H. Wright. 1986. "The Politics of Pollution: Implications for the Black Community." *Phylon* 47 (1): 71–78.

Bureau of Indian Affairs (BIA). 2012. "BIA." U.S. Department of the Interior. Available at http://www.bia.gov/WhoWeAre/BIA/index.htm.

Bureau of Indian Affairs (BIA). 2010a. "Indian Entities Recognized and Eligible to Receive Services from the United States Bureau of Indian Affairs." U.S. Department of the Interior. *Federal Register* 75 (190): 60810.

Bureau of Indian Affairs (BIA). 2010b. "Indian Entities Recognized and Eligible to Receive Services from the United States Bureau of Indian Affairs." U.S. Department of the Interior. *Federal Register* 75 (207): 66124.

Burk, W. 1937. "Juvenile Delinquency and Poor Housing in the Los Angeles Metropolitan Area." Works Progress Administration.

Burke (Olive Ida) v. Isaac Kleiman et al. 1934a. 355 Ill. 390; 189 N.E. 372.

Burke (Olive Ida) v. Isaac Kleiman et al. 1934b. 277 Ill. App. 519 (November 27).

Burlein, M. 2001. *Negrophobia: A Race Riot in Atlanta, 1906*. Encounter Books.

Burlingame Treaty. 1868. 16 Stat. 739 (1848–1871). July 28.

Business Wire. 2012. "Alcoa Confirms EPA Announcement of Remedial Action Plan for Grasse River." October 1.

Buss, L.D. 2008. "The Church and the City: Detroit's Open Housing Movement." Ph.D. dissertation, University of Michigan.

Byrne, J.P. 2011. "Eminent Domain and Racial Discrimination: A Bogus Equation." *Georgetown Law: The Scholarly Commons.* Available at http://scholarship.law.georgetown.edu/facpub/936.

Byrne, J.P. 2003. "Two Cheers for Gentrification." *Howard Law Journal* 46 (3): 405–432.

Cable, S., T.E. Shriver, and T.L. Mix. 2008. "Risk Society and Contested Illness:

The Case of Nuclear Weapons Workers." *American Sociological Review* 73 (3): 380–401.

Cameron, E.H. 1960. *Samuel Slater: Father of American Manufactures.* B. Wheelright.

Cameron, T.A., and I.T. McConnaha. 2006. "Evidence of Environmental Migration." *Land Economics* 82 (2): 273–290.

Campbell, H.E., L.R. Peck, and M.K. Tschudi. 2010. "Justice for All? A Cross-Time Analysis of Toxics Release Inventory Facility Location." *Review of Policy Research* 27 (1, January): 1–25.

Canal Authority of the State of Florida v. Callaway. 1974. 489 F.2d 567 (5th Cir.).

Capeci, D.J., Jr. 1984. *Race Relations in Wartime Detroit.* Temple University Press.

Carey et al. v. City of Atlanta et al. 1915. 143 Ga. 192; 84 S.E. 456 (February 12).

Carle, S.D. 2002. "Race, Class, and Legal Ethics in the Early NAACP (1910–1920)." *Law and History Review* 20 (1): 97–146.

Caro, R.A. 1974. *The Power Broker: Robert Moses and the Fall of New York.* Vintage Books.

Carpenter, D.M., and J.K. Ross. 2010a. "Do Restrictions on Eminent Domain Harm Economic Development?" *Economic Development Quarterly* 24 (4): 337–351.

Carpenter, D.M., and J.K. Ross. 2010b. "Empire State Eminent Domain: Robin Hood in Reverse." Institute for Justice.

Carpenter, D.M., and J.K. Ross. 2009. "Testing O'Connor and Thomas: Does the Use of Eminent Domain Target Poor and Minority Communities?" *Urban Studies* 46 (11, October): 2447–2461.

Carson, R. 1962. *Silent Spring.* Houghton Mifflin.

CBS News. 2010. "'Caucasians Only' Land Advertised in Mass. Town." June 2. Available at http://www.cbsnews.com/2100-201_162-6540876.html.

Center for the American West. 1997. *Atlas of the New West: Portrait of a Changing Region.* Norton.

Centers for Disease Control. 2002. "Cancer Prevention and Control. Cancer Burden Data Fact Sheets, Louisiana."

CERCLA. 1980. *Comprehensive Environmental Response Compensation Liability Act of 1980.* 42 U.S.C. §§ 9601–9657.

Cerrell Associates and J.S. Powell. 1984. *Political Difficulties Facing Waste-to-Energy Conversion Plant Siting.* California Waste Management Board.

Chai, S., and B.H. Kleiner. 2003. "Housing Discrimination Based on Race." *Equal Opportunities International* 22 (3): 16–47.

Chakraborty, J., and M.P. Armstrong. 1997. "Assessing the Impact of Segregation on Environmental Equity Using GIS." CD-ROM. American Congress on Surveying and Mapping.

Chakraborty, J., D.J. Fokenbrock, and L.A. Schweitzer. 1999. "Using GIS to Assess the Environmental Justice Consequences of Transportation System Changes." *Transactions in GIS* 3 (3): 239–258.

Chamber of Commerce of the United States v. Whiting. 2011. 131 S. Ct. 1968 (May 26).

Chambers, J. 1998. "The Supreme Court Has Agreed to Take Up an Issue That Has

Stymied Regulators and Judges: Waste Disposal Facilities Planned for Construction in Minority Areas." *National Law Journal* June 22. B6.

Charest v. Olin. 1981. No. CV 81 434P (Ala. Cir. Ct. October 5).

Chattopadhyay, S., J.B. Braden, and A. Patunru. 2005. "Benefits of Hazardous Waste Cleanup: New Evidence from Survey- and Market-Based Property Value Approaches." *Contemporary Economic Policy* 23 (3): 357–375.

Checker, M. 2005. *Polluted Promises: Environmental Racism and the Search for Justice in a Southern Town.* NYU Press.

Chemical Waste Management. 2005. "Corrective Measures Implementation Plan." Jordan, Jones & Goulding.

Chemical Waste Management v. Broadwater. 1985. 758 F.2d 1538 (U.S. App. April 29).

Chemical Waste Management v. Hunt. 1992. 504 U.S. 334; 112 S. Ct. 2009 (June 1).

Chemical Waste Management v. State of Alabama. 1987. 512 So. 2d 115 (Ala. Civ. App. March 25).

Chicago Bee. 1944. "The CORE Conference." April 9.

Chicago Bee. 1943. "U.S. to Convert Parkway Center into War Homes." August 1.

Chicago Commission on Race Relations. 1922. *The Negro in Chicago: A Study of Race Relations and a Race Riot.* University of Chicago Press.

Chicago Daily News. 1953. "How Some Blocks Keep Blight Away." July 13.

Chicago Defender. 1949. "Housing Project Hands Fire: Charges 'Clearance' of Negroes Is Aim." May 7. P. 4.

Chicago Defender. 1921. "Defender to Give Prizes for Best Kept Lawns." June 4.

Chicago Defender. 1920. "Neighborhood Improvement." January 17.

Choi, S.J., J. Ondrich, and J. Yinger. 2005. "Do Rental Agents Discriminate against Minority Customers? Evidence from the 2000 Housing Discrimination Study." *Journal of Housing Economics* 14 (1): 1–26.

Choldin, H.M. 2005. "Chicago Housing Authority." In *The Encyclopedia of Chicago.* Chicago Historical Society.

Churchill, W. 1993. "Radioactive Colonialism: A Hidden Holocaust in Native North America." In *Struggle for the Land: Indigenous Resistance to Genocide, Ecocide, and Expropriation in Contemporary North America.* Common Courage. Pp. 239–291.

Churchill, W., and W. LaDuke. 1992. "Native North America: The Political Economy of Radioactive Colonialism." In *The State of Native America: Genocide, Colonialism, and Resistance.* M.A. Jaimes, ed. South End. Pp. 241–266.

City of Birmingham v Monk. 1950. 185 F. 2d 859; 341 U.S. 940.

City of Cleburne, Tex., v. Cleburne Living Center. 1985. 473 U.S. 432; 105 S. Ct. 3249; 87 L. Ed. 2d 313.

City of Dallas et al. v. Liberty Annex Corporation. 1929. 19 S.W.2d 845 (Tex. App.)

City of Dallas et al. v. Liberty Annex Corporation. 1927. 295 S.W. 591 (Tex. Com. App.).

City of Hazleton v. Lozano. 2011. 131 S. Ct. 2958. June 6.

City of Memphis v. Wells Fargo. 2011. First Amended Complaint for Declaratory and Injunctive Relief and Damages. No. 2:09-cv-02857x-STA-dkv (W.D. Tenn. April 7).

City of Richmond et al. v. Deans. 1930a. 37 F.2d 712 (U.S. App. January 14).

City of Richmond et al. v. Deans. 1930b. 281 U.S. 704; 50 S. Ct. 407; 74 L. Ed. 1128 (May 19).

City of St. Louis. 1996. "African American History." Available at http://stlouis.missouri .org/government/heritage/history/afriamer.htm.

Civil Rights Act of 1964. 1964. Pub. L. No. 88-352 §§ 78 Stat. 24P, 252–253, 42 U.S.C. § 2000d.

Clark, C.S. 1994. "Housing Discrimination." *CQ Researcher* 5 (February 24): 169–192.

Clark, W.A.V. 1992. "Residential Preferences and Residential Choices in a Multiethnic Context." *Demography* 29:451–466.

Clarke, J.N., and A.K. Gerlak. 1998. "Environmental Racism in Southern Arizona? The Reality beneath the Rhetoric." In *Environmental Injustices, Political Struggles: Race, Class, and the Environment*. D.E. Comacho, ed. Duke University Press. Pp. 82–100.

Clarke, T. 2002. "An Ideographic Analysis of Native American Sovereignty in the State of Utah: Enabling Denotative Dissonance and Constructing Irreconcilable Conflict." *Wicazo Sa Review* 17 (2): 43–63.

Clinard v. City of Winston-Salem. 1940. 217 N.C. 119; 6 S.E.2d 867; 126 A.L.R. 634.

Clingermayer, J.C. 2004. "Heresthetics and Happenstance: Intentional and Unintentional Exclusionary Impacts of the Zoning Decision-Making Process." *Urban Studies* 41 (2): 377–388.

Clingermayer, J.C. 1996. "Quasi-Judicial Decision Making and Exclusionary Zoning." *Urban Affairs Review* 31 (4): 544–553.

Cobb County Times. 1941. "Clay Homes Far Cry from Hollandtown's Disease Ridden Shacks." October 16.

Cole, L.W. 1994. "Environmental Justice Litigation: Another Stone in David's Sling." *Fordham Urban Law Journal* 21:523, 525–530.

Cole, L.W. 1992. "Empowerment as the Key to Environmental Protection: The Need for Environmental Poverty Law." *Ecology Law Quarterly* 19:619–683.

Cole, L.W., and C. Farrell. 2006. "Structural Racism, Structural Pollution and the Need for a New Paradigm." *Washington University Journal of Law and Policy* 20:265–282.

Cole, L.W., and S.H. Foster. 2001. *From the Ground Up: Environmental Racism and the Rise of the Environmental Justice Movement*. NYU Press.

Coleman, J. 1988. "Social Capital in the Creation of Human Capital." *American Journal of Sociology* 94:95–120.

Collin, R.W. 1992. "Environmental Equity: A Law and Planning Approach to Environmental Racism." *Virginia Environmental Law Journal* 11:495.

Collin, R.W., and W. Harris, Sr. 1993. "Race and Waste in Two Virginia Communities." In *Confronting Environmental Racism: Voices from the Grassroots*. R.D. Bullard, ed. South End. Pp. 93–106.

Collins, W.J. 1997. "When the Tide Turned: Immigration and the Delay of the Great Black Migration." *Journal of Economic History* 57 (3): 607–632.

Colten, C.E. 2002. "Basin Street Blues: Drainage and Environmental Equity in New Orleans, 1890–1930." *Journal of Historical Geography* 28 (2): 237–238, 242.

Colten, C.E. 1990. "Historical Hazards: The Geography of Relict Industrial Wastes." *Professional Geographer* 42:143–156.

Comacho, D.E., ed. 1998. *Environmental Injustices, Political Struggles: Race, Class, and the Environment*. Duke University Press.

Comstock, A.P. 1912. "Chicago Housing Conditions: VI. Problems of the Negro." *American Journal of Sociology* 18 (September): 241–257.

Connerly, C.E. 2005. *The Most Segregated City in America: City Planning and Civil Rights in Birmingham, 1920–1980*. University of Virginia Press.

Conoco EDC Litigation. 2002. United States District Court for the Western District of Louisiana, Lake Charles Division. 123 F.Supp.2d 340. November 16.

Conot, R. 1973. *American Odyssey*. Bantam Books.

Cooley, W. 2010. "Moving on Out: Black Pioneering in Chicago, 1915–1950." *Journal of Urban History* 36 (4): 485–506.

Cooley, W. 2008. "Moving Up, Moving Out: Race and Social Mobility in Chicago, 1914–1972." Ph.D. dissertation, University of Illinois.

CorpWatch. 2002. "Concerned Citizens of Norco Reach Agreement with Shell Chemical." June 20. Available at http://www.corpwatch.org/article.php?id=2769.

Corrigan et al. v. Buckley. 1926. 271 U.S. 323; 46 S. Ct. 521; 70 L. Ed. 969 (May 24).

Corrigan et al. v. Buckley. 1924. 55 App. D.C. 30; 299 F. 899 (April 21).

Cory, D.C. 2008. "On Notions of Fairness in Environmental Justice." From *The Selected Works of Dennis C. Cory*. March. Available at http://works.bepress.com/dennis_cory/1.

Costanzo, J. 1999. "No N-Waste: Goshutes Say 25 Join Suit to Have Lease Declared Void." *Deseret News*, March 11.

Costner, P., and J. Thornton. 1991. *Playing with Fire: Hazardous Waste Incineration*. Greenpeace.

Council of the City of Richmond. 1929. *An Ordinance*. February 15.

Coyle, M. 1997a. "EPA Move Makes Tulane the Victor." *National Law Journal*, September 22. P. A13.

Coyle, M. 1997b. "Governor v. Students in $700M Plant Case." *National Law Journal*, September 8. P. A1.

Coyle, M. 1992a. "Company Will Not Build Plant: Lawyers Hail Victory." *National Law Journal*, October 19. P. 3.

Coyle, M. 1992b. "Saying 'No' to Cancer Alley: Community Profile, Wallace, Louisiana." *National Law Journal*, September 21. P. S5.

Coyle, M. 1992c. "When Movements Coalesce: Empowerment, Civil Rights Meets Environmental Rights." *National Law Journal*, September 21. P. S10.

Crawford, C. 1996a. "Analyzing Evidence of Environmental Justice: A Suggestion for Professor Been." *Journal of Land Use and Environmental Law* 12 (1): 103–120.

Crawford, C. 1996b. *Uproar at Dancing Rabbit Creek: Battling over Race, Class, and the Environment*. Addison-Wesley.

Crowder, K. 2000. "The Racial Context of White Mobility: An Individual-Level Assessment of the White Flight Hypothesis." *Social Science Research* 29:223–257.

Crowe, C. 1969. "Racial Massacre in Atlanta, September 22, 1906." *Journal of Negro History* 54 (April): 154–160.

Cutler, D.M., E.L. Glaeser, and J.L. Vigdor. 1999. "The Rise and Decline of the American Ghetto." *Journal of Political Economy* 107:455–506.

Cutter, S.L. 2006. *Hazards Vulnerability and Environmental Justice*. Routledge.

Cutter, S.L., B.J. Boruff, and W. L. Shirley. 2003. "Social Vulnerability to Environmental Hazards." *Social Science Quarterly* 84 (2): 242–261.

Cutter, S.L., D. Holm, and L. Clark. 1996. "The Role of Geographic Scale in Monitoring Environmental Justice." *Risk Analysis* 16 (4): 517–526.

Cypher, M.L., and F.A. Forgey. 2003. "Eminent Domain: An Evaluation Based on Criteria Relating to Equity, Effectiveness, and Efficiency." *Urban Affairs Review* 39: 254–268.

Daines, M. 1940. "Be It Ever So Tumbled—The Story of a Suburban Slum." Detroit Public Library. Detroit Citizens Housing and Planning Council Papers. Box 48. Pp. 6–16.

Dale, L., J.C. Murdoch, M.A. Thayer, and P. Waddell. 1999. "Do Property Values Rebound from Environmental Stigmas? Evidence from Dallas County, Texas." *Land Economics* 75:311–326.

Daley, D.M., and D.F. Layton. 2004. "Policy Implementation and the Environmental Protection Agency: What Factors Influence Remediation at Superfund Sites?" *Policy Studies Journal* 32 (3): 375–392.

Darden, J.T. 1972. "The Spatial Dynamics of Residential Segregation of Afro-Americans in Pittsburgh." Ph.D. dissertation, University of Pittsburgh.

Darden, J.T., R.C. Hill, J. Thomas, and R. Thomas. 1987. *Detroit: Race and Uneven Development*. Temple University Press.

Davidson, P., and D.L. Anderton. 2000. "Demographics of Dumping II: A National Environmental Equity Survey and the Distribution of Hazardous Materials Handlers." *Demography* 37 (4): 461–466.

Davis, L.W. 2004. "The Effect of Health Risk on Housing Values: Evidence from a Cancer Cluster." *American Economic Review* 94 (5): 1693–1704.

Davis, M. 1998. "Utah's Toxic Heaven." *Capitalism, Nature, Socialism: A Journal of Socialist Ecology* 9:35–39.

Davy, B. 1997. *Essential Justice: When Legal Institutions Cannot Resolve Environmental and Land Use Disputes*. Springer-Verlag.

Dear, M. 1992. "Understanding and Overcoming the NIMBY Syndrome." *Journal of the American Planning Association* 58 (3): 288–300.

Deaton, B.J., and J.P. Hoehn. 2004. "Hedonic Analysis of Hazardous Waste Sites in the Presence of Other Urban Disamenities." *Environmental Science & Policy* 7: 499–508.

de Leeuw, M.B., M.K. Whyte, D. Ho, C. Meza, and A. Karteron. 2007. "Residential Segregation and Housing Discrimination in the United States." Poverty & Race Research Action Council. December.

Deloitte Consulting. 2011. *Evaluation of the EPA Office of Civil Rights*.

Denton, N.A., and D.S. Massey. 1991. "Patterns of Neighborhood Transition in a Multi-ethnic World: U.S. Metropolitan Areas, 1970–1980." *Demography* 28:41–63.

Derringer, N.N. 2011. "In a Changing Community, More African Americans Choose Grosse Pointe." *GrossePointeToday.com*, August 8. Available at http://grossepointe today.com/news/002159-changing-community-moreafrican-americans-choose -grosse-pointe.

Detroit Housing Commission. 1939. *Real Property Survey of Detroit, Michigan.* Volume 2. Report on Official Project No. 665-51-3-124. Bureau of Governmental Research.

Devereux, B., Jr. 2005. "Subsidized Housing." In *The Encyclopedia of Chicago.* Chicago Historical Society.

Devereux, B., Jr. 1978. *The Poorhouse: Subsidized Housing in Chicago, 1895–1976.* Southern Illinois University Press.

Dewitt, R. 1991. "Activists Fear New Landfill: Protest Stems from Visit of Choctaw Indians to Emelle." *Tuscaloosa News,* January 30. Pp. 1B–2B.

Dolinoy, D.C., and L. Miranda. 2004. "GIS Modeling of Air Toxics Releases from TRI-Reporting and Non-TRI-Reporting Facilities: Impacts for Environmental Justice." *Environmental Health Perspectives* 112 (17): 1717–1724.

Douglas, D.M. 1995. *Reading, Writing, and Race: The Desegregation of the Charlotte Schools.* University of North Carolina Press.

Douglas, D.M. 1994. "A Quest for Freedom in the Post-*Brown* South: Desegregation and White Self-Interest." *Chicago-Kent Law Review* 70:689–755.

Downey, L. 2007. "US Metropolitan-Area Variation in Environmental Inequality Outcomes." *Urban Studies* 44:953–977.

Downey, L. 2006. "Environmental Racial Inequality in Detroit." *Social Forces* 85 (2): 771–796.

Downey, L. 2005. "The Unintended Significance of Race: Environmental Racial Inequality in Detroit." *Social Forces* 83 (3): 971–1007.

Downey, L. 2003. "Spatial Measurement, Geography, and Urban Racial Inequality." *Social Forces* 81:937–954.

Downey, L., E. Bonds, and K. Clark. 2010. "Natural Resource Extraction, Armed Violence, and Environmental Degradation." *Organization and Environment* 23 (4): 417–445.

Downey, L., S. Dubois, B. Hawkins, and M. Walker. 2008. "Environmental Inequality in Metropolitan America." *Organization and Environment* 21 (3): 270–294.

Downey, L., and S. Strife. 2010. "Inequality, Democracy, and the Environment." *Organization and Environment* 23 (2): 155–188.

Doyle, D.H. 1985. *Nashville since the 1920s.* University of Tennessee Press.

Doyle, J. 2004. *Riding the Dragon: Royal Dutch/Shell and the Fossil Fire.* Common Courage.

Drake, S.C., and H.R. Cayton. [1945] 1993. *Black Metropolis: A Study of Negro Life in a Northern City.* University of Chicago Press.

Dreher, R.G., and J.D. Echeverria. 2006. *Kelo's Unanswered Questions: The Policy Debate over the Use of Eminent Domain for Economic Development.* Georgetown Environmental Law and Policy Institute.

Du Bois, W.E.B. 1972. "Baltimore." In *Darkness at the Dawning: Race and Reform in the Progressive South.* J.T. Kirby, ed. Lippincott. Pp. 23–24.

Ducre, K.A., and E. Moore. 2011. "Extending the Timeline of Environmental Justice Claims: Redlining Map Digitization Project." *Environmental Practice* 13 (4): 325–339.

Dulaney, W.L. 1962. "The Negro and the City." *Journal of Negro Education* 31 (2): 198–201.

Dunn, M. 1997. *Black Miami in the Twentieth Century.* University Press of Florida.

Dymi, A. 2007. "Housing Discrimination: Record of Complaints." *National Mortgage News* 31 (28): 1.

Earnhard, D. 2004. "The Effects of Community Characteristics on Polluter Compliance Levels." *Land Economics* 80 (3): 408–432.

Eason v. Buffaloe. 1930. 152 S.E. 496 (N.C.).

East Bibb Twiggs Neighborhood Association v. Macon-Bibb County Planning and Zoning Commission. 1989. 706 F. Supp. 880 (M.D. Ga.), aff'd, 896 F.2d 1264 (11th Cir.).

Eckerd, A. 2011. "Cleaning Up without Clearing Out? A Spatial Assessment of Environmental Gentrification." *Urban Affairs Review* 47:31–59.

Eheman, C., S.J. Henley, R. Ballard-Barbash, E.J. Jacobs, M.J. Schymura, A.M. Noone, L. Pan, R.N. Anderson, J.E. Fulton, B.A. Kohler, A. Jemal, E. Ward, M. Plescia, L.A.G. Ries, and B.K. Edwards. 2012. "Annual Report to the Nation on the Status of Cancer, 1975–2008, Featuring Cancers Associated with Excess Weight and Lack of Sufficient Physical Activity." *Cancer* 118 (9): 2338–2366.

Eichstaedt, P.H. 1994. *If You Poison Us: Uranium and Native Americans.* Red Crane Books.

Elizabeth Koehler and August Koehler v. Leonard N. Rowland et al. 1918. 275 Mo. 573; 205 S.W. 217 (July 30).

Ellen, I.G. 2000. *Sharing America's Neighborhoods.* Harvard University Press.

Elliott, J.R., and S. Frickel. 2013. "The Historical Nature of Cities: A Study of Urbanization and Hazardous Waste Accumulation." *American Sociological Review* 78 (4): 521–543.

Elliott, J.R., and S. Frickel. 2011. "Environmental Dimensions of Urban Change: Uncovering Relict Industrial Waste Sites and Subsequent Land Use Conversions in Portland and New Orleans." *Journal of Urban Affairs* 33 (1): 61–82.

Ely, R.T. 1885. "Pullman: A Social Study." *Harper's Magazine* 70 (February): 452–466.

Emerson, M.O., G. Yancey, and K.J. Chai. 2001. "Does Race Matter in Residential Segregation? Exploring the Preferences of White Americans." *American Sociological Review* 66:922–935.

Engrossed Senate Bill 6169. 2006. 59th Legislature, 2006 Regular Session. February 13.

Erickson, R.A., and M. Wasylenko. 1980. "Firm Location and Site Selection in Suburban Communities." *Journal of Urban Economics* 8:69–85.

Escobar, A. 1995. *Encountering Development: The Making and Unmaking of the Third World*. Princeton University Press.

Eskew, G.T. 1997. " 'Bombingham': Black Protest in Postwar Birmingham, Alabama." *Historian* 59 (2): 371–390.

Essoka, J.D. 2010. "The Gentrifying Effects of Brownfields Redevelopment." *Western Journal of Black Studies* 34 (3): 299–315.

Evers, M. 2005. "Why I Live in Mississippi." In *The Autobiography of Medgar Evers: A Hero's Life and Legacy Revealed through His Writings, Letters, and Speeches*. M. Evers-Williams and M. Marable, eds. Basic Civitas Books. Pp. 111–121.

Exchange Project. 2006. "Real People—Real Stories: Afton, NC (Warren County)." University of North Carolina, Department of Health Behavior and Health Education. September.

Executive Order 11063. 1962. 3 C.F.R. 261 (Supp. 1962), 42 U.S.C. § 1982 (1964).

Faber, D., and E. Krieg. 2000. "Unequal Exposure to Ecological Hazards: Environmental Injustice in the Commonwealth of Massachusetts." *Environmental Health Perspectives* 110:277–288.

Farley, R., S. Danziger, and H.J. Holzer. 2000. *Detroit Divided*. Russell Sage Foundation.

Farley, R., E. Fielding, and M. Krysan. 1997. "The Residential Preferences of Blacks and Whites: A Four Metropolis Analysis." *Housing Policy Debate* 8:763–800.

Farley, R., and W.H. Frey. 1996. "Latino, Asian, and Black Segregation in the U.S.: Are Multi-ethnic Metros Different?" *Demography* 33:35–50.

Farley, R., and W.H. Frey. 1994. "Changes in the Segregation of Whites from Blacks during the 1980s: Small Steps toward a More Integrated Society." *American Sociological Review* 59 (February): 23–45.

Farley, R., H. Schuman, S. Bianchi, D. Colasanto, and S. Hatchett. 1978. "Chocolate Cities, Vanilla Suburbs: Will the Trend toward Racially Separate Communities Continue?" *Social Science Research* 7:319–344.

Farley, R., C.G. Steeh, M. Krysan, K. Reeves, and T. Jackson. 1994. "Stereotypes and Segregation: Neighborhoods in the Detroit Area." *American Journal of Sociology* 100:750–778.

Farrell, C.R. 2008. "Bifurcation, Fragmentation or Integration? The Racial and Geographical Structure of U.S. Metropolitan Segregation, 1990–2000." *Urban Studies Journal* 45 (3): 467–499.

Farrell, C.R., and B.A. Lee. 2011. "Racial Diversity and Change in Metropolitan Neighborhoods." *Social Science Research* 40:1108–1123.

Farrell, J.L. 2002. "The FHA's Origins: How Its Valuation Method Fostered Racial Segregation and Suburban Sprawl." *Journal of Affordable Housing and Community Development Law* 11 (4): 374–389.

Feagin, J.R., and C.B. Feagin. 2003. *Racial and Ethnic Relations*. Prentice Hall.

Feagin, J.R., and C.B. Feagin. 1986. *Discrimination American Style: Insitutional Racism and Sexism*. 3rd ed. Krieger.

Feagin, J.R., and C.B. Feagin. 1978. *Discrimination American Style: Institutional Racism and Sexism*. 2nd ed. Kreiger.

Federal Housing Administration. 1959. *The FHA Story in Summary, 1934–1959*. Government Printing Office.

Federal Housing Administration. 1939. *Underwriting Manual*. Government Printing Office.

Federal Housing Administration. 1938. *Underwriting Manual*. Government Printing Office.

Federal Reporter. 1890. 43 (August 25): 359–362.

Ferris, D. 1993. "Communities of Color and Hazardous Waste Cleanup: Expanding Public Participation in the Federal Superfund Program." *Fordham Urban Law Journal* 21 (3): 671–687.

Fillilove, M. 2007. *Eminent Domain and African Americans: What Is the Price of the Commons?* Institute for Justice. February.

Fine, S. 1997. "Michigan Housing Discrimination, 1949–1968." *Michigan Historical Review* 23 (2): 81–114.

Fischel, W.A. 2004. "An Economic History of Zoning and a Cure for Its Exclusionary Effects." *Urban Studies* 41 (2): 317–340.

Fischel, W.A. 1998. "Why Judicial Reversal of Apartheid Made a Difference." *Vanderbilt Law Review* 51:975–991.

Fisher, E.M. 1923. *Principles of Real Estate Practice*. Macmillan.

Fisher, J.B., M. Kelly, and J. Romm. 2006. "Scales of Environmental Justice: Combining GIS and Spatial Analysis for Air Toxics in West Oakland, California." *Health and Place* 12:701–714.

Fisher, P. 2005. "Gautreaux Assisted Housing Program." In *The Encyclopedia of Chicago*. Chicago Historical Society.

Fligstein, N. 1981. *Going North: Migration of Blacks and Whites from the South, 1900–1950*. Academic Press.

Freeman, H.M. 1989. *Handbook of Hazardous Waste Treatment and Disposal*. McGraw-Hill.

Freeman, L. 2009. "Neighborhood Diversity, Metropolitan Segregation and Gentrification: What Are the Links in the U.S.?" *Urban Studies* 46 (10): 2079–2101.

Freeman, L. 2006. *There Goes the 'Hood: Views of Gentrification from the Ground Up*. Temple University Press.

Freeman, L. 2005. "Displacement or Succession? Residential Mobility in Gentrifying Neighborhoods." *Urban Affairs Review* 40 (4): 463–491.

Freeman, L., and F. Braconi. 2004. "Gentrification and Displacement in New York City." *Journal of the American Planning Association* 70 (1): 39–52.

Freeman, L., and F. Braconi. 2002a. "Gentrification and Displacement." *Urban Prospect* 8 (1): 1–4.

Freeman, L., and F. Braconi. 2002b. "Gentrification and Displacement: New York City in the 1990s." Unpublished manuscript.

Freeman v. Olin. 1980. No. CV80 M 5057NE (N.D. Ala. March 14).

Freund, D.M. 2007. *Colored Property: State Policy and White Racial Politics in Suburban America*. University of Chicago Press.

Freund, D.M. 2006. "Marketing the Free Market: State Intervention and the Politics of Prosperity in Metropolitan America." In *The New Suburban History*. K.M. Kruse and T.J. Sugrue, eds. University of Chicago Press. Pp. 11–16.

Frey, W.H. 1979. "Central City White Flight: Racial and Nonracial Causes." *American Sociological Review* 44:425–448.

Fricker, R.D., and N.W. Hengartner. 2001. "Environmental Equity and the Distribution of Toxic Release Inventory and Other Environmentally Undesirable Sites in Metropolitan New York City." *Environmental and Ecological Statistics* 8:33–52.

Galster, G.C. 1990. "White Flight from Racially Integrated Neighborhoods in the 1970s: The Cleveland Experience." *Urban Studies* 27:385–399.

Gamble, H.B., R.H. Downing, J.S. Shortle, and D.J. Epp. 1982. *Effects of Solid Waste Disposal Sites on Community Development and Residential Property Values*. Final report for the Bureau of Solid Waste Management. Department of Environmental Resources, Commonwealth of Pennsylvania.

Gamper-Rabindran, S., and C. Timmins. 2011. "Hazardous Waste Cleanup, Neighborhood Gentrification, and Environmental Justice: Evidence from Restricted Access Census Block Data." *American Economic Review* 101 (3): 620–624.

Gandolfo v. Hartman. 1892. 49 F. 181 (C.C.S.D. Cal. January 25).

Gautreaux et al. v. Chicago Housing Authority. 2007. 475 F.3d 845 (7th Cir. January 19).

Gautreaux et al. v. Chicago Housing Authority. 1999. 178 F.3d 951 (7th Cir. June 22).

Gautreaux et al. v. Chicago Housing Authority. 1974. 503 F.2d 930 (7th Cir. September 30).

Gautreaux et al. v. Chicago Housing Authority et al. 1969a. 296 F. Supp. 907 (N.D. Ill. February 10).

Gautreaux et al. v. Chicago Housing Authority. 1969b. 304 F. Supp. 736 (7th Cir. July 1).

Gautreaux et al. v. Pierce. 1982. 690 F.2d 616 (7th Cir. September 30).

Gautreaux et al. v. Romney. 1972. 457 F.2d 124 (7th Cir. April 26).

Gautreaux et al. v. Romney. 1971. 448 F.2d 731 (7th Cir. September 10).

Gayer, T. 2000. "Neighborhood Demographics and the Distribution of Hazardous Waste Risks: An Instrumental Variables Estimation." *Journal of Regulatory Economics* 17 (2): 131–155.

Gayer, T., J.T. Hamilton, and W.K. Viscusi. 2002. "The Market Value of Reducing Cancer Risk: Hedonic Housing Prices with Changing Information." *Southern Economic Journal* 69 (2): 266–289.

Gayer, T., J.T. Hamilton, and W.K. Viscusi. 2000. "Private Values of Risk Tradeoffs at Superfund Sites: Housing Market Evidence on Learning about Risk." *Review of Economics and Statistics* 82 (3): 439–451.

Gedicks, A. 2001. *Resource Rebels: Native Challenges to Mining and Oil Corporations*. South End.

Gedicks, A. 1998. "Corporate Strategies for Overcoming Local Resistance to New Mining Projects." *Race, Gender and Class* 6 (1): 109–123.

Gedicks, A. 1993. *The New Resource Wars: Native and Environmental Struggles against Multinational Corporations*. South End.

Gerrard, M.B., ed. 1999. *The Law of Environmental Justice: Theories, and Procedures to Address Disproportionate Risk*. American Bar Association.

Gibson, C., and K. Jung. 2005. *Historical Census Statistics on Population Totals by Race, 1790 to 1990, and by Hispanic Origin, 1970 to 1990, for Large Cities and Other Urban Places in the United States*. Population Division, Working Paper 76. Washington, DC: Department of Commerce. February.

Glaeser, E., and J. Vigdor. 2012. "The End of the Segregated Century: Racial Separation in America's Neighborhoods, 1890–2010." Civic Report 66. Manhattan Institute. January.

Glick, J. 2008. "Gentrification and the Racialized Geography of Home Equity." *Urban Affairs Review* 44 (2): 280–295.

Glickman, T.S., D. Golding, and R. Hersh. 1995. "GIS-Based Environmental Equity Analysis—A Case Study of TRI Facilities in the Pittsburgh Area." In *Computer Supported Risk Management*. G.E.G. Beroggi and W.A. Wallace, eds. Kluwer Academic. Pp. 95–114.

Glover v. City of Atlanta. 1918. 148 Ga. 285; 96 S.E. 562 (August 13).

Godshalk, D.F. 2005. *Veiled Visions: The 1906 Atlanta Race Riot and the Reshaping of American Race Relations*. University of North Carolina Press.

Goering, J.M. 1986. "Introduction to Section IV: Racial Desegregation and Federal Housing Policies." In *Housing Desegregation and Federal Policy*. J.M. Goering, ed. University of North Carolina Press. Pp. 197–198.

Goetz, E.G. 2000. "The Politics of Poverty Deconcentration and Housing Demolition." *Journal of Urban Affairs* 22 (2): 157–174.

Goetz, S.J., and D.J. Kemlage. 1996. "TSDF Location and Environmental Justice." *Review of Regional Studies* 26:285–299.

Goldman, B.A. 1993. *Not Just Prosperity: Achieving Sustainability with Environmental Justice*. National Wildlife Federation.

Goldman, B.A., and Fitton, L. 1994. *Toxic Waste and Race Revisited*. Center for Policy Alternatives.

Gomillion v. Lightfoot. 1960. 364 U.S. 339; 81 S. Ct. 125; 5 L. Ed. 2d 110 (November 14).

Goodman, M.D., and D.J. Monti. 1999. "Corporate Sponsored Redevelopment Campaigns and the Social Stability of Urban Neighborhoods: St. Louis Revisited." *Journal of Urban Affairs* 21 (1): 101–128.

Gotham, K.F. 2001. "City without Slums: Urban Renewal, Public Housing, and Downtown Revitalization in Kansas City, Missouri." *American Journal of Economics and Sociology* 60 (1): 285–316.

Gould, J. 1986. *The Quality of Life in American Neighborhoods: Levels of Affluence, Toxic Waste, and Cancer Mortality in Residential ZIP Code Areas*. Westview.

Grady v. Garland et al. 1937. 67 App. D.C. 73; 89 F.2d 817.

Graham, J.D., N.D. Beaulieu, D. Sussman, Y. Li, and M. Sadowitz. 1999. "Who Lives Near Coke Plants and Oil Refineries? An Exploration of the Environmental Inequity Hypothesis." *Risk Analysis* 19 (2, April): 171–186.

Graham, Mrs. G.H. 1921. "Editor's Mail." *Chicago Defender*, May 14.

Grant, D., M.N. Trautner, L. Downey, and L. Theibaud. 2010. "Bringing Polluters Back In: Environmental Inequality and the Organization of Chemical Pollution." *American Sociological Review* 75 (4): 479–504.

Great Northern Paper, Inc., et al. v. Penobscot Nation et al. 2001. No. Cum-00-573. 2001 ME 68 (Me. Sup. Jud. Ct. May 1).

Greenberg, M. 1993. "Proving Environmental Inequity in Siting Locally Unwanted Land Uses." *Risk: Issues in Health and Safety* 4 (Spring): 235–252.

Greenberg, M., and R.F. Anderson. 1984. *Hazardous Waste Sites: The Credibility Gap.* Rutgers University, Center for Urban Policy Research.

Greenberg, M., R.F. Anderson, and K. Rosenberger. 1984. "Social and Economic Effects of Hazardous Waste Management Sites." *Hazardous Waste* 1 (3): 387–396.

Greenberg, M., and J. Hughes. 1993. "Impact of Hazardous Waste Sites on Property Value and Land Use: Tax Assessors' Appraisal." *Appraisal Journal* 61 (1): 42–51.

Greenstone, M., and J. Gallagher. 2008. "Does Hazardous Waste Matter? Evidence from the Housing Market and the Superfund Program." *Quarterly Journal of Economics* 123 (3): 951–1003.

Greenstone, M., and J. Gallagher. 2005. "Does Hazardous Waste Matter? Evidence from the Housing Market and the Superfund Program." Working Paper 11790. National Bureau of Economic Research.

Greenwood, M.J., G.H. McClelland, and W.D. Schulze. 1997. "The Effects of Perceptions of Hazardous Waste on Migration: A Laboratory Experimental Approach." *Review of Regional Studies* 27:143–161.

Greer, E. 1979. *Big Steel: Black Politics and Corporate Power in Gary, Indiana.* Monthly Review Press.

Gregory et al. v. Chemical Waste Management. 1996. 38 F. Supp. 2d 598 (W.D. Tenn. December 11).

Grier, G.W. 1967. "The Negro Ghettos and Federal Housing Policy." *Law and Contemporary Problems* 32 (3): 550–560.

Grosse Pointe News. 1961. "Screening Dropped Last May: Defendants in Suit Offer Explanation." January 26. Pp. 1–2.

Grossman, J.R. 2005. "The Great Migration." In *The Encyclopedia of Chicago.* Chicago Historical Society.

Grossman, J.R. 1989. *Land of Hope: Chicago, Black Southerners, and the Great Migration.* University of Chicago Press.

Groves, H.E. 1950–1951. "Judicial Interpretation of the Holdings of the United States Supreme Court in the Restrictive Covenant Cases." *Illinois Law Review* 45:614.

Gunter, B., and M. Williams. 1984. "Emelle, Alabama Toxic Waste Cadillac." *Southern Changes* 6 (4): 1–7.

Gupta, S., G. van Houtven, and M. Cropper. 1996. "Paying for Permanence: An Economic Analysis of EPA's Cleanup Decisions at Superfund Sites." *Rand Journal of Economics* 27 (3): 563–582.

Hafertepe, J. 2001. "Affidavit." State of Texas, County of Dallas. February 5.

Haggerty, M. 1980. "Crisis at Indian Creek." *Atlanta Journal and Constitution Magazine*, January 20. Pp. 14–25.

Half-Century Magazine. 1924. "Here and There." September–October.

Hamilton, J.T. 1995. "Pollution as News: Media and Stock Market Reactions to the Toxics Release Inventory Data." *Journal of Environmental Economics and Management* 28:98–113.

Hamilton, J.T. 1993. "Politics and Social Costs: Estimating the Impact of Collective Action on Hazardous Waste Facilities." *Rand Journal of Economics* 24 (1): 101–125.

Hanchett, T.W. 2000. "Financing Suburbia: Prudential Insurance and the Post–World War II Transformation of the American City." *Journal of Urban History* 26 (3, March): 312–328.

Hanchett, T.W. 1993. "Sorting Out the New South City: Charlotte and Its Neighborhoods." Ph.D. dissertation, University of North Carolina.

Hannink, D.M. 1997. *Principles and Applications of Economic Geography*. Wiley.

Hansberry, L. 1969. *To Be Young, Gifted, and Black*. Prentice Hall.

Hansberry et al. v. Lee et al. 1940. 311 U.S. 32; 61 S. Ct. 115; 85 L. Ed. 22 (November 12).

Harden v. City of Atlanta. 1917. 147 Ga. 248; 93 S.E. 401 (August 31).

Hare, N. 1970. "Black Ecology." *Black Scholar* 1 (April): 2–8.

Harmon, D. 1996. *Beneath the Image of the Civil Rights Movement and Race Relations, Atlanta, Georgia, 1946–1981*. Garland.

Harris, D.R. 1999. "'Property Values Drop When Blacks Move In, Because . . .': Racial and Socioeconomic Determinants of Neighborhood Desirability." *American Sociological Review* 64 (June): 461–479.

Harris, D.R. 1997. "Race, Class, and Social Problems: Determinants of White Residential Mobility." Ph.D. dissertation, Northwestern University.

Harvard Law Review. 1918. "Race Segregation Ordinance Invalid." 31 (3, January): 475–479.

Havlicek, J., Jr., R. Richardson, and L. Davies. 1971. *Measuring the Impacts of Solid Waste Disposal Site Location on Property Values*. Urban Economics Report 65. University of Chicago.

Hawkins, W.A. 1911. "A Year of Segregation in Baltimore." *Crisis* 3 (November): 27–30.

Hazardous and Solid Waste Amendments. 1984. Pub. L. No. 98-616. H.R. Rep. No. 98-198. 98th Cong., 2d sess. 5. Reprinted in 1984 U.S. Code Cong. & Admin. News 5576.

Heathcott, J. 2008. "The City Quiet Remade: National Programs and Local Agendas in the Movement to Clear the Slums, 1942–1952." *Journal of Urban History* 34 (2): 221–242.

Hechter, M. 1994. "Toward a Theory of Ethnic Change." In *Social Stratification: Class, Race, and Gender in Sociological Perspective*. D.B. Grusky, ed. Westview. Pp. 487–500.

Heitgard, J.L., and C.V. Lee. 2003. "A New Look at Neighborhoods Near National Priorities List Sites." *Social Science and Medicine* 57 (6): 1117–1126.

Heitzman, J.H. 1953. Memo dated January 29. Accession 479, Box 13, Folder 2. Civic Unity Committee Collection. University of Washington Libraries, Special Collections.

Hernandez, J. 2009. "Redlining Revisited: Mortgage Lending Patterns in Sacramento 1930–2004." *International Journal of Urban and Regional Research* 33 (2): 291–313.

Higgins, R.R. 1993. "Race and Environmental Equity: An Overview of the Environmental Justice Issue in the Policy Process." *Polity* 26 (2): 281–300.

Highsmith, A.R. 2009. "Demolition Means Progress: Urban Renewal, Local Politics, and State-Sanctioned Ghetto Formation in Flint, Michigan." *Journal of Urban History* 35 (3): 348–368.

Hillier, A.E. 2003. "Redlining and the Home Owners' Loan Corporation." *Journal of Urban History* 29 (4): 394–420.

Hills v. Gautreaux. 1976. 425 U.S. 284 (April 20).

Hines, R. 2001. "African Americans' Struggle for Environmental Justice and the Case of the Shintech Plant: Lessons Learned from a War Waged." *Journal of Black Studies* 31 (6): 777–789.

Hines, T. 1982. "Housing, Baseball, and Creeping Socialism: The Battle of Chavez Ravine, Los Angeles, 1949–1959." *Journal of Urban History* 8 (12): 123–144.

Hird, J.A. 1994. *Superfund: The Political Economy of Environmental Risk.* Johns Hopkins University Press.

Hird, J.A. 1993. "Environmental Policy and Equity: The Case of Superfund." *Journal of Policy Analysis and Management* 12 (2): 232–343.

Hird, J.A. 1990. "Superfund Expenditures and Cleanup Priorities: Distributive Politics or the Public Interest?" *Journal of Policy Analysis and Management* 9 (4): 455–483.

Hird, J.A., and M. Reese. 1998. "The Distribution of Environmental Quality: An Empirical Analysis." *Social Science Quarterly* 79 (4): 693–716.

Hirsch, A.R. [1983] 1998. *Making the Second Ghetto: Race and Housing in Chicago, 1940–1960.* University of Chicago Press.

Hite, D. 2009. "Factors Influencing Differences between Survey and Market-Based Environmental Value Measures." *Urban Studies* 46 (1): 117–138.

Hite, D. 1998. "Information and Bargaining in Markets for Environmental Quality." *Land Economics* 74:303–316.

Hite, D., W. Chern, F. Hitzhusen, A. Randall. 2001. "Property Value Impacts of an Environmental Amenity: The Case of Landfills." *Journal of Real Estate Finance and Economics* 22 (2): 185–202.

Holliman, I.V. 2008. "Techwood Homes." In *The New Georgia Encyclopedia.* Georgia Humanities Council and the University of Georgia Press.

Hollis, M. 1980. "The Persistence of a Poison: Effects of Chemical Plant Still Plague Alabama Town." *Washington Post*, June 15. P. A2.

Hollman v. Cisneros. 1995. Consent Decree. Civ. No. 4-92-712 (D. Minn., 4th Div.).

Holmes, A. 2000. "Neighborhood Racial Composition and Mortgage Redlining: A National Analysis." *Journal of Real Estate Portfolio Management* 6 (1): 37–51.

Hooks, G., and C.L. Smith. 2005. "Treadmills of Production and Destruction: Threats to the Environment Posed by Militarism." *Organization and Environment* 18 (1): 19–37.

Hooks, G., and C.L. Smith. 2004. "Militarism, Environmental Degradation and Native Americans." *American Sociological Review* 69 (4): 558–575.

Hopkins and Others v. City of Richmond and *Coleman v. Town of Ashland*. 1915. 117 Va. 692; 86 S.E. 139 (September 9).

Housing and Home Finance Agency. 1952. *Housing of the Nonwhite Population, 1940–1950*.

Huang, A. 2012. "Environmental Justice and Title VI of the Civil Rights Act: A Critical Crossroads." *American Bar Association Section on Environment, Energy, and Resources Newsletter* 43 (4): 6–7.

Hughes, Langston. 1940. *The Big Sea: An Autobiography*. Knopf.

Hundley et ux. v. Gorewitz et al. 1942. 77 U.S. App. D.C. 48; 132 F.2d 23.

Hunt, D.B. 2001. "What Went Wrong with Public Housing in Chicago? A History of the Robert Taylor Homes." *Journal of the Illinois State Historical Society* 94 (1): 96–123.

Hunt v. Chemical Waste Management. 1991. 584 So. 2d 1367 (July 11).

Hunter, L.M. 2000. "The Spatial Association between U.S. Immigration Residential Concentration and Environmental Hazards." *International Migration Review* 34 (2): 460–488.

Hunter, L.M., and J. Sutton. 2004. "Examining the Association between Hazardous Waste Facilities and Rural 'Brain Drain.'" *Rural Sociology* 69 (2): 197–212.

Hunter, L.M., M.J. White, J.S. Little, and J. Sutton. 2003. "Environmental Hazards, Migration, and Race." *Population and Environment* 25 (1): 23–39.

Hurd, B.H. 2002. "Valuing Superfund Site Cleanup: Evidence of Recovering Stigmatized Property Values." *Appraisal Journal* 70 (4): 426–437.

Hurd et ux. v. Hodge et al. 1948. 334 U.S. 24; 68 S. Ct. 847; 92 L. Ed. 1187 (May 3).

Hurd et al. v. Hodge et al., Uricolo et al. v. Same. 1947. 82 U.S. App. D.C. 180; 162 F.2d 233 (May 26).

Hurley, A. 1997a. "Fiasco at Wagner Electric: Environmental Justice and Urban Geography in St. Louis." *Environmental History* 2 (4): 460–481.

Hurley, A. 1997b. "Floods, Rats, and Toxic Waste: Allocating Environmental Hazards since World War II." In *Common Fields: An Environmental History of St. Louis*. A. Hurley, ed. Missouri Historical Society Press. Pp. 242–261.

Hurley, A. 1995. *Environmental Inequalities: Class, Race, and Industrial Pollution in Gary, Indiana, 1945–1980*. University of North Carolina Press.

Hutcheson, R. 1999. "Bush Explains Racially Restricted Deed on Home." *Spartanburg Herald-Journal*, July 13. P. 20.

Iceland, J. 2004. *The Multigroup Entropy Index (Also Known as Theil's H or the Information Theory Index)*. U.S. Bureau of the Census.

Ihlanfeldt, K.R., and L.O. Taylor. 2004. "Externality Effects of Small-Scale Hazardous Waste Sites: Evidence from Urban Commercial Property Markets." *Journal of Environmental Economic Management* 47:117–139.

Illinois Association for Criminal Justice. 1929. *The Illinois Crime Survey.* Blakely.

Indianapolis Freeman. 1924a. March 1.

Indianapolis Freeman, 1924b. July 26.

Indianapolis Recorder. 1926. November 27.

Indianapolis World. 1921. May 6.

Industrial Safety Equipment Assoc., Inc. v. U.S. Environmental Protection Agency. 1988. 656 F. Supp. 852, *aff'd,* 837 F.2d 1115 (D.C.C.).

Innis Arden Covenant. 1941. No. 3187136, Vol. 1992. Recorded August 28, 1941. Available at http://depts.washington.edu/civilr/Innis%20Arden.htm.

In re Lee Sing & In re Sing Too Quan. 1890. 43 F. 359 (C.C.D. Cal. August 25).

Ishiyama, N., and K. TallBear. 2001. "Changing Notions of Environmental Justice in the Decision to Host a Nuclear Fuel Storage Facility on the Skull Valley Goshute Reservation." Paper presented at the 2001 Waste Management Symposium. Boston, MA.

Jackson, K.T. 1985. *Crabgrass Frontier: The Suburbanization of the United States.* Oxford University Press.

Jackson, K.T. [1967] 1992. *The Ku Klux Klan in the City, 1915–1930.* Ivan R. Dee.

Jackson, M.I. 2008. *Model City Blues: Urban Space and Organized Resistance in New Haven.* Temple University Press.

Jackson v. State. 1918. 132 Md. 311; 103 A. 910.

Jacobs, M. 2009. "Preston Hollow Adding Bushes to List of High-Profile Residents." *Dallas Morning News,* January 7.

Jaimes, M.A., ed. 1992. *The State of Native America: Genocide, Colonization, and Resistance.* South End.

James v. Olin. 1979. No. CA79 PT 5128NE (N.D. Ala. July 9).

Jeffreys, K. 1994. "Environmental Racism: A Skeptic's View." *Journal of Civil Rights and Economic Development* 9 (2): 677–691.

Jenkins, R., K. Maguire, and C. Morgan. 2004. "Host Community Compensation and Municipal Solid Waste Landfills." *Land Economics* 80 (4): 513–528.

Johansen, B. 1994. "Akwesasne's Toxic Turtles." In *Ecocide of Native America: Environmental Destruction of Indian Lands and People.* D.A. Grinde and B.E. Johansen, eds. Clear Light. Pp. 175–199.

Jones-Correa, M. 2000–2001. "The Origins and Diffusion of Racial Restrictive Covenants." *Political Science Quarterly* 115 (4): 541–568.

Journal of the Common Council of the City of Indianapolis, Indiana, from January 1, 1926, to December 1, 1926. 1927.

Kamps, K. 2006. "Hard Won Victory against Environmentally Racist Nuke Waste Dump Targeted at Native Lands." Nuclear Information and Resource Service. September 18.

Kansas City Call. 1954. "Segregation in Housing Must Go." April 2. P. 22.

Kaplan, D.H., and S.R. Holloway. 2001. "Scaling Ethnic Segregation: Causal Processes and Contingent Outcomes in Chinese Residential Patterns." *GeoJournal* 53:59–70.

Karlin, W. 1937. "New York Slum Clearance and the Law." *Political Science Quarterly* 52 (2, June): 241–258.

Kasarda, J.D. 1972. "The Theory of Ecological Expansion: An Empirical Test." *Social Forces* 51:165–175.

Katahdin Foundation. 2005. *Homeland: Four Portraits of Native Action*. Documentary film produced and directed by D. Taylor, R. Grossman, and L.B. Thomas.

Kathan v. Williams. 1944. 309 Mich. 219; 15 N.W.2d 137 (June 30).

Keating, L., and C.A. Flores. 2000. "Sixty and Out: Techwood Homes Transformed by Enemies and Friends." *Journal of Urban History* 26 (3): 275–311.

Kelleher, D.T. 1970. "St. Louis' 1916 Residential Segregation Ordinance." *Bulletin—Missouri Historical Society* 26 (3): 239–248.

Kennickell, A., M. Starr-McCluer, and A. Suden. 1997. "Family Finances in the U.S.: Recent Evidence from the Survey of Consumer Finances." *Federal Reserve Bulletin* 83:1–24.

Ketar, K. 1992. "Hazardous Waste Sites and Property Values in the State of New Jersey." *Applied Economics* 24 (6): 647–659.

Kiel, K.A. 1995. "Measuring the Impact of the Discovery and Cleaning of Identified Hazardous Waste Sites on House Values." *Land Economics* 71 (4): 428–435.

Kiel, K.A., and M. Williams. 2007. "The Impact of Superfund Sites on Local Property Values: Are All Sites the Same?" *Journal of Urban Economics* 61 (1): 170–192.

King, P.E. 1978. "Exclusionary Zoning and Open Housing: A Brief Judicial History." *Geographical Review* 68 (4, October): 459–469.

Kirkland, E. 2008. "What's Race Got to Do with It? Looking for the Racial Dimensions of Gentrification." *Western Journal of Black Studies* 32 (2): 18–30.

Klarman, M.J. 2004. *From Jim Crow to Civil Rights: The Supreme Court and the Struggle for Racial Equality*. Oxford University Press.

Kmiec, D.W. 2007. "Hitting Home: The Supreme Court Earns Public Notice Opining on Public Use." *University of Pennsylvania Journal of Constitutional Law* 9:501–543.

Knight, R.R., and J.R. Powell. 2001. *Occurrence and Distribution of Organochlorine Pesticides, Polychlorinated Biphenyls, and Trace Elements in Fish Tissue in the Lower Tennessee River Basin, 1980–98*. U.S. Geological Survey.

Knowles, L., and K. Prewitt. 1970. *Institutional Racism in America*. Prentice Hall.

Kochhar, R., A. Gonzalez-Barrera, and D. Dockterman. 2009. "Through Boom and Bust: Minorities, Immigrants, and Homeownership." Pew Research Center.

Koeppel, B. 1999. "Cancer Alley Louisiana." *The Nation* 269 (15, November): 16–23.

Kohlhase, J.E. 1991. "The Impact of Toxic Waste Sites on Housing Values." *Journal of Urban Economics* 30 (July): 1–26.

Kraft, M.E., and R. Kraut. 1988. "Citizen Participation and Hazardous Waste Policy Implementation." In *Dimensions of Hazardous Waste Policy*. C.E. Davis and J.P. Lester, eds. Greenwood. Pp. 63–80.

Kranish, M. 1999. "Bush Home Had Racial Restriction." *Boston Globe*, July 14. P. A3.

Kratt, M.N., and T. Hanchett. 2009. *Legacy: The Myers Park Story*. Duke Mansion.

Kraus, N. 2004. "The Significance of Race in Urban Politics: The Limitations of Regime Theory." *Race and Society* 7 (2): 95–111.

Kreiss, K., M.M. Zack, R.D. Kimbrough, L.L. Needham, A.L. Smrek, and B.T. Jones. 1981. "Cross-Sectional Study of a Community with Exceptional Exposure to DDT." *Journal of the American Medical Association* 245 (19): 1926–1930.

Krieg, E.J. 1995. "A Socio-historical Interpretation of Toxic Waste Sites: The Case of Greater Boston." *American Journal of Economics and Sociology* 54:1–14.

Krivo, L.J., and R.L. Kaufman. 2004. "Housing and Wealth Inequality: Racial-Ethnic Differences in Home Equity in the United States." *Demography* 41 (3): 585–605.

Kruse, K.M. 2005. *White Flight: Atlanta and the Making of Modern Conservatism.* Princeton University Press.

Krysan, M. 2002. "Whites Who Say They'd Flee: Who Are They, and Why Would They Leave?" *Demography* 39 (4): 675–696.

Kuehn, R. 1994. "Remedying the Unequal Enforcement of Environmental Laws." *St. John's Journal of Legal Commentary* 9 (2): 625–668.

Kuletz, V. 1998. *The Tainted Desert: Environmental and Social Ruin in the American West.* Routledge.

LaBalme, J. 1988. "Dumping on Warren County." In *Environmental Politics: Lessons from the Grassroots.* B. Hall, ed. Institute for Southern Studies. Pp. 25–30.

LaBalme, J. 1987. *A Road to Walk: A Struggle for Environmental Justice.* Regulator.

LaDuke, W. 1999. *All Our Relations: Native Struggles for Land and Life.* South End.

LaDuke, W. 1993. "A Society Based on Conquest Cannot Be Sustained: Native Peoples and the Environmental Crisis." In *Toxic Struggles: The Theory and Practice of Environmental Justice.* R. Hofrichter, ed. New Society. Pp. 98–106.

LaDuke, W. 1979. "The History of Uranium Mining." *Black Hills / Paha Sapa Report* 1 (1): 2.

Lake, R.W. 1981. *The New Suburbanites: Race and Housing in the Suburbs.* Center for Urban Policy Research, Rutgers University.

Lancaster, A.G. 1944. "Protests Housing Project." *Chicago Defender*, March 18. P. 12.

Land Development Company of Louisiana v. City of New Orleans. 1927. 17 F.2d 1016 (C.C.A. April 1).

Land Development Company of Louisiana v. City of New Orleans. 1926. 13 F.2d 898 (D.D.C. July 8).

LaRoss, D., and D. Reeves. 2012. "EPA Adding Anti-discrimination to Multi-year Environmental Justice Plan." *Inside EPA Weekly Report* 33 (March 16): 11.

Lashley, S., and D.E. Taylor. 2010. "Why Can't They Work Together? A Framework for Understanding Conflict and Collaboration in Two Environmental Disputes in Southeast Michigan." *Research in Social Problems and Public Policy* 18:409–449.

LatinoJustice. 2008. "Hazleton." Available at http://latinojustice.org/civil_rights/Hazleton_story/.

Lavelle, M., and M. Coyle. 1993. "Unequal Protection: The Racial Divide in Environmental Law." In *Toxic Struggles: The Theory and Practice of Environmental Justice.* R. Hofrichter, ed. New Society. Pp. 136–143.

Lavelle, M., and M. Coyle. 1992. "The Racial Divide in Environmental Law: Unequal Protection." *National Law Journal*, Special Supplement, September 21.

Leahy, P.J. 1985. "Are Racial Factors Important for the Allocation of Mortgage Money?" *American Journal of Economics and Sociology* 44:186–196.

Leavenworth, S. 1993. "State Planning to Drain Water from Toxic Landfill." *Raleigh News & Observer*, May 15. P. A6.

Lee (Anna M.) et al. v. Carl A. Hansberry et al. 1939. 372 Ill. 369; 24 N.E.2d 37 (December 13).

Lee (Anna M.) et al. v. Carl A. Hansberry et al. 1937. 291 Ill. App. 517; 10 N.E.2d 406 (October 7).

Lee, B.A., and K.E. Campbell. 1997. "Common Ground? Urban Neighborhoods as Survey Respondents See Them." *Social Science Quarterly* 78:922–936.

Lee, B.A., J. Iceland, and G. Sharp. 2012. "Racial and Ethnic Diversity Goes Local: Charting Change in American Communities over Three Decades." American Communities Project, Brown University. September.

Lee, B.A., S.F. Reardon, G. Firebaugh, C.R. Farrell, S.A. Matthews, and D. O'Sullivan. 2008. "Beyond the Census Tract: Patterns and Determinants of Racial Segregation at Multiple Geographic Scales." *American Sociological Review* 73 (October): 766–971.

Lee, B.A., and P.H. Wood. 1991. "Is Neighborhood Racial Succession Place-Specific?" *Demography* 28:21–40.

Lee, C. 1993. "Beyond Toxic Wastes and Race." In *Confronting Environmental Racism: Voices from the Grassroots*. R.D. Bullard, ed. South End. Pp. 41–52.

Lee, M.A., and K.F. Ferraro. 2007. "Neighborhood Residential Segregation and Physical Health among Hispanic Americans: Good, Bad, or Benign." *Journal of Health and Social Behavior* 48 (2): 131–148.

Lee, S., and P. Mohai. 2011. "Racial and Socioeconomic Assessments of Neighborhoods Adjacent to Small-Scale Brownfield Sites in the Detroit Region." *Environmental Practice* 13 (4): 340–353.

Lejano, R.P., and H. Iseki. 2001. "Environmental Justice: Spatial Distribution of Hazardous Waste Treatment Storage and Disposal Facilities in Los Angeles." *Journal of Urban Planning and Development* 127 (2): 51–62.

Leonard, K.I. 1994. *Making Ethnic Choices: California's Punjabi Mexican Americans.* Temple University Press.

Lerner, S. 2005. *Diamond: A Struggle for Environmental Justice in Louisiana's Chemical Corridor.* MIT Press.

Levine, D.A. 1976. *Internal Combustion: The Races in Detroit, 1915–1926.* Greenwood.

Liberty Annex Corporation v. City of Dallas et al. 1926. 289 S.W. 1067 (Tex. Civ. App.)

Lichter, D.T. 2007. "Municipal Underbounding? Annexation and Racial Exclusion in Southern Small Towns." *Rural Sociology* 72 (1): 47–68.

Light, S.A., and K.R.L. Rand. 1996. "Is Title VI a Magic Bullet? Environmental Racism in the Context of Political-Economic Processes and Imperatives." *Michigan Journal of Race & Law* 2:1.

Linder, D. 2000. "The Sweet Trials." *Jurist*. Available at http://jurist.law.pitt.edu/
famoustrials/sweet.php.

Little, M.H. 1994. "Civil Rights." In *The Encyclopedia of Indianapolis*. D.J. Bodenhamer
and R.G. Barrows, eds. Indiana University Press. Pp. 438–441.

Logan, J.R. 2011. "Separate and Unequal: The Neighborhood Gap for Blacks, Hispanics, and Asians in Metropolitan America." American Communities Project, Brown
University.

Logan, J.R. 2001. "Ethnic Diversity Grows, Neighborhood Integration Lags Behind."
Lewis Mumford Center for Comparative Urban and Regional Research, Brown
University.

Logan, J.R., and H.L. Molotch. 1987. "Homes: Exchange and Sentiment in the Neighborhood." In *Urban Fortunes: The Political Economy of Place*. J.R. Logan, ed. University of California Press. Pp. 367–387.

Logan, J.R., and B.J. Stults. 2011. "The Persistence of Segregation in the Metropolis: New
Findings from the 2010 Census." American Communities Project, Brown University.

Logan, J.R., and W.C. Zhang. 2011. "Global Neighborhoods: New Evidence from Census 2010." American Communities Project, Brown University.

Logan, J.R., and W.C. Zhang. 2010. "Global Neighborhoods: New Pathways to Diversity
and Separation." *American Journal of Sociology* 115 (4): 1069–1109.

Lopez, R. 2002. "Segregation and Black / White Differences in Exposure to Air Toxics
in 1990." *Environmental Health Perspectives* 110 (April): 289–295.

Los Angeles Investment Company v. Alfred Gary et al. 1919. 181 Cal. 680; 186 P. 596
(December 11).

Louisiana Bucket Brigade. 2012. "Norco: Profile." Available at http://www.labucket
brigade.org/section.php?id=23.

Louisiana Department of Environmental Quality. 2009. *Annual Report 09*.

Louisiana Economic Development. 2012. "Industrial Tax Exemption." Available
at http://www.louisianaeconomicdevelopment.com/incentives/industrial-tax
-exemption.aspx?id=0.

Louisiana Environmental Action Network and Greenpeace USA. 1999. "Shintech Environmental Racism." September 1.

*Louis Kraemer and Fern E. Kraemer v. J.D. Shelley and Ethel Lee Shelley, and Josephine
Fitzgerald*. 1948. 358 Mo. 364; 214 S.W.2d 525 (November 8).

*Louis Kraemer and Fern E. Kraemer v. J.D. Shelley and Ethel Lee Shelley, and Josephine
Fitzgerald*. 1946. 355 Mo. 814; 198 S.W.2d 679 (December 9).

Louisville Courier-Journal. 1913. November 15. P. 4.

Lowry, R.C. 1998. "All Hazardous Waste Politics Is Local: Grassroots Advocacy and
Public Participation in Siting and Cleanup Decisions." *Policy Studies Journal* 26 (4):
748–759.

Luarkie, R. 2012. "Testimony on H.R. 785, to Amend the Surface Mining Control and
Reclamation Act of 1977 to Clarify That Uncertified States and Indian Tribes Have
the Authority to Use Certain Payments for Certain Noncoal Reclamation Projects."

House Committee on Natural Resources, Subcommittee on Energy and Mineral Resources. February 17.

Luebben, R.A. 1972. "Prejudice and Discrimination against Navahos in a Mining Community." In *Native Americans Today: Sociological Perspectives*. B.A. Chadwick, R.C. Day, and H.M. Bahr, eds. Harper and Row. Pp. 89–100.

Lui, F. 2001. *Environmental Justice Analysis: Theories, Methods, and Practice*. CRC.

Lynch, M., P.B. Stretesky, and R.G. Burns. 2004. "Determinants of Environmental Law Violation Fines against Petroleum Refineries: Race, Ethnicity, Income, and Aggregation Effects." *Society and Natural Resources* 17 (4): 333–347.

Maantay, J. 2002. "Zoning Law, Health, and Environmental Justice: What's the Connection?" *Journal of Law, Medicine & Ethics* 30:572–593.

Majumdar, R.D. 2006–2007. "Racially Restrictive Covenants in the State of Washington: A Primer for Practitioners." *Seattle University Law Review* 30 (4): 1095–1117.

Mank, B.C. 1999. "Title VI." In *The Law of Environmental Justice: Theories and Procedures to Address Disproportionate Risks*. M.B. Gerrard, ed. American Bar Association. Pp. 23–68.

Maraniss, D., and M. Weisskopf. 1987. "Jobs and Illness in Petrochemical Corridor: In Louisiana, Pollution Is Familiar but Pattern of Disease Is New." *Washington Post*, December 22. P. A1.

Marcuse, P. 1986. "Abandonment, Gentrification, and Displacement: The Linkages in New York City." In *Gentrification and the City*. N. Smith and P. Williams, eds. Unwin Hyman. Pp. 153–177.

Markham, W.T., and E. Rufa. 1997. "Class, Race, and the Disposal of Urban Waste: Locations of Landfills, Incinerators, and Sewage Treatment Plants." *Sociological Spectrum* 17:235–248.

Martino-Taylor, L. 2011. "The Manhattan-Rochester Coalition, Research on the Health Effects of Radioactive Materials, and Tests on Vulnerable Populations without Consent in St. Louis, 1945–1970." Ph.D. dissertation, University of Missouri–Columbia.

Martino-Taylor, L. 2008. "The Military-Industrial-Academic Complex and a New Social Autism." *Journal of Political and Military Sociology* 36 (1): 37–52.

Maskovsky, J. 2006. "Governing the 'New Hometowns': Race, Power, and Neighborhood Participation in the New Inner City." *Identities: Global Studies in Culture and Power* 13:73–99.

Massey, D.S., and N.A. Denton. 1993. *American Apartheid: Segregation and the Making of the Underclass*. Harvard University Press.

Maynard, Cooper & Gale, P.C. 1995. "Fish-Monitoring Data for the Huntsville Spring Branch-Indian Creek System Released." *Environmental Compliance Update* 3 (9, October).

Mays et al. v. Burgess et al. 1945. 79 U.S. App. D.C. 343; 147 F.2d 869 (January 29).

McClelland, G.H., W.D. Schulze, and B. Hurd. 1990. "The Effect of Risk Beliefs on

Property Values: A Case Study of a Hazardous Waste Site." *Risk Analysis* 10 (4): 485–497.

McCluskey, J.J., and G.C. Rausser. 2001. "Estimation of Perceived Risk and Its Effect on Property Values." *Land Economics* 77 (1): 42–55.

McCord, S. 2012. "Hyde Park Residents Still Waiting to Be Moved." *Augusta Chronicle*, September 15.

McCord, S. 2011. "Commission Approves Relocation, Compensation for Hyde Park Residents." *Augusta Chronicle*, October 18.

McDermott, C.J. 1994. "Balancing the Scales of Environmental Justice." *Fordham Urban Law Journal* 21 (3): 687–705.

McDermott, C.J. 1993. Testimony of Waste Management, Inc. U.S. House of Representatives, Judiciary Committee, Subcommittee on Civil and Constitutional Rights. 103d Cong., 1st sess. March 3.

McGhee et ux. v. Sipes et al. 1947. 331 U.S. 804; 67 S. Ct. 1754; 91 L. Ed. 1826 (June 23).

McGovern, F.E. 1997. "The Defensive Use of Federal Class Actions in Mass Torts." *Arizona Law Review* 39:595–614.

McGovern, F.E. 1990. "The Alabama DDT Settlement Fund." *Law and Contemporary Problems* 53 (4): 61–78.

McKinnish, T., R. Wals, and K. White. 2008. "Who Gentrifies Low-Income Neighborhoods?" Working Paper 14036. National Bureau of Economic Research. Available at http://www.nber/org/papers/w14036.

McMichael, S.L. 1931. *McMichael's Appraising Manual: A Real Estate Appraising Handbook for Field Work and Advanced Study Courses.* Prentice Hall.

McMillen, D.P., and P. Thorsnes. 2003. "The Aroma of Tacoma: Time-Varying Average Derivatives and the Effect of a Superfund Site on House Prices." *Journal of Business & Economic Statistics* 21 (2l): 237–246.

McNulty, T.L., and S.R. Holloway. 2000. "Race, Crime, and Public Housing in Atlanta: Testing a Conditional Effect Hypothesis." *Social Forces* 79 (2): 707–729.

Melvin, D. 1994. "Hazardous Waste Site Complaint Charges Environmental Racism." *Sun-Sentinel*, March 20.

Mennis, J.L., and L. Jordan. 2005. "The Distribution of Environmental Equity: Exploring Spatial Nonstationarity in Multivariate Models of Air Toxic Releases." *Annals of the Association of American Geographers* 95 (2): 249–268.

Metropolitan Housing Council of Chicago. 1935. *Finding New Homes for Families Who Will Leave PWA Reconstruction Areas in Chicago.*

Meyer, D.R. 1973. "Blacks in Slum Housing." *Journal of Black Studies* 4 (2, December): 139–152.

Meyer, S.G. 2001. *As Long as They Don't Move Next Door: Segregation and Racial Conflict in American Neighborhoods.* Rowman and Littlefield.

Miller, L. 1965. "The Protest against Housing Segregation." *Annals of the American Academy of Political and Social Science* 357 (January): 73–79.

Mills, C.W. 1994. "The Power Elite." In *Social Stratification: Class, Race, and Gender in Sociological Perspective.* D. Grusky, ed. Westview. Pp. 161–170.

Mincer, J. 1987. "National Notebook: Kansas City, Mo.; Failed Project Demolished." *New York Times*, March 8.

Ming, W.R. 1949. "Racial Restriction and the Fourteenth Amendment: The Restrictive Covenant Cases." *University of Chicago Law Review* 16 (Winter): 203–238.

Mississippi Development Authority. 2012. "Industrial Property Tax Exemption." Available at http://www.mississippi.org/mda-library-resources/finance -tax-info/tax-exemptions-incentives-and-credits/industrial-property-tax -exemption.html.

Mixom, G. 2005. *The Atlanta Riot: Race, Class, and Violence in a New South City*. University Press of Florida.

Mohai, P. 1996. "Environmental Justice or Analytic Justice? Reexamining Historical Hazardous Waste Landfill Siting Patterns in Metropolitan Texas." *Social Science Quarterly* 77:500–507.

Mohai, P. 1995. "The Demographics of Dumping Revisited: Examining the Impact of Alternative Methodologies in Environmental Justice Research." *Virginia Environmental Law Journal* 14:615–653.

Mohai, P., and B. Bryant. 1992. "Environmental Racism: Reviewing the Evidence." In *Race and the Incidence of Environmental Hazards: A Time for Discourse*. B. Bryant and P. Mohai, eds. Westview. Pp. 162–176, 245–246.

Mohai, P., D. Pellow, and J.T. Roberts. 2009. "Environmental Justice." *Annual Review of Environment and Resources* 34:405–430.

Mohai, P., and R. Saha. 2007. "Racial Inequality in the Distribution of Hazardous Waste: A National-Level Assessment." *Social Problems* 54 (3): 343–370.

Mohai, P., and R. Saha. 2006. "Reassessing Racial and Socioeconomic Disparities in Environmental Justice Research." *Demography* 43:383–399.

Mohl, R.A. 1995. "Making the Second Ghetto in Metropolitan Miami, 1940–1960." *Journal of Urban History* 21 (3): 395–427.

Mohl, R.A. 1987. "Black Immigrants: Bahamians in Early Twentieth-Century Miami." *Florida Historical Quarterly* 65 (3): 271–297.

Morell, D., and C. Magorian. 1982. *Siting Hazardous Waste Facilities: Local Opposition and the Myth of Preemption*. Ballinger.

Morello-Frosch, R., and B. Jesdale. 2006. "Separate and Unequal: Residential Segregation and Air Quality in the Metropolitan U.S." *Environmental Health Perspectives* 113:386–393.

Morello-Frosch, R., and R. Lopez. 2006. "The Riskscape and the Color Line: Examining the Role of Segregation in Environmental Health Disparities." *Environmental Research* 102 (2): 181–196.

Morrill, D.L. 2004. *Historic Charlotte: An Illustrated History of Charlotte-Mecklenburg*. Historical Publishing Network.

Motavalli, J. 1998. "Toxic Targets: Polluters That Dump on Communities of Color Are Finally Being Brought to Justice—Environmental Racism." *E: The Environmental Magazine*, July–August, 1–11.

Mrsa v. Reynolds. 1947. 317 Mich. 632; 27 N.W.2d 40 (April 17).

Mushkatel, A., and K. Nakhleh 1978. "Eminent Domain: Land-Use Planning and the Powerless in the United States and Israel." *Social Problems* 26 (2): 147–159.

Myrdal, G. 1944. *An American Dilemma: The Negro Problem in Modern Democracy.* Harper Brothers.

NAACP (National Association for the Advancement of Colored People). 1927. *Seventeenth Annual Report.*

NAACP v. Gorsuch. 1982. No. 82-768-CIV-5 (E.D.N.C. August 10).

NAACP v. U.S. Department of Housing and Urban Development. 1987. 817 F.2d 149 (1st Cir. March 19).

Nabokov, P. 1991. *Native American Testimony.* Penguin.

National Center for Health Statistics, Centers for Disease Control. 2002. *Preventing and Controlling Cancer: Addressing the Nation's Second Leading Cause of Death.*

National Institutes of Health (NIH). 1997. "NCI and University of Alabama in Huntsville to Conduct Breast Cancer Study, Offer Screening Exams in Triana, Alabama." December 22.

National Park Service. 1993. "Historic American Buildings Survey: Techwood Homes." HABS No. GA-2257. U.S. Department of the Interior.

National Register of Historic Places. 2004. "The Civil Rights Movement in Birmingham, Alabama, 1933–1979." U.S. Department of the Interior, National Park Service.

National Register of Historic Places. 1999. "Historic and Architectural Resources of The Ville, St. Louis (Independent City), Missouri." U.S. Department of the Interior, National Park Service. August 17.

National Solid Wastes Management Association and Chemical Waste Management v. Alabama Department of Environmental Management. 1990a. 729 F. Supp. 792 (N.D. Ala. January 12).

National Solid Wastes Management Association and Chemical Waste Management v. Alabama Department of Environmental Management. 1990b. 910 F. Supp. 713 (11th Cir. August 8).

Native Action. 2012. "Our Staff." Available at http://www.nativeaction.org/staff.html.

Neal, D.E., V.E. Famira, and V. Miller-Travis. 2010. *Now Is the Time: Environmental Injustice in the U.S. and Recommendations for Eliminating Disparities.* Lawyers' Committee for Civil Rights Under Law. June.

Nelson, A.C., J. Genereux, and M.M. Genereux. 1992. "Price Effects of Landfills on House Values." *Land Economics* 68 (4, November): 359–365.

Nesbitt, G.B. 1949. "Relocating Negroes from Urban Slum Clearance Sites." *Land Economics* 25 (3, August): 275–288.

Neumann, C., D. Forman, and J. Rothlein. 1998. "Hazard Screening of Chemical Releases and Environmental Equity Analysis of Populations Proximate to Toxic Release Inventory Facilities in Oregon." *Environmental Health Perspectives* 106 (4): 217–226.

Newman, K., and E.K. Wyly. 2006. "The Right to Stay Put, Revisited: Gentrification and Resistance to Displacement in New York City." *Urban Studies* 43 (1): 23–57.

Newman, R.J., and D.H. Sullivan. 1987. "Econometric Analysis of Business Tax Impacts on Industrial Location: What Do We Know and How Do We Know It?" *Journal of Urban Economics* 23:215–234.

New York City Housing Authority v. Mueller. 1936. 270 N.Y. 333.

New York Power Authority. 2012. "St. Lawrence–Franklin D. Roosevelt Power Project." Available at http://www.nypa.gov/facilities/stlaw.htm.

New York Times. 1982a. "Carolinians Angry over PCB Landfill." August 11. P. 17.

New York Times. 1982b. "Carolinians See Governor in PCB Landfill Dispute." October 10. P. 31.

New York Times. 1982c. "Congressman and 120 Arrested at PCB Protest." September 28.

New York Times. 1913. "Building Height and Its Legality." March 2. P. XX2.

New York Times. 1910. "Baltimore Tries Drastic Plan of Race Segregation." December 25. Pp. 10–11.

Nielsen, K. 1998. "The Wall: How Can You Tell Where White Coconut Grove Ends and Black Coconut Grove Begins? Just Look for the Barbed Wire." *Miami New Times*, February 5.

Noland, T. 1979. "Triana Fish Story." *Southern Changes* 1 (8): 14–15.

Noonan, D.S. 2008. "Evidence of Environmental Justice: A Critical Perspective on the Practice of EJ Research and Lessons for Policy Design." *Social Science Quarterly* 89 (5, December): 1153–1174.

Noonan, D.S., D.J. Krupka, and B.M. Baden. 2007. "Neighborhood Dynamics and Price Effects of Superfund Site Clean-Up." *Journal of Regional Science* 47 (4): 665–692.

Noonan, D.S., R.M.R. Turaga, and B.M. Baden. 2009. "Superfund, Hedonics, and the Scales of Environmental Justice." *Environmental Management* 44 (5): 909–920.

Northwest Civic Association v. Sheldon. 1947. 317 Mich. 416; 27 N.W.2d 36 (April 17).

Nossiter, A. 1991. "Toxic Waste Firms Dangle Sweet Deals, Officials Promise Jobs, Plenty of Perks to Poor Miss. County." *Atlanta Journal-Constitution*, May 31. P. A3.

Nuclear Information and Resource Service. 2006. "Private Fuel Storage Targets High-Level Radioactive Waste Dump at Skull Valley Goshute Indian Reservation, Utah." Radioactive Waste Project.

Nuclear Waste Policy Act. 1982. Pub. L. 97-425, 96 Stat. 2202.

Oakes, J.M., D.L. Anderton, and A.B. Anderson. 1996. "A Longitudinal Analysis of Environmental Equity in Communities with Hazardous Waste Facilities." *Social Science Research* 25 (2): 125–148.

Olin v. Insurance Company. 1992. 966 F.2d 718 (2d Cir. June 1).

Olin v. Insurance Company. 1991. 762 F. Supp. 548 (S.D.N.Y.).

Oliver, M.L., and T. Shapiro. 1995. *Black Wealth / White Wealth: A New Perspective on Racial Inequality*. Routledge.

Oliveri, R.C. 2009. "Between a Rock and a Hard Place: Landlords, Latinos, Anti-Illegal Immigrant Ordinances, and Housing Discrimination." *Vanderbilt Law Review* 62 (1): 55–124.

O'Neil, S.G. 2007. "Superfund: Evaluating the Impact of Executive Order 12898." *Environmental Health Perspectives* 115 (7): 1087–1093.

Oregon Real Estate News. 1956. "NAREB Code of Ethics." Oregon Historical Society. February.

Ottinger, G.E. 2005. "Grounds for Action: Community and Science in Environmental Justice Controversy." Ph.D. dissertation, University of California–Berkeley.

Padres Hacia Una Vida Mejor v. Jackson. 2011. No. 1:11-cv01094 (E.D. Cal.).

Palmer, C. 1955. *Adventures of a Slum Fighter.* Tupper and Love.

Palmquist, R.B., and V.K. Smith. 2002. "The Use of Hedonic Property Value Techniques for Policy and Litigation." In *The International Yearbook of Environmental and Resource Economics.* T. Tietenberg and H. Folmer, eds. Edward Elgar. Pp. 115–164.

Parcus v. Olin. 1980. No. CV80 M 5098NE (N.D. Ala. March 17).

Pardo, M. 1998. *Mexican American Women Activists: Identity and Resistance in Two Los Angeles Communities.* Temple University Press.

Park, L.S., and D.N. Pellow. 2011. *The Slums of Aspen: Immigrants vs. the Environment in America's Eden.* NYU Press.

Parker, B.J. 2003. *Solid Waste Landfills and Residential Property Values.* National Solid Wastes Management Association.

Parmalee v. Morris. 1922. 218 Mich. 625; 188 N.W. 330 (June 5).

Pastor, M., R. Morello-Frosch, J. Sadd. 2006. "Breathless: Air Quality, Schools, and Environmental Justice in California." *Policy Studies Journal* 34 (3): 337–362.

Pastor, M., and J.L. Sadd. 2004. "Waiting to Inhale: The Demographics of Toxic Air Release Facilities in 21st-Century California." *Social Science Quarterly* 85 (2): 420–440.

Pastor, M., J.L. Sadd, and J. Hipp. 2001. "Which Came First? Toxic Facilities, Minority Move-In, and Environmental Justice." *Journal of Urban Affairs* 23 (1): 1–21.

Patterson, O. 1997. *The Ordeal of Integration: Progress and Resentment in America's Racial Crisis.* Counterpoint.

Pedro Lozano et al. v. City of Hazleton. 2013. D.C. No. 3:06-cv-01586.

Pedro Lozano et al. v. City of Hazleton. 2011. 131 S. Ct. 2958.

Pedro Lozano et al. v. City of Hazleton. 2010. 620 F.3d 170 (3d Cir.).

Pedro Lozano et al. v. City of Hazleton. 2007. 496 F. Supp. 2d 477 (M.D. Pa.).

Pellow, D.N. 2002. *Garbage Wars.* MIT Press.

Perlin, S.A, K. Sexton, and D.W.S. Wong. 1999. "An Examination of Race and Poverty for Populations Living Near Industrial Sources of Air Pollution." *Journal of Exposure Analysis and Environmental Epidemiology* 9 (1): 29–48.

Perlin, S.A., D. Wong, and K. Sexton. 2001. "Residential Proximity to Industrial Sources of Air Pollution: Interrelationships among Race, Poverty, and Age." *Journal of the Air & Waste Management Association* 51 (3): 406–421.

Petition to the Mayor and City Council. 1910. Baltimore City Archives. Mahool Files. File 406. July 5.

Pettigrew, T. 1973. "Attitudes on Race and Housing: A Social Psychological View." In *Segregation in Residential Areas.* A. Hawley and V.P. Rock, eds. National Academy of Sciences.

Pettus, T. 1948. "Seattle Is Blighted by Restrictive Covenants." *New World*, January 15. P. 1.

Phillips v. Naff. 1952. 332 Mich. 389; 52 N.W.2d 158 (Mich. Sup. Ct.).

Phillips v. Wearn. 1946. 226 N.C. 290; 37 S.E.2d 895.

Philpott, T.L. [1978] 1991. *The Slum and the Ghetto: Neighborhood Deterioration and Middle-Class Reform.* Wadsworth.

Pietila, A. 2010. *Not in My Neighborhood: How Bigotry Shaped a Great American City.* Ivan R. Dee.

Pinderhughes, R. 1996. "The Impact of Race on Environmental Quality: An Empirical and Theoretical Discussion." *Sociological Perspectives* 39 (2): 231–248.

Piore, M.J. 1994. "The Dual Labor Market: Theory and Implications." In *Social Stratification: Class, Race, and Gender in Sociological Perspective.* D. Grusky, ed. Westview. Pp. 359–361.

Plasencia, A.J. 2011. "A History of West Coconut Grove from 1925: Slum Clearance, Concrete Monsters, and the Dichotomy of East and West Coconut Grove." Master's thesis, Clemson University.

Plessy v. Ferguson. 1896. 163 U.S. 537.

Plotkin, W. 1999. "Deeds of Mistrust: Race, Housing and Restrictive Covenants in Chicago, 1900–1953." Ph.D. dissertation, University of Illinois at Chicago.

Plyler v. Doe. 1982. 457 U.S. 202; 102 S. Ct. 2382; 72 L. Ed. 2d 786.

Poletown Neighborhood Council v. City of Detroit. 1981. 410 Mich. 616; 304 N.W.2d 444.

Pollock, P.H., and M.E. Vittas. 1995. "Who Bears the Burdens of Environmental Pollution? Race, Ethnicity, and Environmental Equity in Florida." *Social Science Quarterly* 76 (2): 294–310.

Popkin, S.J., G.C. Galster, K. Temkin, C. Herbig, D.K. Levy, and E.K. Reicher. 2003. "Obstacles to Desegregating Public Housing: Lessons Learned from Implementing Eight Consent Decrees." *Journal of Policy Analysis and Management* 22 (2): 179–199.

Portney, K.E. 1991. *Siting Hazardous Waste Treatment Facilities: The NIMBY Syndrome.* Auburn House.

Power, G. 1984. "High Society: The Building Height Limitation on Baltimore's Mt. Vernon Place." *Maryland Historical Magazine* 79 (3): 197–219.

Power, G. 1983. "Apartheid Baltimore Style: The Residential Segregation Ordinances of 1910–1913." *Maryland Law Review* 42 (Winter): 289–328.

Press, R. M. 1981. " 'Love Canal South': Alabama DDT Residue Will Cost Millions to Clean Up," *Christian Science Monitor*, June 12. P. 11.

Preston, J. 2010. "Court Rejects a City's Efforts to Restrict Immigrants." *New York Times*, September 10. P. A12.

Pritchett, W.E. 2003. "The 'Public Menace' of Blight: Urban Renewal and the Private Uses of Eminent Domain." *Yale Law and Policy Review* 21:1–52.

Public Works Administration. 1935. *America Builds.* Government Printing Office.

Pulido, L. 1996. "A Critical Review of the Methodology of Environmental Racism Research." *Antipode* 28 (2): 142–159.

Putnam, R. 2000. *Bowling Alone: The Collapse and Revival of American Community*. Simon and Schuster.

Quigley, D. 2001. "Ethical Considerations in Research Methodologies for Exposure Assessment of Toxic and Radioactive Contaminants in Native Communities." Syracuse University.

Rabin, Y. 1990. "Expulsive Zoning: The Inequitable Legacy of Euclid." In *Zoning and the American Dream*. C.M. Haar and J.S. Kayden, eds. APA Planners.

Radford, G. 2005. "Housing Reform." In *The Encyclopedia of Chicago*. Chicago Historical Society.

Rae, D.W. 2003. *City: Urbanism and Its End*. Yale University Press.

Raja, S., C. Ma, and P. Yadav. 2008. "Beyond Food Deserts: Measuring and Mapping Racial Disparities in Neighborhood Food Environments." *Journal of Planning Education and Research* 27 (4): 469–482.

Ready, R.C. 2010. "Do Landfills Always Depress Nearby Property Values?" *Journal of Real Estate Research* 32 (3): 321–339.

Real Estate Board of Chicago. 1917. *Chicago Real Estate Bulletin* 25 (4): 313–317.

Reardon, S.F., S.A. Matthews, D. O'Sullivan, B.A. Lee, G. Firebaugh, C.R. Farrell, and K. Bischoff. 2008. "The Geographic Scale of Metropolitan Racial Segregation." *Demography* 45 (3): 489–514.

Reardon, S.F., and D. O'Sullivan. 2004. "Measures of Spatial Segregation." *Sociological Methodology* 34 (1): 121–162.

Record-Herald (Chicago). 1909. August 21.

Redstone Arsenal. 2002. "Redstone Arsenal Complex Chronology, Part IIIB, 1980–1989." Huntsville, AL.

Reeves, D. 2012. "EPA Plan Expected to Limit New Title VI Petitions Though Backlog Remains." *Inside EPA Weekly Report* 33 (April 20): 16.

Reeves, D. 2011. "EPA, DOJ Crafting Agreement to Boost Environmental Justice Cooperation." *Inside EPA Weekly Report* 32 (June 15): 28.

Reich, A.R., J.L. Perkins, and G. Cutter. 1985. "DDT Contamination of a North Alabama Aquatic Ecosystem." *Environmental Toxicology and Chemistry* 5 (8): 725–736.

Reichert, A.K. 1997. "Impact of Toxic Waste Superfund Site on Property Values." *Appraisal Journal* 65 (4): 381–392.

Reichert, A.K., M. Small, and S. Mohanty. 1992. "The Impact of Landfills on Residential Property Values." *Journal of Real Estate Research* 7 (3): 297–314.

Relman, J.P. 2008. "Foreclosures, Integration, and the Future of the Fair Housing Act." *Indiana Law Review* 41 (3): 629–652.

Reynolds, B. 1980. "Triana, Alabama: The Unhealthiest Town in America." *National Wildlife* 18 (August): 33.

Rice, C.P., and P. O'Keefe. 1995. "Sources, Pathways, and Effects of PCBs, Dioxins, and Dibenzofurans." In *Handbook of Ecotoxicology*. B.A. Rattner, G.A. Burton, J. Cairns, and D.J. Hoffman, eds. Lewis. Pp. 424–468.

Rice, R.R. 1966. *The Housing Environment as a Factor in Child Development*. Office of Economic Opportunity.

Richards, B. 1988. "EPA Orders Unit of Waste Management to Begin Tests at Big Dump in Alabama." *Wall Street Journal*, April 5. P. A12.

Richey, W. 2011. "Supreme Court Demands Review of Ruling in Anti-Illegal Immigration Case." *Christian Science Monitor*, June 6.

Rinquist, E.J. 2005. "Assessing Evidence of Environmental Inequities: A Meta-Analysis." *Journal of Policy Analysis and Management* 24 (2): 223–247.

Rinquist, E.J. 2000. "Environmental Justice: Normative Concerns and Empirical Evidence." In *Environmental Policy*, 4th ed. N.J. Vig and M.E. Kraft, eds. CQ. Pp. 232–256.

Rinquist, E.J. 1998. "A Question of Justice: Equity in Environmental Litigation, 1974–1991." *Journal of Politics* 60 (4): 1148–1165.

R.I.S.E., Inc., et al. v. Robert A. Kay Jr. et al. 1992. 977 F.2d 573 (4th Cir. October 15).

R.I.S.E., Inc., et al. v. Robert A. Kay Jr. et al. 1991. 768 F. Supp. 1144 (E.D. Va.).

Ritzdorf, M. 1997. "Locked Out of Paradise: Contemporary Exclusionary Zoning, the Supreme Court, and African Americans, 1970 to the Present." In *Urban Planning and the African American Community: In the Shadows*. J.M. Thomas and M. Ritzdorf, eds. Sage. Pp. 43–57.

Robbins, R.L. 1992. "Self-Determination and Subordination: The Past, Present, and Future of American Indian Governance." In *The State of Native America: Genocide, Colonization, and Resistance*. M.A. Jaimes, ed. South End. Pp. 87–121.

Roberts, D.R., L.L. Laughlin, P. Hsheih, and L.J. Legters. 1997. "DDT, Global Strategies, and a Malaria Control Crisis in South America." *Emerging Infectious Diseases* 3 (3): 295–302.

Roberts, T.J., and M.M. Toffolon-Weiss. 2001. *Chronicles from the Environmental Justice Frontline*. Cambridge University Press.

Robinson, W.P. 1992. "Uranium Production and Its Effects on Navajo Communities along the Rio Puerco in Western New Mexico." In *Race and the Incidence of Environmental Hazards: A Time for Discourse*. B. Bryant and P. Mohai, eds. Westview. Pp. 153–162, 244.

Rolfes, A. 2000. "Shell Games: Divide and Conquer in Norco's Diamond Community; The Case for a Fair and Just Relocation." *CorpWatch*, November 1. Available at http://www.corpwatch.org/article.php?id=404.

Rollins Environmental Services v. the Parish of St. James. 1985. 775 F.2d 627 (5th Cir. November 1).

Roscoe, R.J., J.A. Deddens, A. Salvan, and T.M. Schnorr. 1995. "Mortality among Navajo Uranium Miners." *American Journal of Public Health* 85 (4): 535–541.

Rose, H.M. 1965. "The All-Negro Town: Its Evolution and Function." *Geographical Review* 55 (3, July): 362–381.

Rose, J. 2010. "Hidden in Old Home Deeds, a Segregationist Past." WFAE 90.7 Charlotte National Public Radio. January 11.

Rosemere Neighborhood Association v. U.S. Environmental Protection Agency, 2009. 581 F.3d 1169 (9th Cir.).

Rosenbaum, E. 2012. "Home Ownership's Wild Ride, 2001–2011." American Communities Project, Brown University.

Rosner, D., and J. Markovitz. 2002. *Deceit and Denial: The Deadly Politics of Industrial Pollution*. University of California Press.

Ross, S.L., and M.A. Turner. 2005. "Housing Discrimination in Metropolitan America: Explaining Changes between 1989 and 2000." *Social Problems* 52 (2): 152–180.

Rothstein, R. 2012. "A Comment on Bank of America / Countrywide's Discriminatory Mortgage Lending and Its Implications for Racial Segregation." Economic Policy Institute. January 23.

Rothstein, R., and M. Santow. 2012. "The Cost of Living Apart." *American Prospect*, August 22.

Ruechel, F. 1997. "New Deal Public Housing, Urban Poverty, and Jim Crow: Techwood and University Homes in Atlanta." *Georgia Historical Quarterly* 81 (5): 915–937.

Rugh, J.S., and D.S. Massey, 2010. "Racial Segregation and the American Foreclosure Crisis." *American Sociological Review* 74 (5): 629–651.

Rusiecki, J.A., J. Cash, C. Raines, L. Brinton, S. Zahm, T. Mason, L. Needham, A. Blair, S. Sieber, and R. Hoover. 2006. "Serum Concentrations of Organochlorine Compounds and Mammographic Density in a Highly Exposed Population in Triana, Alabama." *Epidemiology* 17 (6, November): S89.

Sack, K. 1991. "Alcoa to Pay New York State $7.5 Million in Waste Fines. *New York Times*, July 12.

Sadd, J. L., M. Pastor, J.T. Boer, and L.D. Snyder. 1999. "Every Breath You Take . . . : The Demographics of Toxic Air Releases in Southern California." *Economic Development Quarterly* 13 (2): 107–123.

Saha, R.K., and P. Mohai 2005. "Historical Context and Hazardous Waste Facility Siting: Understanding Temporal Patterns in Michigan." *Social Problems* 52 (4): 618–648.

Samet, J.M., D.M. Kutvirt, R.J. Waxweiler, and C.R. Key. 1984. "Uranium Mining and Lung Cancer in Navajo Men." *New England Journal of Medicine* 310 (23): 1481–1484.

Sampson, R.J., S.W. Raudenbush, and F. Earls. 1997. "Neighborhoods and Violent Crime: A Multilevel Study of Collective Efficacy." *Science* 277 (August 15): 918–924.

Sanders, W., and J. Getzels, 1987. *The Planning Commission: Its Composition and Function*. Planning Advisor Service Report 400. American Planning Association.

Sastry, N., A. Pebley, and M. Zonta. 2002. "Neighborhood Definitions and the Spatial Dimension of Daily Life in Los Angeles." CCPR Working Paper 033-04. California Center for Population Research, UCLA.

Schell, L.M., and A.M. Tarbell. 1998. "A Partnership Study of PCBs and Health of Mohawk Youth: Lessons from Our Past and Guidelines for Our Future." *Environmental Health Perspectives* 106 (3): 833–840.

Schelly, D., and P. Stretesky. 2009. "An Analysis of the 'Path of Least Resistance'

Argument in Three Environmental Justice Success Cases." *Society and Natural Resources* 22 (4): 369–380.

Schlosberg, D. 2007. *Defining Environmental Justice: Theories, Movements, and Nature.* Oxford University Press.

Schmidt, B.C., Jr., 1982. "Principle and Prejudice: The Supreme Court and Race in the Progressive Era, Part I: The Heyday of Jim Crow." *Columbia Law Review* 82 (April): 444–524.

Schneider, K. 1993. "Plan for Toxic Dump Pits Blacks against Blacks." *New York Times,* December 13. P. A7.

Schneider v. D.C. Redevelopment Land Agency. 1953. 117 F. Supp. 705 (D.D.C. 1953).

Schulte v. Starks. 1927. 238 Mich. 102; 213 N.W. 102 (April 1).

Schutze, J. 1986. *The Accommodation: The Politics of Race in an American City.* Citadel.

Schwab, J. 1994. *Deeper Shades of Green: The Rise of Blue-Collar and Minority Environmentalism.* Sierra Club Books.

Schweitzer, L., and M. Stephenson Jr. 2007. "Right Answers, Wrong Questions: Environmental Justice as Urban Research." *Urban Studies* 44 (2): 319–337.

Sengupta, S. 2001. "From a Dump, a Legacy of Illness and Debate." *New York Times,* April 7. P. 11.

Shaikh, S.L., and J.B. Loomis. 1999. "An Investigation into the Presence and Causes of Environmental Inequity in Denver, Colorado." *Social Science Journal* 36 (1): 77–92.

Sharp, E.B., and D. Haider-Markel. 2008. "At the Invitation of the Court: Eminent Domain Reform in State Legislatures in the Wake of the *Kelo* Decision." *Plubius: The Journal of Federalism* 38 (3): 556–575.

Sheets v. Dillon. 1942. 221 N.C. 426; 20 S.E.2d 344.

Shell. 2012. "Norco Refinery." Available at http://www.shell.us/home/content/usa/aboutshell/projects_locations/norco/.

Shelley et ux. v. Kraemer et ux. 1948. 334 U.S. 1; 68 S. Ct. 836; 92 L. Ed. 1161 (May 3).

Sheppard, E., R. McMaster, H. Leitner, H. Tian. 1999. "GIS-Based Measures of Environmental Equity: Exploring Their Sensitivity and Significance." *Journal of Exposure Analysis and Environmental Epidemiology* 9 (1): 18–28.

Shlay, A.B. 1987. *Maintaining the Divided City: Residential Lending Patterns in the Baltimore SMSA.* Maryland Alliance for Responsible Investment. March.

Shores, A. 1974. "Bombings Fail to Intimidate Shores." Interview conducted by Jack Bass on July 17, 1974. Interview A-0021. Southern Oral History Program Collection (4007), University of North Carolina.

Shoup, D. 2008. "Graduated Density Zoning." *Journal of Planning Education and Research* 28 (2): 161–179.

Sicotte, D., and S. Swanson. 2007. "Whose Risk in Philadelphia? Proximity to Unequally Hazardous Industrial Facilities." *Social Science Quarterly* 88 (2): 515–534.

Sigman, H. 2001. "The Pace of Progress at Superfund Sites: Policy Goals and Interest Group Influence." *Journal of Law and Economics* 44 (1): 315–343.

Silva, C. 2009. "Racial Restrictive Covenants: Enforcing Neighborhood Segregation in

Seattle." Seattle Civil Rights and Labor History Project, University of Washington. Available at http://depts.washington.edu/civilr/covenants_report.htm.

Silver, C. 1997. "The Racial Origins of Zoning in American Cities." In *Urban Planning and the African American Community: In the Shadows*. J.M. Thomas and M. Ritzdorf, eds. Sage. Pp. 23–42.

Silver, C., and J.V. Moeser. 1995. *The Separate City: Black Communities in the Urban South, 1940–1968*. University Press of Kentucky.

Simons, R.A., W. Bowen, and A. Sementall. 1997. "The Effect of Underground Storage Tanks on Residential Property Values in Cuyahoga County, Ohio." *Journal of Real Estate Research* 14 (1): 29–42.

Singleton, E. 2009. "Race-Restrictive Covenant Draws Attention of NAACP: Myers Park Clause Ruled Discriminatory by Community Relations Committee." *Charlotte Post* 37 (1, December 15).

Sipes v. McGhee. 1947. 316 Mich. 614; 25 N.W.2d 638 (January 7).

Smith, C.L. 2007. "Economic Deprivation and Environmental Inequality in Postindustrial Detroit." *Organization & Environment* 20 (1): 25–44.

Smith, P.H., II. 2000. "The Quest for Racial Democracy: Black Civic Ideology and Housing Interests in Postwar Chicago." *Journal of Urban History* 26 (2): 131–157.

Smith v. City of Atlanta. 1926. 161 Ga. 769, 132 S.E. 66.

Smith, V.K., and W.H. Desvousges. 1986. "The Value of Avoiding a LULU: Hazardous Waste Disposal Sites." *Review of Economics and Statistics* 68:293–299.

Smolen, G.E., G. Moore, and L.V. Conway. 1992. "Hazardous Waste Landfill Impacts on Local Property Values." *Real Estate Appraiser* 58 (1): 4–11.

Sobotta, R.R., H.E. Campbell, and B.J. Owens. 2007. "Aviation Noise and Environmental Justice: The Barrio Barrier." *Journal of Regional Science* 47 (1): 125–154.

South Camden Citizens in Action v. New Jersey Department of Environmental Protection. 2001a. 145 F. Supp. 2d 446 (D.N.J.).

South Camden Citizens in Action v. New Jersey Department of Environmental Protection. 2001b. 274 F.3d 771 (3d Cir.).

South, S.J., and K.D. Crowder. 1998. "Leaving the 'Hood: Residential Mobility between Black, White, and Integrated Neighborhoods." *American Sociological Review* 63 (1): 17–26.

South, S.J., and K.D. Crowder. 1997. "Residential Mobility between Cities and Suburbs: Race, Suburbanization, and Back-to-the-City Moves." *Demography* 34 (4): 525–538.

South, S.J., and G.D. Deane. 1993. "Race and Residential Mobility: Individual Determinants and Structural Constraints." *Social Forces* 72 (1): 147–167.

Spear, A.H. 1967. *Black Chicago: The Making of a Negro Ghetto, 1890–1920*. University of Chicago Press.

Squires, G.D., S. Friedman, and C.E. Saidat. 2002. "Experiencing Residential Segregation: A Contemporary Study of Washington, D.C." *Urban Affairs Review* 38 (2): 155–183.

Squires, G.D., D.S. Hyra, and R.N. Renner. 2009. *Segregation and the Subprime Lending*

Crisis. Economic Policy Institute Briefing Paper 244. November 4. Available at http://www.epi.org/page/-/pdf/110409-briefingpaper244.pdf.

State of Alabama v. U.S. Environmental Protection Agency. 1989. 871 F.2d 1548 (11th Cir. April 18).

State of Alabama v. U.S. Environmental Protection Agency. 1988a. Civil Action No. 88V-987-N (M.D. Ala. October 21).

State of Alabama v. U.S. Environmental Protection Agency. 1988b. 711 F. Supp. 574 (M.D. Ala. December 15).

State of Alabama et al. v. U.S. Environmental Protection Agency. 1990. 911 F.2d 499 (11th Cir. August 23).

State of Florida v. Wilson. 1946. 157 Fla. 342; 25 So. 2d 860.

State of Maryland v. John H. Gurry. 1913. 121 Md. 534; 88 A. 546 (Ct. App. Md. October 7).

State v. William Darnell. 1914. 166 N.C. 300; 81 S.E. 338.

Sternberg, M.A. [1996] 2001. *Along River Road: Past and Present on Louisiana's Historic Byway*. Louisiana State University Press.

Sterns, L.B., and J.R. Logan. 1986. "The Racial Structuring of the Housing Market and Segregation in Suburban Areas." *Social Forces* 65 (1, September): 28–42.

St. John, C., and N.A. Bates. 1990. "Racial Composition and Neighborhood Evaluation." *Social Science Research* 19 (1): 47–61.

St. Louis Real Estate Bulletin. 1923. "Segregation of Negro Districts Approved by Realtors' Referendum." Real Estate Board of St. Louis. September 1.

St. Louis Union Trust Co. v. Foster. 1937. 211 N.C. 331; 190 S.E. 522.

Stocking, B. 1993. "Old Landfill Fears Far from Buried: Warren County Residents Fear That Water inside PCB Dump Poses Danger." *Raleigh News & Observer*, July 11. P. A1.

Stoiber, J. 1999. "Historic Apartments' New Future: The Carl Mackley Houses, Popular for Many Decades, Have Undergone a Revival." *Philadelphia Inquirer*, June 25. P. 36.

Stretesky, P., and M.J. Hogan. 1998. "Environmental Justice: An Analysis of Superfund Sites in Florida." *Social Problems* 45 (2): 268–287.

Stretesky, P., and M. Lynch. 2002. "Environmental Hazards and School Segregation in Hillsborough County, Florida, 1987–1999." *Sociological Quarterly* 43 (4): 553–573.

Sugrue, T.J. 1996. *The Origins of the Urban Crisis: Race and Inequality in Postwar Detroit*. Princeton University Press.

Sullivan, D.M. 2007. "Reassessing Gentrification: Measuring Residents' Options Using Survey Data." *Urban Affairs Review* 42 (4): 583–592.

Susette Kelo et al. v. City of New London et al. 2005. 545 U.S. 469; 268 Conn. 1; 843 A.2d 500.

Swerczek, M. 2002. "Residents to Learn to Test Air Quality: Devices to Check Chemicals on Display." *New Orleans Times-Picayune*, October 18. P. 1.

Szasz, A., and M. Meuser. 2000. "Unintended and Inexorable: The Production of Environmental Inequalities in Santa Clara County, California." *American Behavioral Scientist* 43 (4): 602–632.

Szasz, A., and M. Meuser. 1997. "Environmental Inequalities." *Current Sociology* 45 (3): 99–120

Sze, J., and J.K. London. 2008. "Environmental Justice at the Crossroads." *Sociology Compass* 2 (4): 1331–1354.

Taggart, H.T., and Smith, K.W. 1981. "Redlining: An Assessment of the Evidence of Disinvestment in Metropolitan Boston." *Urban Affairs Quarterly* 17 (1): 91–107.

TallBear, K. 2000. "Comments of Kimberly TallBear Regarding Private Fuel Storage Project on the Skull Valley Band of Goshute Reservation." Nuclear Regulatory Commission Atomic Safety and Licensing Board Public Hearing. Salt Lake City. June 24–25.

Taylor, D. 1999. "Talking Trash: The Economic and Environmental Issues of Landfills." *Environmental Health Perspectives* 107 (8): A404–A409.

Taylor, D.E. 2011. "The Evolution of Environmental Justice Activism, Research, and Scholarship." *Environmental Practice* 13 (4): 280–301.

Taylor, D.E. 2010. "Introduction." *Research in Social Problems and Public Policy* 18:3–28.

Taylor, D.E. 2009. *The Environment and the People in American Cities: Disorder, Inequality, and Social Change.* Duke University Press.

Taylor, D.E. 2000. "The Rise of the Environmental Justice Paradigm: Injustice Framing and the Social Construction of Environmental Discourses." *American Behavioral Scientist* 43 (4): 508–580.

Taylor, Q. 2003. *The Forging of a Black Community: Seattle's Central District from 1870 through the Civil Rights Era.* University of Washington Press.

Taylor, R.S. 1948. "Federated Clubs: Block Organizations Are Becoming Popular." *Chicago Defender*, June 5.

Teaford, J.C. 1990. *The Rough Road to Renaissance: Urban Revitalization in America, 1940–1985.* Johns Hopkins University Press.

Tedeschi, B. 2010. "Bias Accord as Harbinger." *New York Times*, April 23.

Temple, C., and J. Hansen. 2000. "Ministers' Homes, Churches among Bomb Targets." *Birmingham News*, July 16.

Tex. Rev. Civ. Stat. Ann. art. 1015-b. 1927.

Thayer, M., H. Albers, and M. Rahmatian. 1992. "The Benefits of Reducing Exposure to Waste Disposal Sites: A Hedonic Housing Value Approach." *Journal of Real Estate Research* 7 (3): 265–282.

Thernstrom, S., and A. Thernstrom. 1997. *America in Black and White: One Nation, Indivisible.* Simon and Schuster.

Thomas, J. 2005. "Home Ownership, Self-Determination, Restrictive Covenants, Redistricting." *Kansas City Star*, February 13.

Thomas, J.K., D. Fannin, and E.J. Rossman. 2010. "Native American Reservations and Toxic Wastes, 2000–2008." Paper presented at the 2010 National Training Conference on the Toxics Release Inventory and Environmental Conditions in Communities: Connecting Communities and Decision-Makers with Environmental Information. Washington, DC. November 1–4.

Thomas, J.M. 1997. *Redevelopment and Race: Planning a Finer City in Postwar Detroit.* Johns Hopkins University Press.

Thometz, C.E. 1963. *The Decision-Makers: The Power Structure of Dallas.* Southern Methodist University Press.

Thompson, E. 1988. "Poor Country Sees Victory with PCB Clean-Up Funds." (*Durham, NC*) *Herald Sun,* May 31. P. A3.

Thompson v. U.S. Department of Housing and Urban Development. 2005. 348 F. Supp. 2d 398 (D. Md.).

Thornbrough, E.L. 2000. "The Twenties: Increased Segregation." In *Indiana Blacks in the Twentieth Century.* L. Ruegamer, ed. Indiana University Press. Pp. 47–70.

Thornbrough, E.L. 1961. "Segregation in Indiana during the Klan Era of the 1920's." *Mississippi Valley Historical Review* 47 (4): 594–618.

Thornbrough, E.L. [1957] 1993. *The Negro in Indiana before 1900: A Study of a Minority.* Indiana University Press.

Thorpe, G. 1996. "Our Homes Are Not Dumps: Creating Nuclear-Free Zones." *Natural Resources Journal* 36:715–723.

Tolnay, S., and E.M. Beck. 1991. "Rethinking the Role of Racial Violence in the Great Migration." In *Black Exodus: The Great Migration from the American South.* A. Harrison, ed. University of Mississippi Press. Pp. 20–35.

Trifun, N.M. 2009. "Residential Segregation after the Fair Housing Act." *Human Rights* 36 (4): 14–20.

Trotter, J.W., and J.N. Day. 2010. *Race and Renaissance: African Americans in Pittsburgh since World War II.* University of Pittsburgh Press.

Tsai, S.P., K.M. Cardarelli, J.K. Wendt, and A.E. Fraser. 2004. "Mortality Patterns among Residents in Louisiana's Industrial Corridor, USA, 1970–1999." *Occupational and Environmental Medicine* 61 (4): 295–304.

Tsai, S.P., V.W. Chen, E.E. Fox, J.K. Wendt, W.X. Cheng, D.E. Foster, and A.E. Fraser. 2004. "Cancer Incidence among Refinery and Petrochemical Employees in Louisiana, 1983–1999." *Annals of Epidemiology* 14 (9): 722–730.

Tso, H., and L.M. Shields. 1980. "Navajo Mining Operations: Early Hazards and Recent Interventions." *New Mexico Journal of Science* 20 (1): 11–17.

Turnbull, L. 2005. "Homeowners Find Records Still Hold Blot of Racism." *Seattle Times,* June 3, P. A1.

Tuttle, W.M. 1970. *Race Riot: Chicago in the Red Summer of 1919.* Atheneum.

Twitty v. State of North Carolina. 1987. 85 N.C. App. 42; 354 S.E.2d 296 (April 7).

Twitty v. State of North Carolina. 1981. 527 F. Supp. 778 (E.D.N.C. November 25).

Tyler v. Harmon. 1926. 150 La. 943; 107 So. 704 (March 5).

Tyler v. Harmon. 1925. 158 La. 439; 104 So. 200 (March 2).

UCC (United Church of Christ). 1987. *Toxic Wastes and Race in the United States.*

United States Steel Corporation v. Russell E. Train II. 1977. 556 F.2d 822 (7th Cir. May 13).

United States v. Burns. 1986. 793 F.2d 1294 (6th Cir. May 5).

United States v. City of Blackjack. 1974. 508 F.2d 1179 (8th Cir. December 27).

United States v. Countrywide Financial Corporation et al. 2011a. Complaint. CV11-10540-PSG (AJW) (C.D. Cal. December 21). Available at http://www.justice.gov/crt/about/hce/documents/countrywidecomp.pdf.

United States v. Countrywide Financial Corporation et al. 2011b. Proposed Settlement Agreement. Document 4. No. 2:11-cv-10540-PSG-AJW (C.D. Cal. December 28). Available at http://www.justice.gov/crt/about/hce/documents/countrywidesettle.pdf.

United States v. Olin Corp. 1980. CV 80-PT-5300-NE (N.D. Ala.).

United States v. Ward. 1985. 618 F. Supp. 884 (E.D.N.C. September 9).

United States v. Ward. 1984. 22 ERC (BNA) 1235; 14 ELR 2084 (E.D.N.C. May 11).

United States v. Ward. 1982a. 793 F.2d 551 (3rd Cir.).

United States v. Ward. 1982b. 676 F.2d 94 (4th Cir.).

United States v. Ward. 1982c. 459 U.S. 835; 103 S. Ct. 79; 74 L. Ed. 2d 76 (October 5).

University of North Carolina Center for Civil Rights. 2006. "Invisible Fences: Municipal Underbounding in Southern Moore County."

USA Today. 2012. "Wells Fargo Settles Lending Bias Case." July 13. P. B1.

U.S. Cancer Statistics Working Group. 2012. *United States Cancer Statistics: 1999–2008 Incidence and Mortality Web-Based Report.* Centers for Disease Control and Prevention and National Cancer Institute. Available at www.cdc.gov/uscs.

U.S. Census Bureau. 2010. "Profile of General Population and Housing Characteristics: 2010." U.S. Department of Commerce.

U.S. Census Bureau. 2006–2010. "American Community Survey." U.S. Department of Commerce.

U.S. Census Bureau. 2004. "Residential Segregation of Blacks or African Americans: 1980–2000." In *Racial and Ethnic Residential Segregation in the United States: 1980–2000.* U.S. Department of Commerce, Housing and Household Economic Statistics Division.

U.S. Census Bureau. 2001. *Did You Know? Homes Account for 44 Percent of All Wealth: Findings from the SIPP.* Census Population Reports, Series P70, No. 75, Household Economics Studies. U.S. Department of Commerce.

U.S. Census Bureau. 2000. Census 2000 Summary File 3 (SF 1) Sample Data. U.S. Department of Commerce.

U.S. Census Bureau. 1995. "Population of Counties by Decennial Census: 1900–1990." U.S. Department of Commerce.

U.S. Census Bureau. 1990. Summary Tape File 1. U.S. Department of Commerce.

U.S. Census Bureau. 1980. "Profile of General Population and Housing Characteristics: 1980." U.S. Department of Commerce.

U.S. Census Bureau. 1973. *Census of the Population: 1970.* Vol. 1 (Part 24). U.S. Department of Commerce.

U.S. Commission on Civil Rights. 1973. *Understanding Fair Housing.* Clearinghouse Publication 42. Government Printing Office. February.

U.S. Department of Housing and Urban Development. 2000. *Treasury Task Force on Predatory Lending Report.* Available at http://archives.hud.gov/reports/treasrpt.pdf.

U.S. Department of Justice, Civil Division. 2009. "Radiation Exposure Compensation System." November 17.

U.S. District and Bankruptcy Courts, Southern District of Texas. 2011. "History of the District." Available at http://www.txs.uscourts.gov/research/history.htm.

U.S. Environmental Protection Agency. 2012a. "Aluminum Company of America." EPA Region 2 Superfund. Available at http://www.epa.gov/region2/superfund/npl/aluminumcompany/.

U.S. Environmental Protection Agency. 2012b. "Aluminum Company of America: NPL Listing History." EPA Region 2. February 8. Available at http://www.epa.gov/region2/superfund/npl/0201690c.pdf.

U.S. Environmental Protection Agency. 2012c. "G.M. Massena: St. Lawrence County, NY." EPA Region 2 Superfund. Available at http://www.epa.gov/region2/superfund/npl/gmmassena/index.html.

U.S. Environmental Protection Agency. 2012d. "Grasse River Superfund Site." Public meeting held at the Office for Aging-Seniors Dining Hall, Akwesasne. November 15. Available at http://www.epa.gov/region2/superfund/npl/aluminumcompany/pdf/grasseriver_akwesasnepubmtg_final.pdf.

U.S. Environmental Protection Agency. 2011a. "General Motors (Central Foundry Division) New York: NPL Listing History." EPA Region 2. March 29. Available at http://www.epa.gov/region2/superfund/npl/0201644c.pdf.

U.S. Environmental Protection Agency. 2011b. *Health and Environmental Impacts of Uranium Contamination: EPA Progress in Implementing a Five-Year Cleanup Plan.* August.

U.S. Environmental Protection Agency. 2011c. *Plan EJ 2014: Considering Environmental Justice in Permitting.* Available at http://www.epa.gov/compliance/ej/resources/policy/plan-ej-2014/plan-ej-permitting-2011-09.pdf.

U.S. Environmental Protection Agency. 2011d. "Release Reports." TRI Explorer. Available at http://iaspub.epa.gov/triexplorer/tri_release.chemical.

U.S. Environmental Protection Agency. 2011e. "2011 State Fact Sheet: Louisiana." TRI Explorer. Available at http://iaspub.epa.gov/triexplorer/tri_broker_statefs.broker?p_view=STCO&trilib=TRIQ1&state=LA&SFS=YES&year=2011.

U.S. Environmental Protection Agency. 2010. *2010 Toxics Release Inventory National Analysis Overview.*

U.S. Environmental Protection Agency. 2008. *Health and Environmental Impacts of Uranium Contamination: Five-Year Plan.* June 9.

U.S. Environmental Protection Agency. 2003. *Sensitive Environments and the Siting of Hazardous Waste Management Facilities.*

U.S. Environmental Protection Agency. 2002. *Land Cleanup and Wastes: Alabama NPL/NPL Caliber Cleanup Site Summaries.*

U.S. Environmental Protection Agency. 2000a. "Response to Comments Documents Hazardous Waste Listings Determination for Chlorinated Aliphatics Production Wastes (Final Rule)." Pp. 1-70–1-71.

U.S. Environmental Protection Agency. 2000b. "Toxic Release Inventory, Louisiana."

U.S. Environmental Protection Agency. 1998. "Final EPA Supplemental Projects Policy Issued." *Federal Register* 63:24796–24804.

U.S. Environmental Protection Agency. 1986a. *Guidance on Determining a Violator's Ability to Pay a Civil Penalty.*

U.S. Environmental Protection Agency. 1986b. *Report on the Remedial Action to Isolate DDT from People and the Environment in the Huntsville Spring Branch–Indian Creek System Wheeler Reservoir, Alabama.* Region IV. July.

U.S. Environmental Protection Agency. 1983. "Olin Agrees to Clean Up DDT in Triana, Alabama Area." April 21.

U.S. General Accounting Office. 1995. *Hazardous and Non-hazardous Waste: Demographics of People Living Near Waste Facilities.*

U.S. General Accounting Office. 1983. *Siting of Hazardous Waste Landfills and Their Correlation with the Racial and Socio-Economic Status of Surrounding Communities.*

Utah Division of Indian Affairs. 2012. "Skull Valley Band Goshute Tribal Profile." Available at http://indian.utah.gov/utah_tribes/skullvalley_goshute.html.

Vernon v. R.J. Reynolds Realty Co. 1945. 226 N.C. 58; 36 S.E.2d 710.

Vig, N.J., and M.E. Kraft. 2006. *Environmental Policy: New Directions for the Twenty-First Century.* CQ.

Vigdor, J. 2002. "Does Gentrification Harm the Poor?" *Brookings-Wharton Papers on Urban Affairs.* Brookings Institute. Pp. 133–173.

Village of Arlington Heights v. Metropolitan Housing Development Corporation. 1977. 97 S. Ct. 555; 50 L. Ed. 2d 450.

Vine, P. 2004. *One Man's Castle: Clarence Darrow in Defense of the American Dream.* HarperCollins.

Vose, C.E. 1959. *Caucasians Only: The Supreme Court, the NAACP, and the Restrictive Covenant Cases.* University of California Press.

Walker v. U.S. HUD. 1989. 734 F. Supp. 1289 (N.D. Tex.).

Wang, F., and Y.C. Feliberty. 2010. "Spatial Distribution of Toxic Release Inventory Sites in Chicago Area: Is There Environmental Inequality?" In *Geospatial Techniques in Urban Hazard and Disaster Analysis.* P. Showalter and Y. Lu, eds. Springer. Pp. 157–177.

Ware, C.F. 1931. *The Early New England Cotton Manufacture.* Houghton Mifflin.

Warren County v. State of North Carolina. 1981. 528 F. Supp. 276 (E.D.N.C. November 25).

Washington Department of Ecology v. United States Environmental Protection Agency. 1985. 752 F.2d 1465 (9th Cir.).

Washington Post. 1978. "N.J. Cancer Testing." April 16. P. C7.

Washington v. Davis. 1976. 426 U.S. 229; 96 S. Ct. 2040; 48 L. Ed. 2d 597.

Wash. Sess. Laws. 2006. Ch. 58 (S.B. 6169).

Waterhouse, C. 2009. "Abandon All Hope Ye That Enter: Title VI, Equal Protection, and the Divine Comedy of Environmental Justice." *Fordham Environmental Law Review* 20 (Spring): 51–89.

Weaver, J., ed. 1997. *Defending Mother Earth: Native American Perspectives on Environmental Justice.* Orbis Books.

Weaver, R.C. 1953. "The Relative Status of the Housing of Negroes in the United States." *Journal of Negro Education* 22 (3): 343–354.

Weaver, R.C. 1944. "Race Restrictive Housing Covenants." *Journal of Land and Public Utility Economics* 20 (3): 183–193.

Weil, J.H. 2009. "Finding Housing: Discrimination and Exploitation of Latinos in the Post-Katrina Rental Market." *Organization and Environment* 22 (4): 491–502.

Weinberg, P. 1999. "Equal Protection." In *The Law of Environmental Justice: Theories and Procedures to Address Disproportionate Risks.* M.B. Gerrard, ed. American Bar Association. Pp. 3–22.

Weise, A. 2004. *Places of Their Own: African American Suburbanization in the Twentieth Century.* University of Chicago Press.

Weiss, M.A. 1987. *The Rise of the Community Builders: The American Real Estate Industry and Urban Land Planning.* Columbia History of Urban Life. Columbia University Press.

Wellman, W.T. 1977. *Portraits of White Racism.* Cambridge University Press.

Wheeler, L. 2009. "Birmingham: 'The Symbol of Segregation.'" *Qcitymetro*, March 10. Available at http://www.qcitymetro.com/news/articles/birmingham--the-symbol-of-segregation-104711722.cfm.

White, H.L. 1992. "Hazardous Waste Incineration and Minority Communities." In *Race and the Incidence of Environmental Hazards: A Time for Discourse.* B. Bryant and P. Mohai, eds. Westview. Pp. 126–139, 240–242.

White, M.J. 1984. "Racial and Ethnic Succession in Four Cities." *Urban Affairs Quarterly* 20 (2): 165–183.

Wilder, M.G., and J.E. Stigter. 1989. "Rethinking the Role of Judicial Scrutiny in Eminent Domain." *Journal of the American Planning Association* 55 (1): 57–65.

Williams, R.Y. 2004. *The Politics of Public Housing: Black Women's Struggles against Urban Inequality.* Oxford University Press.

Wilonsky, R. 2008. "From the Bushes' New Bushes Near Preston Hollow, a History Lesson." *Unfair Park* (blog), *Dallas Observer*, December 8. Available at http://blogs.dallasobserver.com/unfairpark/2008/12/history_lessons_and_scared_nei.php.

Wilson, M. 1998. "Feds Finally Admit That Nerve Agent Was Found Near 1968 Sheep Kill. *Salt Lake Tribune*, January 2.

WMX Technologies. 1991. Study conducted by the National Planning Data Corporation. December.

Wolcott, V.W. 1993. "Defending the Home: Ossian Sweet and the Struggle against Segregation in 1920s Detroit." *Organization of American Historians Magazine of History* 7 (4): 23–27.

Wolf, E.P., and C.N. Lebeaux. 1967. "On the Destruction of Poor Neighborhoods by Urban Renewal." *Social Problems* 15 (1): 3–8.

Wright, B. 2005. "Living and Dying in Louisiana's 'Cancer Alley.'" In *The Quest for*

Environmental Justice: Human Rights and the Politics of Pollution. R.D. Bullard, ed. Sierra Club Books. Pp. 87–107.

Wright, G.C. 1985. *Life behind a Veil: Blacks in Louisville, Kentucky, 1865–1930.* Louisiana State University Press.

Wright, G.C. 1980. "The NAACP and Residential Segregation in Louisville, Kentucky, 1914–1917. *Register of the Kentucky Historical Society* 78:39–54.

Wyly, E.K., M. Atia, and D.J. Hammel. 2004. "Has Mortgage Capital Found an Inner-City Fix?" *Housing Policy Debate* 15 (3): 623–686.

Wyly, E.K., and D.J. Hammel. 2004. Gentrification, Segregation and Discrimination in the American System." *Environment and Planning A* 36:1215–1241.

Wyly, E.K., and D.J. Hammel. 2000. "Capital's Metropolis: Chicago and the Transformation of American Housing Policy." *Geografiska Annaler* 82 (B, 4): 181–206.

Yandle, T., and D. Burton. 1996. "Reexamining Environmental Justice: A Statistical Analysis of Historical Hazardous Landfill Siting Patterns in Metropolitan Texas." *Social Science Quarterly* 77 (3): 477–492.

Yick Wo v. Hopkins. 1886. 118 U.S. 356; 6 S. Ct. 1064; 30 L. Ed. 220.

Yinger, J. 1995. *Closed Doors, Opportunities Lost: The Continuing Costs of Housing Discrimination.* Russell Sage Foundation.

Yinger, J. 1986. "Measuring Discrimination with Fair Housing Tests: Caught in the Act." *American Economic Review* 76 (5): 881–893.

Yinger, J. 1979. "Prejudice and Discrimination in the Urban Housing Market." In *Current Issues in Urban Economics.* P. Mieszkowski and M. Straszheim, eds. Johns Hopkins University Press. Pp. 430–468.

Yinger, J., G. Galster, B. Smith, and F. Eggers. 1978. *The Status of Research into Racial Discrimination and Segregation in American Housing Markets.* U.S. Department of Housing and Urban Development.

Young, L.C. 2005. "Breaking the Color Line: Zoning and Opportunity in America's Metropolitan Areas." *Journal of Gender, Race and Justice* 8 (3): 667–710.

Zahran, S., D.W. Hastings, and S.D. Brody. 2008. "Rationality, Inequity, and Civic Vitality: The Distribution of Treatment, Storage, and Disposal Facilities in the Southeast." *Society and Natural Resources* 21 (3): 179–196.

Zeiss, C., and J. Atwater. 1989. "Waste Facility Impacts on Residential Property Values." *Journal of Urban Planning and Development* 115 (2): 64–80.

Zenk, S.N., A.J. Schulz, B.A. Israel, S.A. James, S. Bao, and M.L. Wilson. 2006. "Fruit and Vegetable Access Differs by Community Racial Composition and Socioeconomic Position in Detroit, Michigan." *Ethnicity & Disease* 16 (1): 275–280.

Zenk, S.N., A.J. Schulz, B.A. Israel, S.A. James, S. Bao, and M.L. Wilson. 2005. "Neighborhood Racial Composition, Neighborhood Poverty, and the Spatial Accessibility of Supermarkets in Metropolitan Detroit." *American Journal of Public Health* 95 (4): 660–667.

Zhao, B., J. Ondrich, and J. Yinger. 2006. "Why Do Real Estate Brokers Continue to Discriminate? Evidence from the 2000 Housing Discrimination Study." *Journal of Urban Economics* 59 (3): 394–419.

Zimmerman, R. 1994. "Issues of Classification in Environmental Equity: How We Manage Is How We Measure." *Fordham Urban Law Journal* 21 (3): 633–669.

Zunz, O. 1982. *The Changing Face of Inequality: Urbanization, Industrial Development, and Immigrants in Detroit: 1880–1920*. University of Chicago Press.

of Colored People (NAACP): Baltimore racial ordinance, 158; Birmingham public housing, 249; Birmingham racial ordinance, 174–176; complaint against Myers Park racial covenant, 198, 223; Detroit racially restrictive covenant, 214; Medgar Evers, 2; housing discrimination, 221; high-interest loans to Blacks, 269; Indianapolis racial ordinance, 180–181; legal challenges to racially restrictive covenants, 194; Louisville racial ordinance, 161–162; Noxubee County, 136–141; Oklahoma City racial ordinance, 172; Richmond racial ordinance, 167; St. Louis racial ordinance, 168; Warren County landfill, 17

National Association of Real Estate Boards (NAREB): code of ethics, 210; founding of and housing discrimination, 207, 237; response to anti-discrimination law suits, 222; removing racially restrictive clauses, 225; eminent domain, 229

National priorities list (NPL), study of sites, 44; Carver Terrace, 116; cluster analysis, 81; length of time for site cleanup, 100, 104; likelihood of placement on, 102–103; minority displacement, 88; Mohawk reservation, 64; neighborhood demographic change, 87; number of sites, 101; property values, 76–80; Pueblo reservation, 60; site remediation, 90–92

Native Action, 2, 67
Navajo, 51, 54, 56–59
Neal, D. E., 95, 120–122
Nelson, A. C., 76
Nesbitt, G. B., 210, 249–250, 254
Neumann, C., 40
Newman, K., 89
Newman, R. J., 70
New Orleans, 20, 27, 47, 93, 154, 168–169, 181–182, 219, 265, 277
New York, 62, 64, 88–89, 93, 116, 154–155, 173, 179, 186–187, 219, 229, 234, 238, 242–243, 250, 252, 265, 274
Noonan, D. S., 3, 44, 76, 78, 80, 88
Norco, 27–30, 38, 49, 143–144
Norfolk, 153–154, 167
Noxious, 1–2, 31, 37, 47–48, 75, 122, 142, 147, 150, 191, 255, 260, 275, 279
Noxubee County, 134–141
NPL. See National priorities list

Oakes, J. M., 39–40, 44, 70, 86, 103
Oklahoma City, 72, 171–172, 277
Olin, 7–12
Oliver, M. L., 275–276
Oliveri, R. C., 188–189
O'Neil, S. G., 103

Palmer, C., 244
Palmquist, R. B., 76
Pardo, M., 38
Paris, Wendell, 133
Park, L. S., 185
Pastor, M., 40, 44, 81, 83, 85–86
Path of least resistance, 34, 81–83
Patterson, O., 73
PCBs. See Polychlorinated biphenyls
Pellow, D. N., 3, 142, 145, 185, 190
Penobscot Reservation, 67
PEON. See Protect the Environment of Noxubee
Perlin, S. A., 20, 40
Petrochemical Corridor, 20
Pettigrew, T., 74
Philadelphia, 154–155, 189–190, 219, 238, 243, 265
Philpott, T. L., 209
Phoenix, 70, 81, 85, 265, 277
Pietila, A., 157
Pinderhughes, R., 3
Pine Ridge Reservation, 61,
Piore, M. J., 52
Plaquemine, 31
Plotkin, W., 195, 209
Pollock, P. H., 40
Polychlorinated biphenyls (PCBs): Alsen and St. James Parish, 25; Emelle, 127–129; Hyde Park, 96; Mohawk reservation, 61–65; in Triana, 12–13; Warren County, 13–18
Popkin, S. J., 254–255
Portland, 88–89, 93, 265, 277
Portney, K. E., 82
Power, G., 155–159
Pritchett, W. E., 228–231, 249–250, 253
Property values, 29, 34, 70, 72–79, 86, 91–92, 97, 110, 114, 143–144, 152, 157, 161, 181, 183, 193, 203, 206–207, 209–210, 222, 237, 259, 275, 279–280
Protect the Environment of Noxubee (PEON): formation of and opposition to waste facility, 136; waste facility siting, 140–141

ABOUT THE AUTHOR

Dorceta E. Taylor is Professor in the School of Natural Resources and Environment at the University of Michigan, where she also serves as Field of Studies Coordinator for the Environmental Justice program. She graduated from Yale University with doctorates in sociology and forestry and environmental studies. Her previous books include *The Environment and the People in American Cities: 1600s–1900s* and *Disorder, Inequality, and Social Change*, which won the 2010 Allan Schnaiberg Outstanding Publication Award from the Environment and Technology Section of the American Sociological Association.